Viz Graphic Novel

Vol. 1

Action Edition

Story and Art by
Nobuyuki Anzai

Flame of Recca

Vol. 1
Action Edition

Story and Art by
Nobuyuki Anzai

English Adaptation/Lance Caselman
Translation/Joe Yamazaki
Touch-up & Lettering/Kelle Han
Graphics & Cover Design/Sean Lee
Editor/Eric Searleman

Managing Editor/Annette Roman
Editor-in-Chief/William Flanagan
Director of Licensing and Acquisitions/Rika Inouye
Sr. VP of Sales & Marketing/Rick Bauer
Sr. VP of Editorial/Hyoe Narita
Publisher/Seiji Horibuchi

Published by VIZ, LLC
P.O. Box 77064
San Francisco, CA 94107

Action Edition
10 9 8 7 6 5 4 3 2 1
First printing, July 2003

For advertising rates or media kit, e-mail advertising@viz.com

store.viz.com

www.viz.com

www.animerica-mag.com

Viz Graphic Novel

FLAME OF RECCA™

Vol. 1

Story & Art by Nobuyuki Anzai

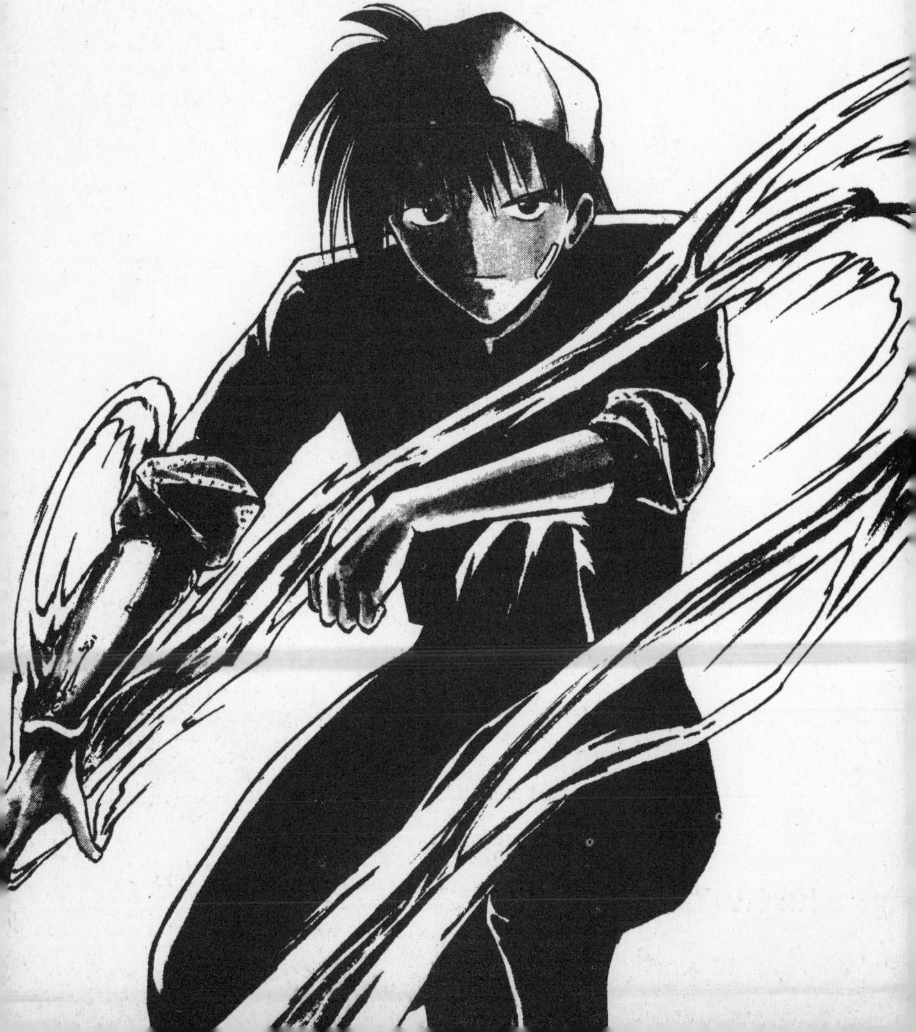

Contents

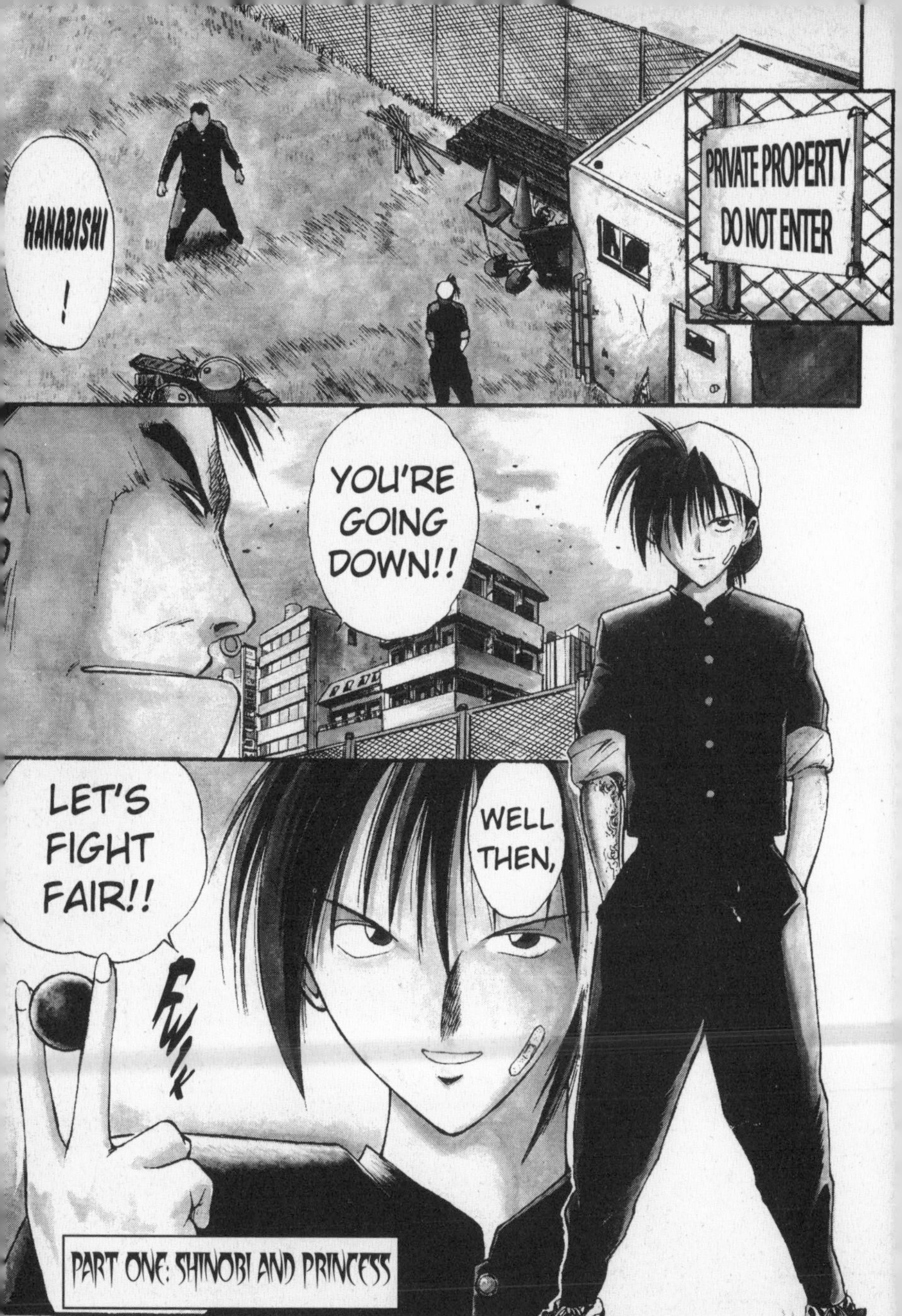
PRIVATE PROPERTY DO NOT ENTER
HANABISHI!
YOU'RE GOING DOWN!!
WELL THEN,
LET'S FIGHT FAIR!!
FWIK
PART ONE: SHINOBI AND PRINCESS

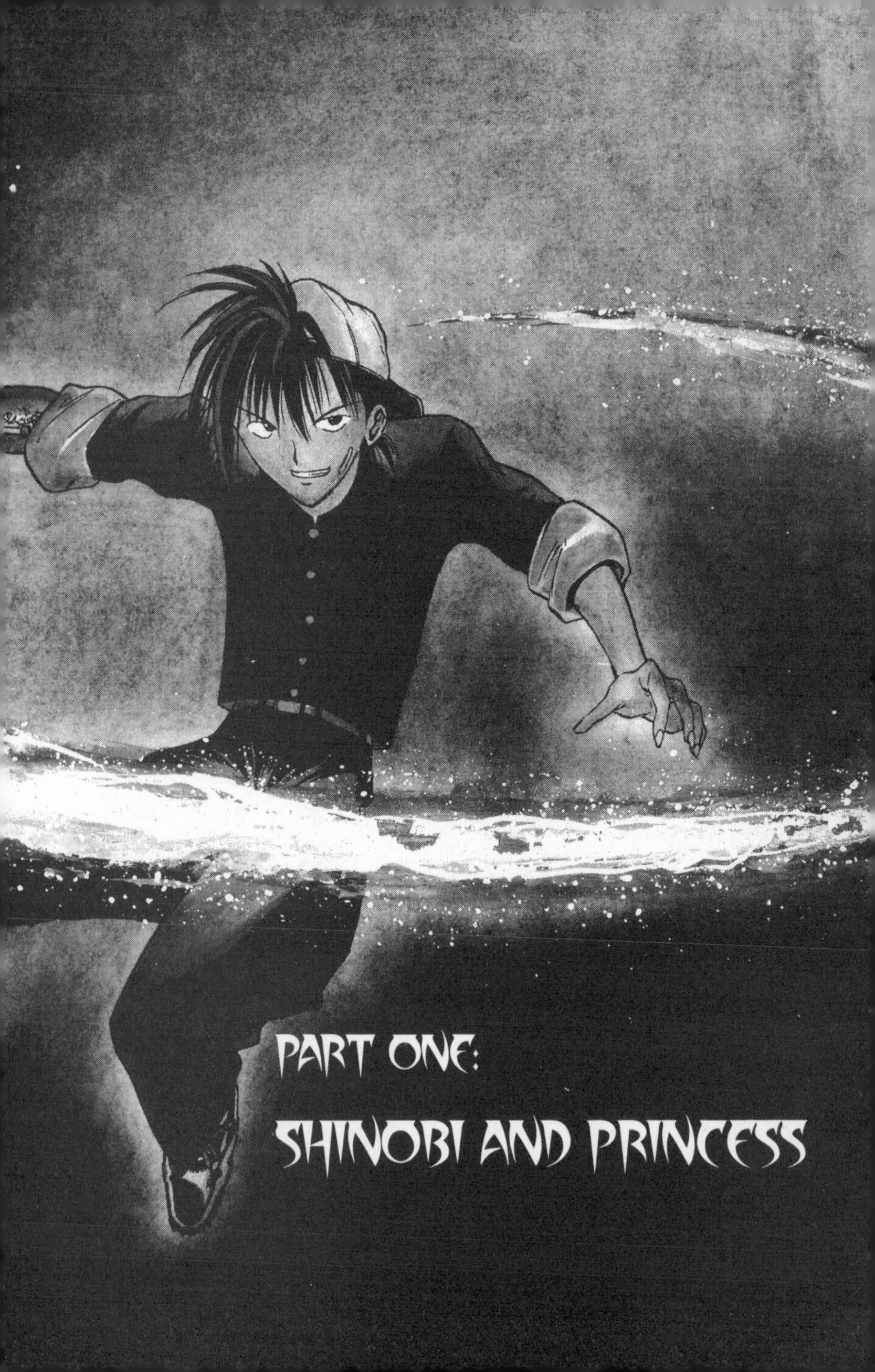
PART ONE:
SHINOBI AND PRINCESS

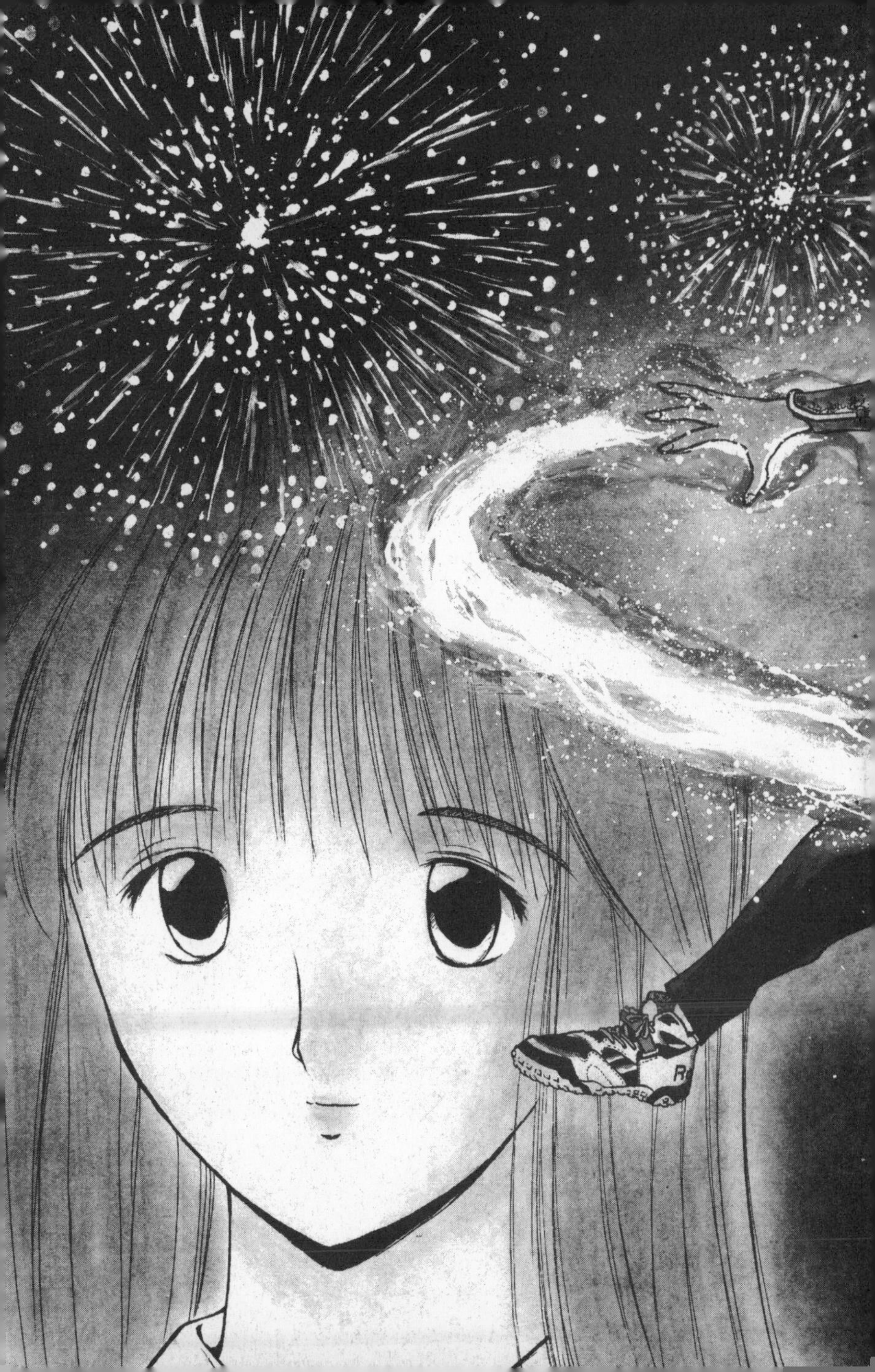

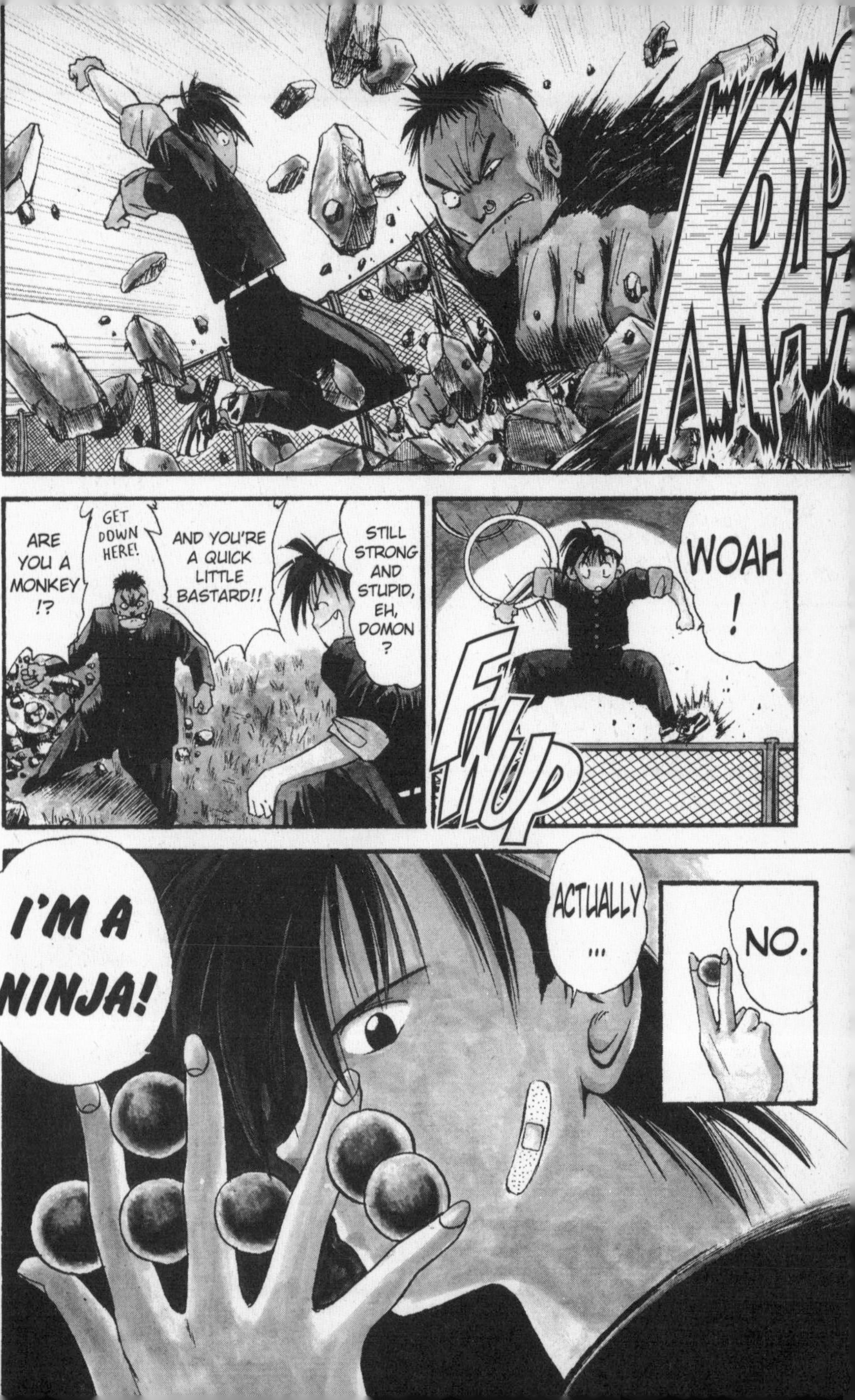
WOAH!
FWUP
STILL STRONG AND STUPID, EH, DOMON?
AND YOU'RE A QUICK LITTLE BASTARD!!
GET DOWN HERE!
ARE YOU A MONKEY!?
NO.
ACTUALLY ...
I'M A NINJA!

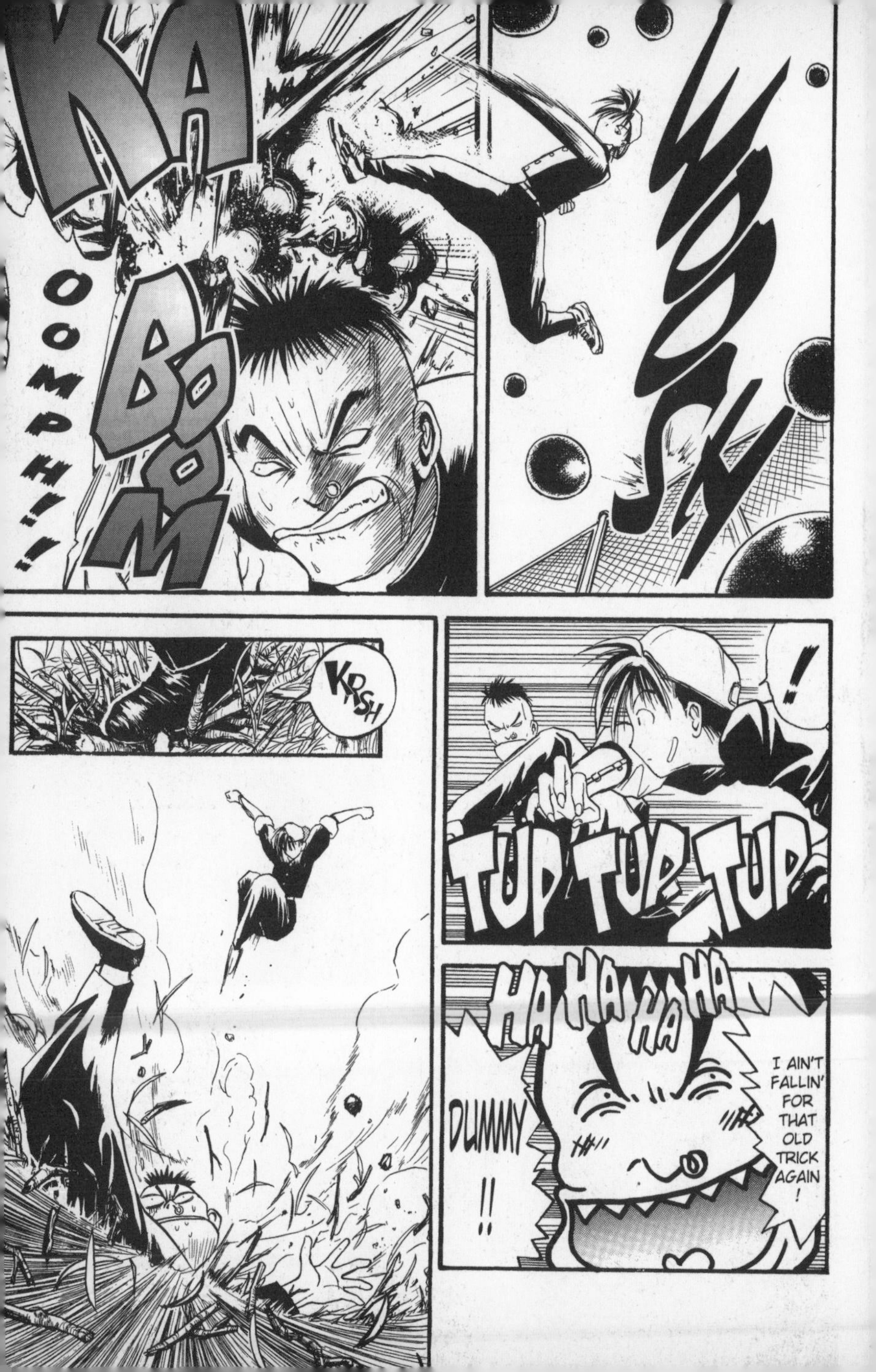

WOOSH
KA
BOOM
OOMPH!!!
!
TUP TUP TUP
KRSH
HA HA HA HA
I AIN'T FALLIN' FOR THAT OLD TRICK AGAIN!
DUMMY !!

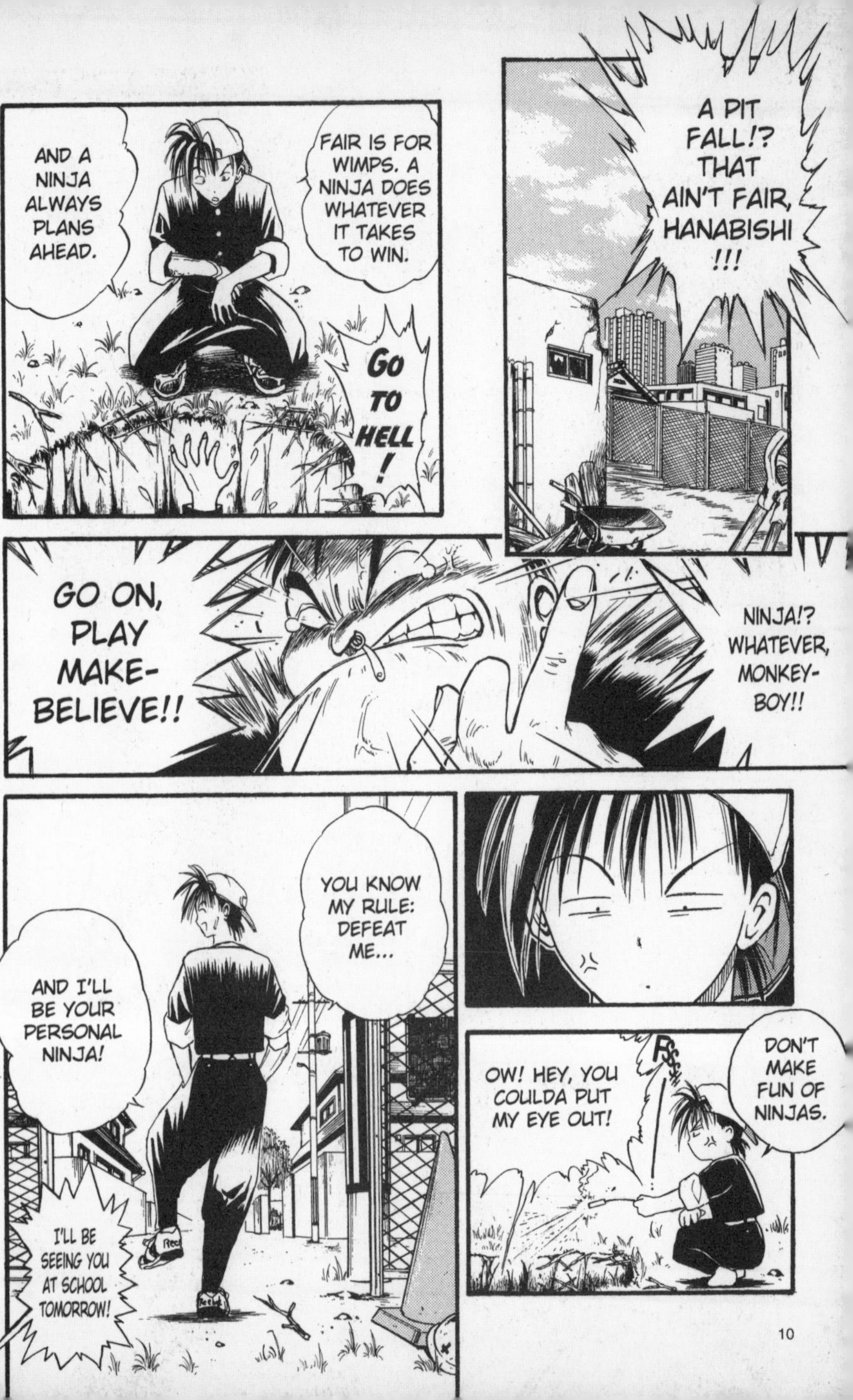
A PIT FALL!? THAT AIN'T FAIR, HANABISHI !!!
FAIR IS FOR WIMPS. A NINJA DOES WHATEVER IT TAKES TO WIN.
AND A NINJA ALWAYS PLANS AHEAD.
GO TO HELL!
NINJA!? WHATEVER, MONKEY-BOY!!
GO ON, PLAY MAKE-BELIEVE!!
DON'T MAKE FUN OF NINJAS.
FSSSH
OW! HEY, YOU COULDA PUT MY EYE OUT!
YOU KNOW MY RULE: DEFEAT ME...
AND I'LL BE YOUR PERSONAL NINJA!
I'LL BE SEEING YOU AT SCHOOL TOMORROW!

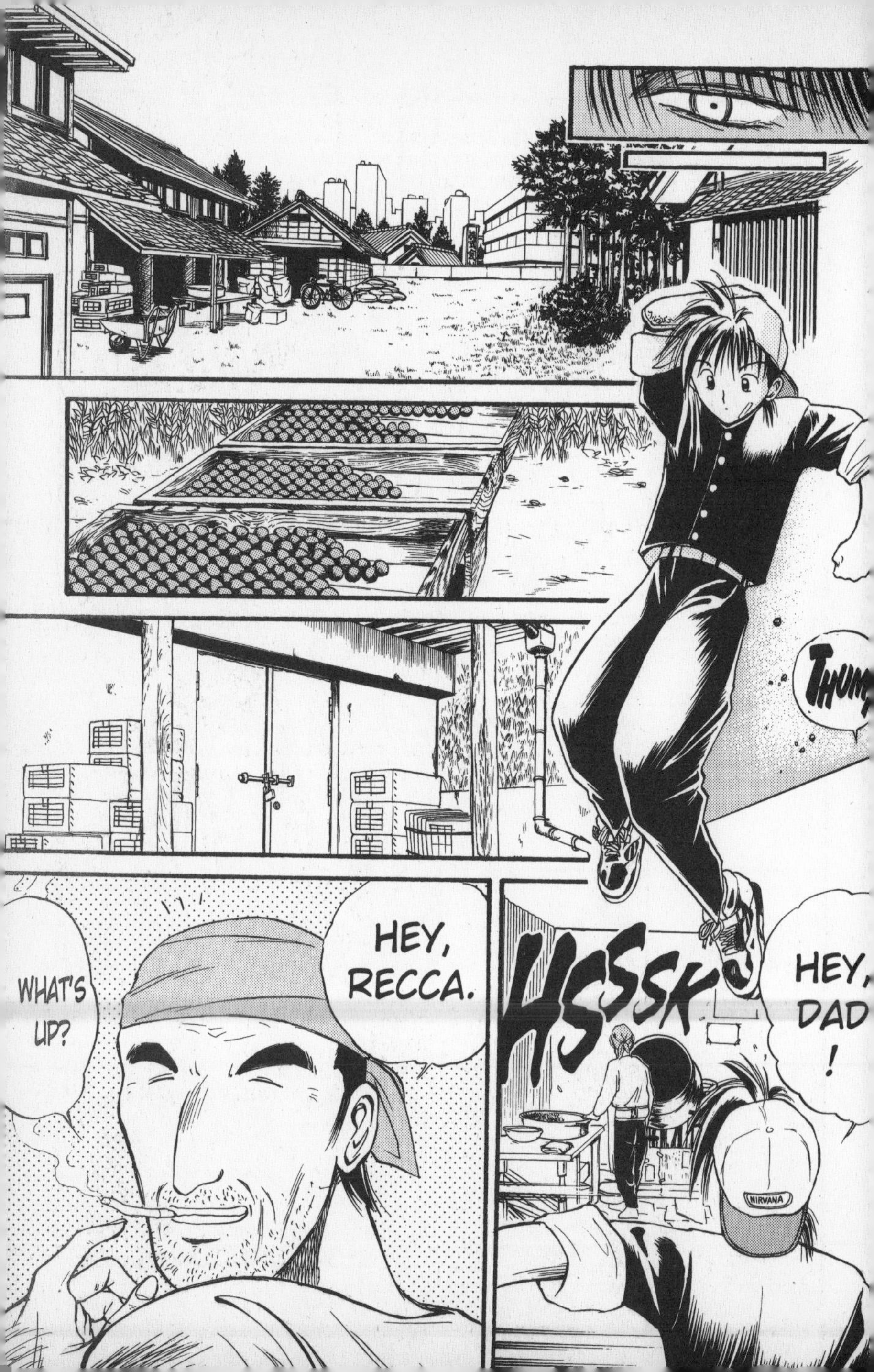
THUM
HSSK
HEY, DAD!
NIRVANA
HEY, RECCA.
WHAT'S UP?

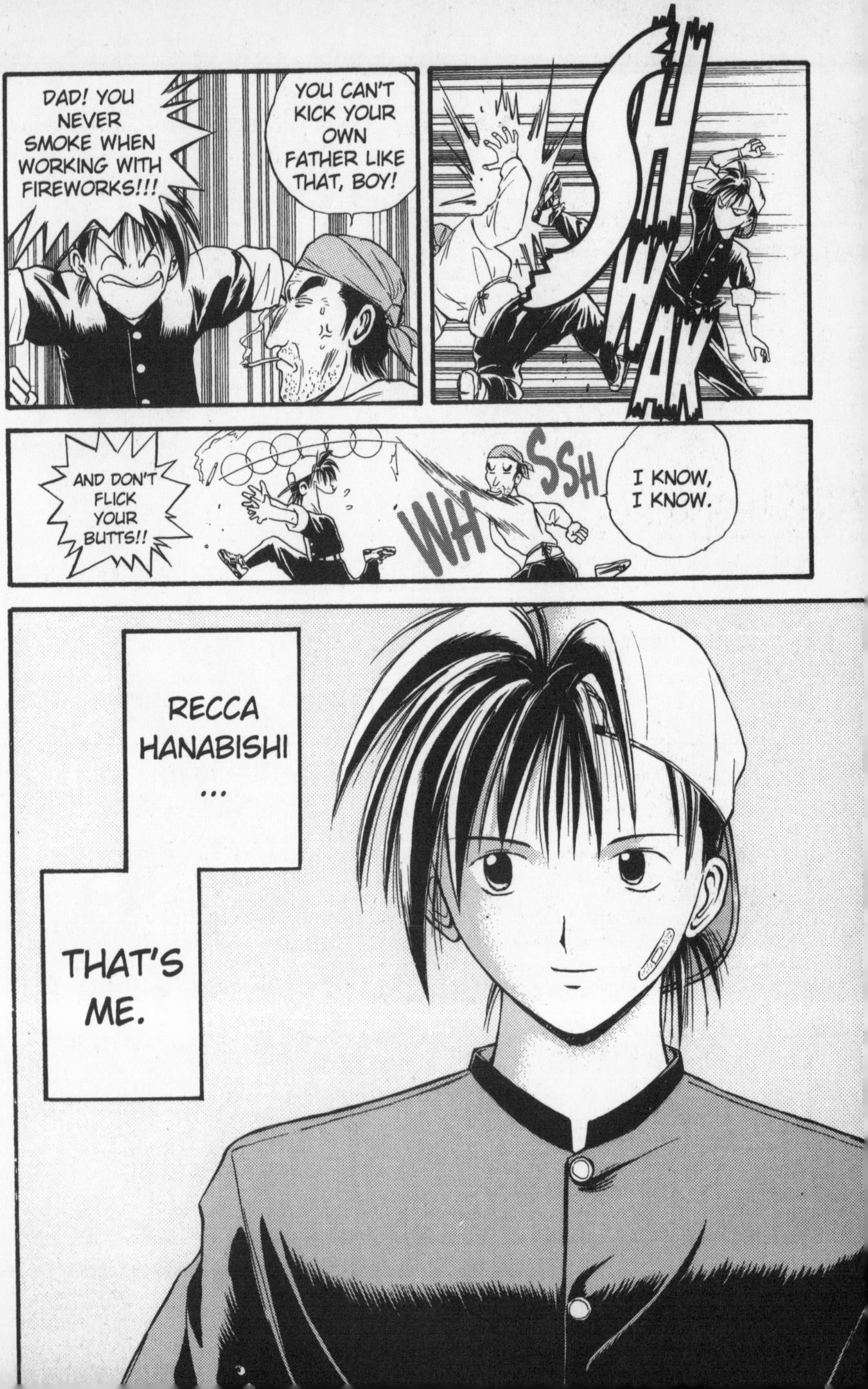
SHWAK
YOU CAN'T KICK YOUR OWN FATHER LIKE THAT, BOY!
DAD! YOU NEVER SMOKE WHEN WORKING WITH FIREWORKS!!!
I KNOW, I KNOW.
WHSSH
AND DON'T FLICK YOUR BUTTS!!
RECCA HANABISHI ...
THAT'S ME.

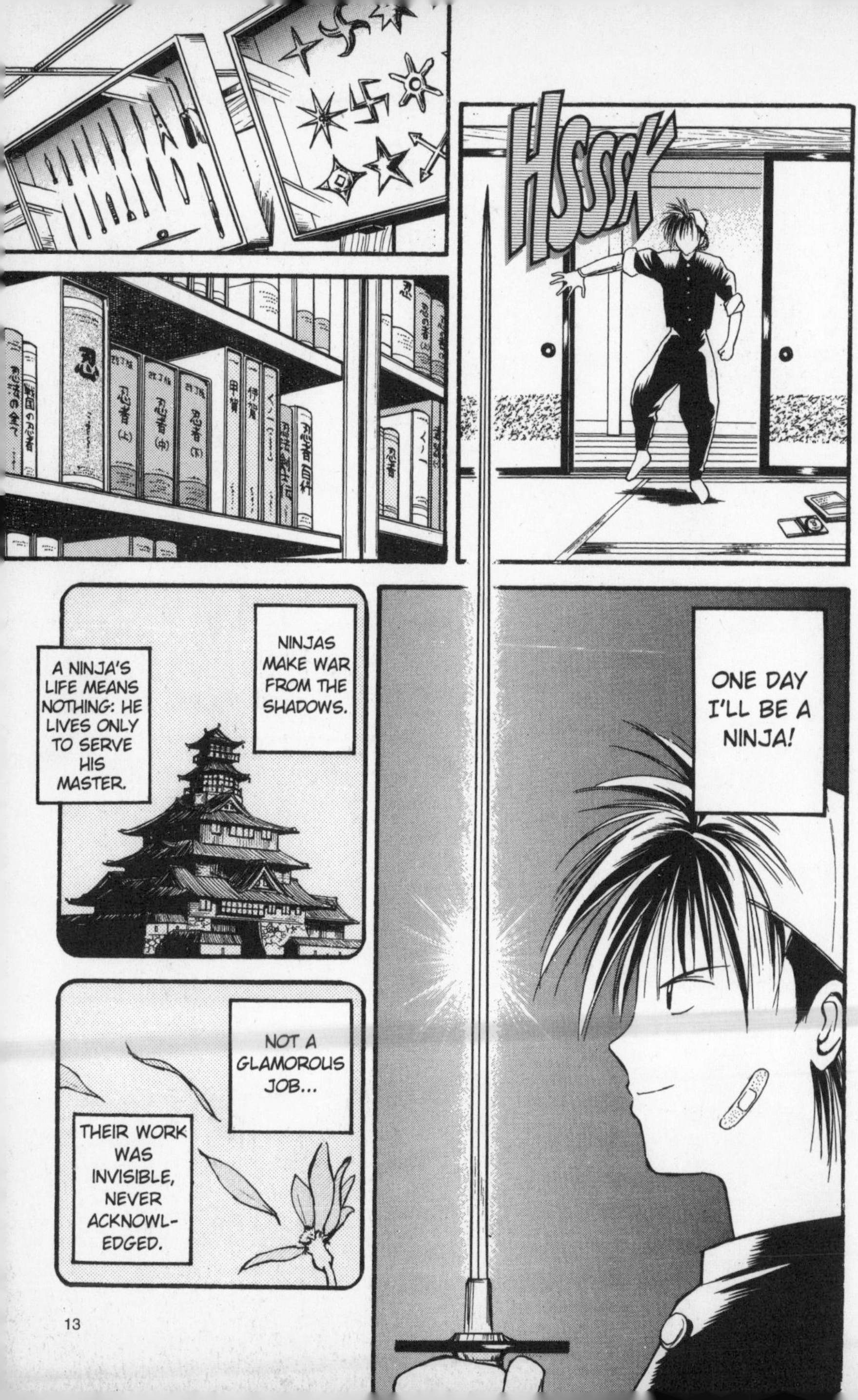
HSSSK
ONE DAY I'LL BE A NINJA!
NINJAS MAKE WAR FROM THE SHADOWS.
A NINJA'S LIFE MEANS NOTHING: HE LIVES ONLY TO SERVE HIS MASTER.
NOT A GLAMOROUS JOB...
THEIR WORK WAS INVISIBLE, NEVER ACKNOWL-EDGED.

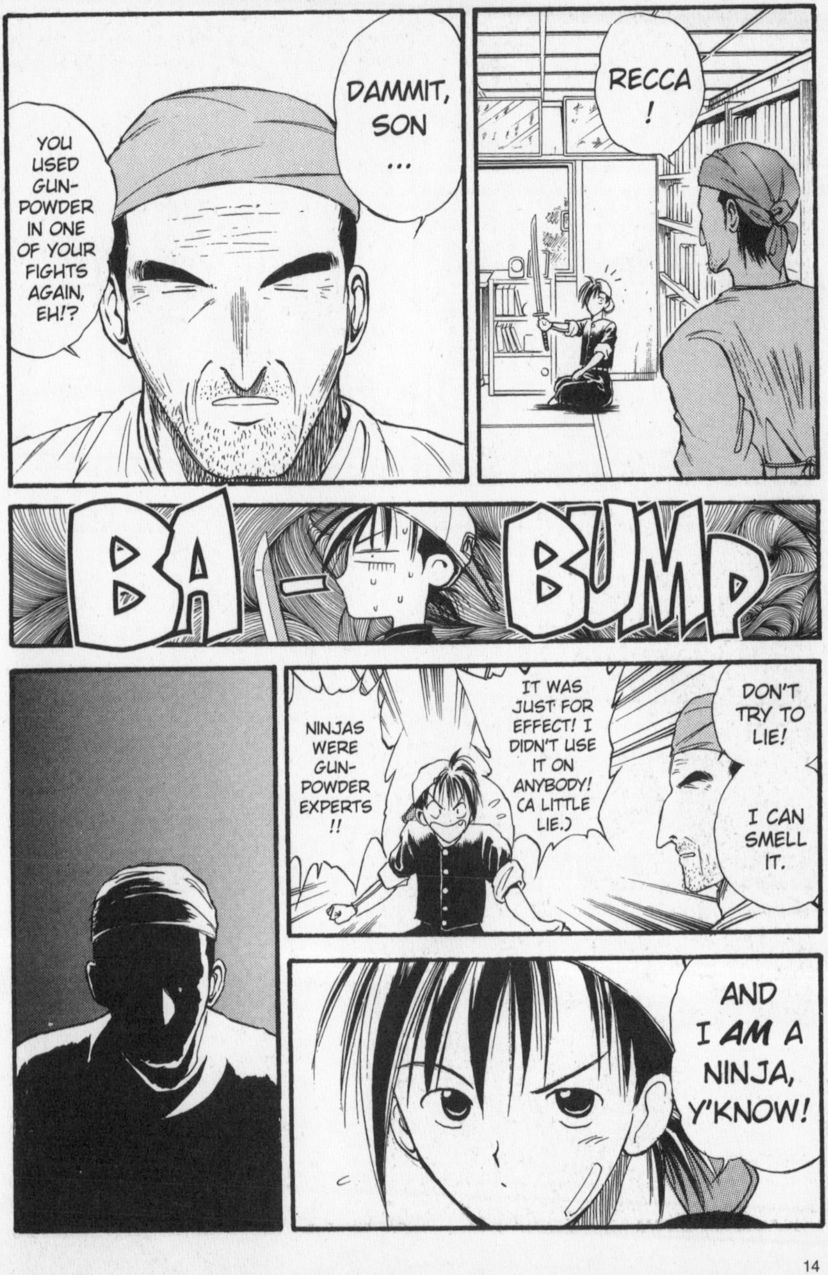
RECCA !
DAMMIT, SON ...
YOU USED GUN-POWDER IN ONE OF YOUR FIGHTS AGAIN, EH!?
BA-BUMP
DON'T TRY TO LIE!
I CAN SMELL IT.
IT WAS JUST FOR EFFECT! I DIDN'T USE IT ON ANYBODY! (A LITTLE LIE.)
NINJAS WERE GUN-POWDER EXPERTS !!
AND I AM A NINJA, Y'KNOW!

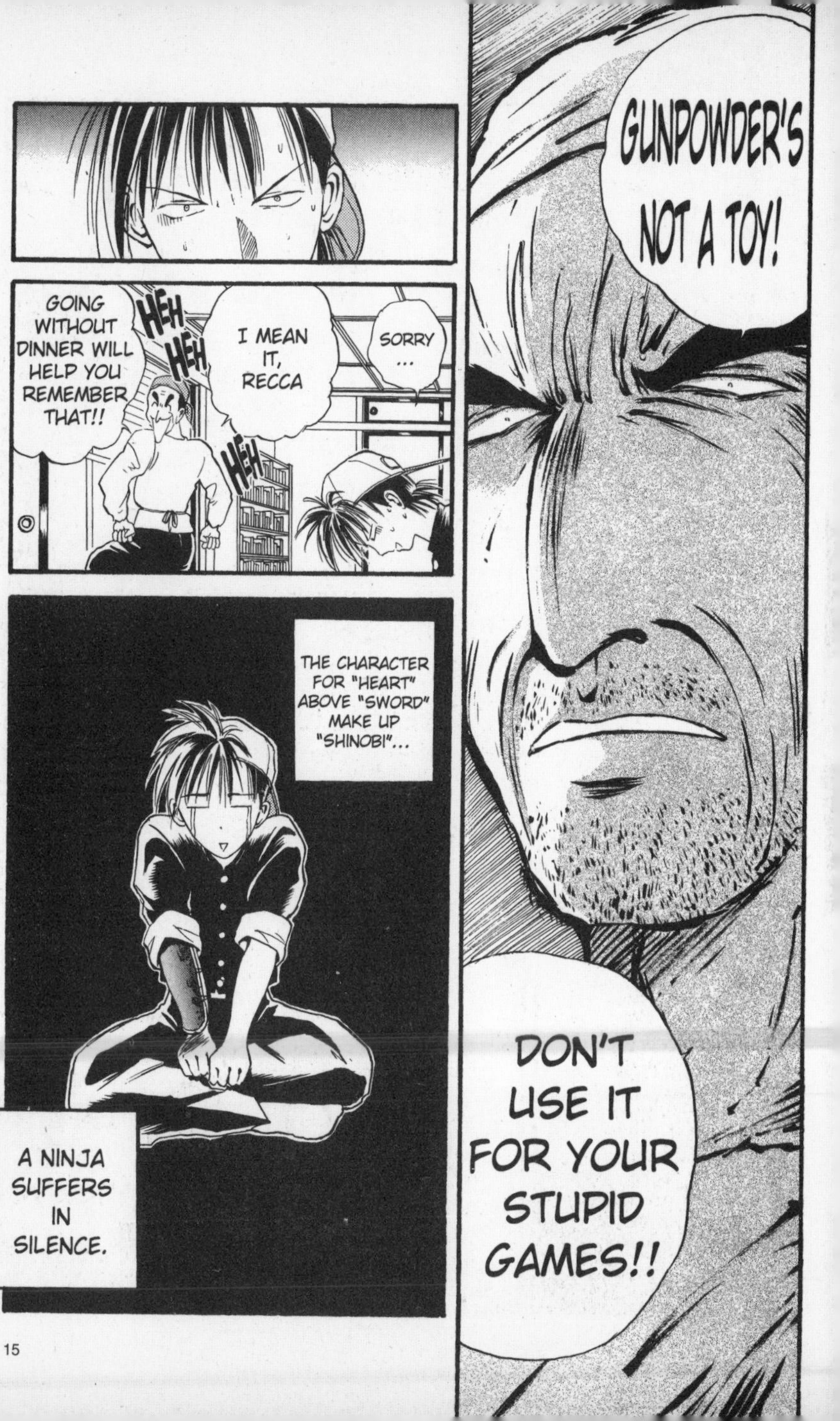
GUNPOWDER'S NOT A TOY!
DON'T USE IT FOR YOUR STUPID GAMES!!
SORRY ...
I MEAN IT, RECCA
HEH HEH HEH
GOING WITHOUT DINNER WILL HELP YOU REMEMBER THAT!!
THE CHARACTER FOR "HEART" ABOVE "SWORD" MAKE UP "SHINOBI"...
A NINJA SUFFERS IN SILENCE.

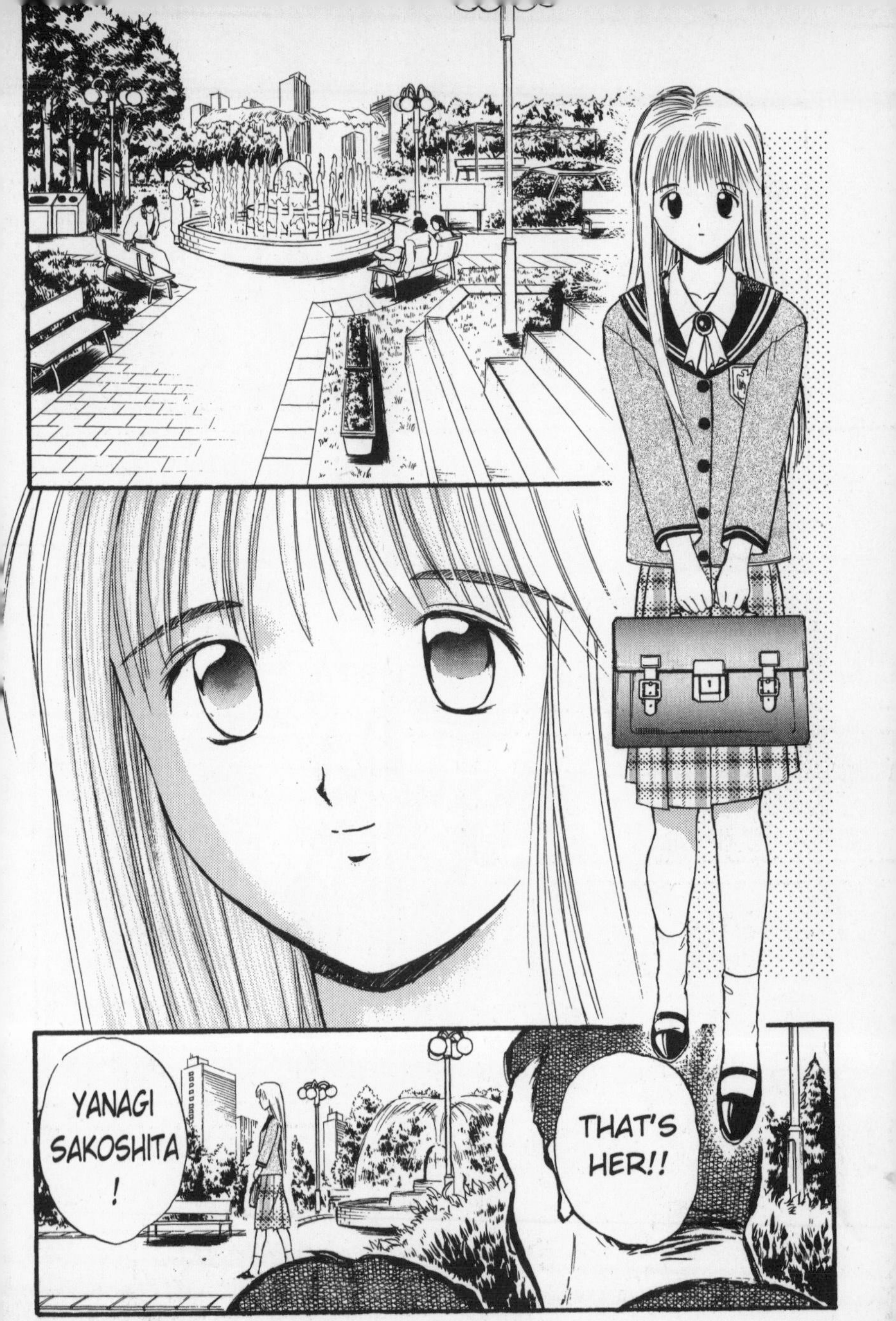
THAT'S HER!!
YANAGI SAKOSHITA !

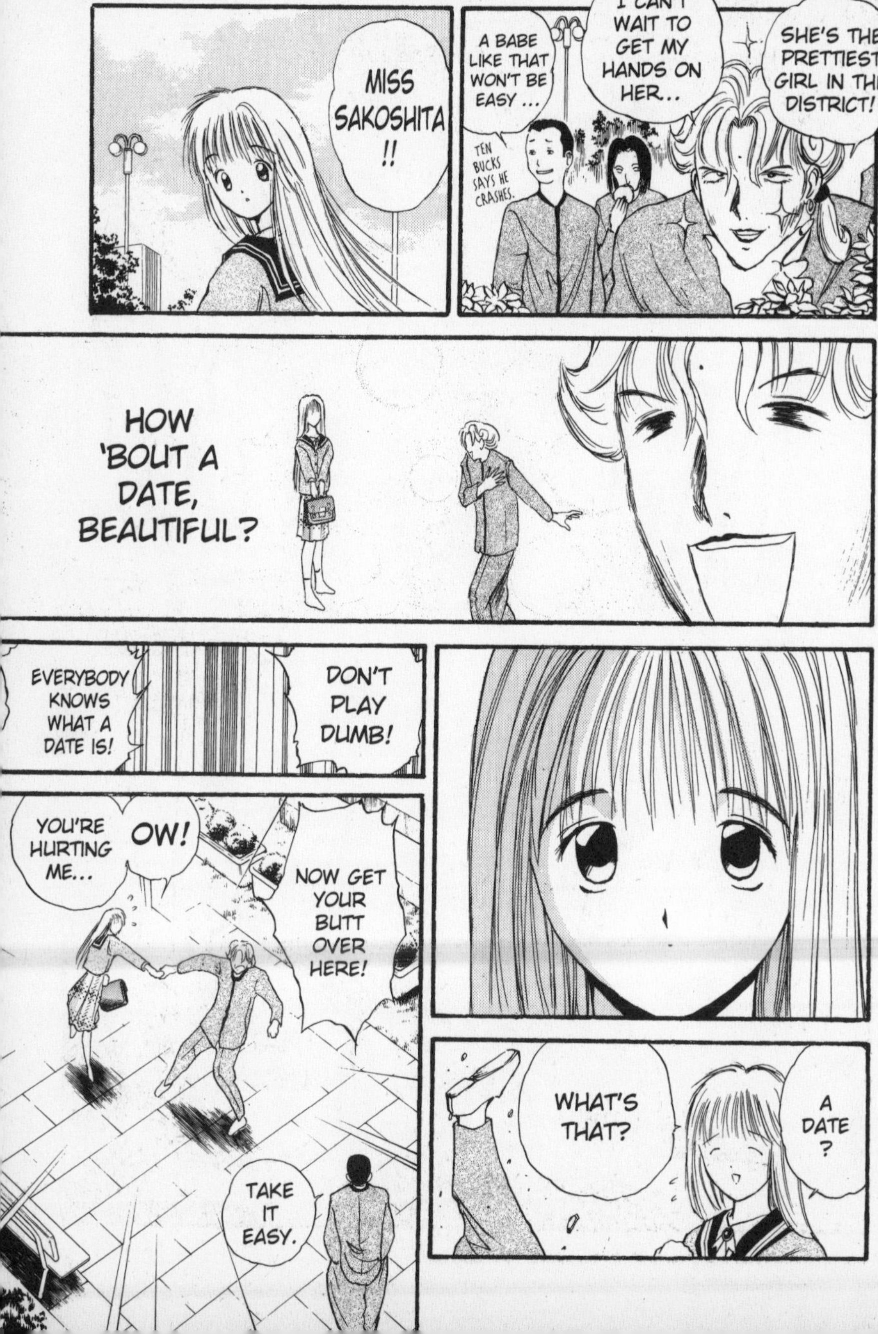
SHE'S THE PRETTIEST GIRL IN THE DISTRICT!
I CAN'T WAIT TO GET MY HANDS ON HER...
A BABE LIKE THAT WON'T BE EASY...
TEN BUCKS SAYS HE CRASHES.
MISS SAKOSHITA!!
HOW 'BOUT A DATE, BEAUTIFUL?
A DATE?
WHAT'S THAT?
DON'T PLAY DUMB!
EVERYBODY KNOWS WHAT A DATE IS!
NOW GET YOUR BUTT OVER HERE!
OW!
YOU'RE HURTING ME...
TAKE IT EASY.

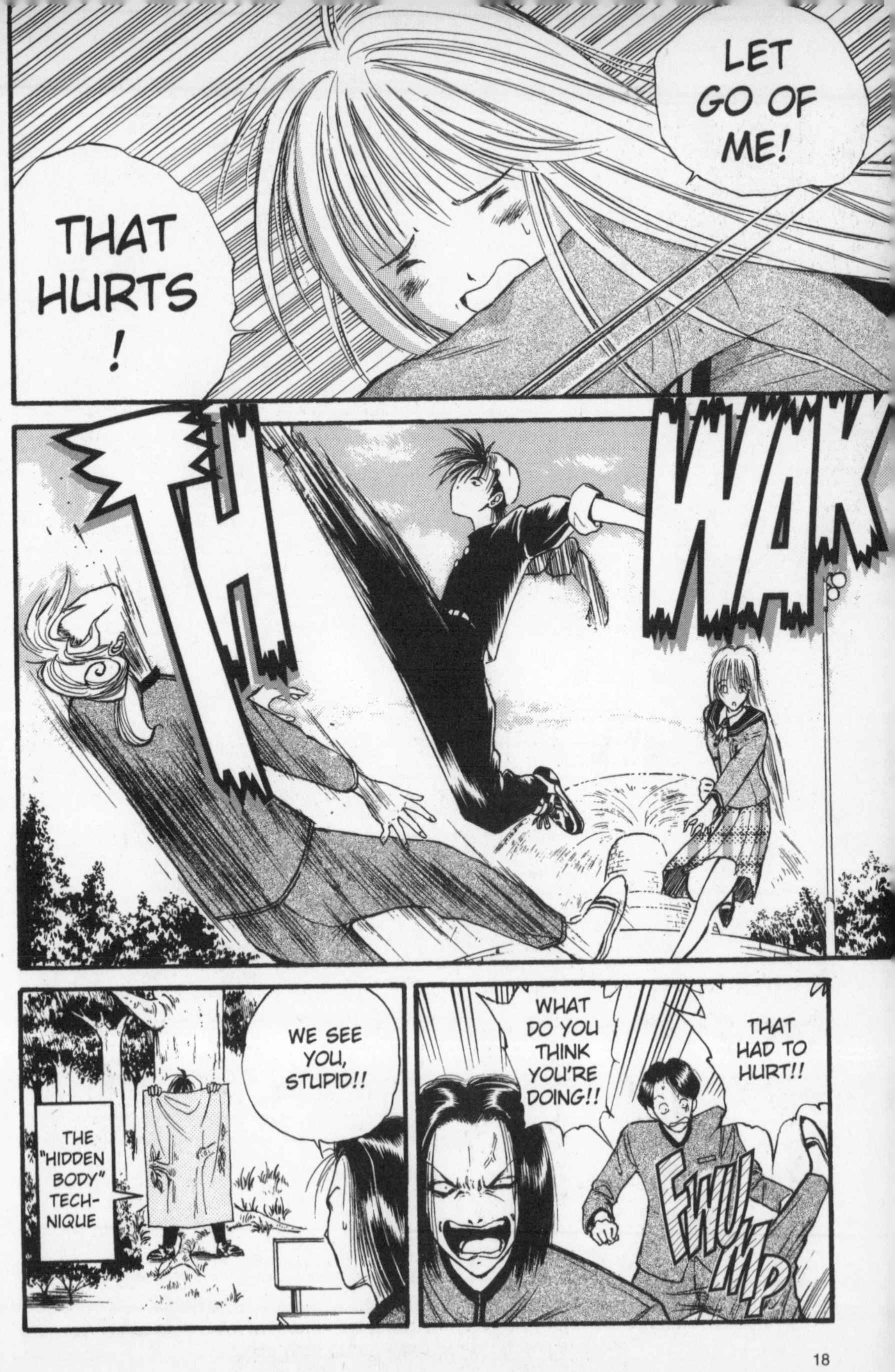
LET GO OF ME!
THAT HURTS!
TH
WAK
THAT HAD TO HURT!!
WHAT DO YOU THINK YOU'RE DOING!!
FWUMP
WE SEE YOU, STUPID!!
THE "HIDDEN BODY" TECHNIQUE

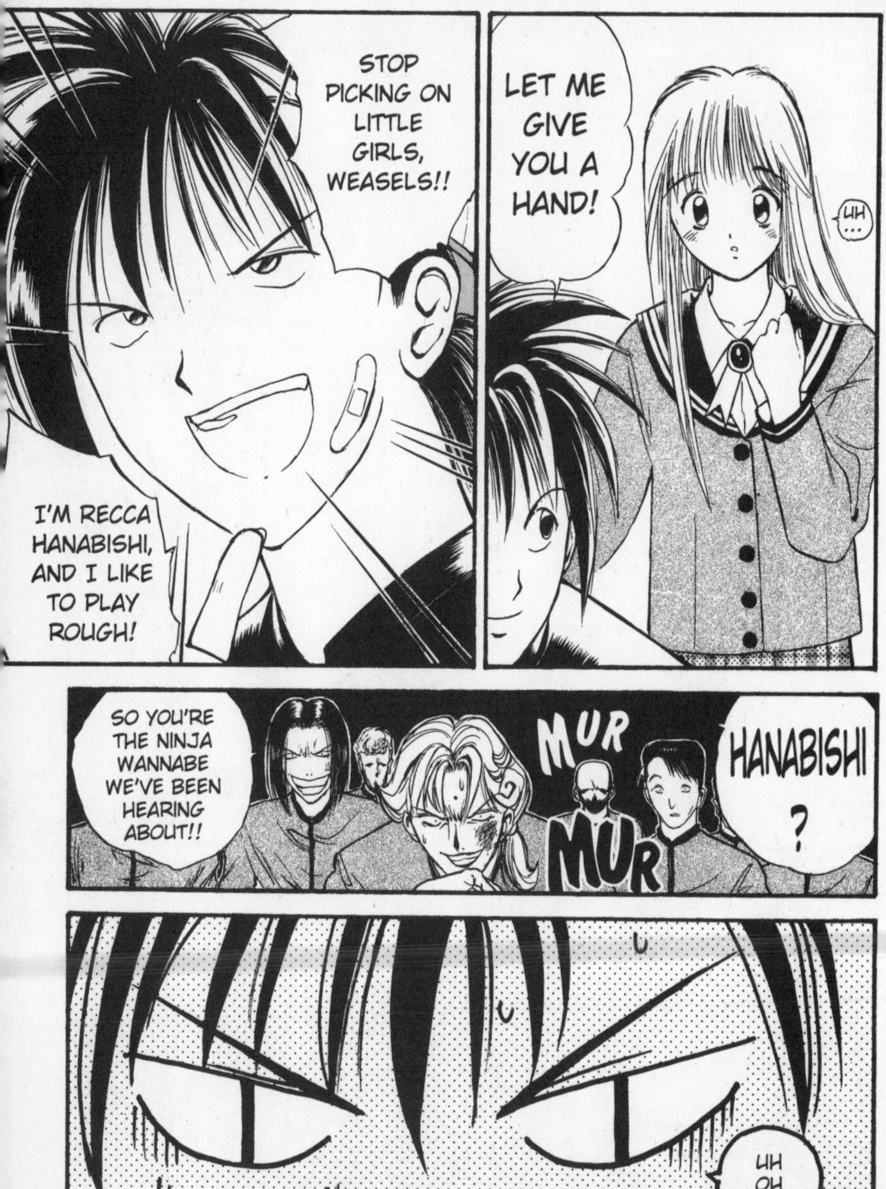
LET ME GIVE YOU A HAND!
UH ...
STOP PICKING ON LITTLE GIRLS, WEASELS!!
I'M RECCA HANABISHI, AND I LIKE TO PLAY ROUGH!
HANABISHI ?
MUR
MUR
SO YOU'RE THE NINJA WANNABE WE'VE BEEN HEARING ABOUT!!
UH OH ...

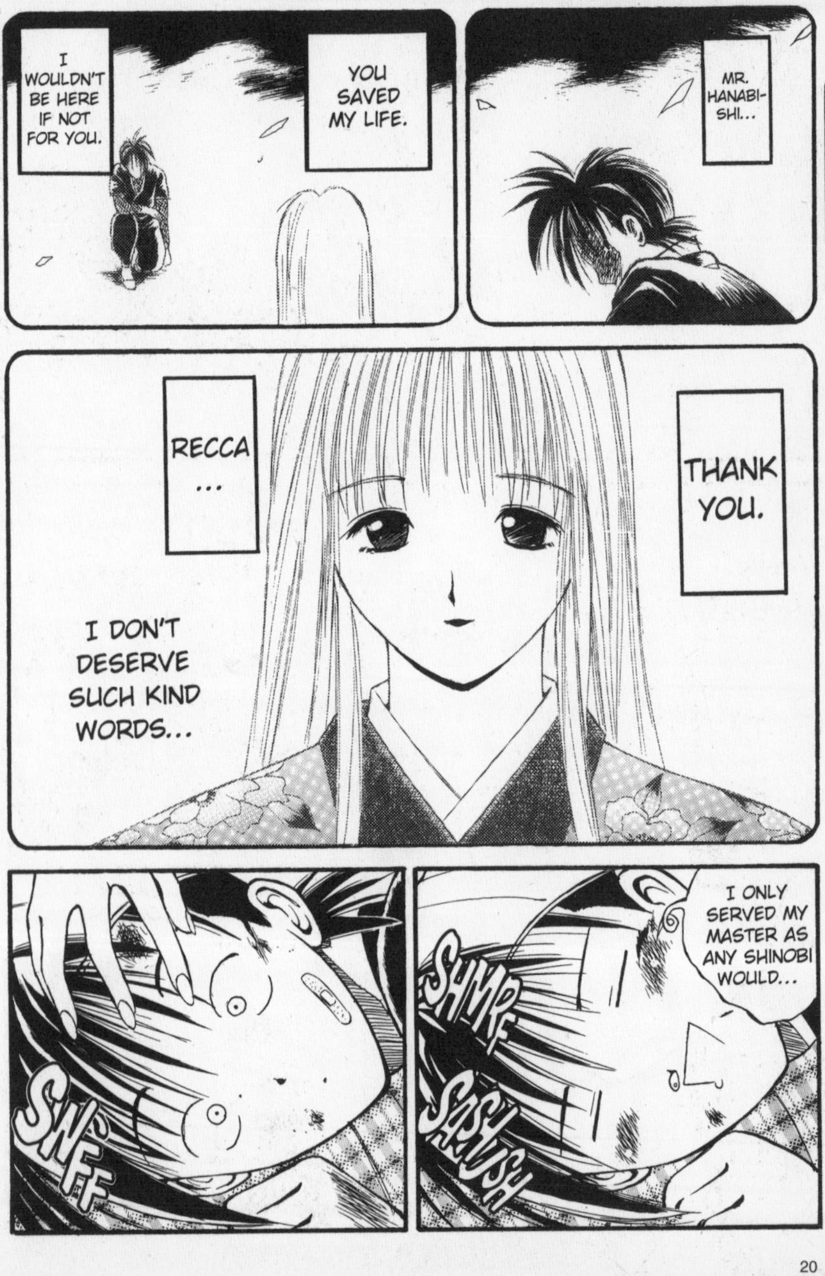
MR. HANABI-SHI...
YOU SAVED MY LIFE.
I WOULDN'T BE HERE IF NOT FOR YOU.
RECCA...
THANK YOU.
I DON'T DESERVE SUCH KIND WORDS...
I ONLY SERVED MY MASTER AS ANY SHINOBI WOULD...
SHMF
SASHSH
SNIFF

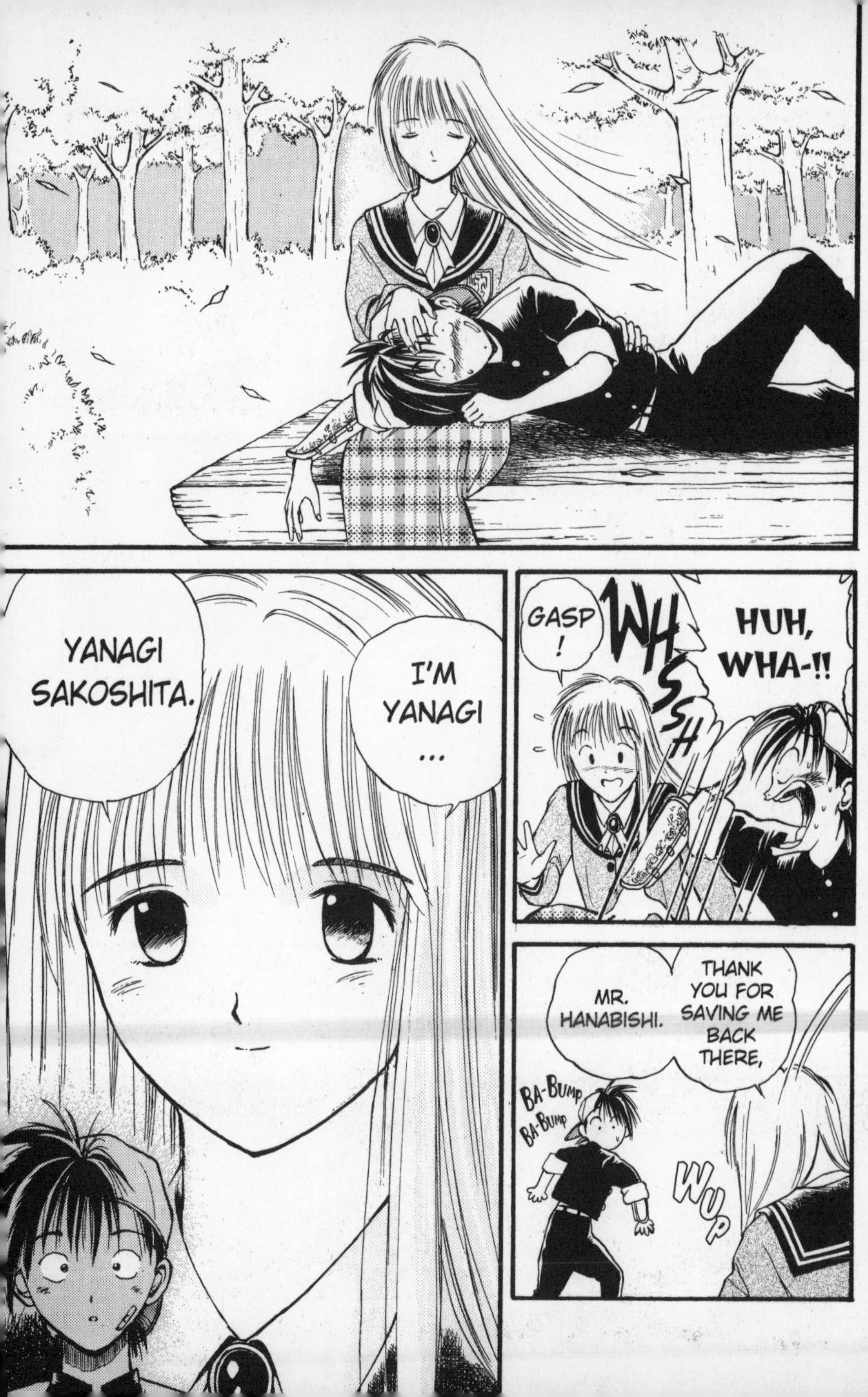
HUH, WHA-!!
WHSSH
GASP!
THANK YOU FOR SAVING ME BACK THERE,
MR. HANABISHI.
BA-BUMP BA-BUMP
WUP
I'M YANAGI ...
YANAGI SAKOSHITA.

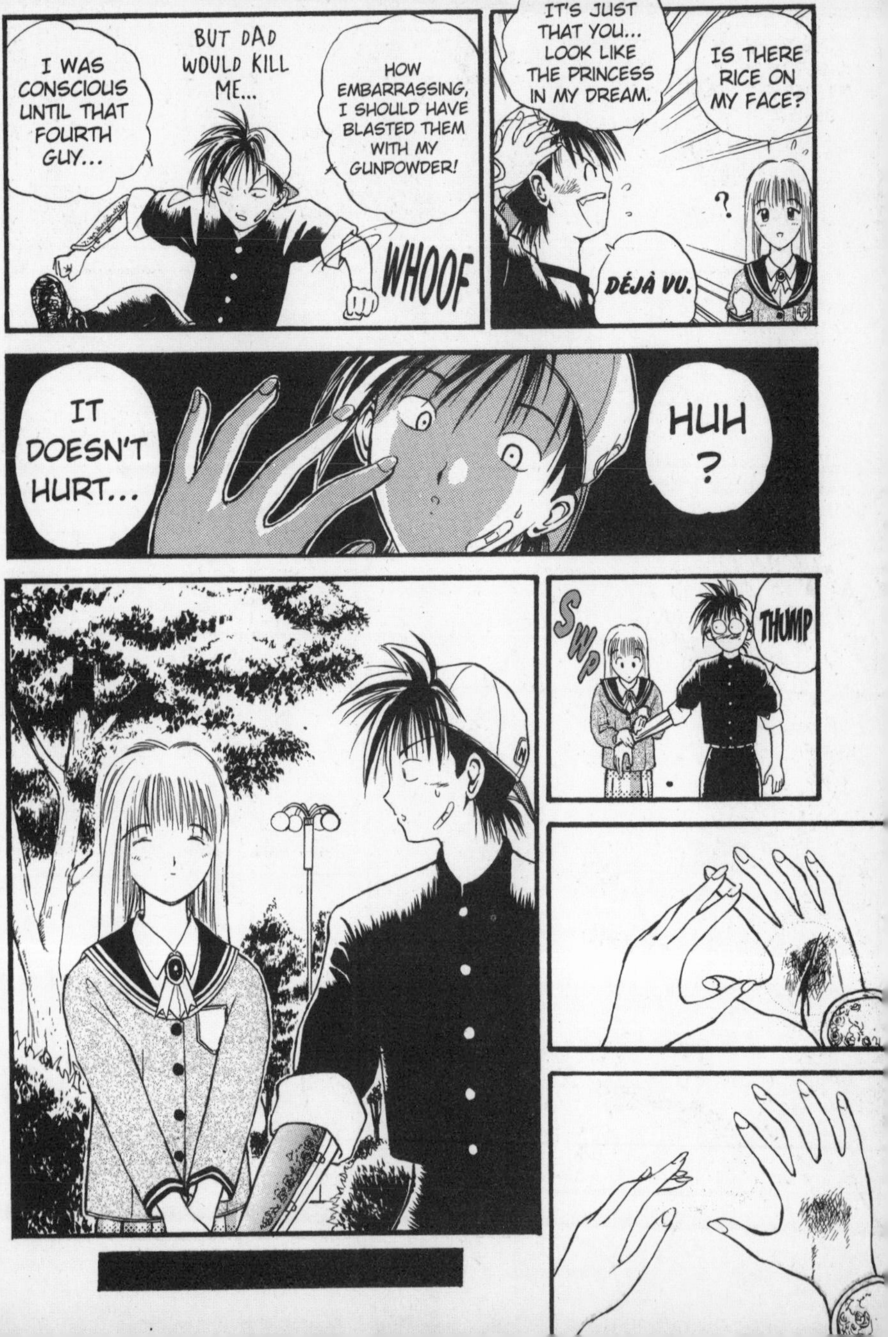
IS THERE RICE ON MY FACE?
HUH? NO. IT'S JUST THAT YOU... LOOK LIKE THE PRINCESS IN MY DREAM.
DÉJÀ VU.
HOW EMBARRASSING, I SHOULD HAVE BLASTED THEM WITH MY GUNPOWDER!
BUT DAD WOULD KILL ME...
I WAS CONSCIOUS UNTIL THAT FOURTH GUY...
WHOOF
HUH ?
IT DOESN'T HURT...
THUMP
SWP

[redacted]

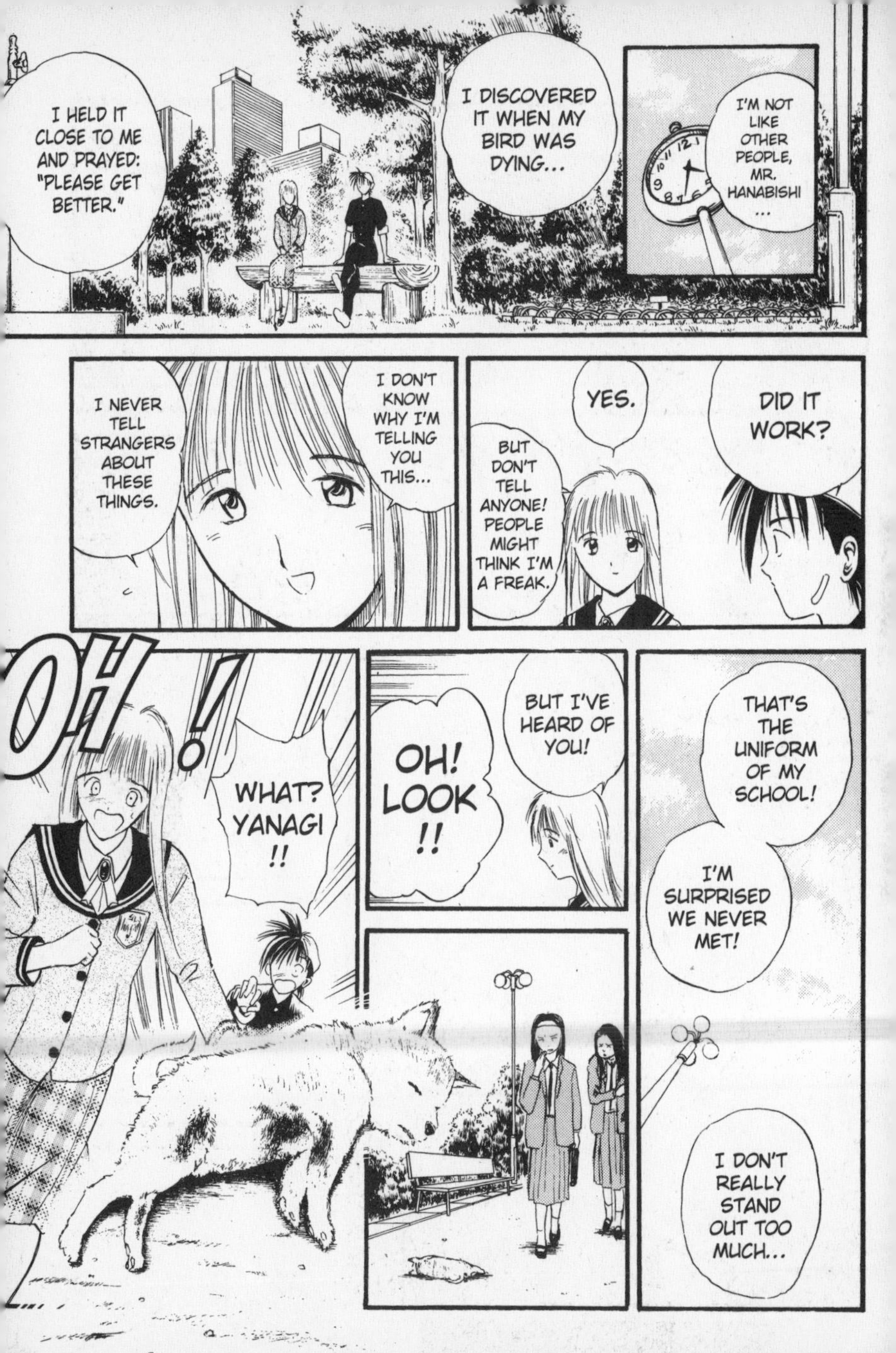
I'M NOT LIKE OTHER PEOPLE, MR. HANABISHI...
I DISCOVERED IT WHEN MY BIRD WAS DYING...
I HELD IT CLOSE TO ME AND PRAYED: "PLEASE GET BETTER."
DID IT WORK?
YES.
BUT DON'T TELL ANYONE! PEOPLE MIGHT THINK I'M A FREAK.
I DON'T KNOW WHY I'M TELLING YOU THIS...
I NEVER TELL STRANGERS ABOUT THESE THINGS.
THAT'S THE UNIFORM OF MY SCHOOL!
I'M SURPRISED WE NEVER MET!
I DON'T REALLY STAND OUT TOO MUCH...
BUT I'VE HEARD OF YOU!
OH! LOOK!!
OH!
WHAT? YANAGI!!

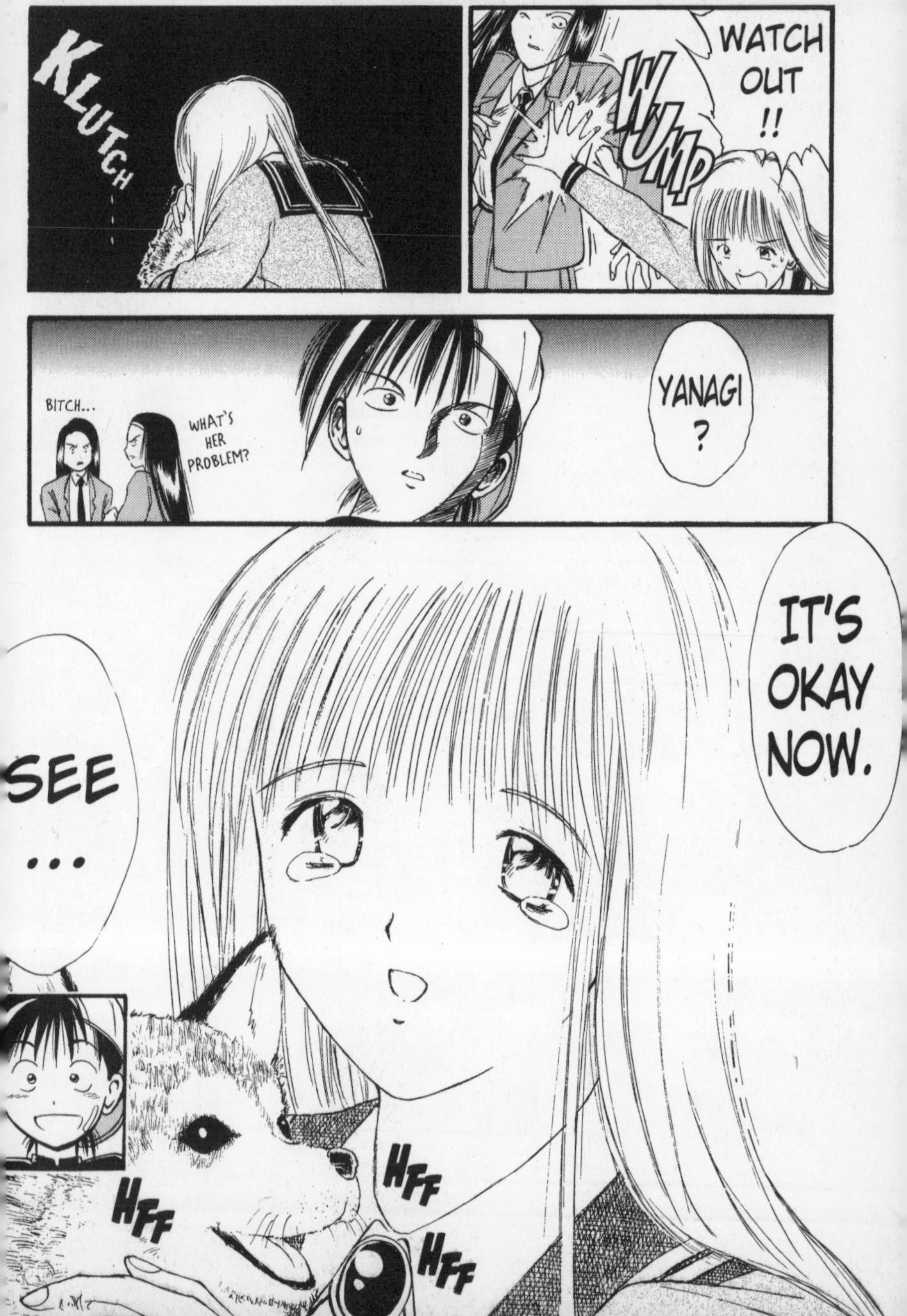
WATCH OUT !!
WUMP
KLUTCH
YANAGI ?
WHAT'S HER PROBLEM?
BITCH...
IT'S OKAY NOW.
SEE ...
HFF
HFF
HFF

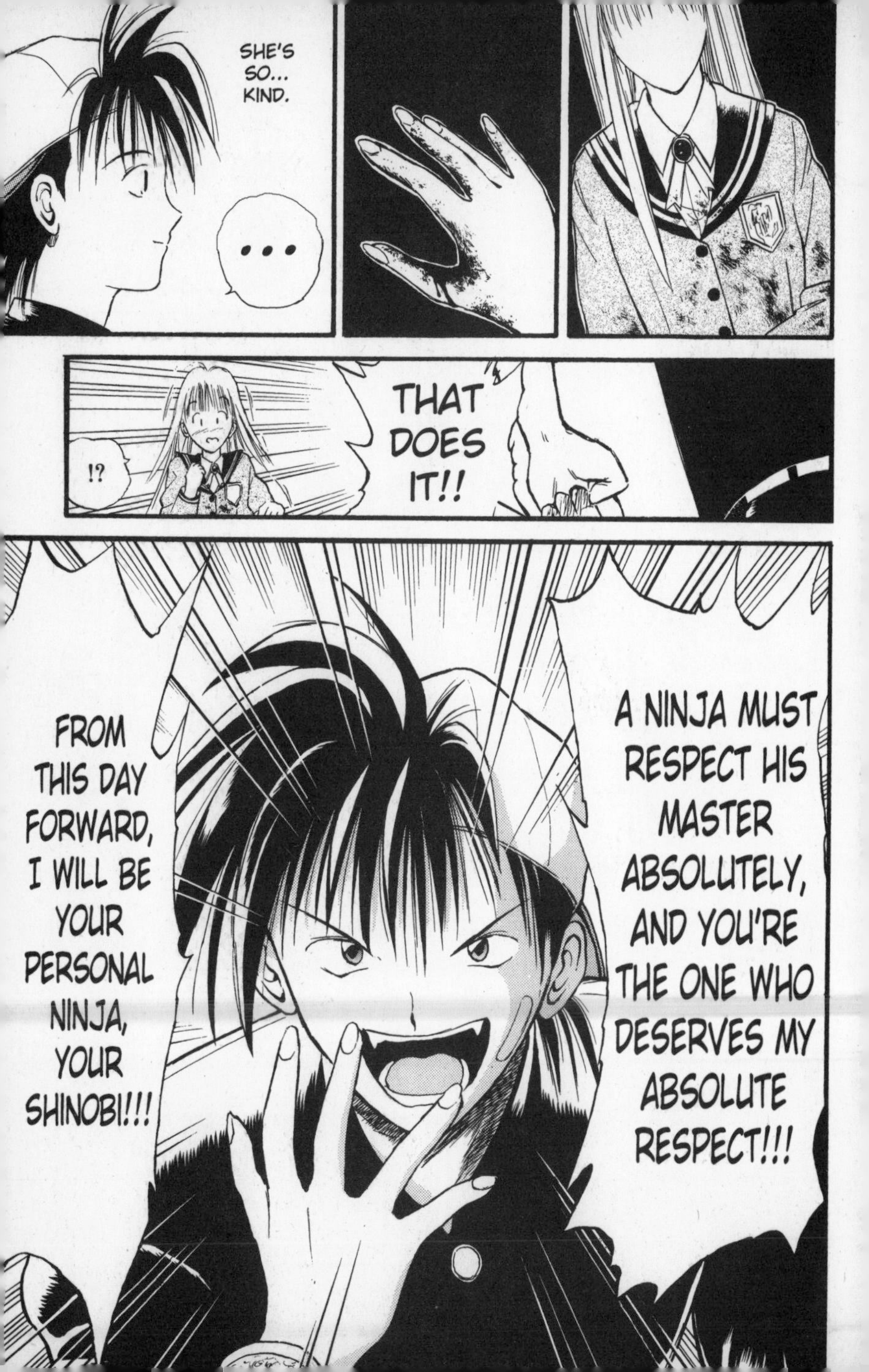
SHE'S SO... KIND.
...
THAT DOES IT!!
!?
A NINJA MUST RESPECT HIS MASTER ABSOLUTELY, AND YOU'RE THE ONE WHO DESERVES MY ABSOLUTE RESPECT!!!
FROM THIS DAY FORWARD, I WILL BE YOUR PERSONAL NINJA, YOUR SHINOBI!!!

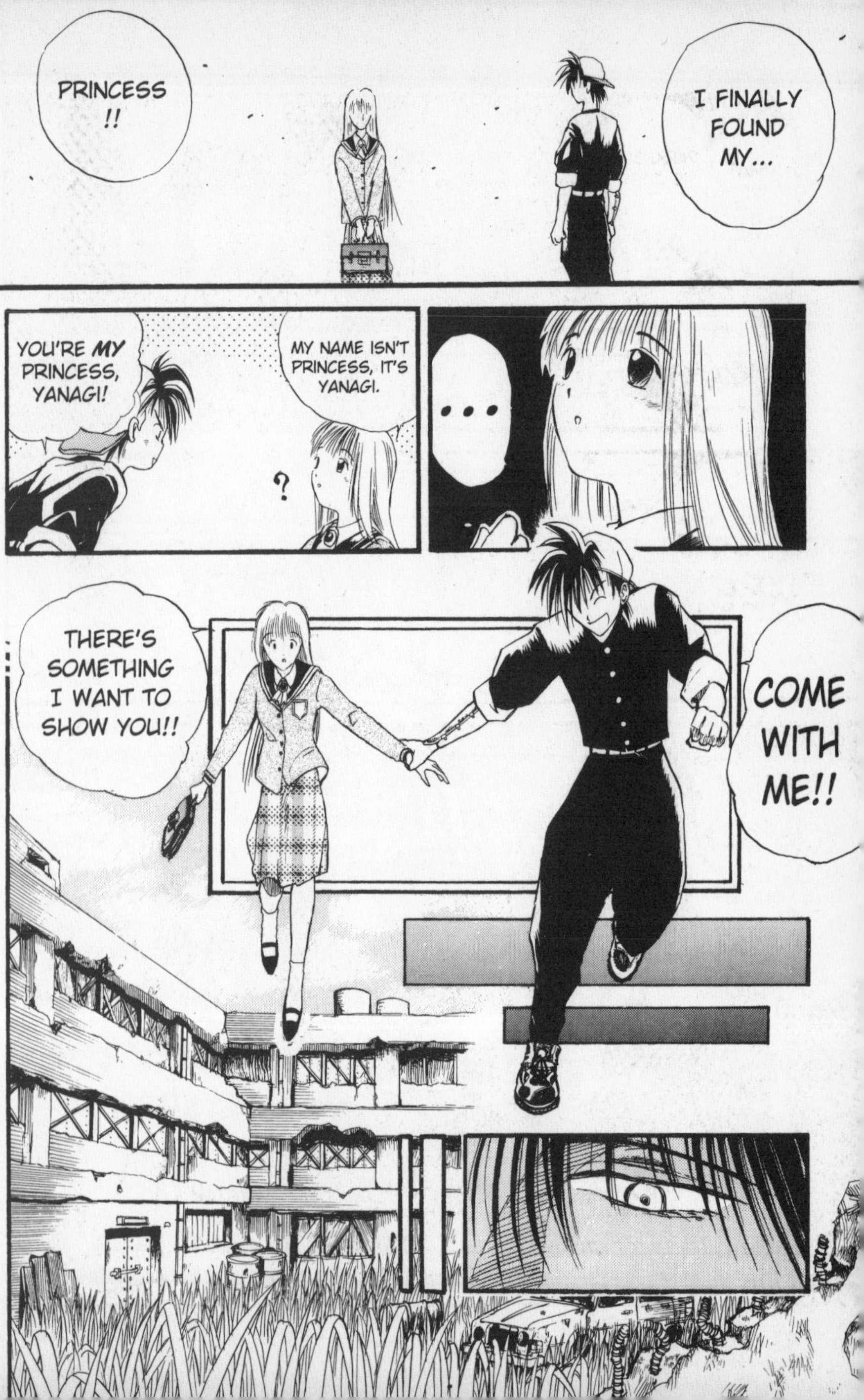
I FINALLY FOUND MY...
PRINCESS !!
...
MY NAME ISN'T PRINCESS, IT'S YANAGI.
?
YOU'RE *MY* PRINCESS, YANAGI!
COME WITH ME!!
THERE'S SOMETHING I WANT TO SHOW YOU!!

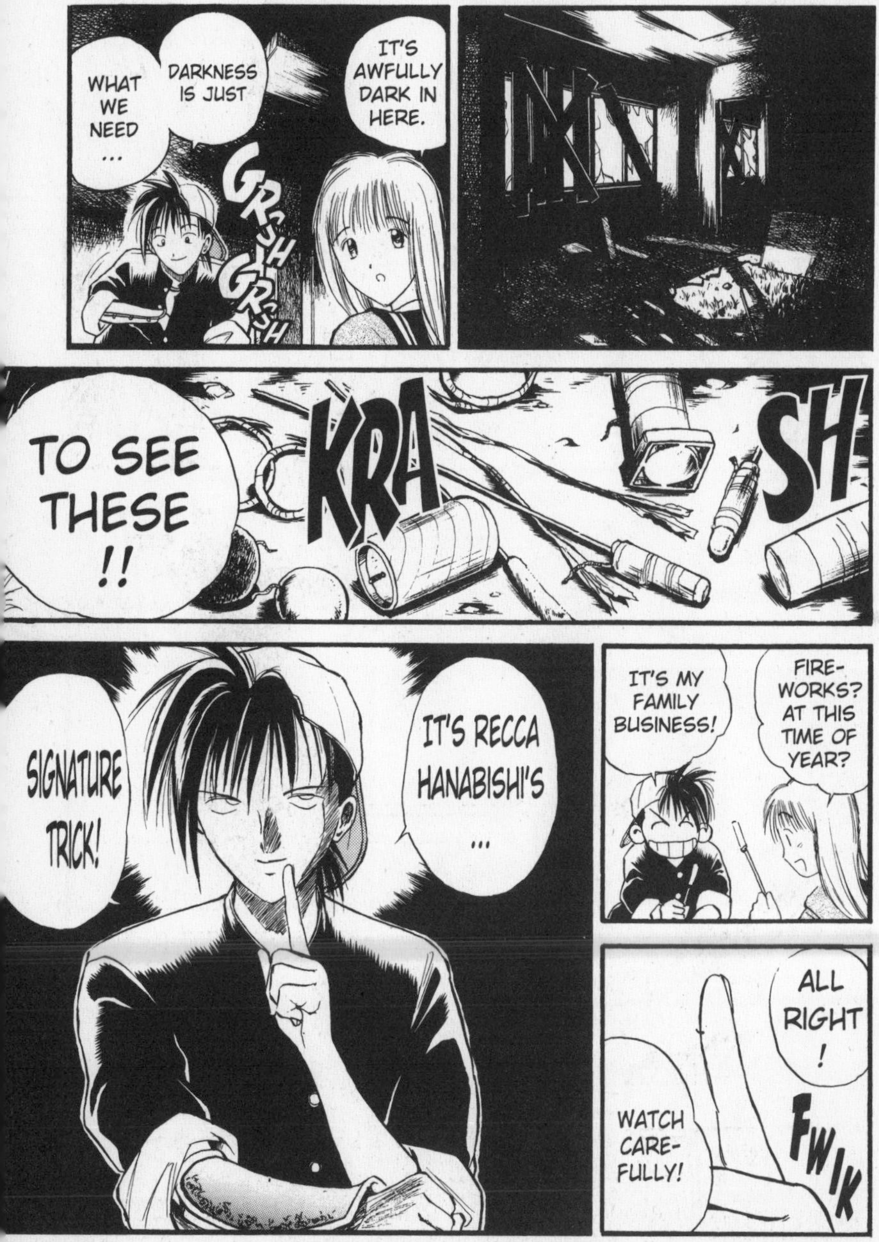
IT'S AWFULLY DARK IN HERE.
DARKNESS IS JUST
WHAT WE NEED ...
GRSH GRSH
SH
KRA
TO SEE THESE !!
FIRE-WORKS? AT THIS TIME OF YEAR?
IT'S MY FAMILY BUSINESS!
ALL RIGHT !
FWIK
WATCH CARE-FULLY!
IT'S RECCA HANABISHI'S ...
SIGNATURE TRICK!

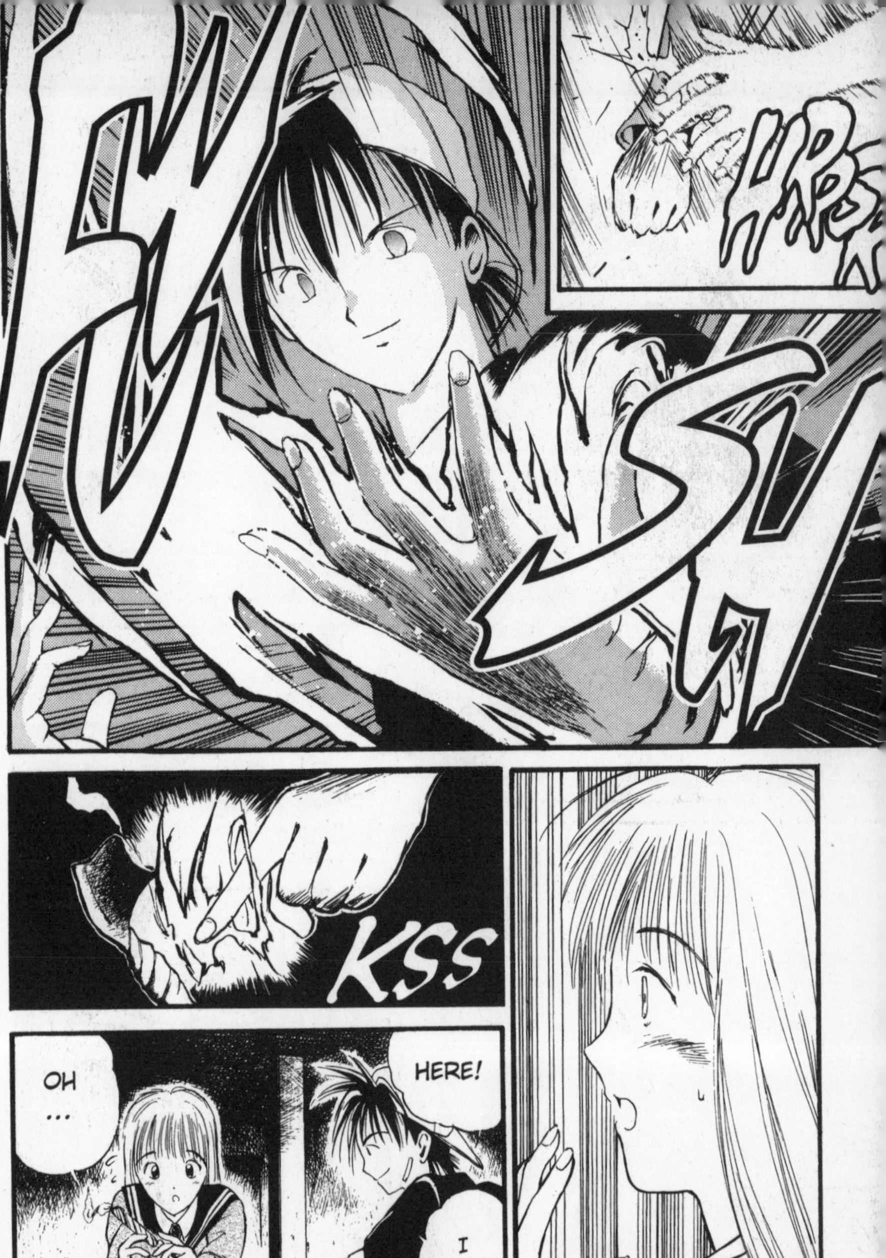
KSS
HERE!
I MADE IT MYSELF !!
OH ...

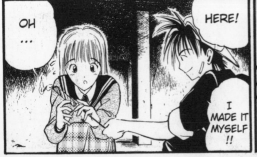

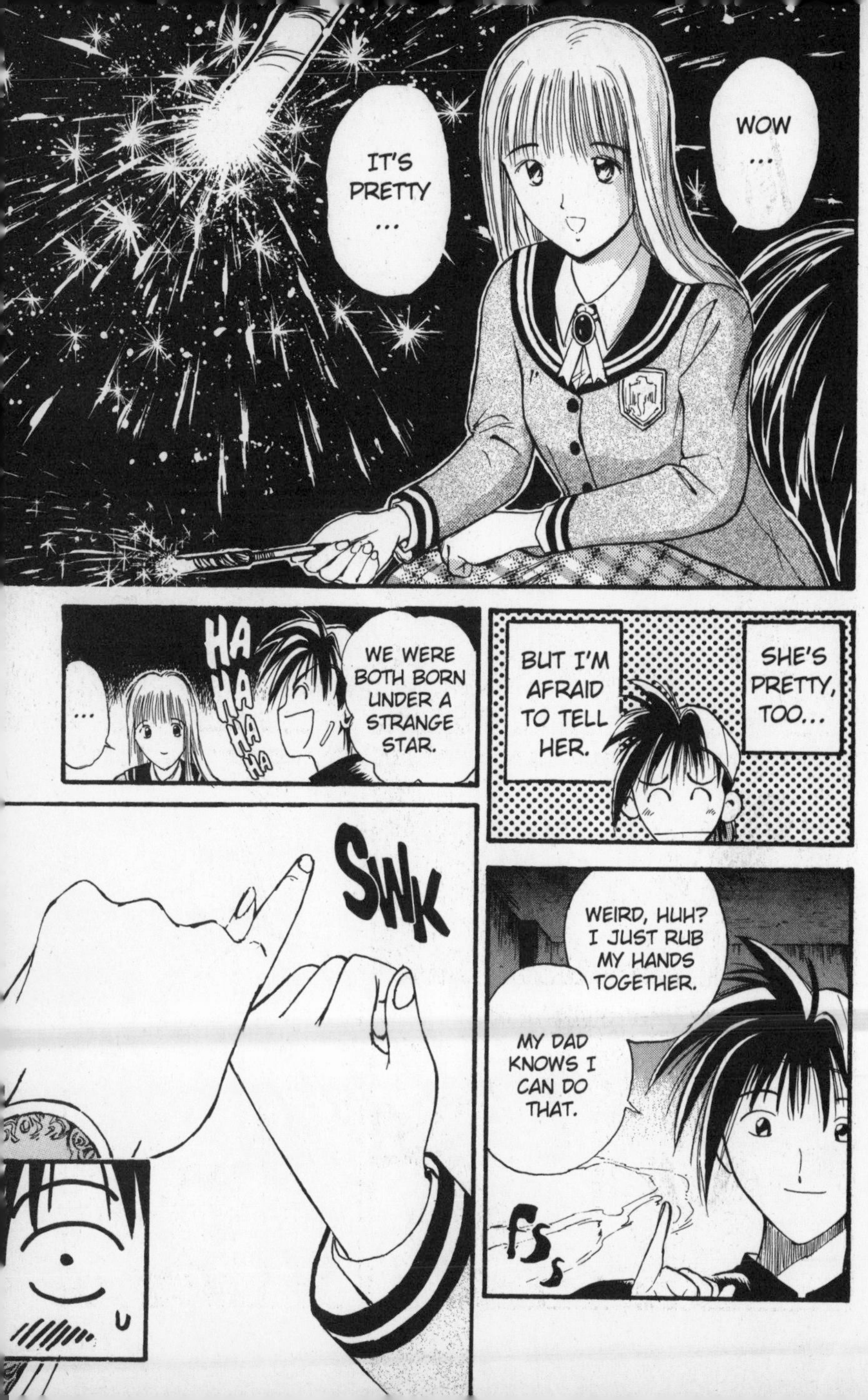
WOW ...
IT'S PRETTY ...
SHE'S PRETTY, TOO...
BUT I'M AFRAID TO TELL HER.
WE WERE BOTH BORN UNDER A STRANGE STAR.
HA HA HA HA HA
...
WEIRD, HUH? I JUST RUB MY HANDS TOGETHER.
MY DAD KNOWS I CAN DO THAT.
FSS
SINK

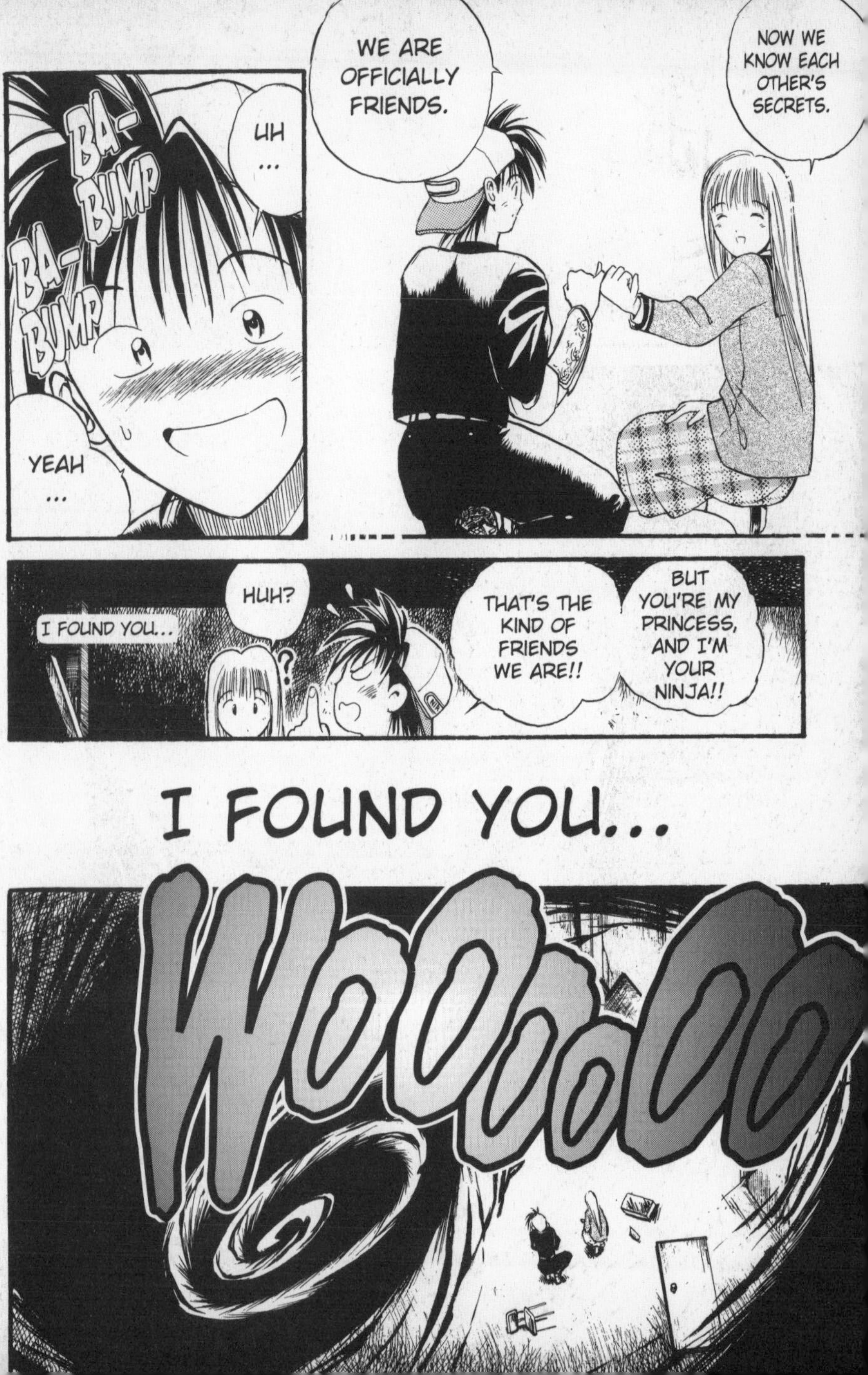
NOW WE KNOW EACH OTHER'S SECRETS.
WE ARE OFFICIALLY FRIENDS.
UH ...
BA-BUMP
BA-BUMP
YEAH ...
BUT YOU'RE MY PRINCESS, AND I'M YOUR NINJA!!
THAT'S THE KIND OF FRIENDS WE ARE!!
HUH?
I FOUND YOU...
I FOUND YOU...
WOOooOO

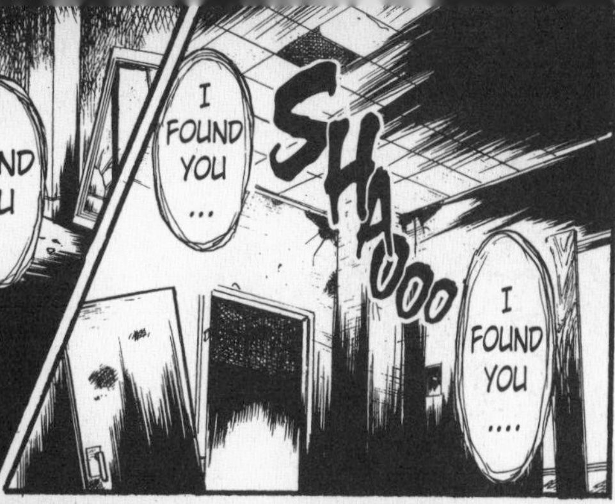
I FOUND YOU ...
SHAOOO
I FOUND YOU ....
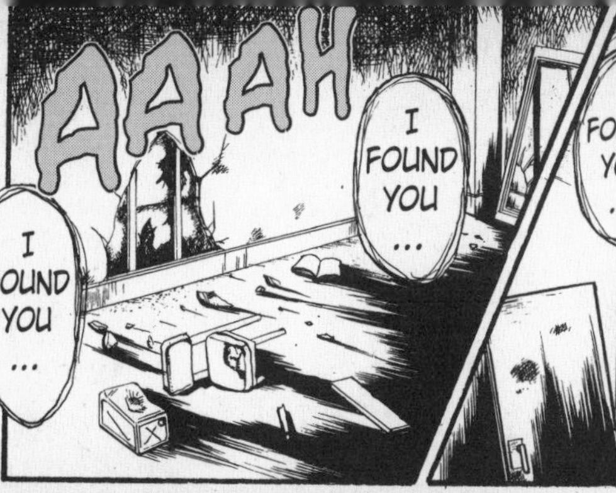
I FOUND YOU ...
AAAH
I FOUND YOU ...
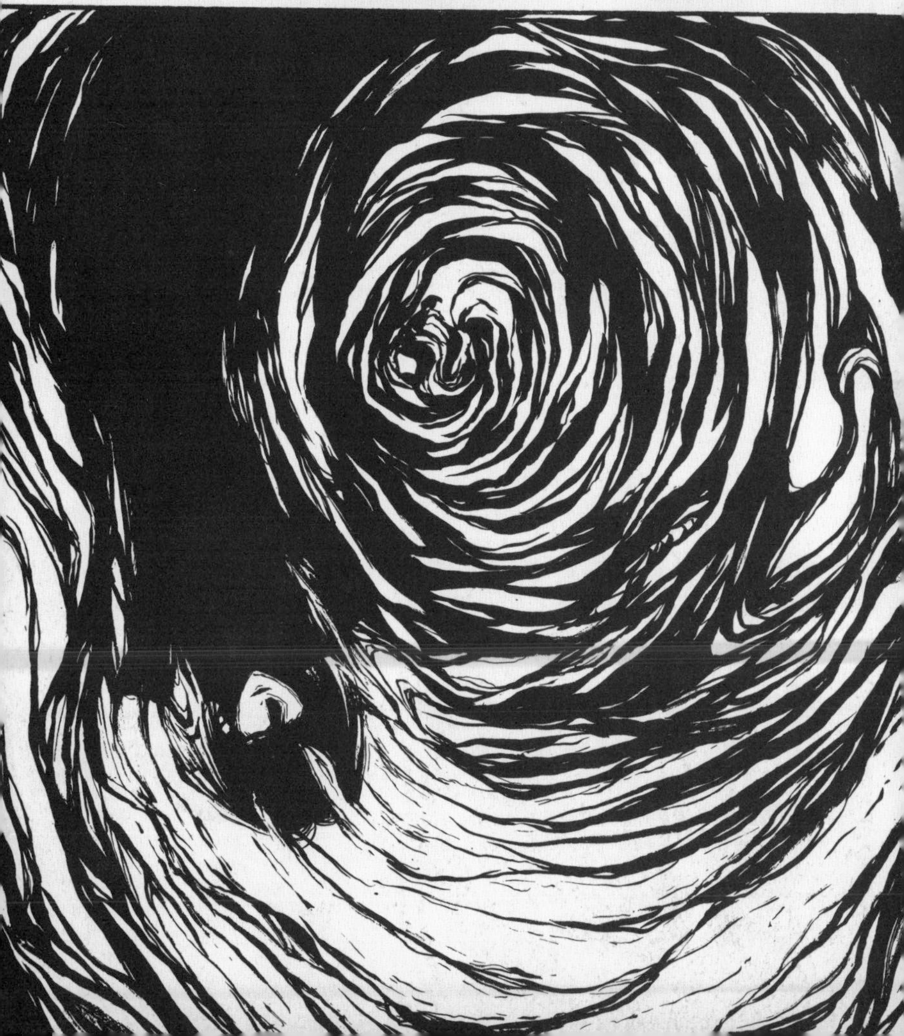

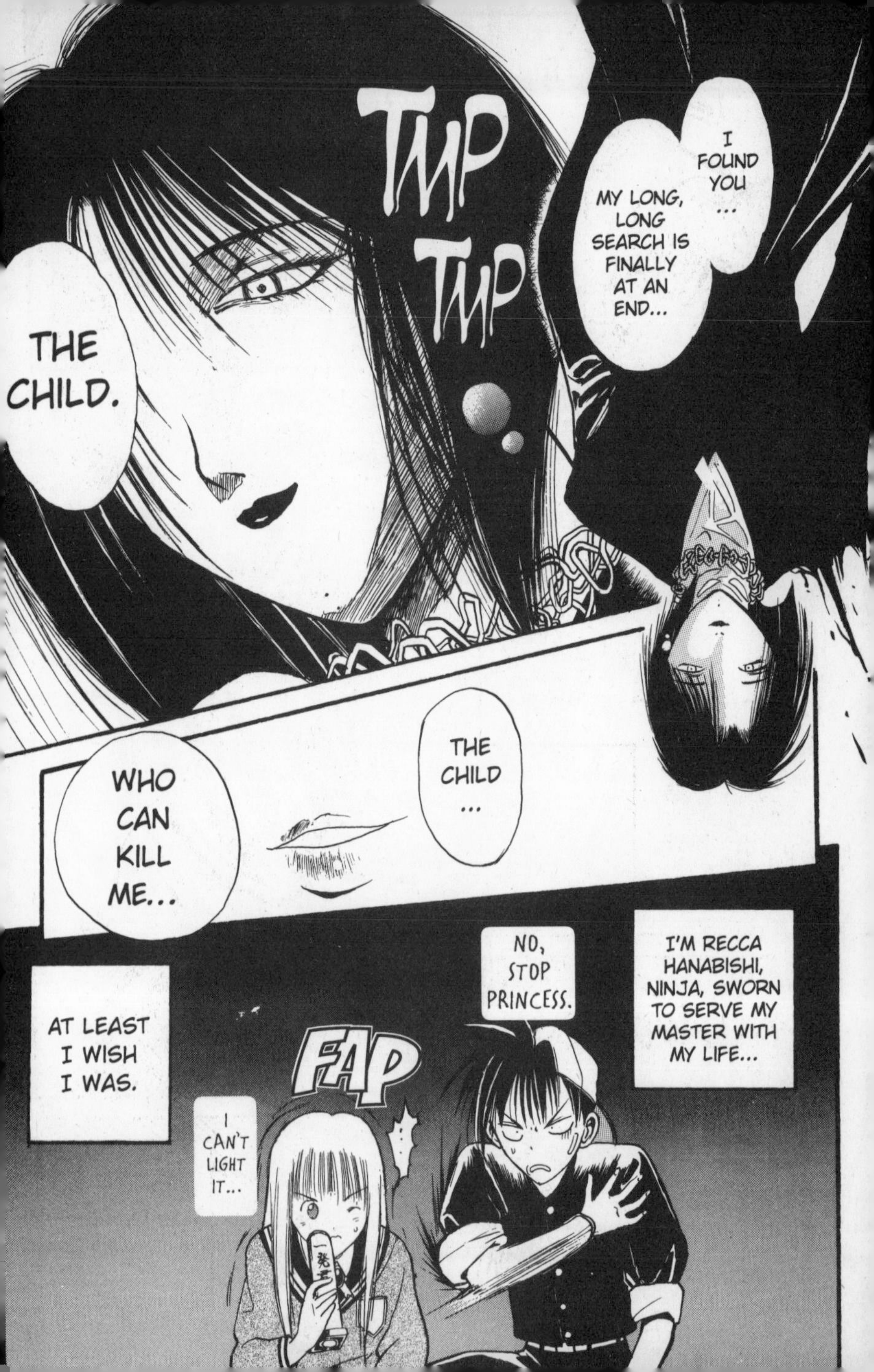
I FOUND YOU ...
MY LONG, LONG SEARCH IS FINALLY AT AN END...
TMP TMP
THE CHILD.
THE CHILD ...
WHO CAN KILL ME...
I'M RECCA HANABISHI, NINJA, SWORN TO SERVE MY MASTER WITH MY LIFE...
NO, STOP PRINCESS.
AT LEAST I WISH I WAS.
FAP
I CAN'T LIGHT IT...

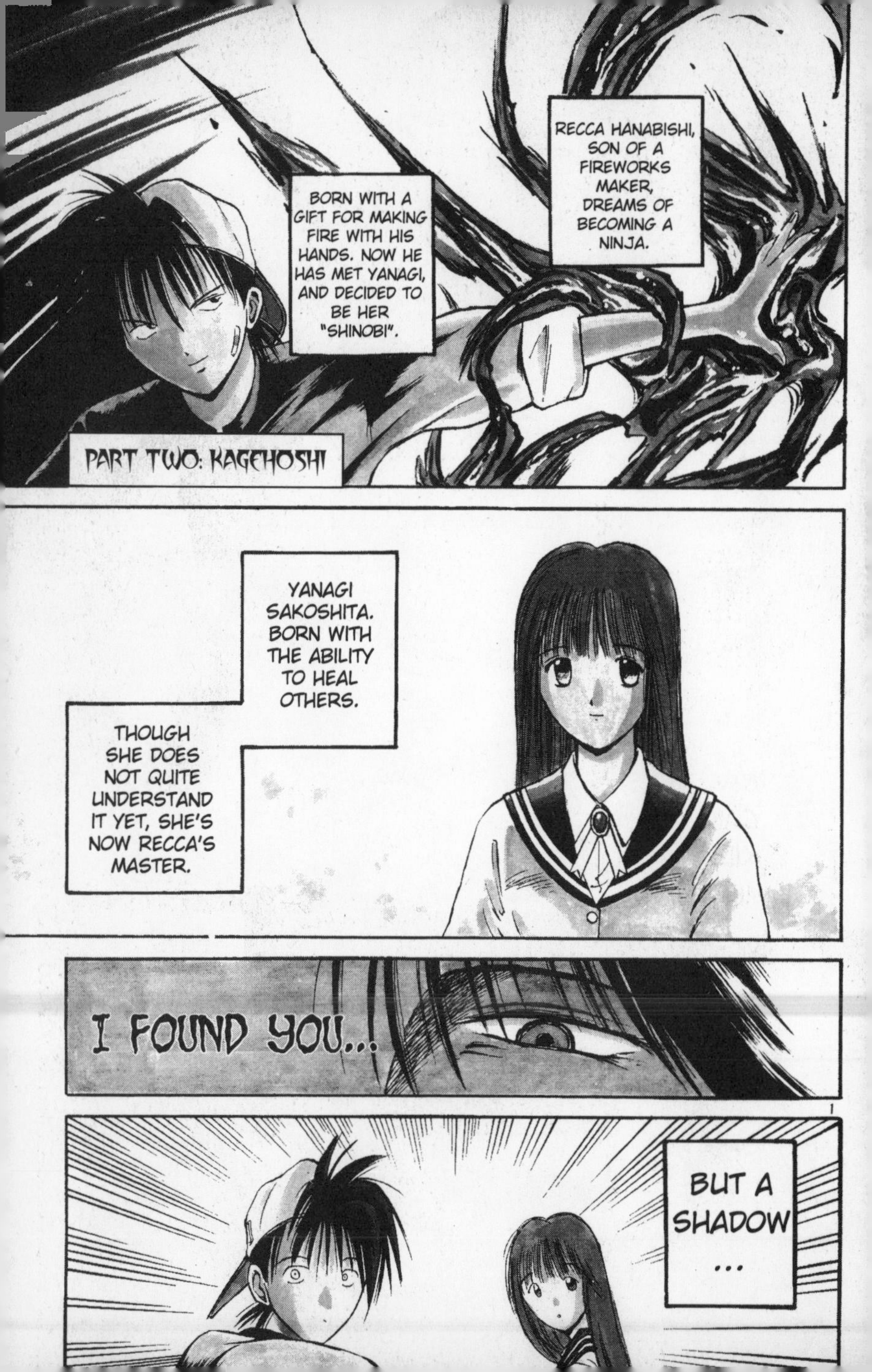
RECCA HANABISHI, SON OF A FIREWORKS MAKER, DREAMS OF BECOMING A NINJA.
BORN WITH A GIFT FOR MAKING FIRE WITH HIS HANDS. NOW HE HAS MET YANAGI, AND DECIDED TO BE HER "SHINOBI".
PART TWO: KAGEHOSHI
YANAGI SAKOSHITA. BORN WITH THE ABILITY TO HEAL OTHERS.
THOUGH SHE DOES NOT QUITE UNDERSTAND IT YET, SHE'S NOW RECCA'S MASTER.
I FOUND YOU...
BUT A SHADOW ...

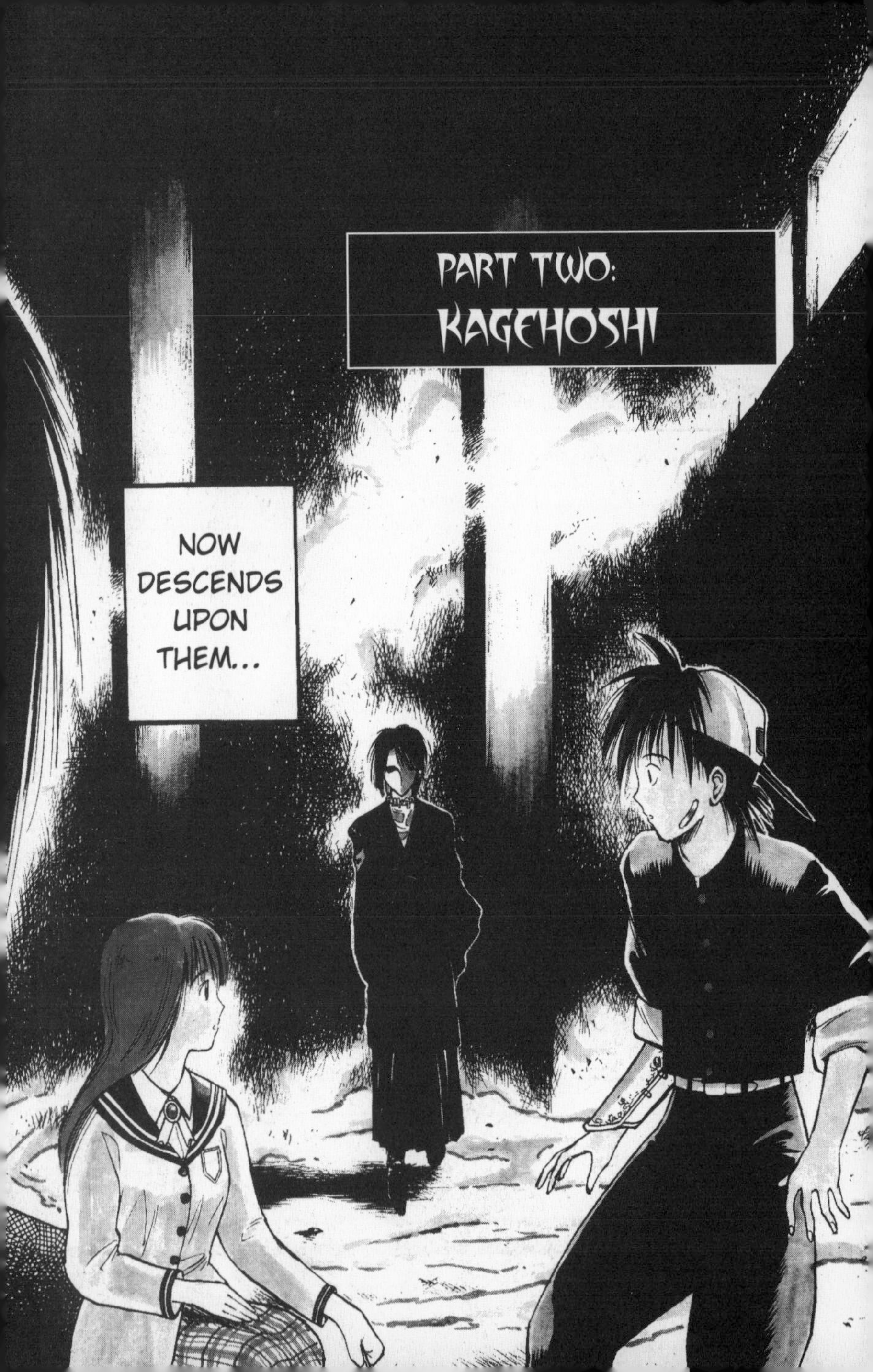
PART TWO:
KAGEHOSHI
NOW DESCENDS UPON THEM...

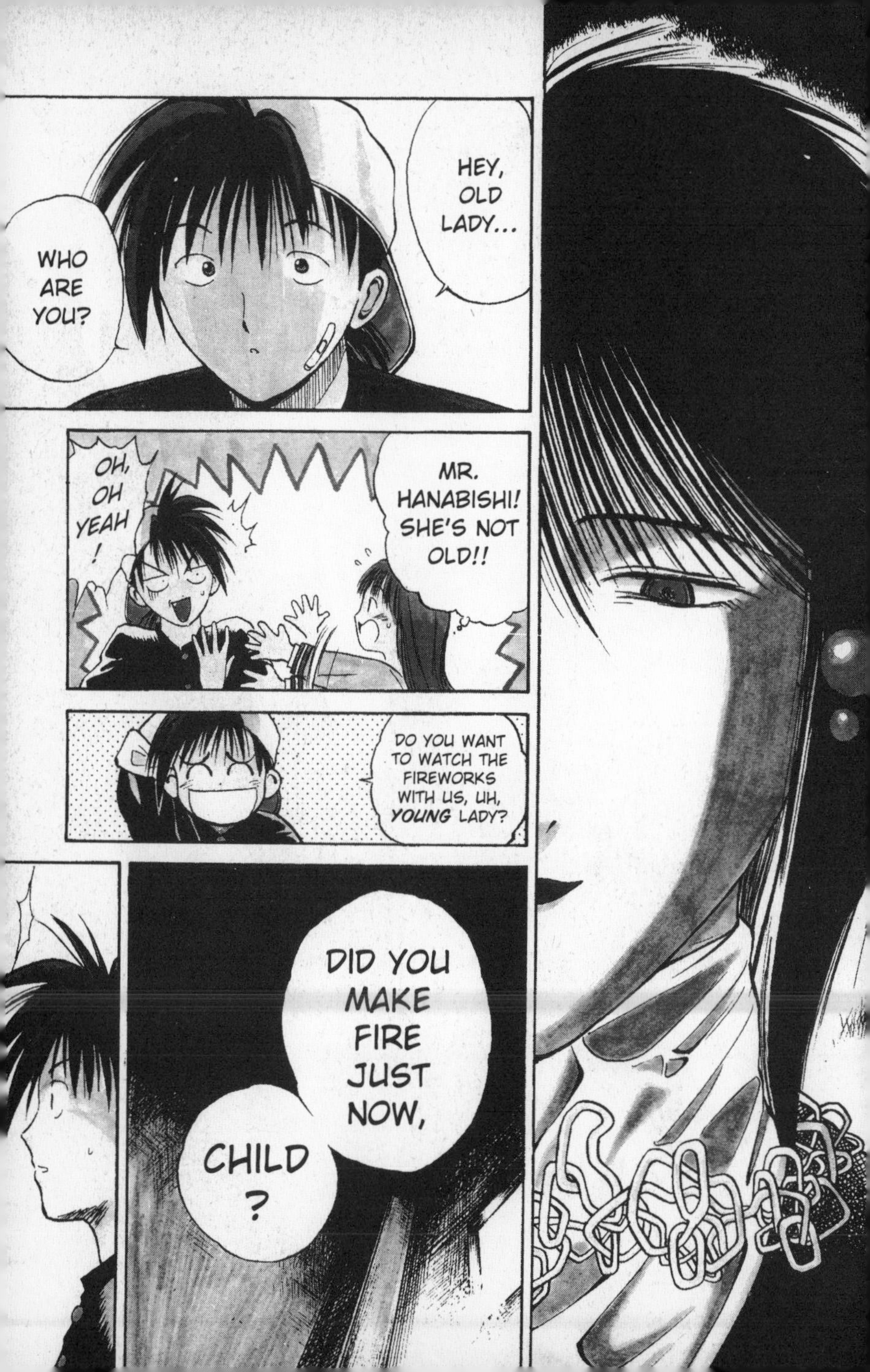
HEY, OLD LADY...
WHO ARE YOU?
MR. HANABISHI! SHE'S NOT OLD!!
OH, OH YEAH!
DO YOU WANT TO WATCH THE FIREWORKS WITH US, UH, *YOUNG* LADY?
DID YOU MAKE FIRE JUST NOW,
CHILD?

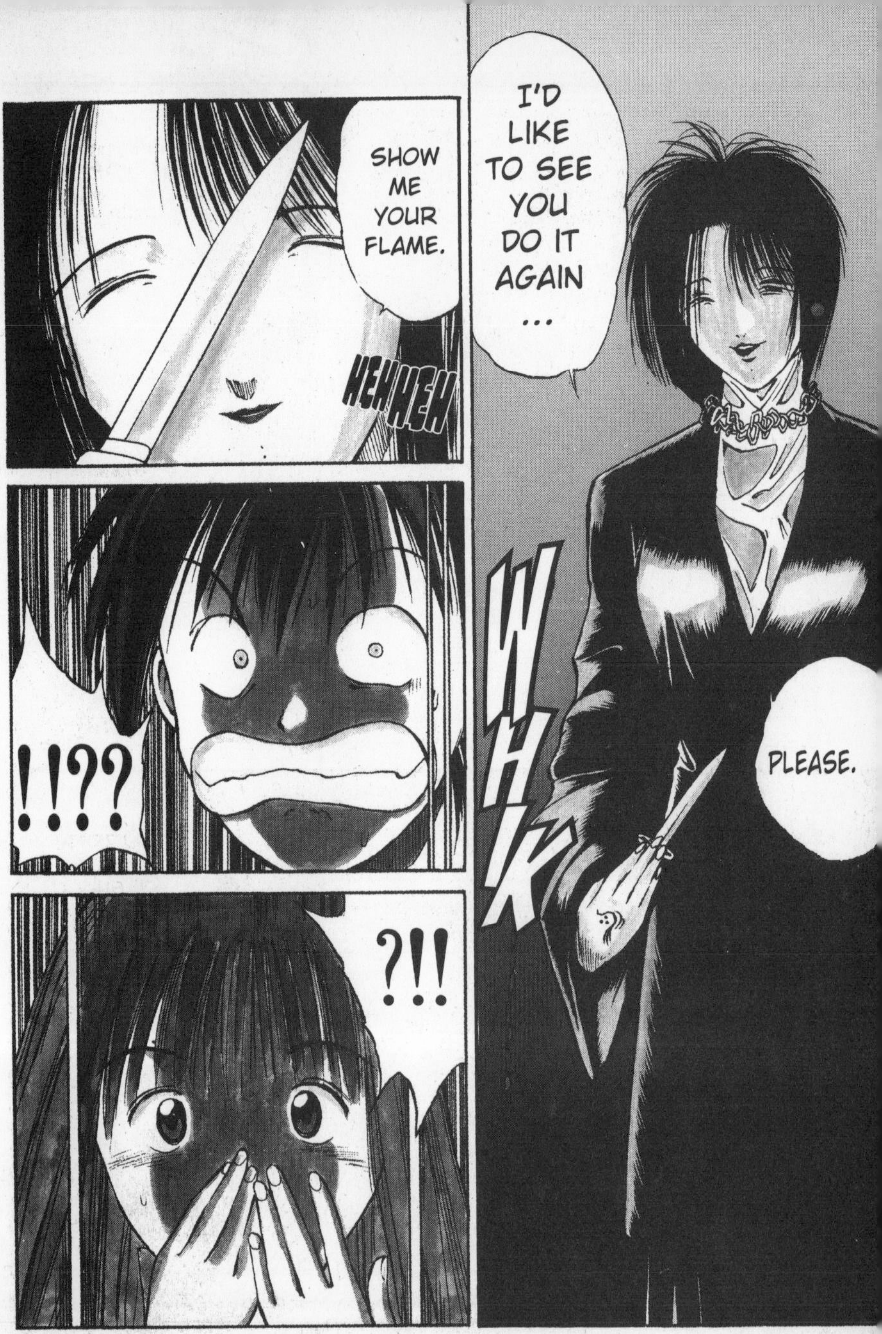
I'D LIKE TO SEE YOU DO IT AGAIN ...
WHIK
PLEASE.
SHOW ME YOUR FLAME.
HEH HEH
!!??
?!!

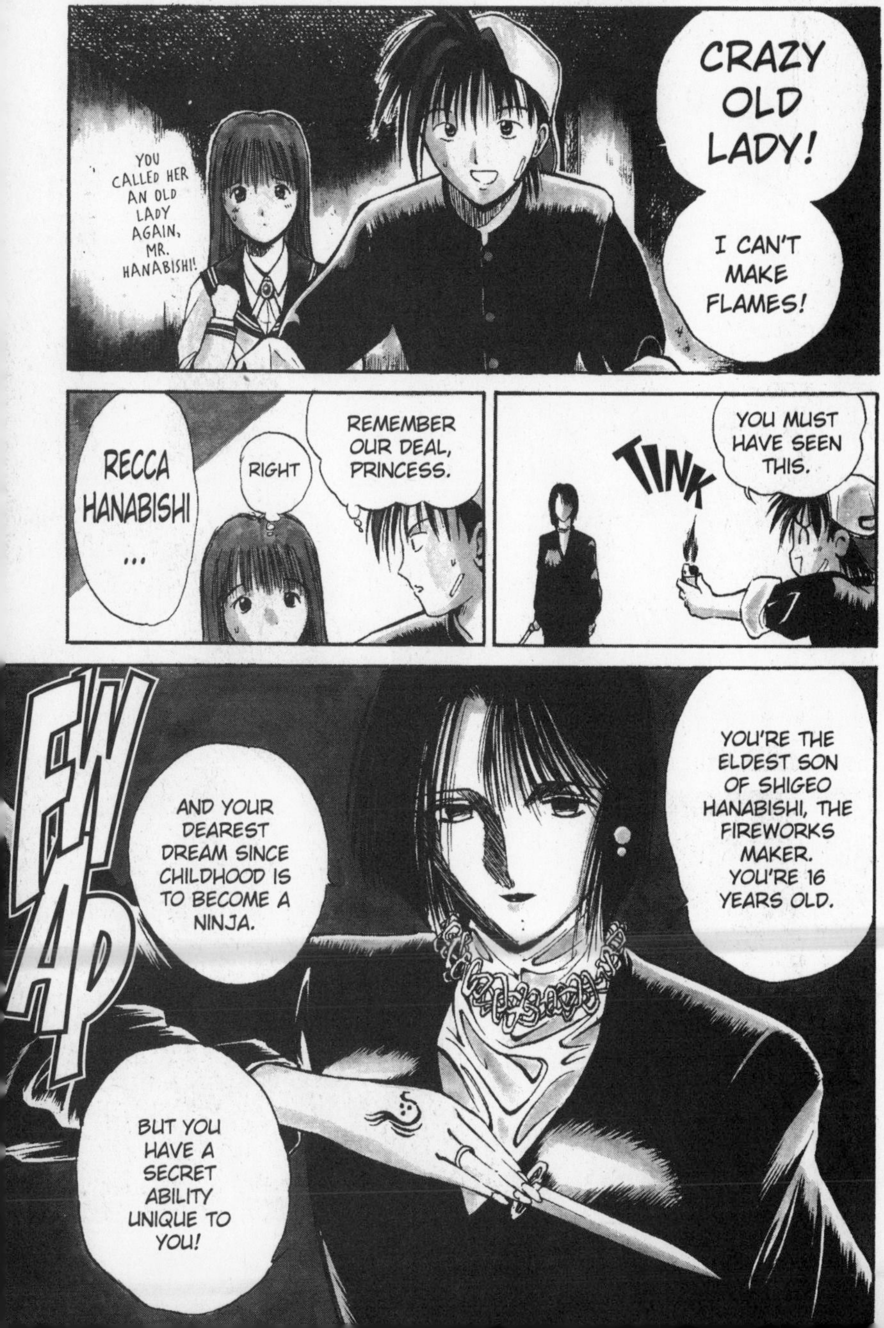
CRAZY OLD LADY!
I CAN'T MAKE FLAMES!
YOU CALLED HER AN OLD LADY AGAIN, MR. HANABISHI!
YOU MUST HAVE SEEN THIS.
TINK
REMEMBER OUR DEAL, PRINCESS.
RIGHT
RECCA HANABISHI ...
YOU'RE THE ELDEST SON OF SHIGEO HANABISHI, THE FIREWORKS MAKER. YOU'RE 16 YEARS OLD.
AND YOUR DEAREST DREAM SINCE CHILDHOOD IS TO BECOME A NINJA.
FWAP
BUT YOU HAVE A SECRET ABILITY UNIQUE TO YOU!

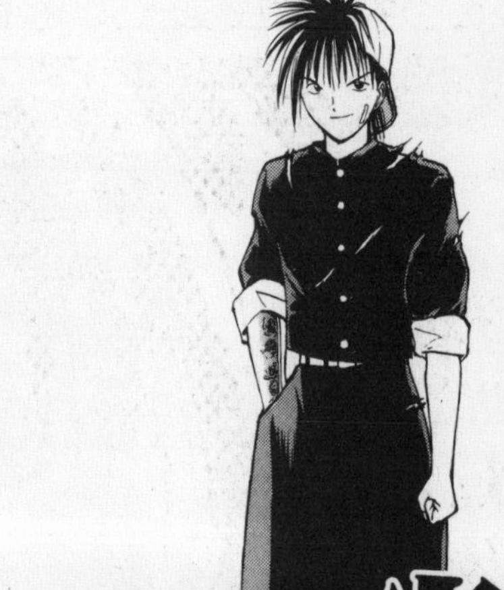
烈火(れっか)の炎(ほのお)
~FLAME OF RECCA~

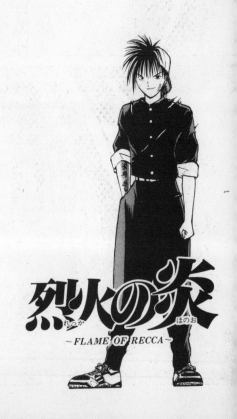

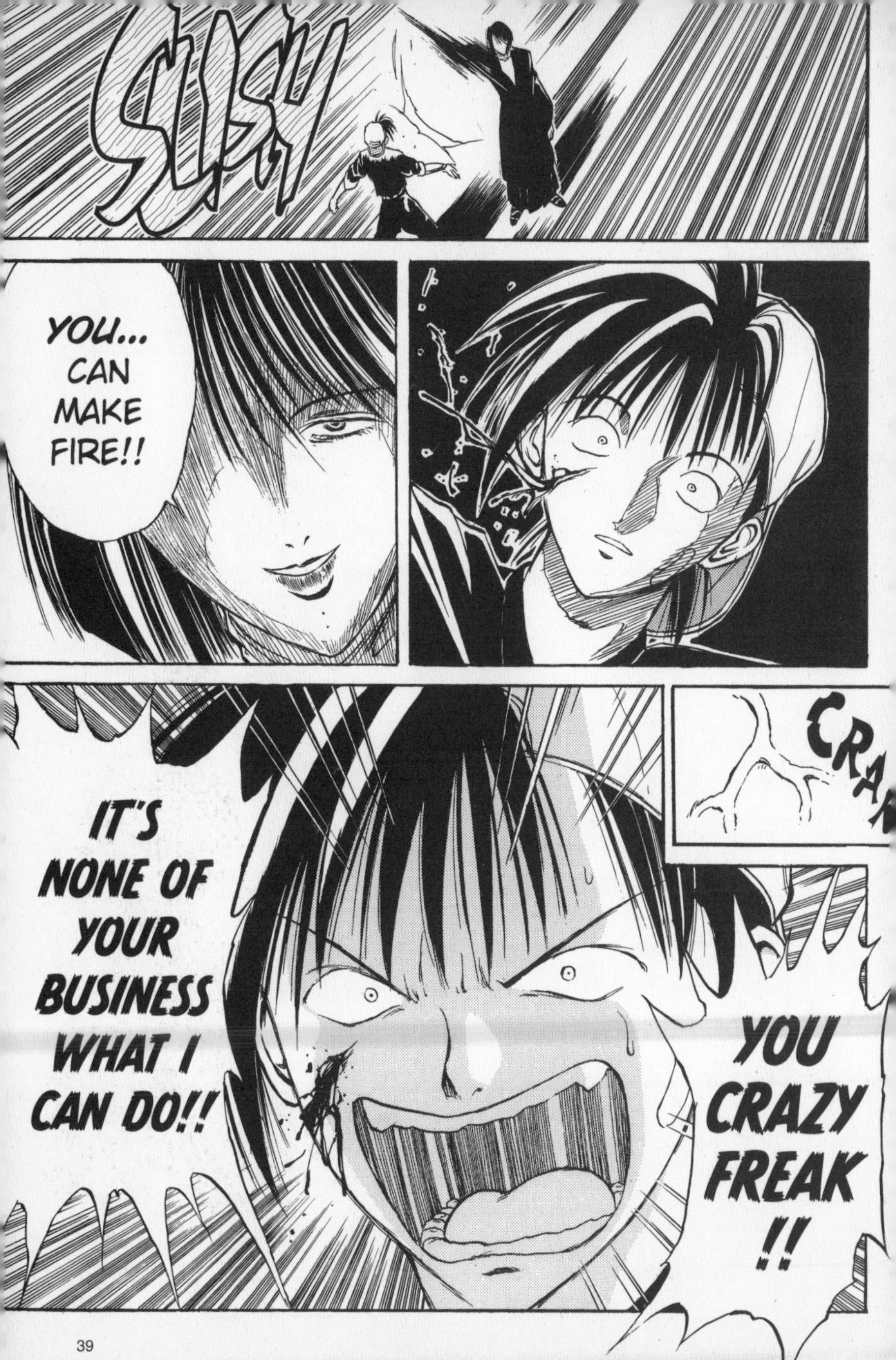
YOU... CAN MAKE FIRE!!
YOU CRAZY FREAK !!
IT'S NONE OF YOUR BUSINESS WHAT I CAN DO!!

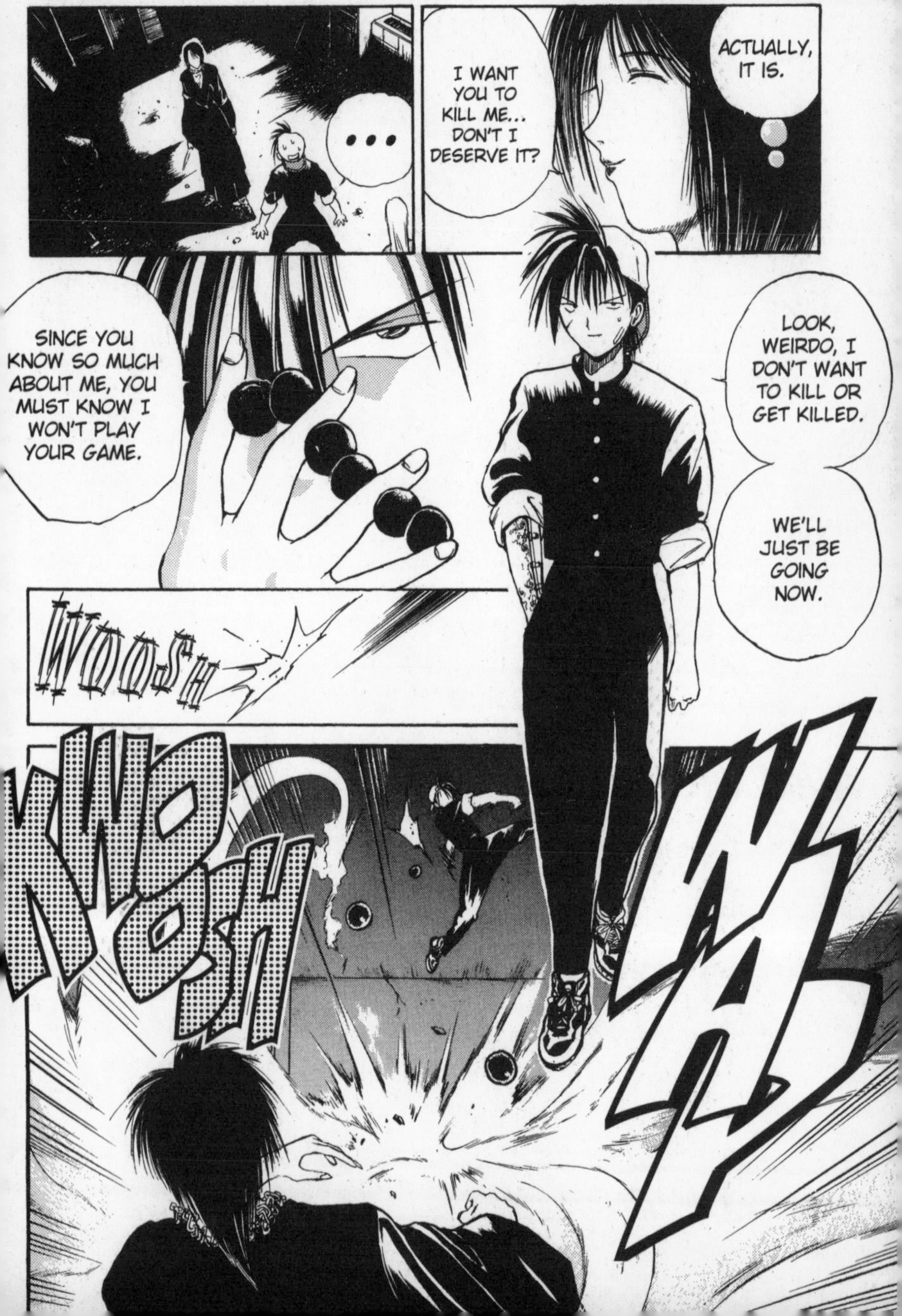
I WANT YOU TO KILL ME... DON'T I DESERVE IT?
ACTUALLY, IT IS.
...
LOOK, WEIRDO, I DON'T WANT TO KILL OR GET KILLED.
WE'LL JUST BE GOING NOW.
SINCE YOU KNOW SO MUCH ABOUT ME, YOU MUST KNOW I WON'T PLAY YOUR GAME.
WOOSH

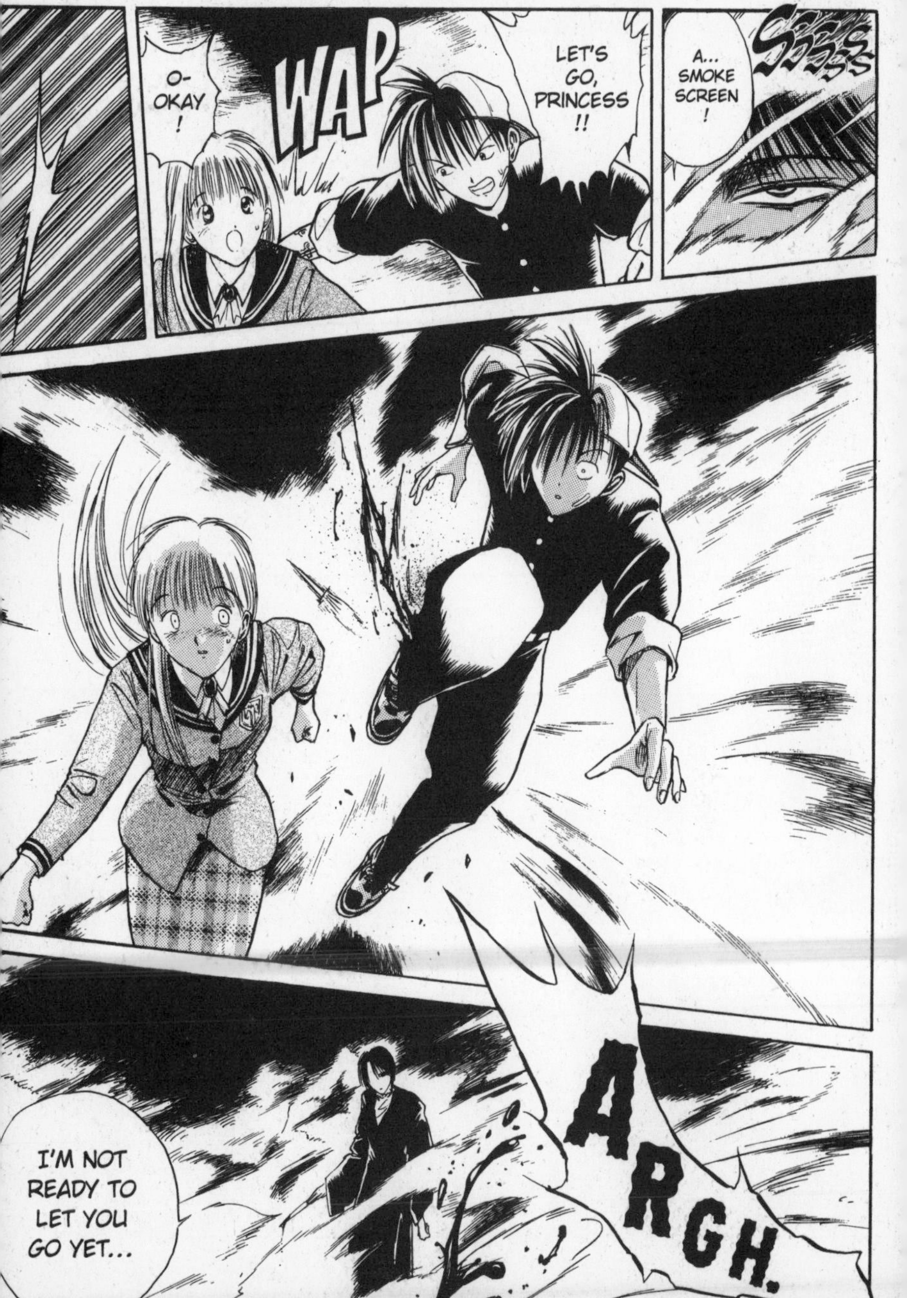
A... SMOKE SCREEN!
LET'S GO, PRINCESS!!
WAP
O-OKAY!
ARGH.
I'M NOT READY TO LET YOU GO YET...

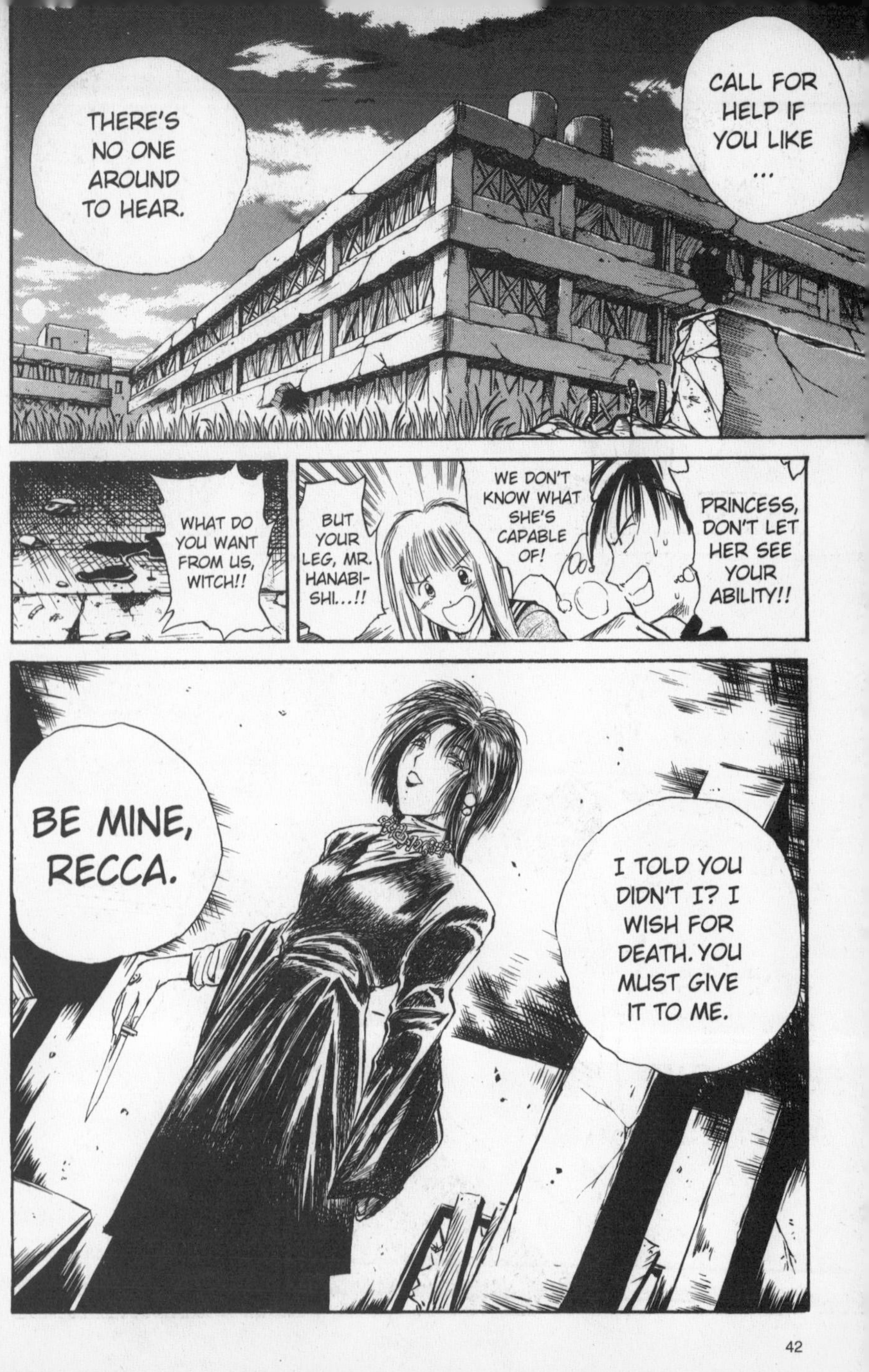
CALL FOR HELP IF YOU LIKE ...
THERE'S NO ONE AROUND TO HEAR.
PRINCESS, DON'T LET HER SEE YOUR ABILITY!!
WE DON'T KNOW WHAT SHE'S CAPABLE OF!
BUT YOUR LEG, MR. HANABI-SHI...!!
WHAT DO YOU WANT FROM US, WITCH!!
I TOLD YOU DIDN'T I? I WISH FOR DEATH. YOU MUST GIVE IT TO ME.
BE MINE, RECCA.

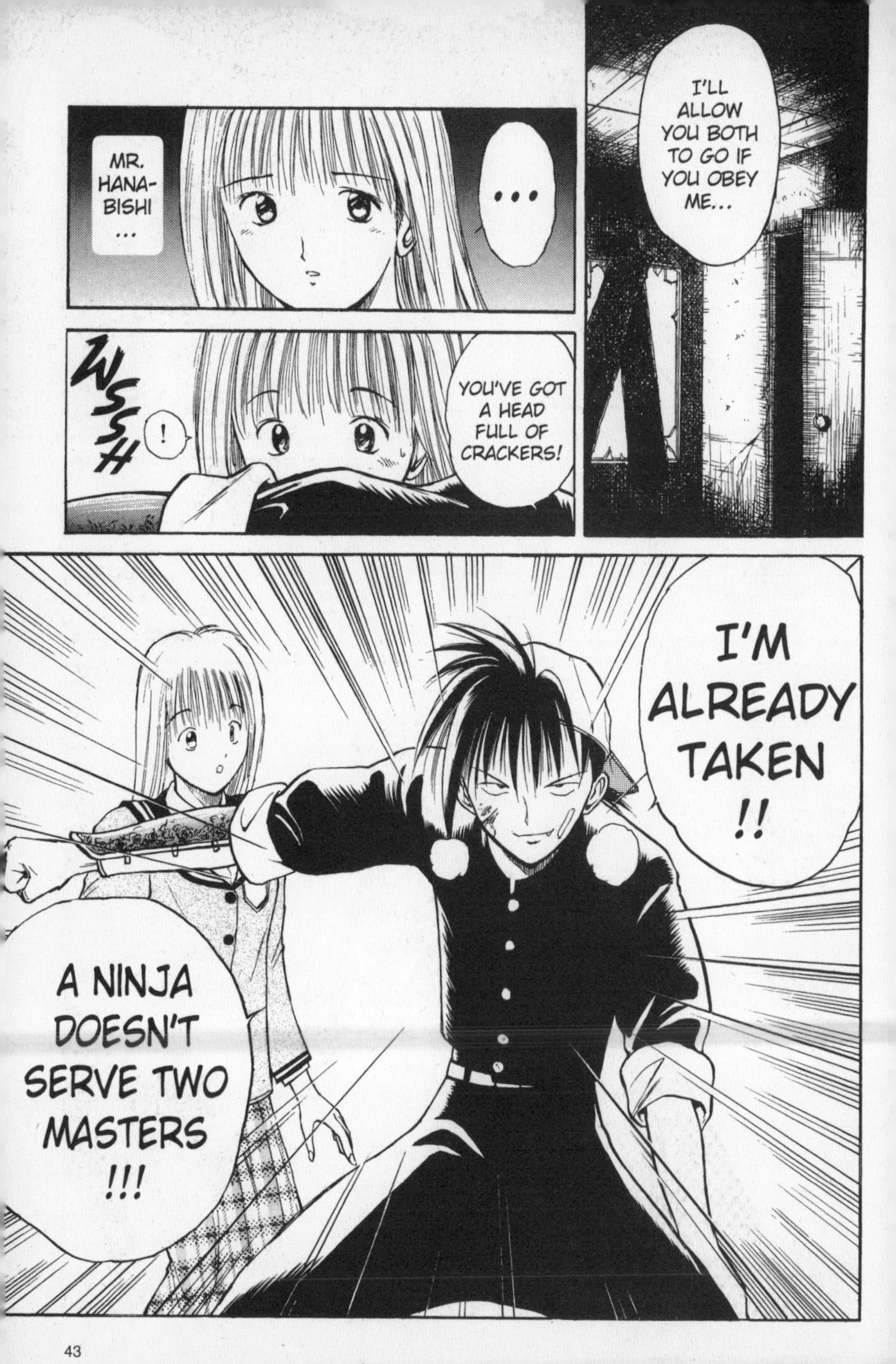
I'LL ALLOW YOU BOTH TO GO IF YOU OBEY ME...
...
MR. HANA-BISHI ...
YOU'VE GOT A HEAD FULL OF CRACKERS!
!
WSSH
I'M ALREADY TAKEN !!
A NINJA DOESN'T SERVE TWO MASTERS !!!

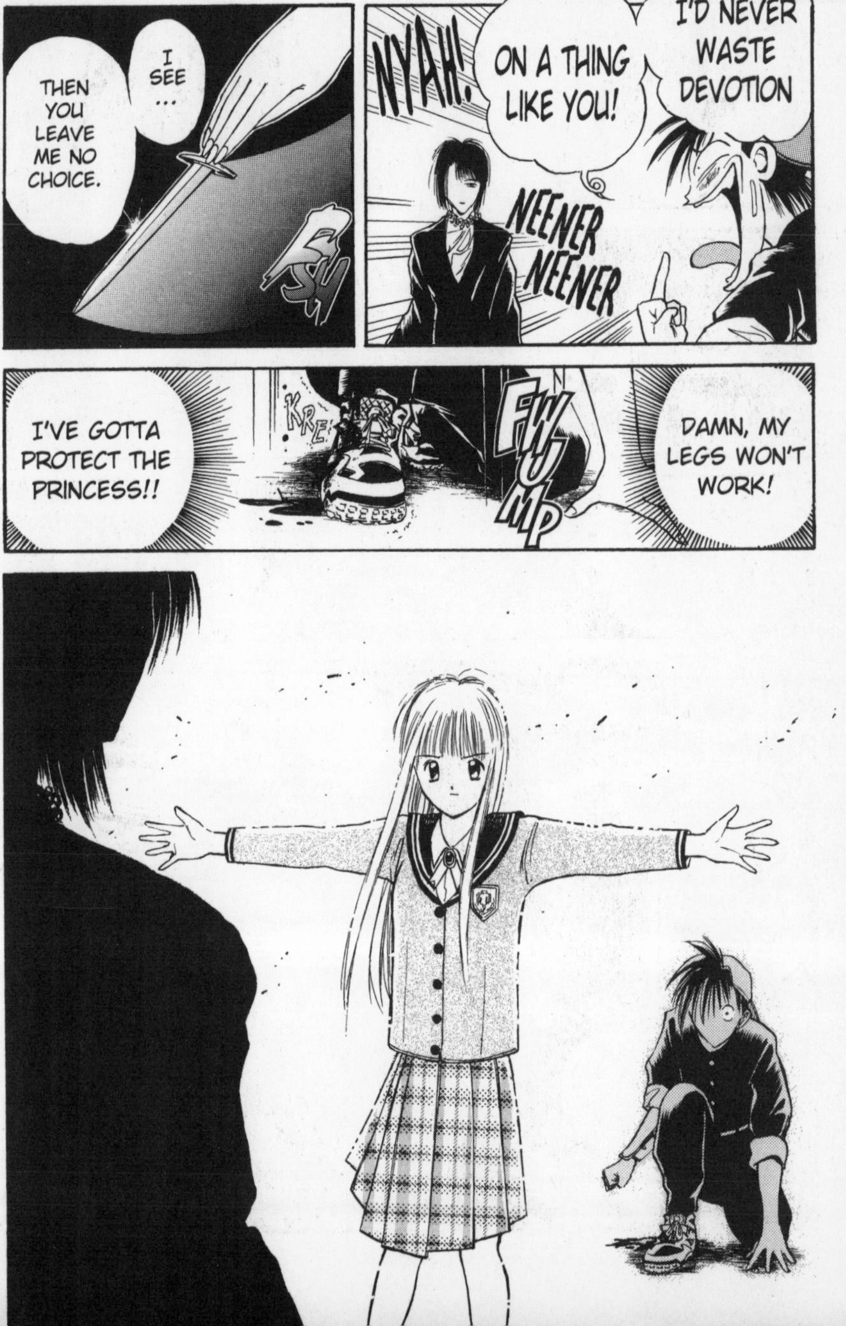
I'D NEVER WASTE DEVOTION
ON A THING LIKE YOU!
NYAH!
NEENER NEENER
I SEE ...
THEN YOU LEAVE ME NO CHOICE.
FSH
DAMN, MY LEGS WON'T WORK!
FWUMP
KRE
I'VE GOTTA PROTECT THE PRINCESS!!

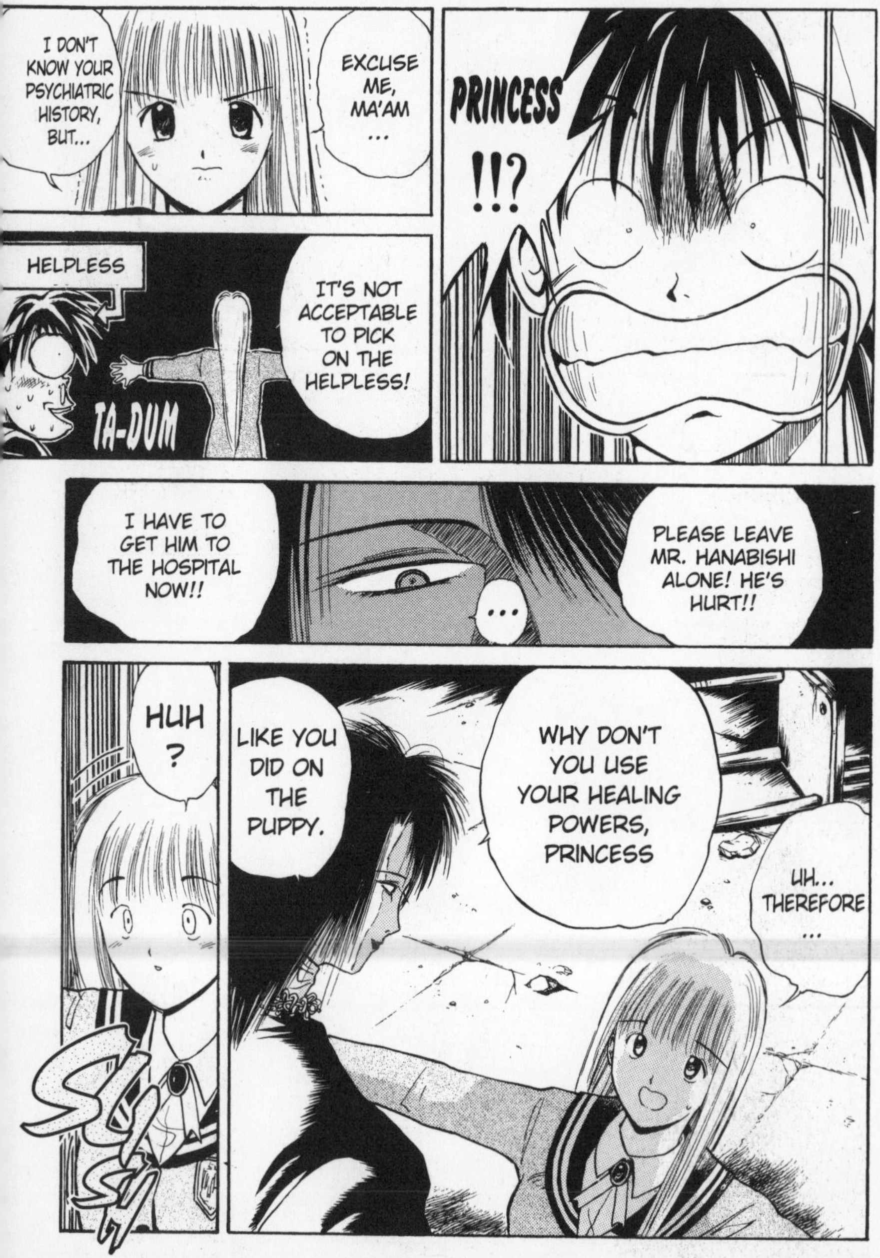
PRINCESS
!!?
EXCUSE ME, MA'AM ...
I DON'T KNOW YOUR PSYCHIATRIC HISTORY, BUT...
IT'S NOT ACCEPTABLE TO PICK ON THE HELPLESS!
HELPLESS
TA-DUM
PLEASE LEAVE MR. HANABISHI ALONE! HE'S HURT!!
...
I HAVE TO GET HIM TO THE HOSPITAL NOW!!
UH... THEREFORE ...
WHY DON'T YOU USE YOUR HEALING POWERS, PRINCESS
LIKE YOU DID ON THE PUPPY.
HUH ?

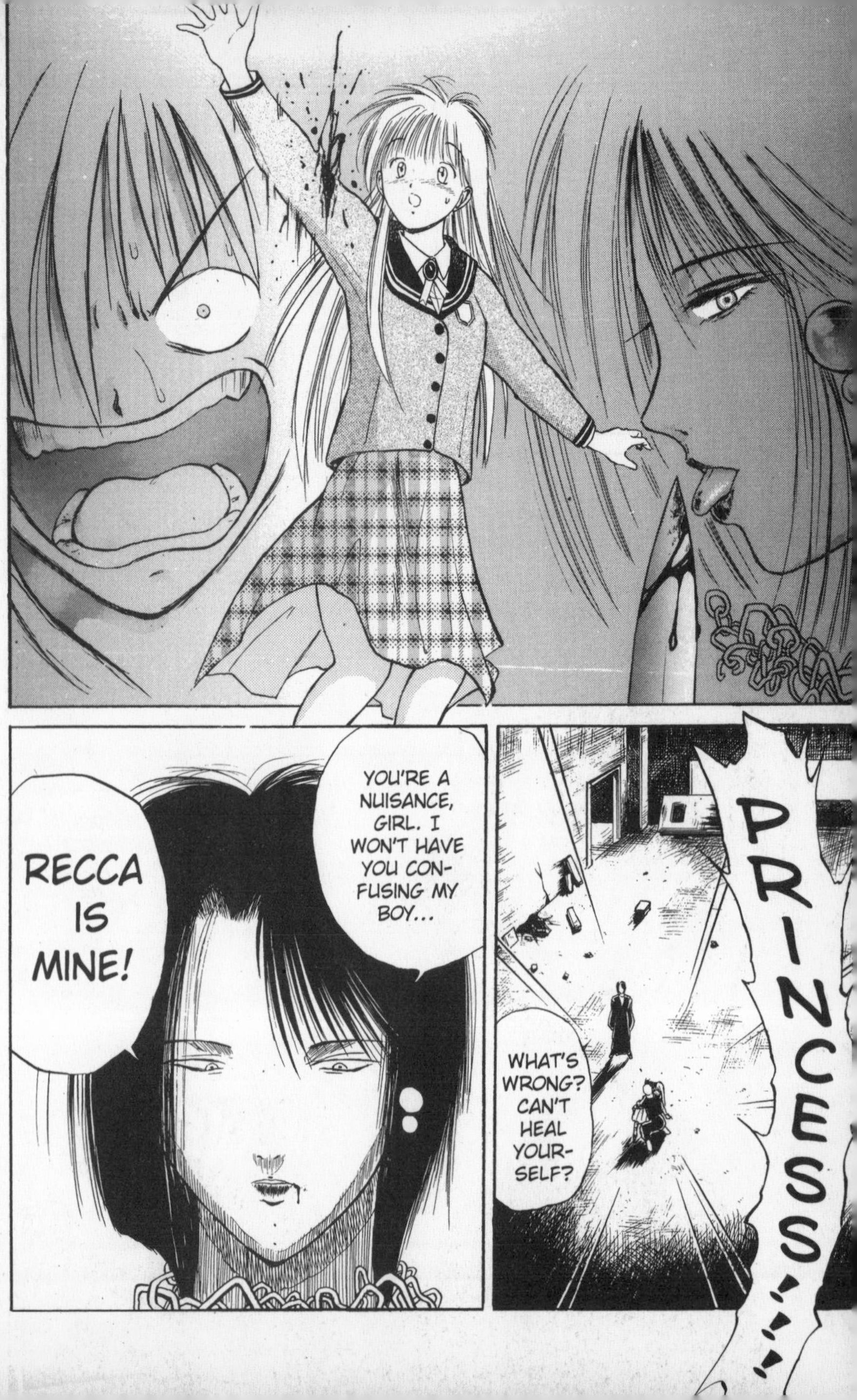
PRINCESS!!!
WHAT'S WRONG? CAN'T HEAL YOURSELF?
YOU'RE A NUISANCE, GIRL. I WON'T HAVE YOU CONFUSING MY BOY...
RECCA IS MINE!

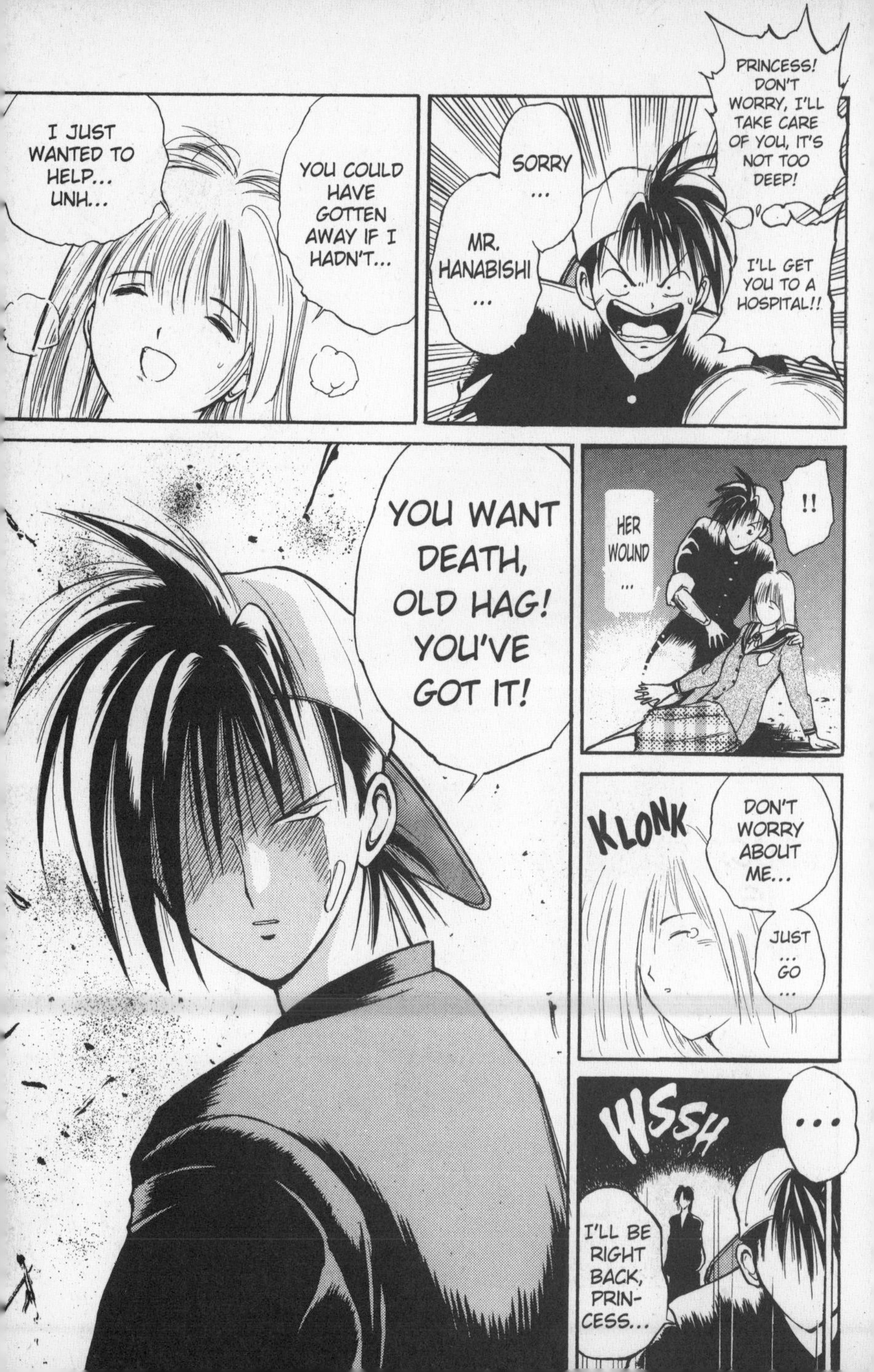

PRINCESS! DON'T WORRY, I'LL TAKE CARE OF YOU, IT'S NOT TOO DEEP!
I'LL GET YOU TO A HOSPITAL!!
SORRY ...
MR. HANABISHI ...
YOU COULD HAVE GOTTEN AWAY IF I HADN'T...
I JUST WANTED TO HELP... UNH...
!!
HER WOUND ...
KLONK
DON'T WORRY ABOUT ME...
JUST ... GO ...
...
WSSH
I'LL BE RIGHT BACK, PRIN-CESS...
YOU WANT DEATH, OLD HAG! YOU'VE GOT IT!

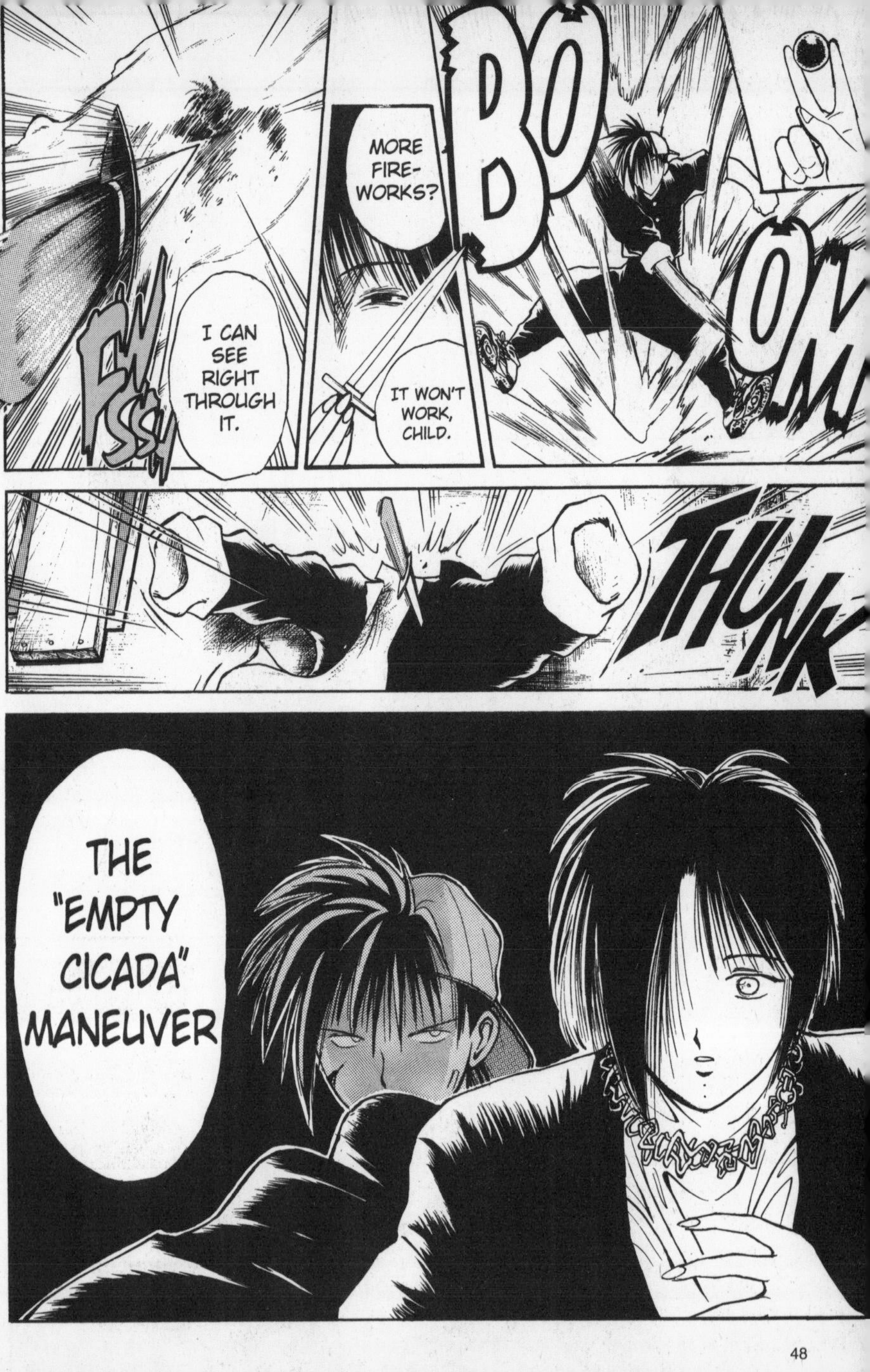
BOOM
MORE FIRE-WORKS?
IT WON'T WORK, CHILD.
I CAN SEE RIGHT THROUGH IT.
THUNK
THE "EMPTY CICADA" MANEUVER

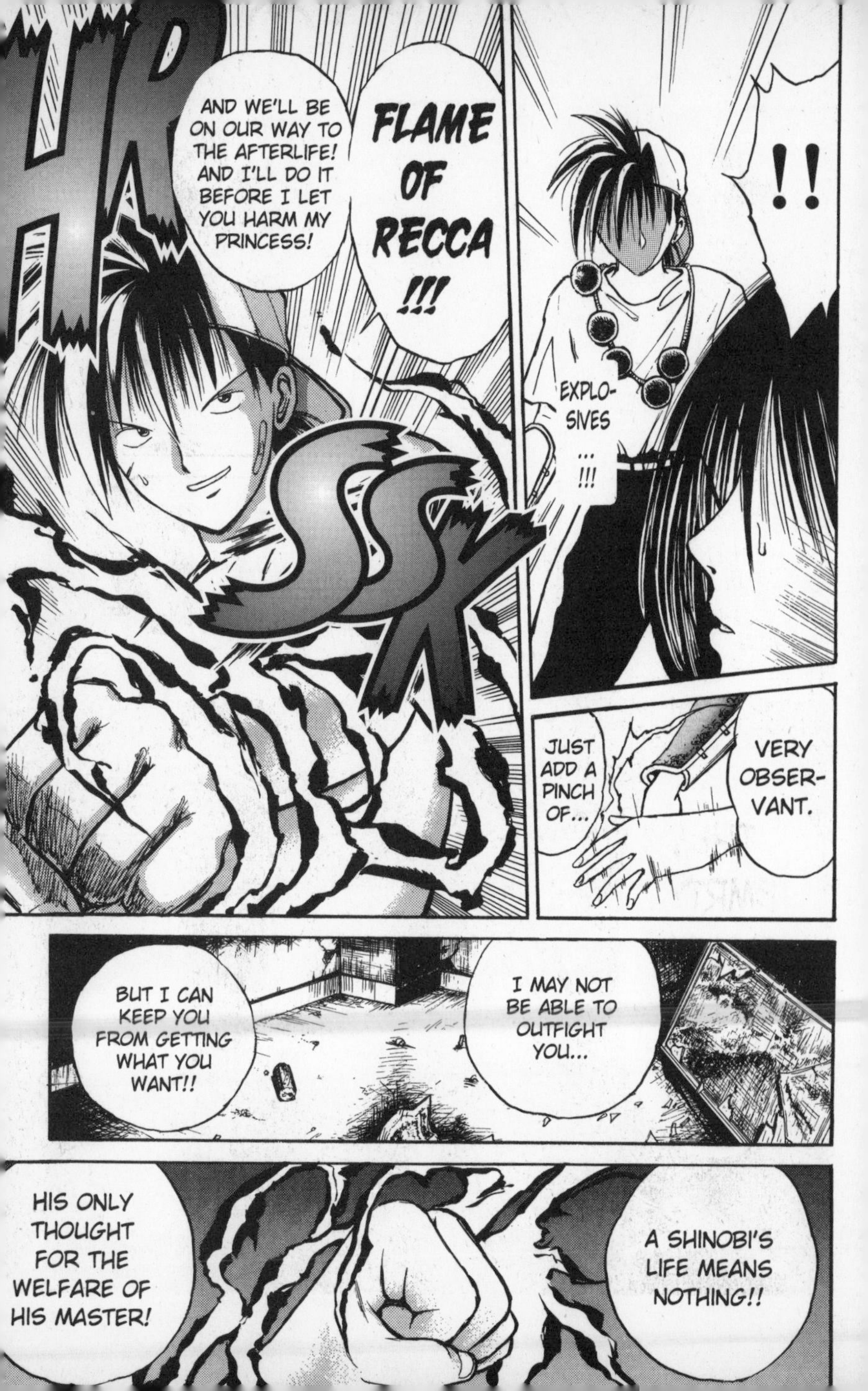
!!
EXPLO-SIVES ... !!!
VERY OBSER-VANT.
JUST ADD A PINCH OF...
FLAME OF RECCA !!!
AND WE'LL BE ON OUR WAY TO THE AFTERLIFE! AND I'LL DO IT BEFORE I LET YOU HARM MY PRINCESS!
I MAY NOT BE ABLE TO OUTFIGHT YOU...
BUT I CAN KEEP YOU FROM GETTING WHAT YOU WANT!!
A SHINOBI'S LIFE MEANS NOTHING!!
HIS ONLY THOUGHT FOR THE WELFARE OF HIS MASTER!

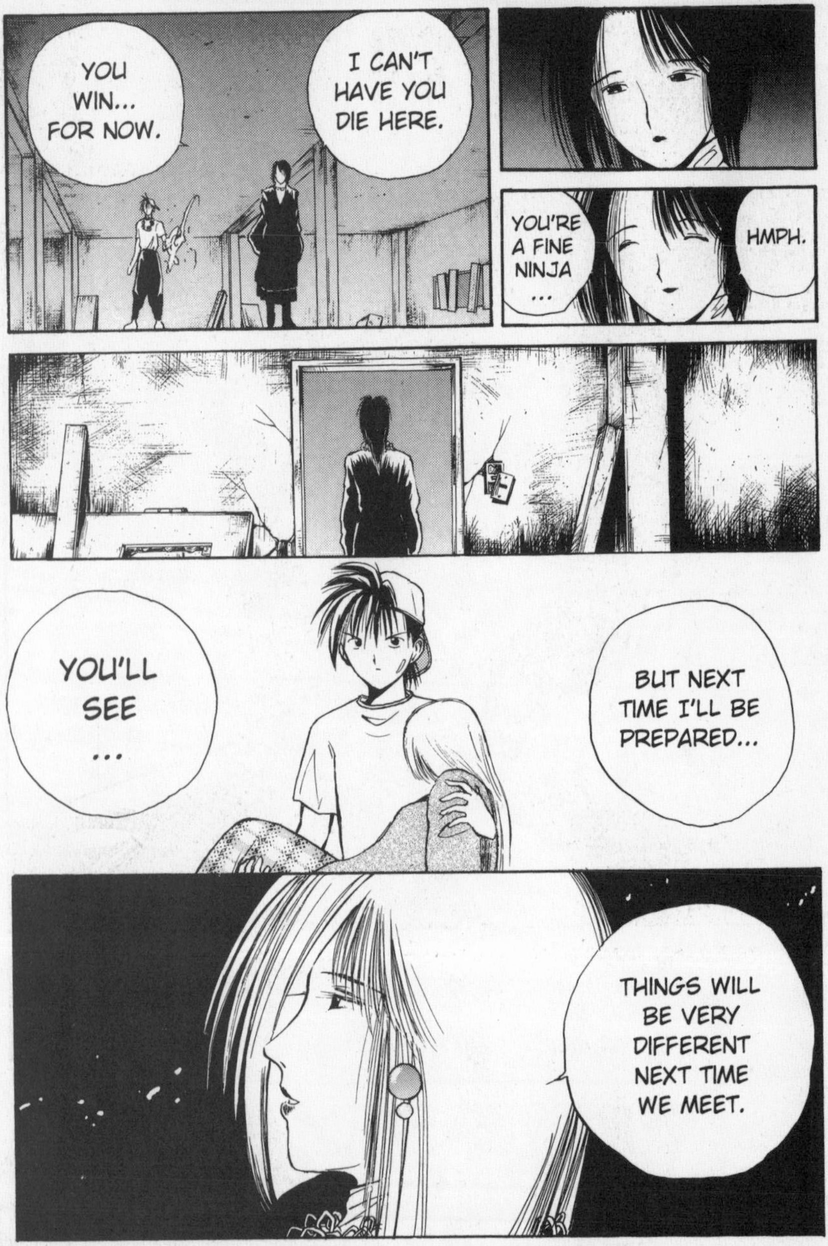
HMPH.
YOU'RE A FINE NINJA ...
I CAN'T HAVE YOU DIE HERE.
YOU WIN... FOR NOW.
BUT NEXT TIME I'LL BE PREPARED...
YOU'LL SEE ...
THINGS WILL BE VERY DIFFERENT NEXT TIME WE MEET.

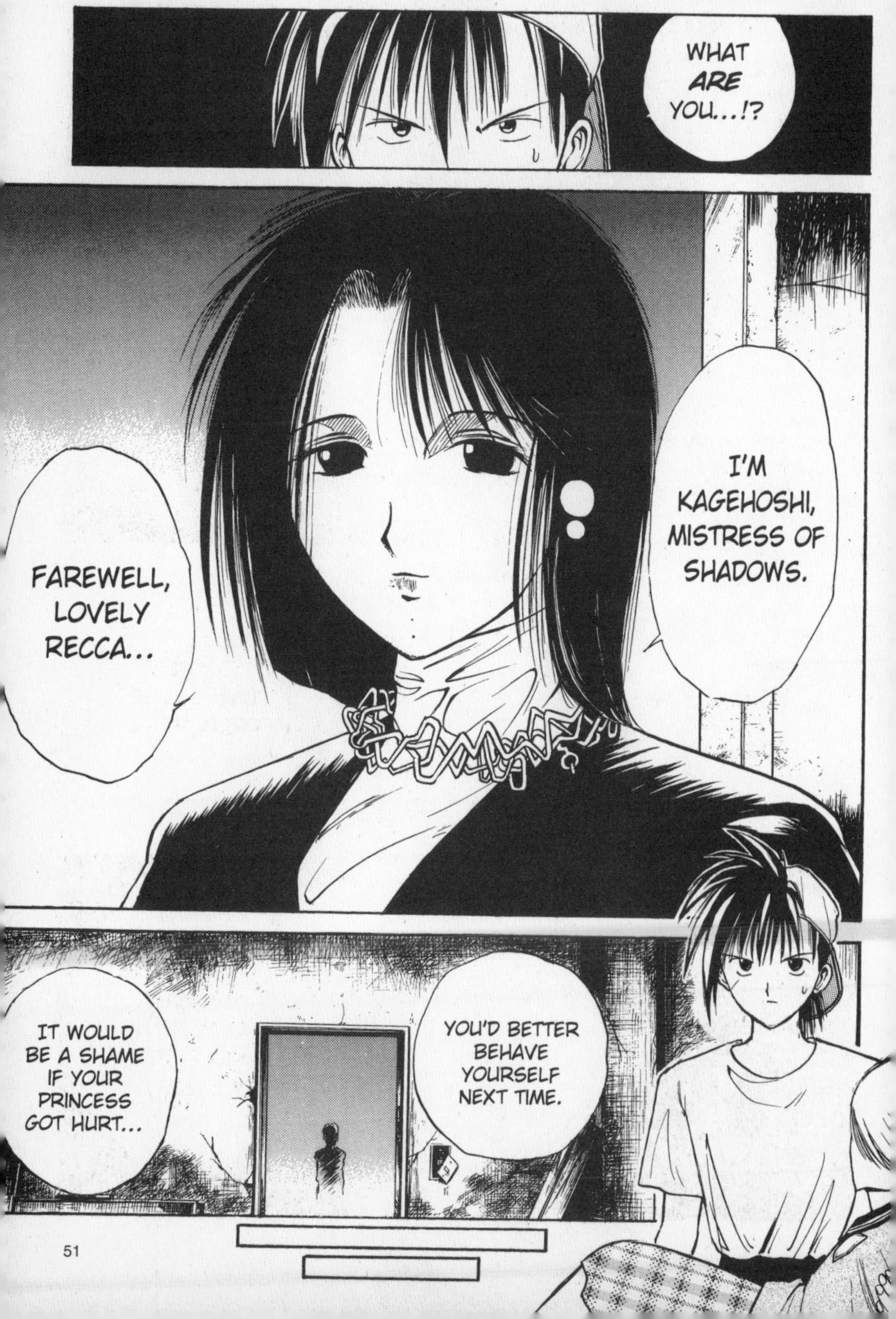
WHAT **ARE** YOU...!?
I'M KAGEHOSHI, MISTRESS OF SHADOWS.
FAREWELL, LOVELY RECCA...
YOU'D BETTER BEHAVE YOURSELF NEXT TIME.
IT WOULD BE A SHAME IF YOUR PRINCESS GOT HURT...

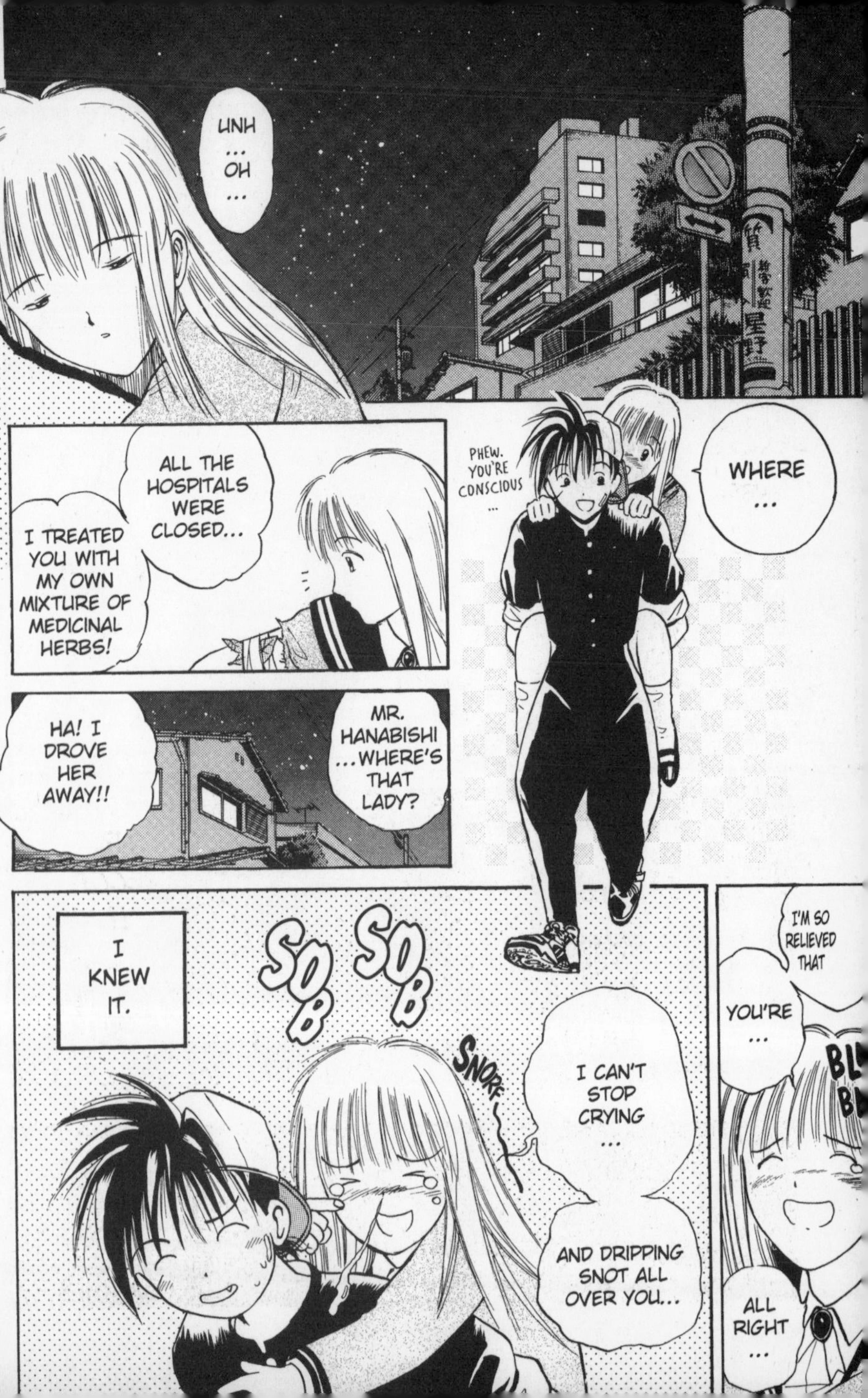
UNH ... OH ...
WHERE ...
PHEW. YOU'RE CONSCIOUS ...
ALL THE HOSPITALS WERE CLOSED...
I TREATED YOU WITH MY OWN MIXTURE OF MEDICINAL HERBS!
MR. HANABISHI ...WHERE'S THAT LADY?
HA! I DROVE HER AWAY!!
I'M SO RELIEVED THAT
YOU'RE ...
ALL RIGHT ...
I CAN'T STOP CRYING ...
AND DRIPPING SNOT ALL OVER YOU...
SNORF
SOB SOB
I KNEW IT.

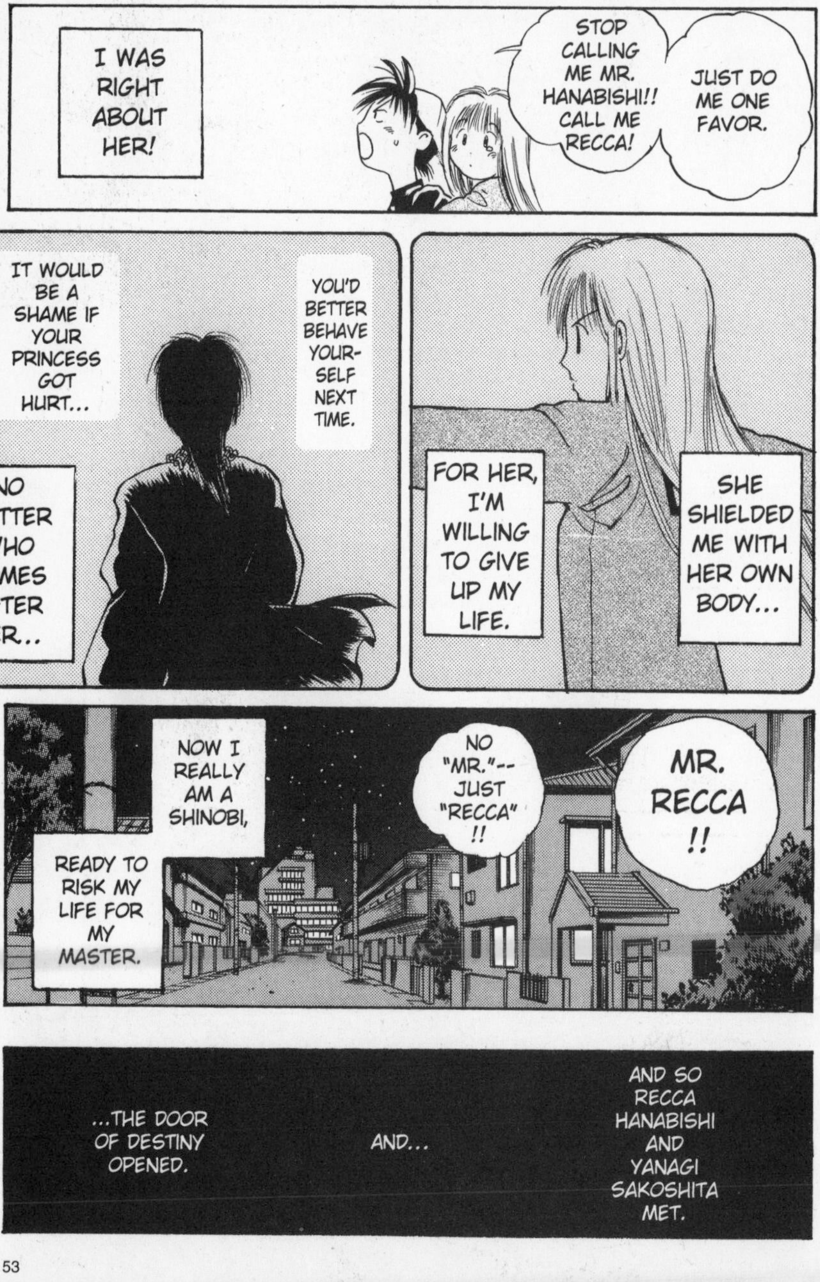
JUST DO ME ONE FAVOR.
STOP CALLING ME MR. HANABISHI!! CALL ME RECCA!
I WAS RIGHT ABOUT HER!
SHE SHIELDED ME WITH HER OWN BODY...
FOR HER, I'M WILLING TO GIVE UP MY LIFE.
YOU'D BETTER BEHAVE YOUR-SELF NEXT TIME.
IT WOULD BE A SHAME IF YOUR PRINCESS GOT HURT...
NO MATTER WHO COMES AFTER HER...
MR. RECCA !!
NO "MR."-- JUST "RECCA" !!
NOW I REALLY AM A SHINOBI,
READY TO RISK MY LIFE FOR MY MASTER.
AND SO RECCA HANABISHI AND YANAGI SAKOSHITA MET.
AND...
...THE DOOR OF DESTINY OPENED.

烈火の炎
~FLAME OF RECCA~

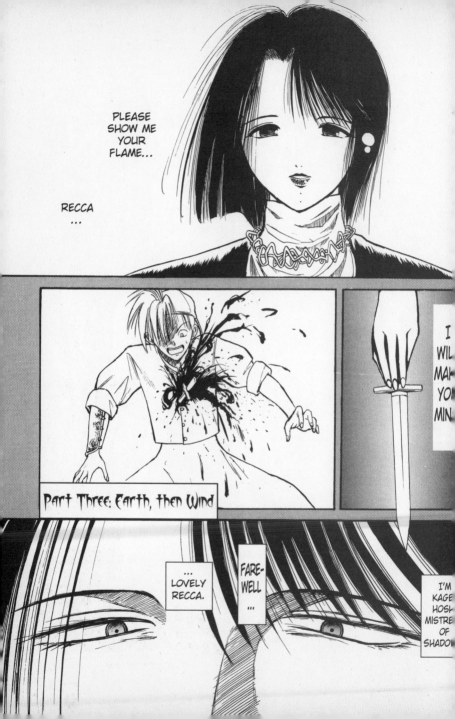

PLEASE SHOW ME YOUR FLAME...

RECCA ...

I WIL MAK YO MIN

Part Three: Earth, then Wind

... LOVELY RECCA.

FARE-WELL ...

I'M KAGE HOSI MISTRE OF SHADO

Part Three:
Earth, then Wind

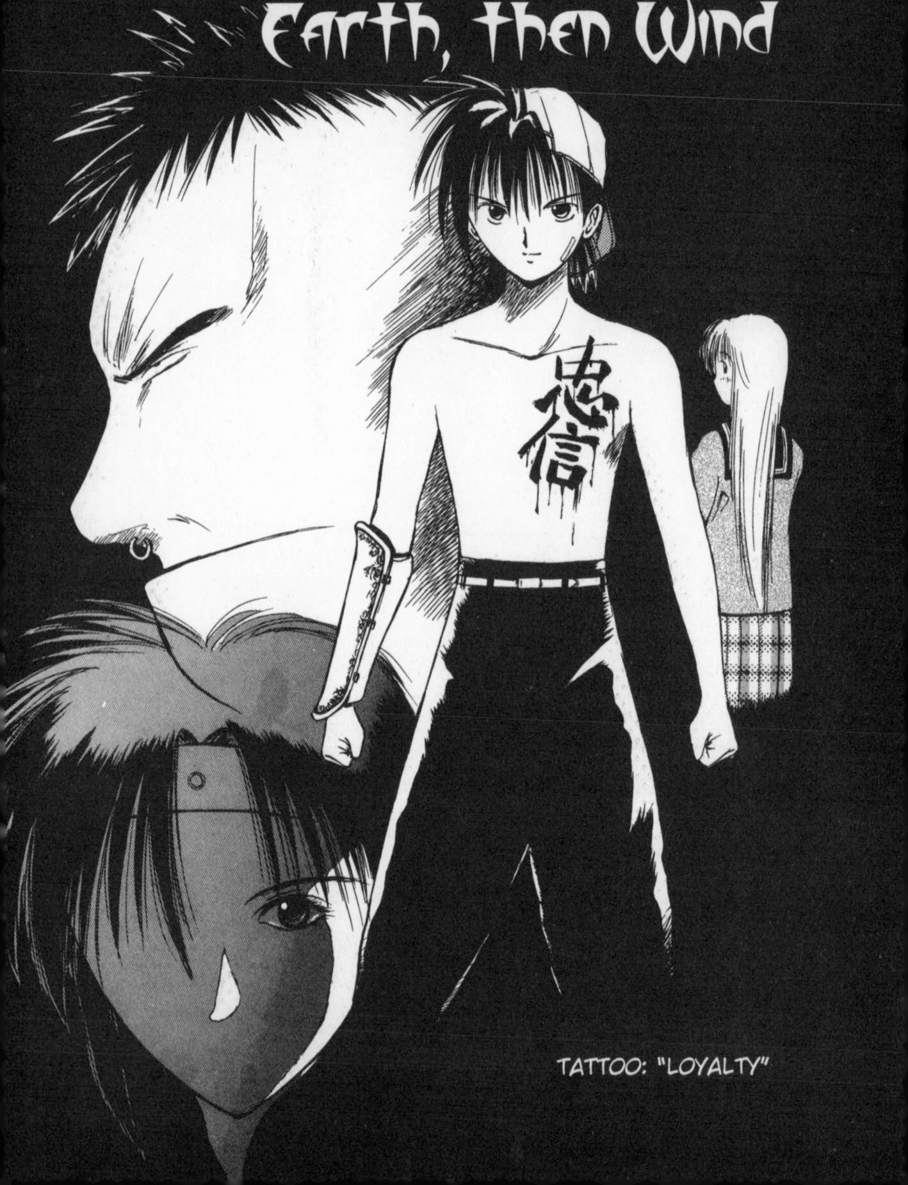
忠信
TATTOO: "LOYALTY"

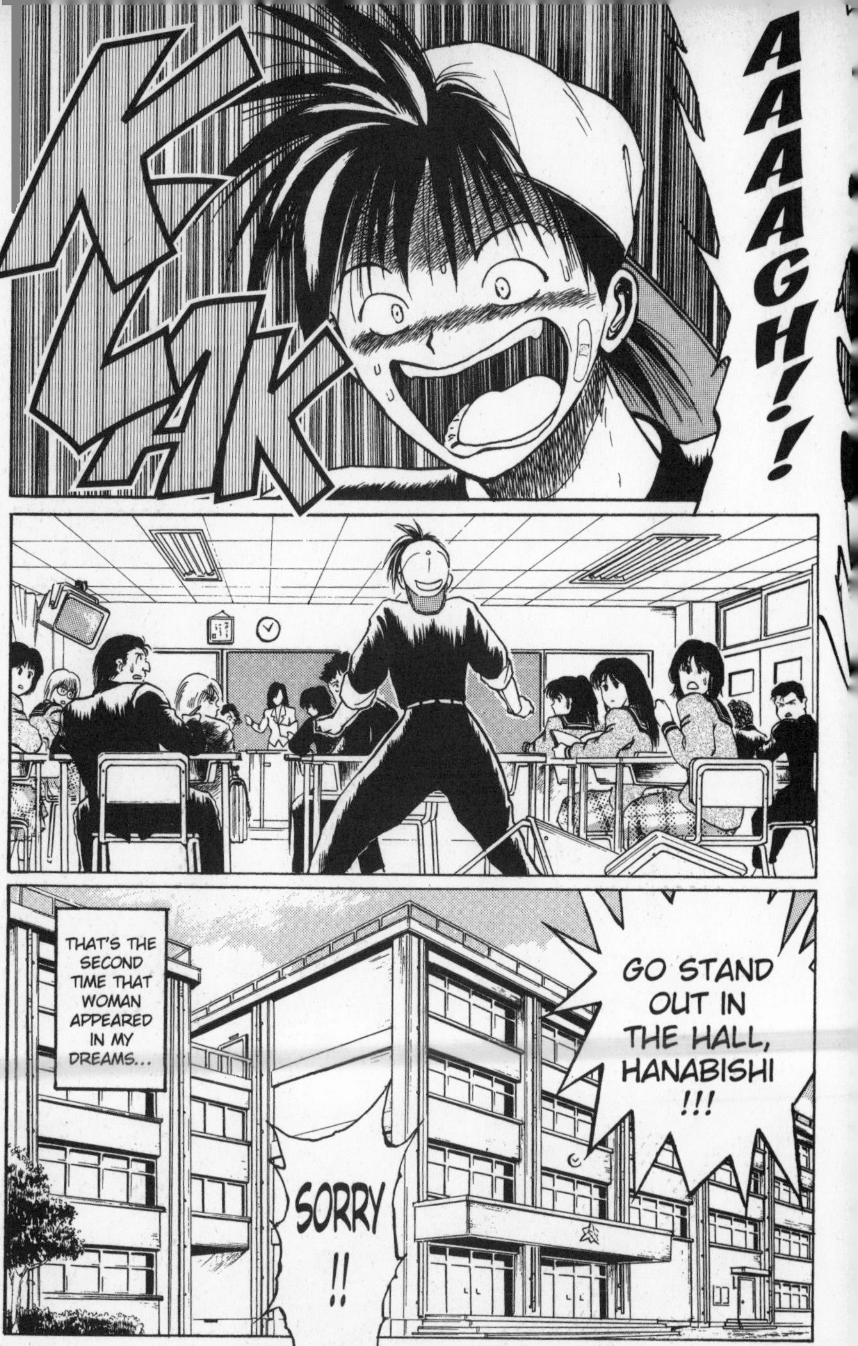
AAAAGH!!!
GO STAND OUT IN THE HALL, HANABISHI!!!
SORRY!!
THAT'S THE SECOND TIME THAT WOMAN APPEARED IN MY DREAMS...

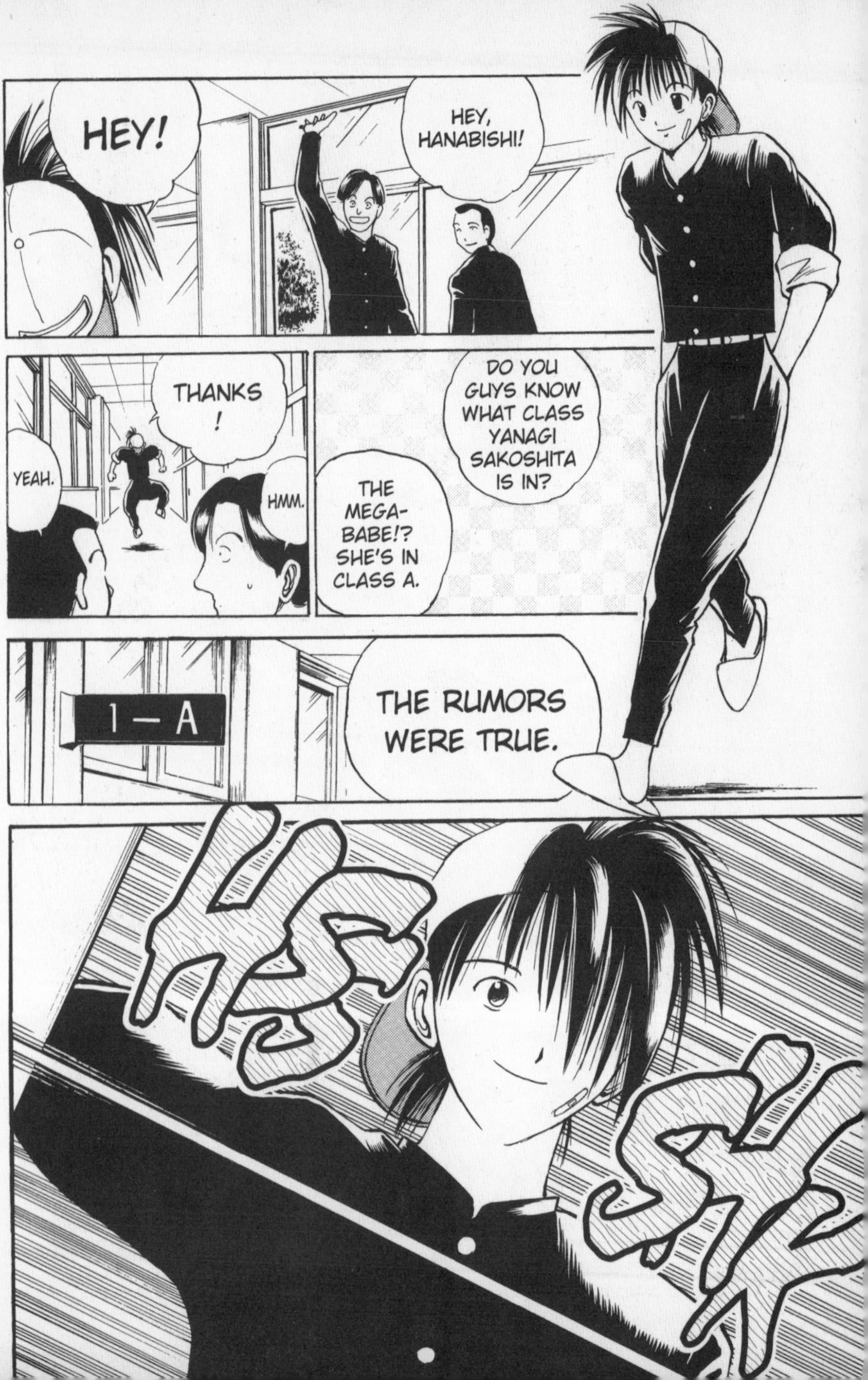
HEY, HANABISHI!
HEY!
DO YOU GUYS KNOW WHAT CLASS YANAGI SAKOSHITA IS IN?
THE MEGA-BABE!? SHE'S IN CLASS A.
HMM.
THANKS!
YEAH.
THE RUMORS WERE TRUE.
1—A

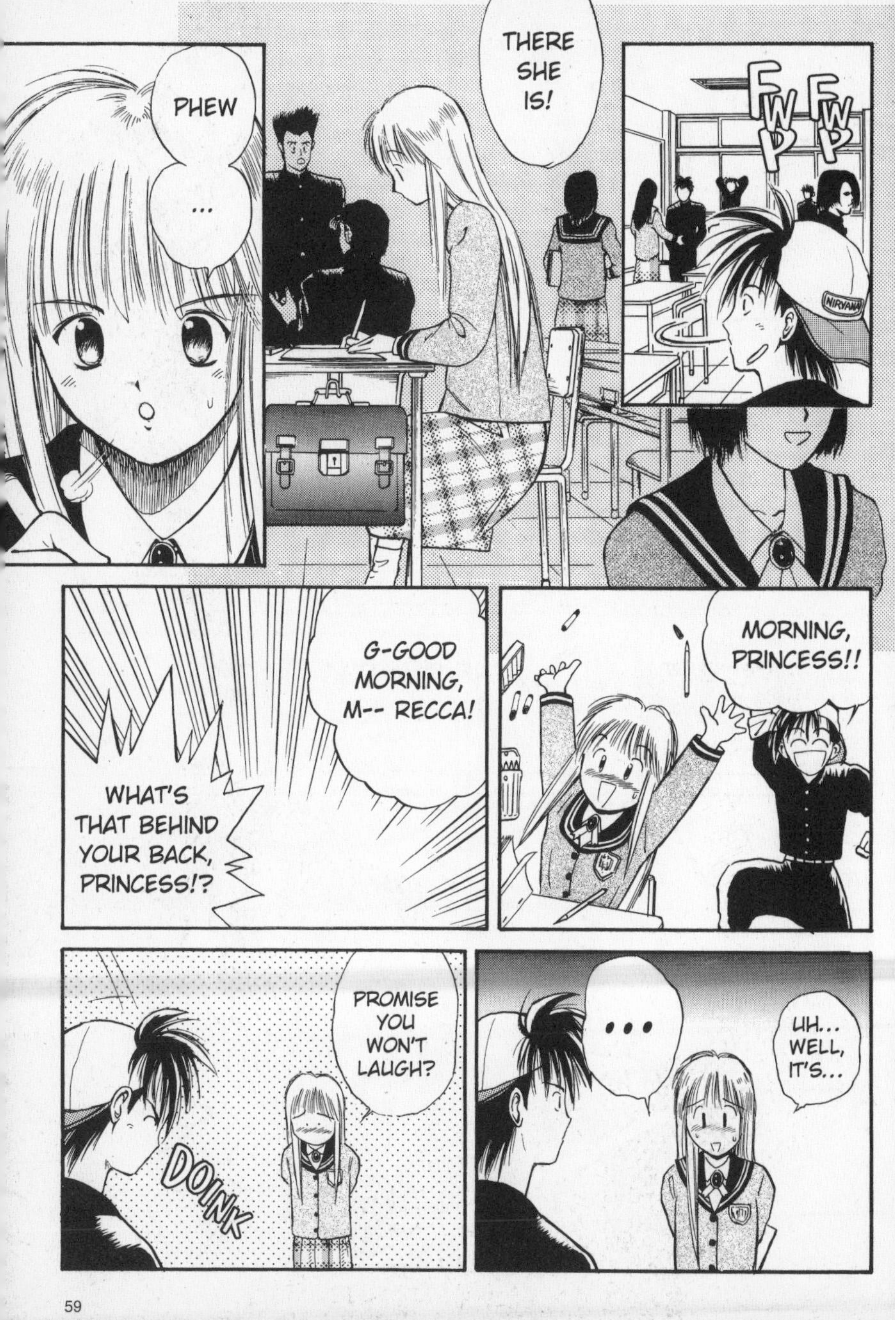
FWP FWP
THERE SHE IS!
PHEW
...
MORNING, PRINCESS!!
G-GOOD MORNING, M-- RECCA!
WHAT'S THAT BEHIND YOUR BACK, PRINCESS!?
UH... WELL, IT'S...
...
PROMISE YOU WON'T LAUGH?
DOINK

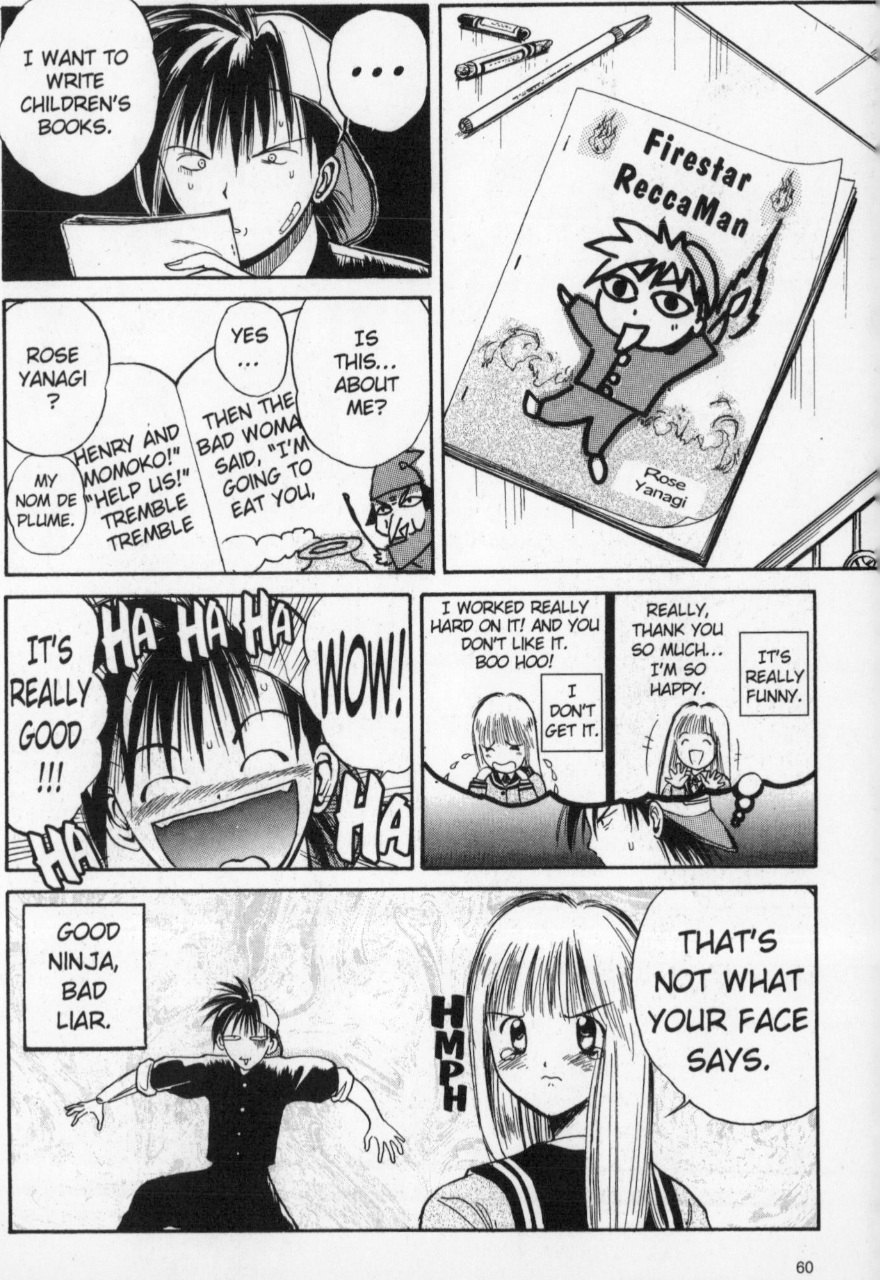

Firestar ReccaMan
Rose Yanagi
...
I WANT TO WRITE CHILDREN'S BOOKS.
IS THIS... ABOUT ME?
YES ...
THEN THE BAD WOMA SAID, "I'M GOING TO EAT YOU,
HENRY AND MOMOKO!" "HELP US!" TREMBLE TREMBLE
ROSE YANAGI ?
MY NOM DE PLUME.
REALLY, THANK YOU SO MUCH... I'M SO HAPPY.
IT'S REALLY FUNNY.
I WORKED REALLY HARD ON IT! AND YOU DON'T LIKE IT. BOO HOO!
I DON'T GET IT.
WOW!
HA HA HA
IT'S REALLY GOOD !!!
HA
HA
THAT'S NOT WHAT YOUR FACE SAYS.
HMPH
GOOD NINJA, BAD LIAR.

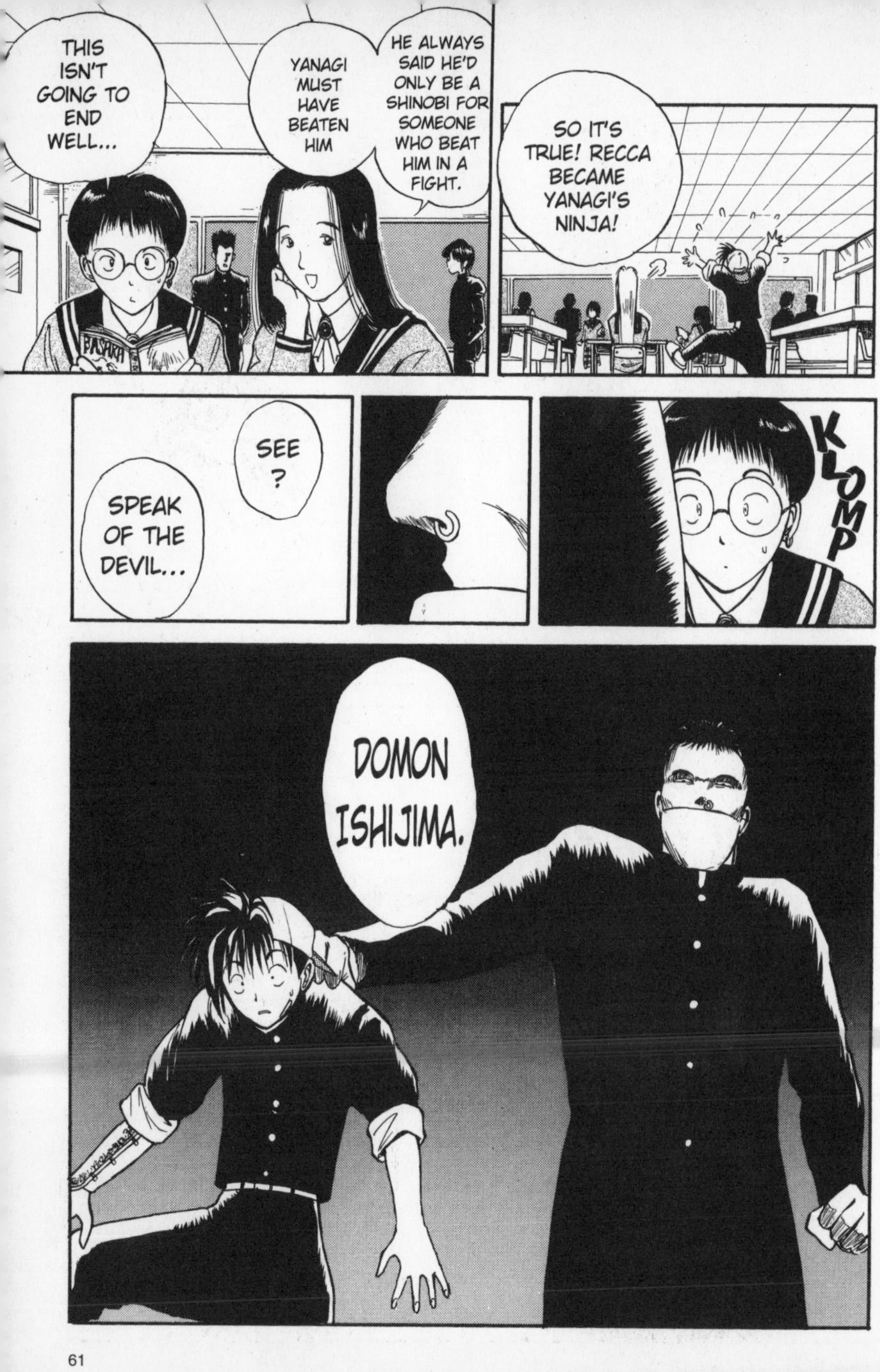
SO IT'S TRUE! RECCA BECAME YANAGI'S NINJA!
HE ALWAYS SAID HE'D ONLY BE A SHINOBI FOR SOMEONE WHO BEAT HIM IN A FIGHT.
YANAGI MUST HAVE BEATEN HIM
THIS ISN'T GOING TO END WELL...
KLOMP
SEE?
SPEAK OF THE DEVIL...
DOMON ISHIJIMA.

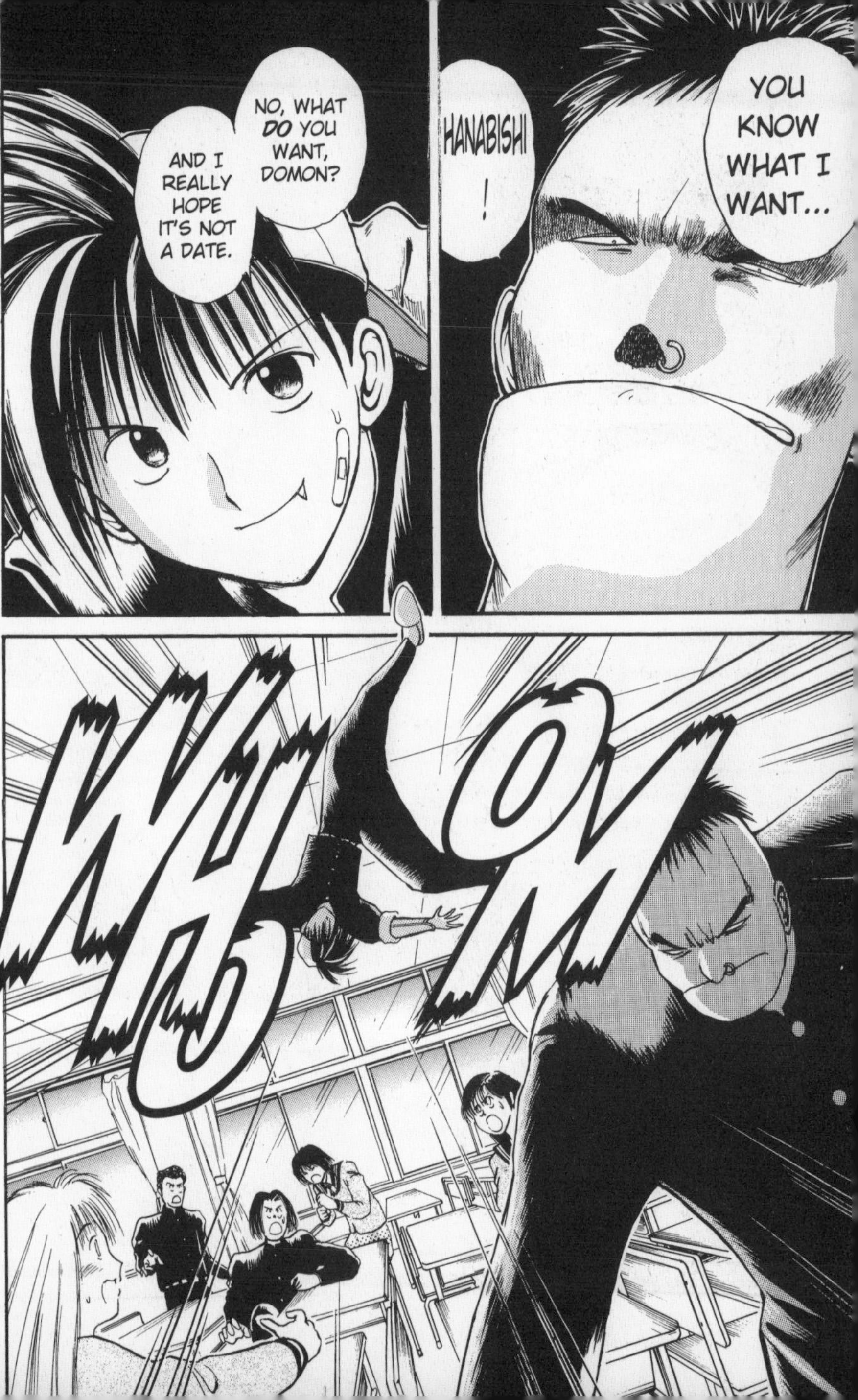
YOU KNOW WHAT I WANT...
HANABISHI!
NO, WHAT DO YOU WANT, DOMON?
AND I REALLY HOPE IT'S NOT A DATE.
WHOOM

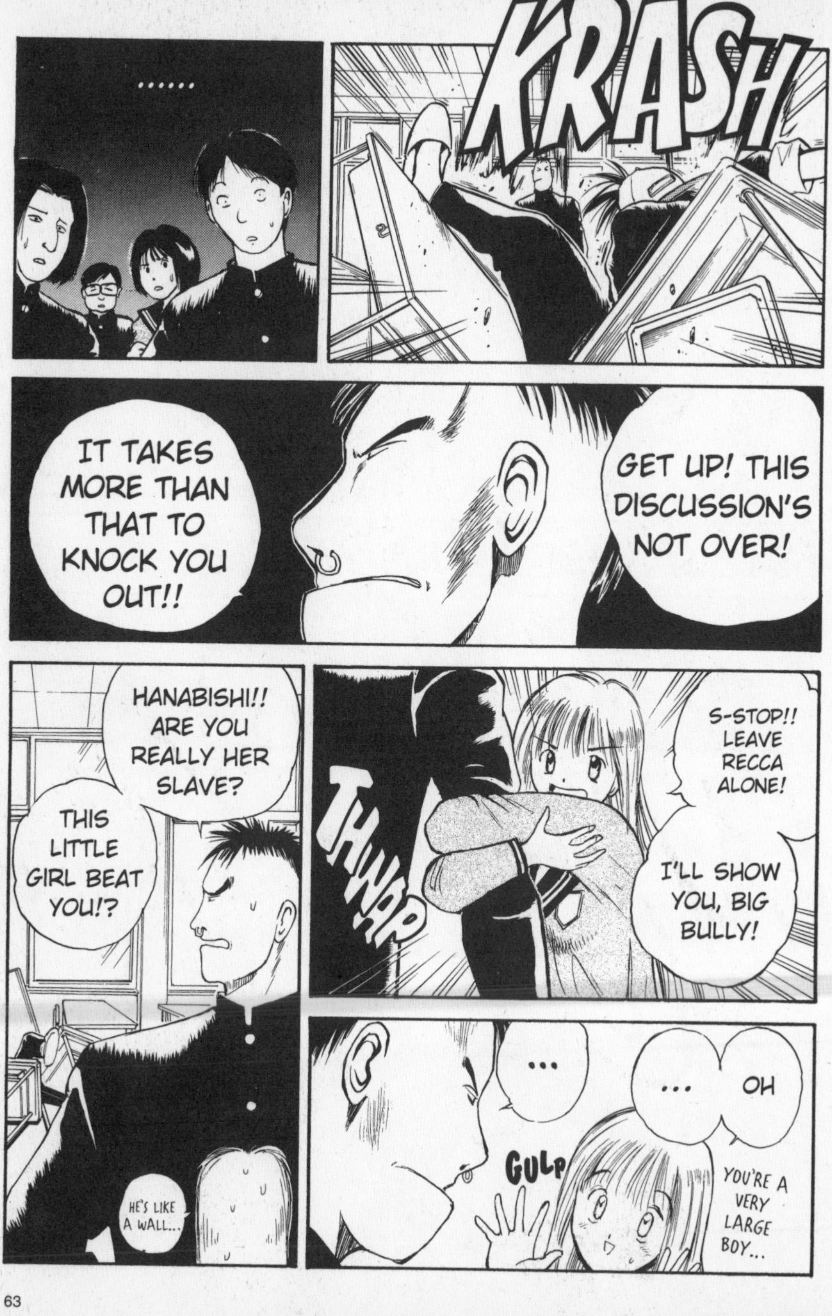
KRASH
......
GET UP! THIS DISCUSSION'S NOT OVER!
IT TAKES MORE THAN THAT TO KNOCK YOU OUT!!
S-STOP!! LEAVE RECCA ALONE!
THWAP
I'LL SHOW YOU, BIG BULLY!
... OH
...
GULP
YOU'RE A VERY LARGE BOY...
HANABISHI!! ARE YOU REALLY HER SLAVE?
THIS LITTLE GIRL BEAT YOU!?
HE'S LIKE A WALL...

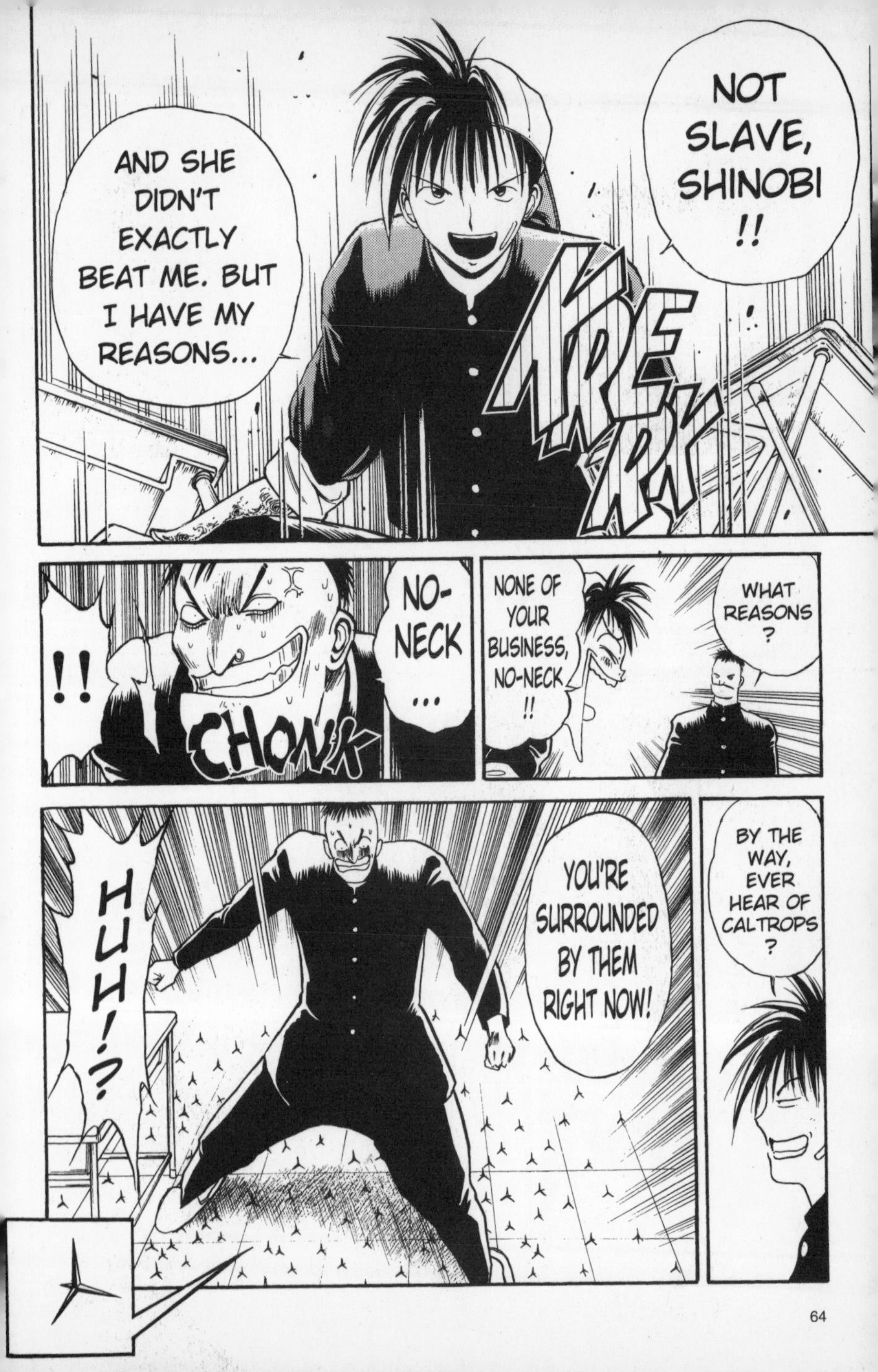
NOT SLAVE, SHINOBI !!
AND SHE DIDN'T EXACTLY BEAT ME. BUT I HAVE MY REASONS...
WHAT REASONS ?
NONE OF YOUR BUSINESS, NO-NECK !!
NO-NECK ...
!!
CHONK
BY THE WAY, EVER HEAR OF CALTROPS ?
YOU'RE SURROUNDED BY THEM RIGHT NOW!
HUH!?

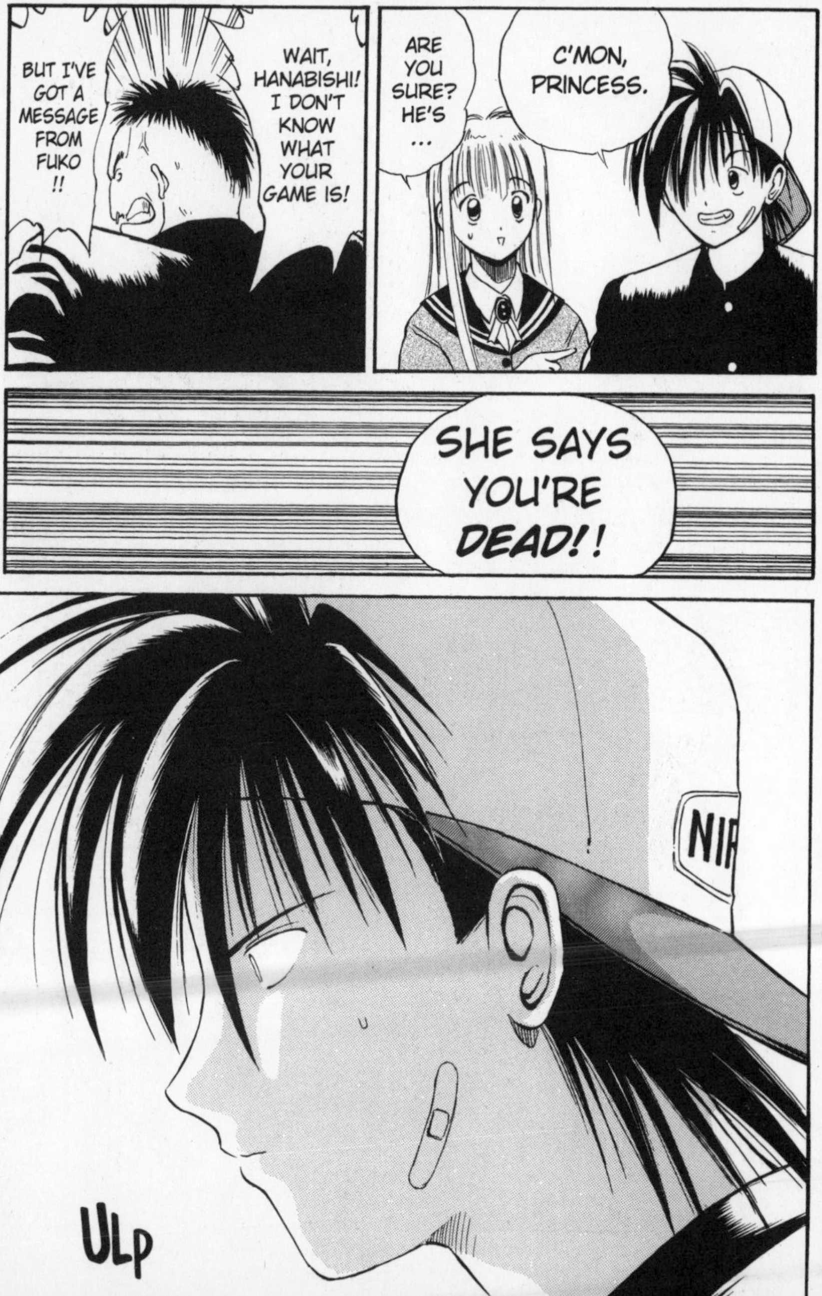
C'MON, PRINCESS.
ARE YOU SURE? HE'S ...
WAIT, HANABISHI! I DON'T KNOW WHAT YOUR GAME IS!
BUT I'VE GOT A MESSAGE FROM FUKO !!
SHE SAYS YOU'RE DEAD!!
ULP
NIF

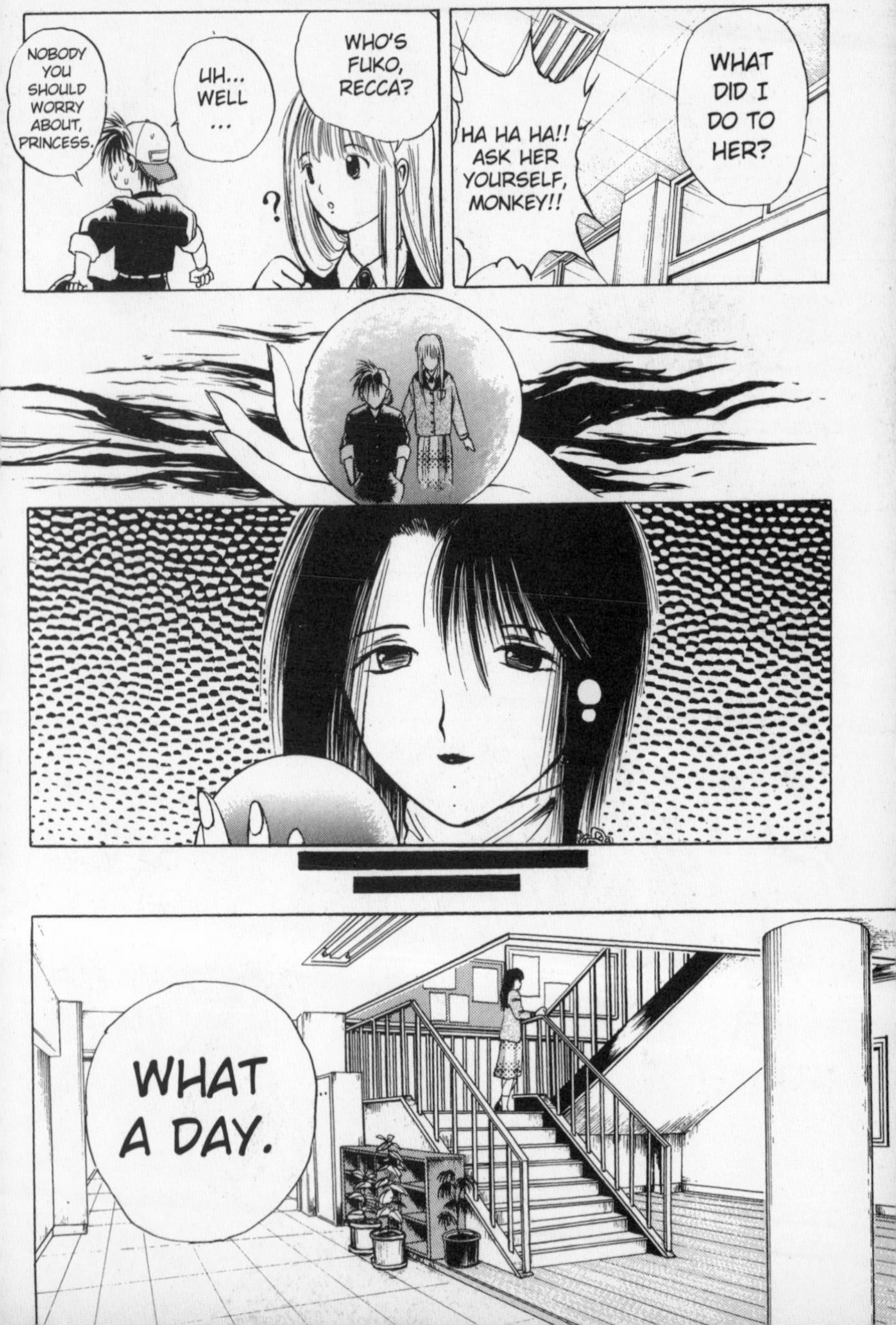
WHAT DID I DO TO HER?
HA HA HA!! ASK HER YOURSELF, MONKEY!!
WHO'S FUKO, RECCA?
UH... WELL ...
?
NOBODY YOU SHOULD WORRY ABOUT, PRINCESS.
WHAT A DAY.

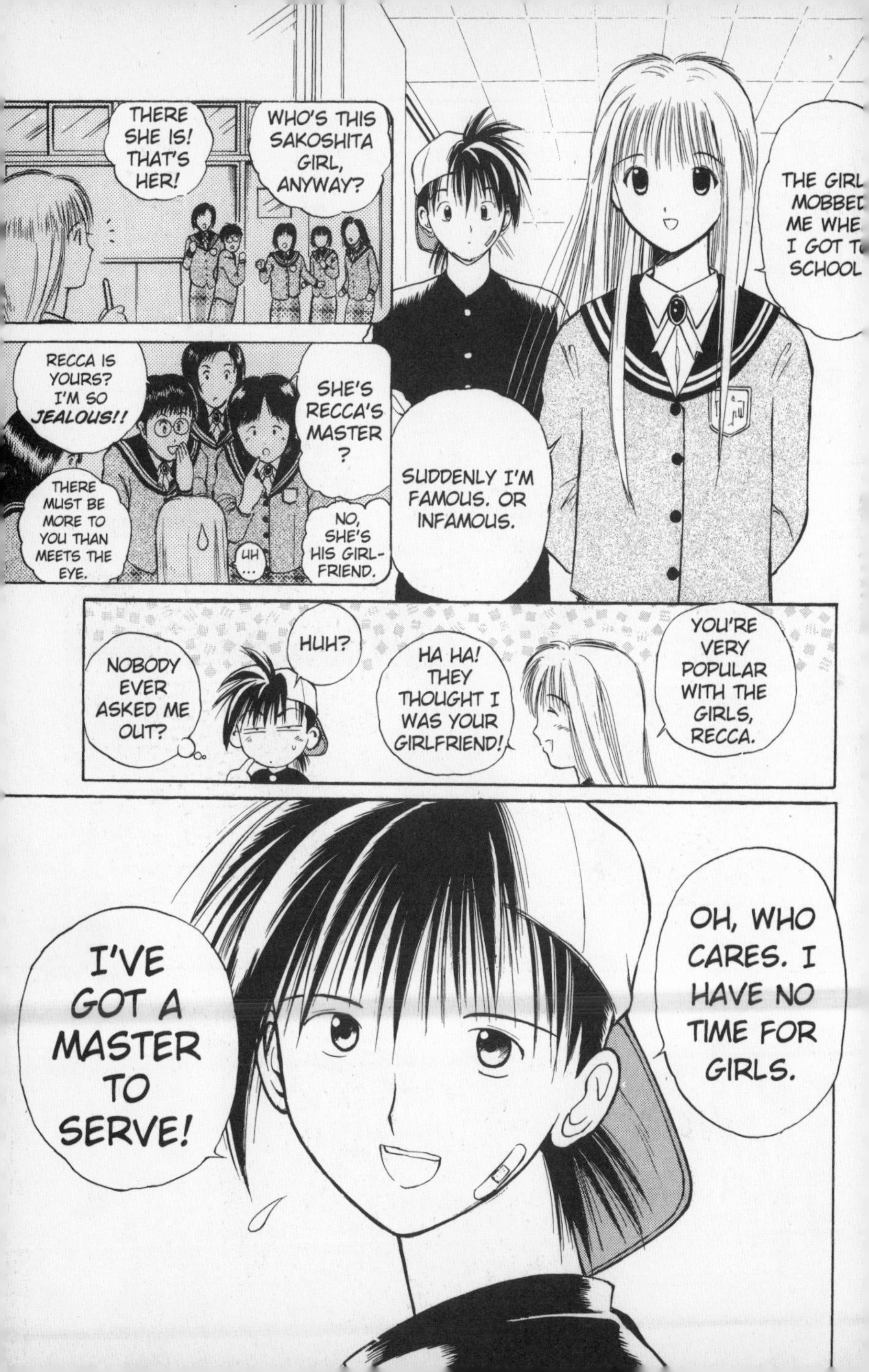
THE GIRL MOBBEI ME WHE I GOT T SCHOOL
SUDDENLY I'M FAMOUS. OR INFAMOUS.
WHO'S THIS SAKOSHITA GIRL, ANYWAY?
THERE SHE IS! THAT'S HER!
SHE'S RECCA'S MASTER?
NO, SHE'S HIS GIRL-FRIEND.
RECCA IS YOURS? I'M SO *JEALOUS!!*
UH ...
THERE MUST BE MORE TO YOU THAN MEETS THE EYE.
YOU'RE VERY POPULAR WITH THE GIRLS, RECCA.
HA HA! THEY THOUGHT I WAS YOUR GIRLFRIEND!
HUH?
NOBODY EVER ASKED ME OUT?
OH, WHO CARES. I HAVE NO TIME FOR GIRLS.
I'VE GOT A MASTER TO SERVE!

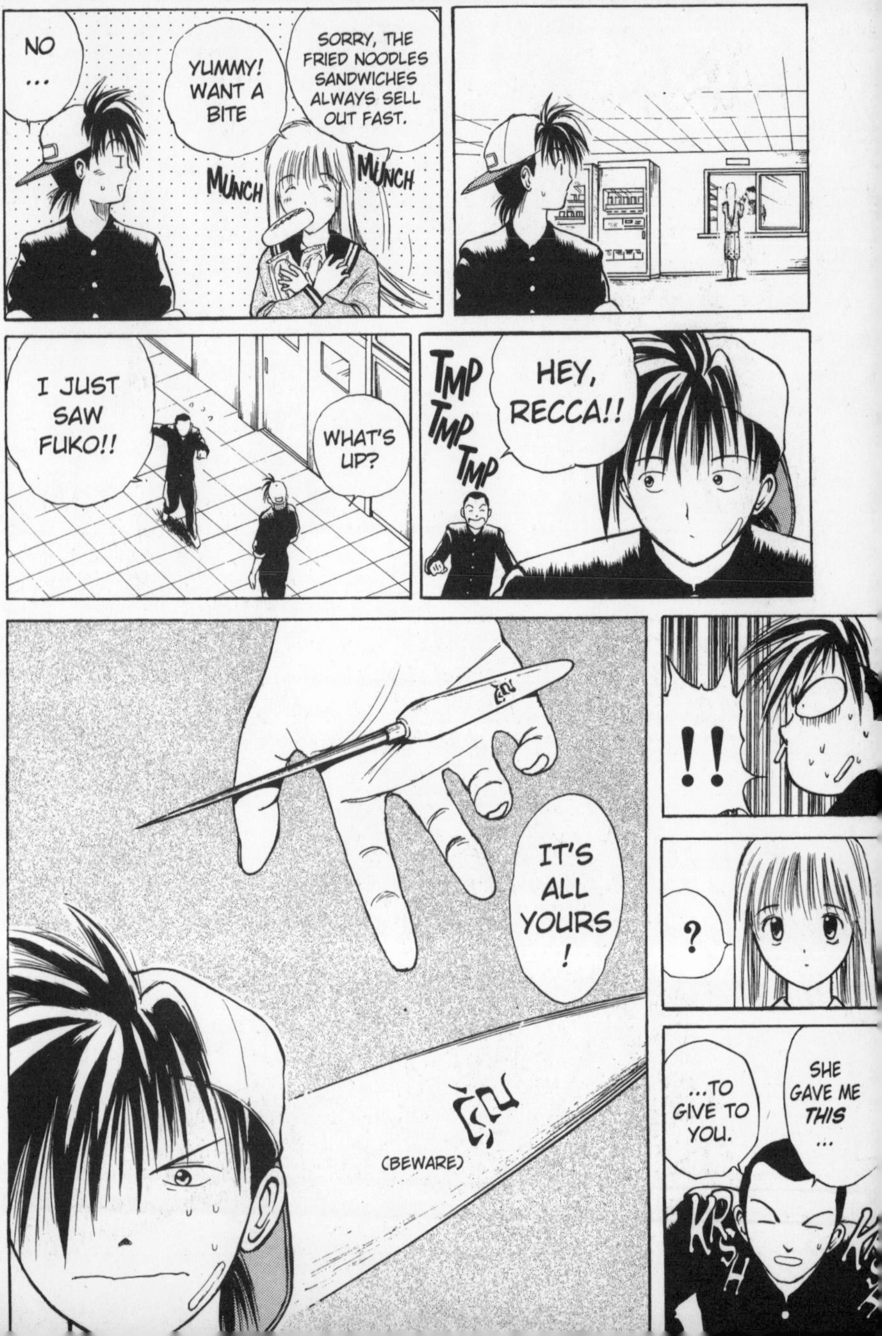
SORRY, THE FRIED NOODLES SANDWICHES ALWAYS SELL OUT FAST.
MUNCH
MUNCH
YUMMY! WANT A BITE
NO ...
TMP TMP TMP
HEY, RECCA!!
WHAT'S UP?
I JUST SAW FUKO!!
!!
?
SHE GAVE ME THIS ...
...TO GIVE TO YOU.
KRSH
IT'S ALL YOURS!
(BEWARE)

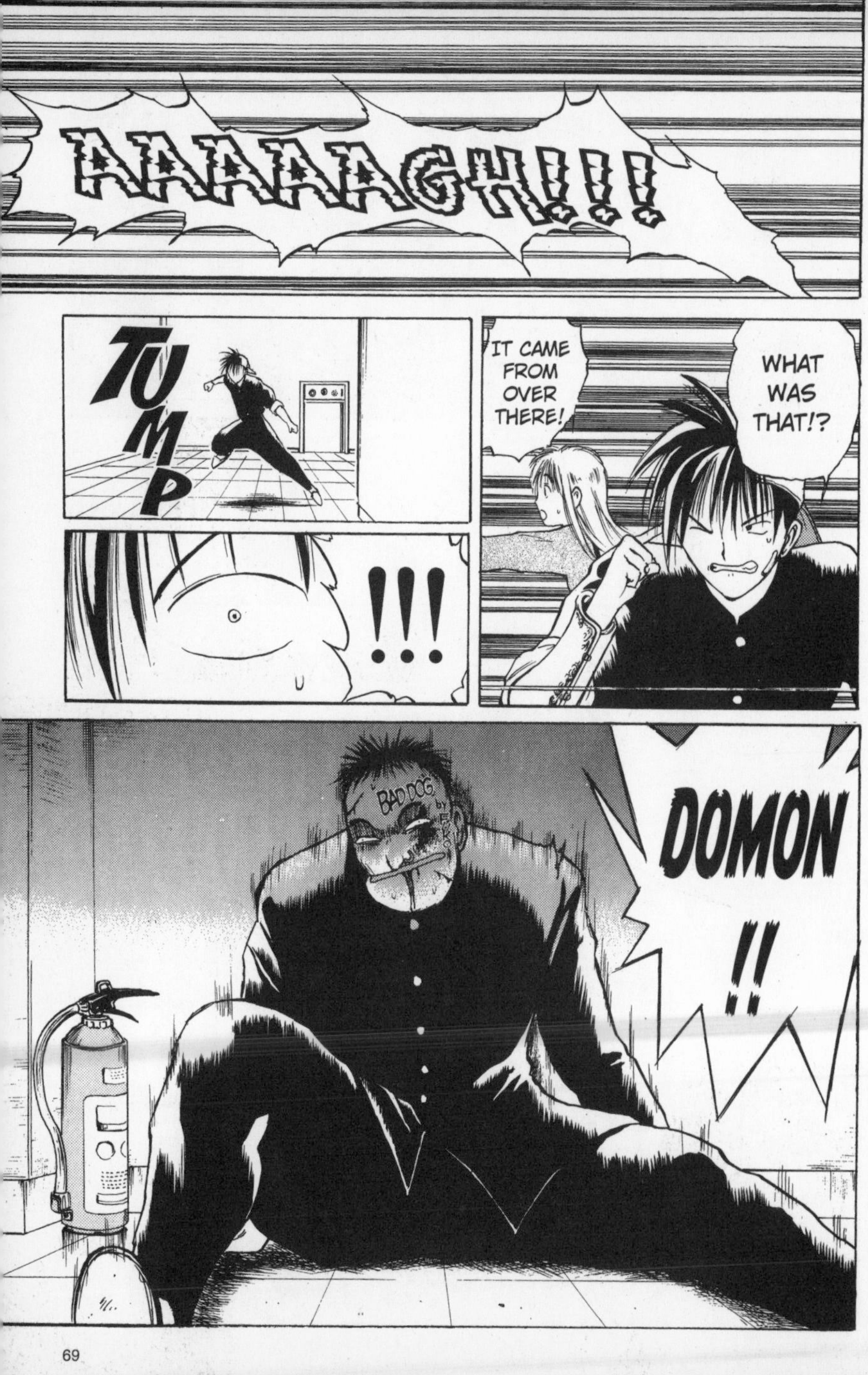
AAAAAGH!!!
WHAT WAS THAT!?
IT CAME FROM OVER THERE!
TUMP
!!!
DOMON !!
BAD DOG
by

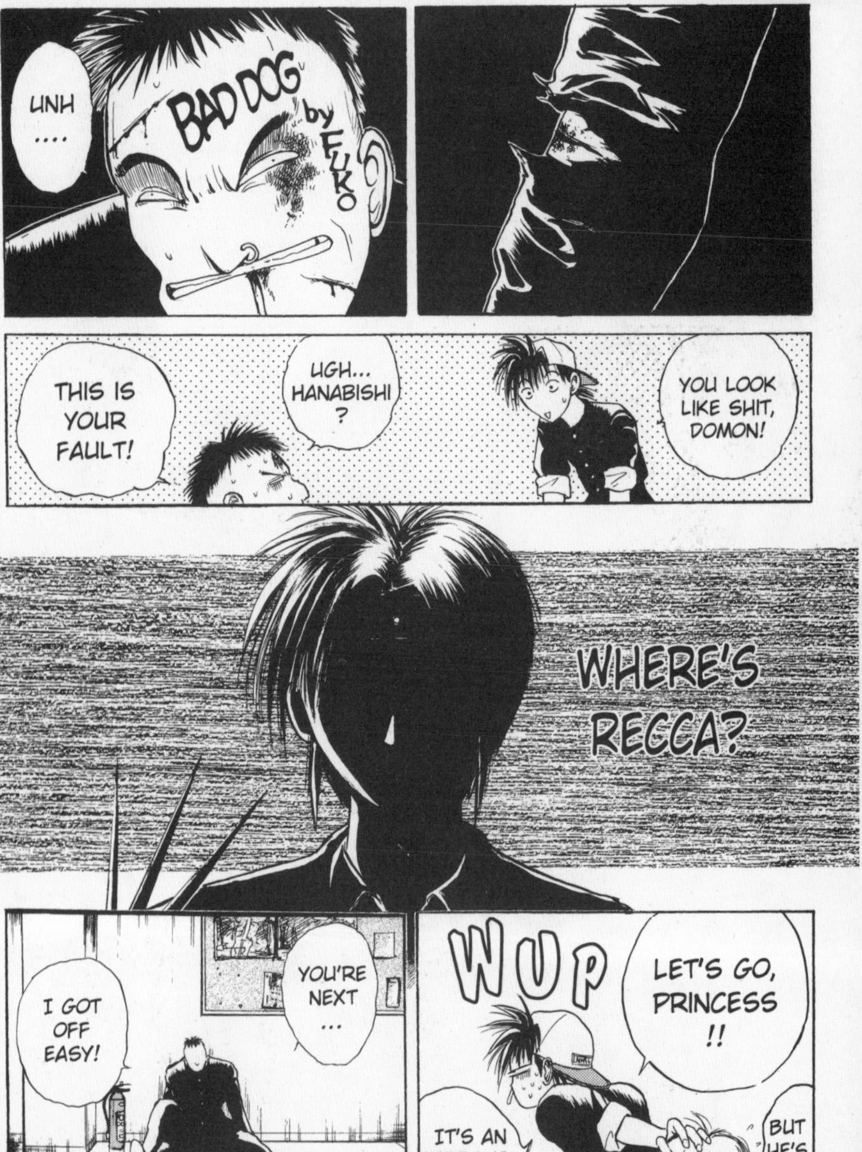
BAD DOG by FUKO
UNH ....
YOU LOOK LIKE SHIT, DOMON!
UGH... HANABISHI ?
THIS IS YOUR FAULT!
WHERE'S RECCA?
WUP
LET'S GO, PRINCESS !!
BUT HE'S ...
IT'S AN IMPROVE-MENT, C'MON!
YOU'RE NEXT ...
I GOT OFF EASY!

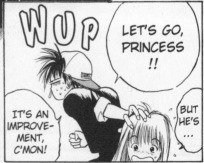

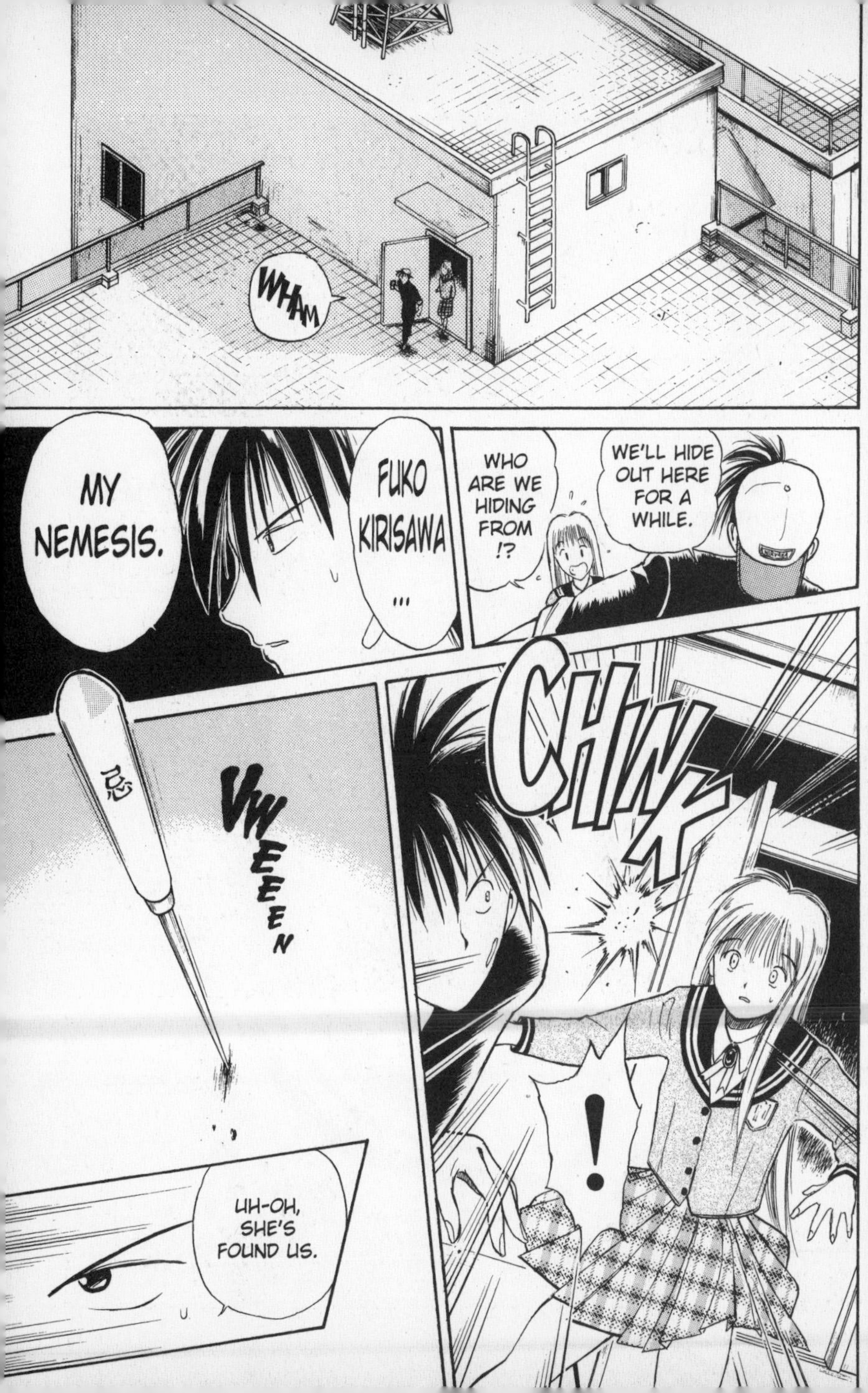
WHAM
WE'LL HIDE OUT HERE FOR A WHILE.
WHO ARE WE HIDING FROM !?
FUKO KIRISAWA ...
MY NEMESIS.
CHINK
!
忍
VWEEEEN
UH-OH, SHE'S FOUND US.

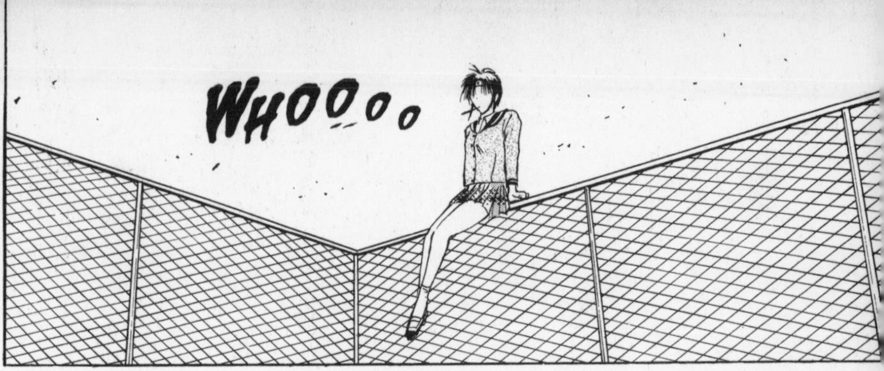
WHOOOOO

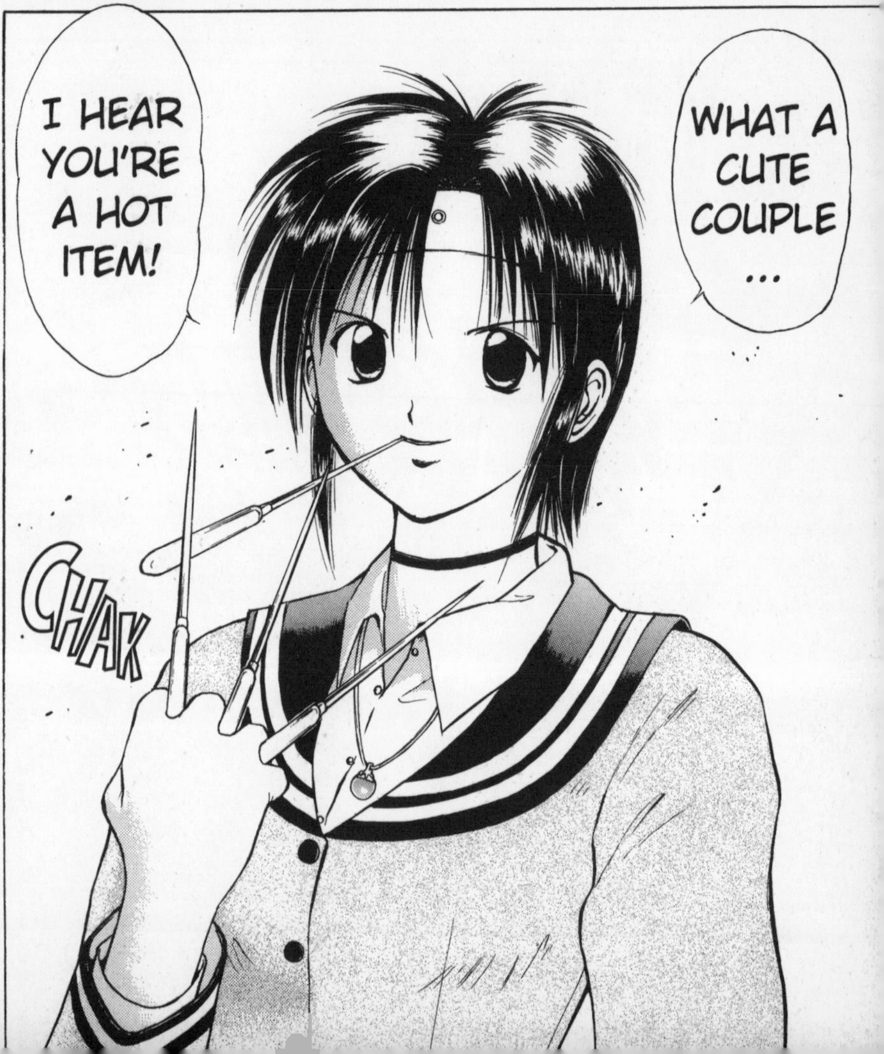
WHAT A CUTE COUPLE ...
I HEAR YOU'RE A HOT ITEM!
CHAK

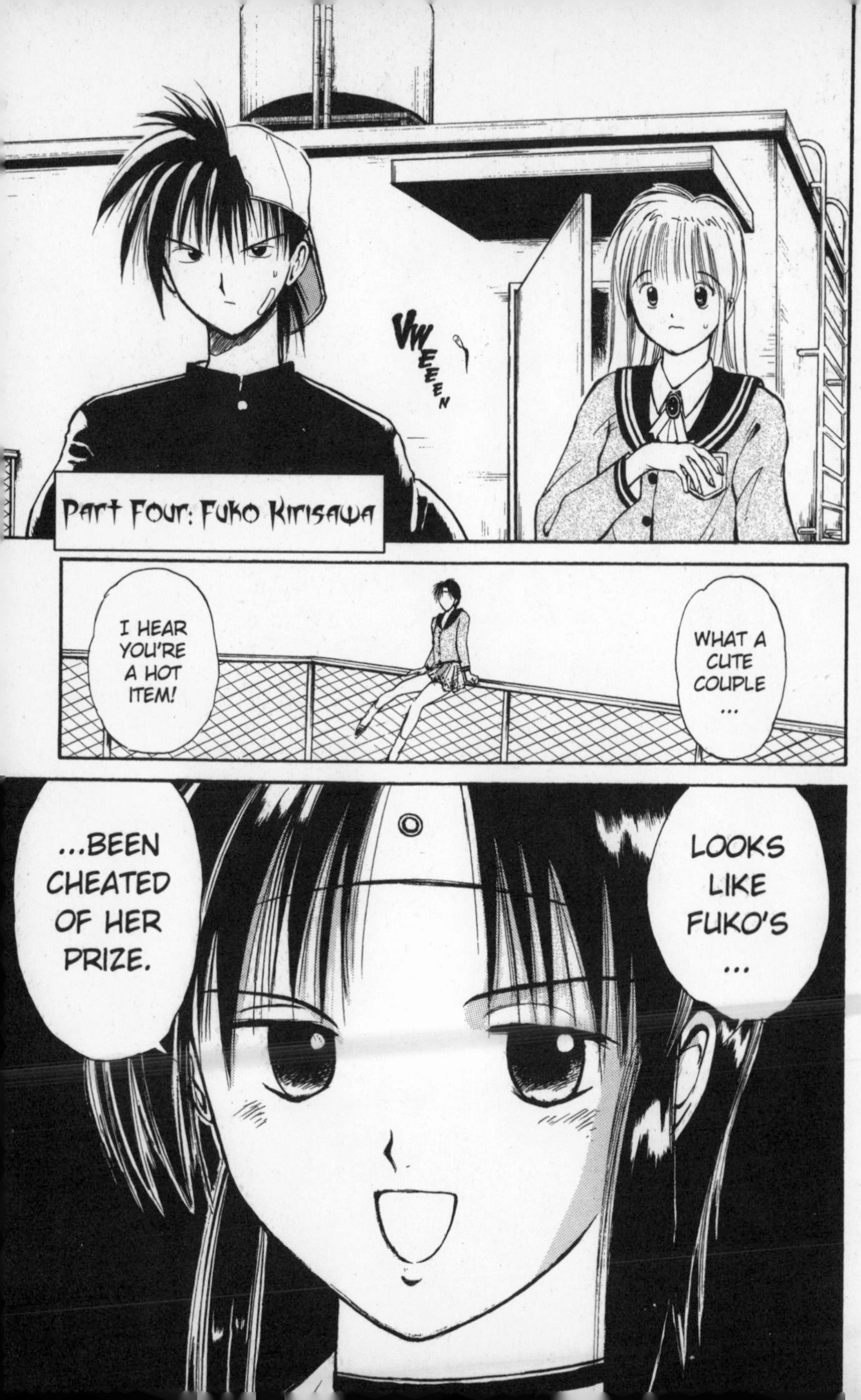
VWEEEEN
Part Four: Fuko Kirisawa
WHAT A CUTE COUPLE ...
I HEAR YOU'RE A HOT ITEM!
LOOKS LIKE FUKO'S ...
...BEEN CHEATED OF HER PRIZE.

Part 4: Fuko Kirisawa

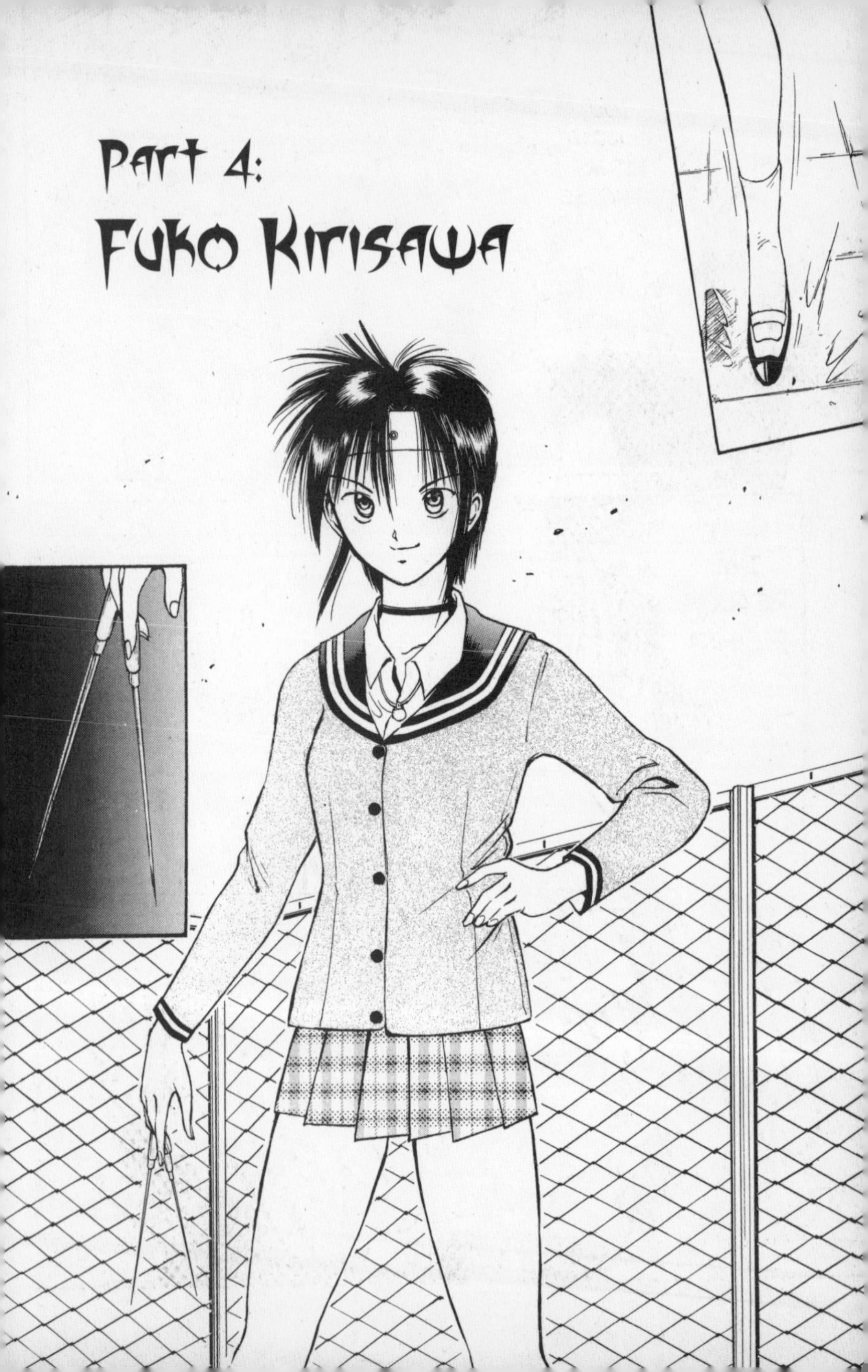

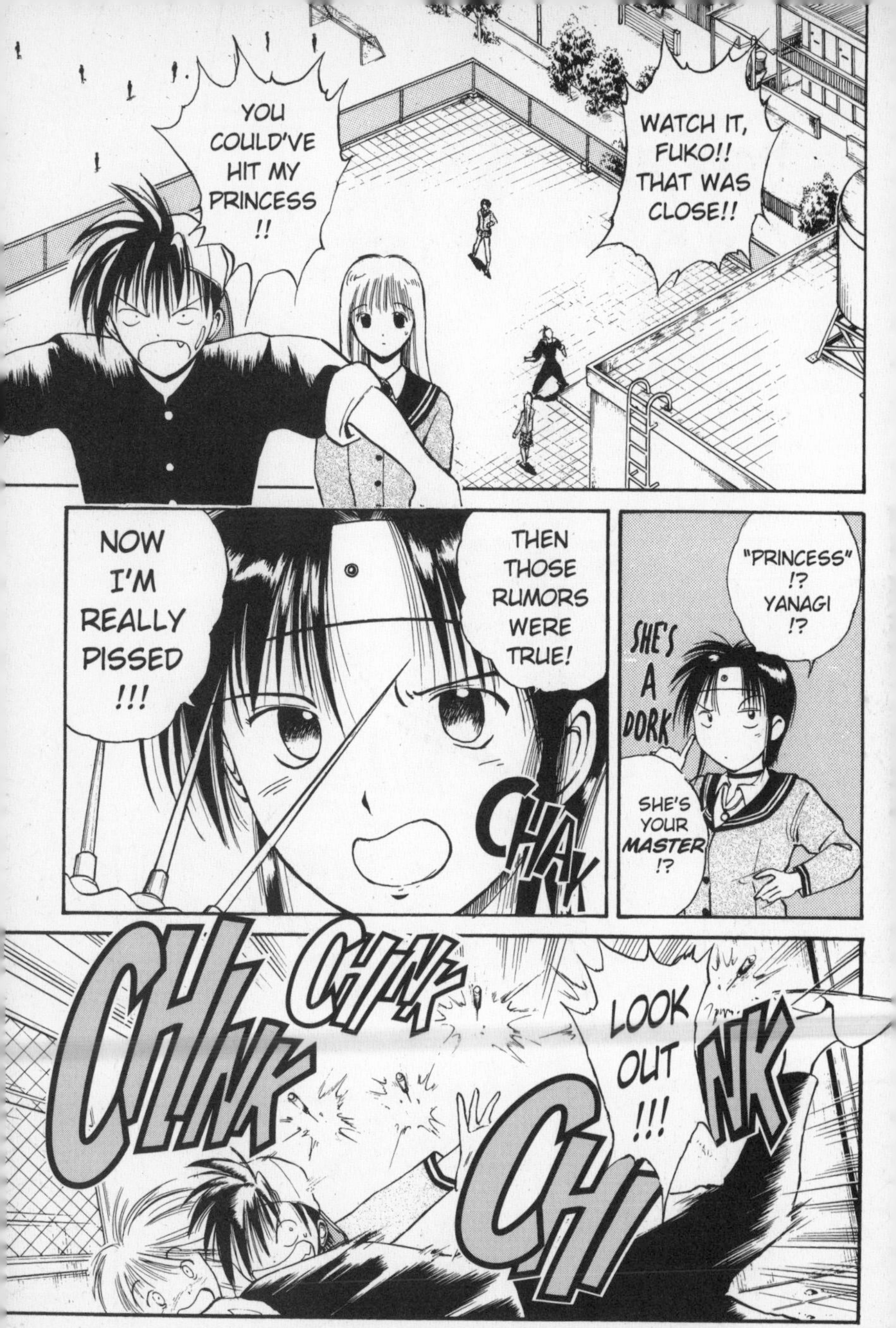
WATCH IT, FUKO!! THAT WAS CLOSE!!
YOU COULD'VE HIT MY PRINCESS!!
"PRINCESS"!? YANAGI!?
SHE'S A DORK
SHE'S YOUR MASTER!?
THEN THOSE RUMORS WERE TRUE!
NOW I'M REALLY PISSED!!!
CHAK
LOOK OUT!!!
NK
CHI
CHINK
CHINK

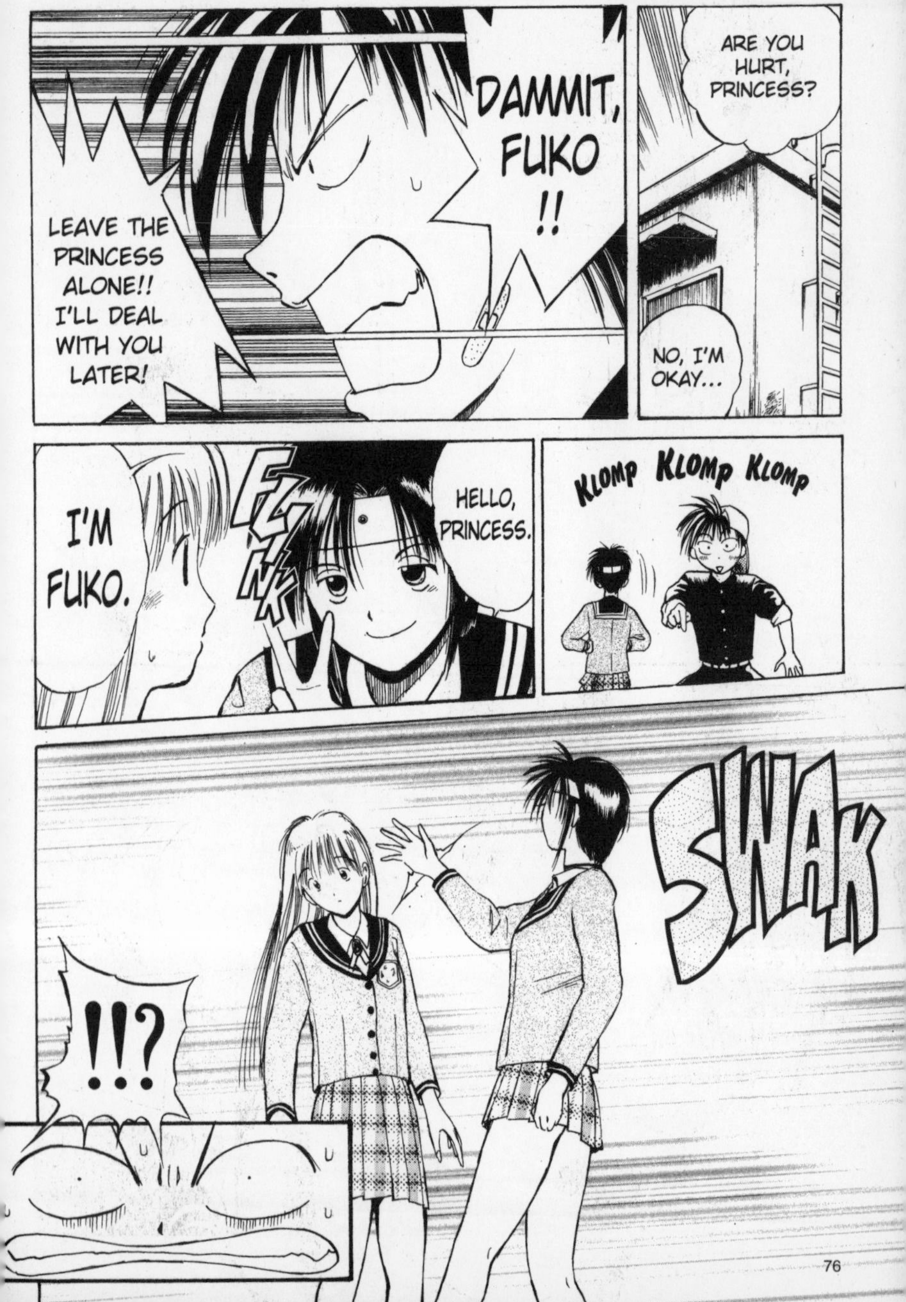
ARE YOU HURT, PRINCESS?
NO, I'M OKAY...
DAMMIT, FUKO !!
LEAVE THE PRINCESS ALONE!! I'LL DEAL WITH YOU LATER!
KLOMP KLOMP KLOMP
HELLO, PRINCESS.
I'M FUKO.
SWAK
!!?

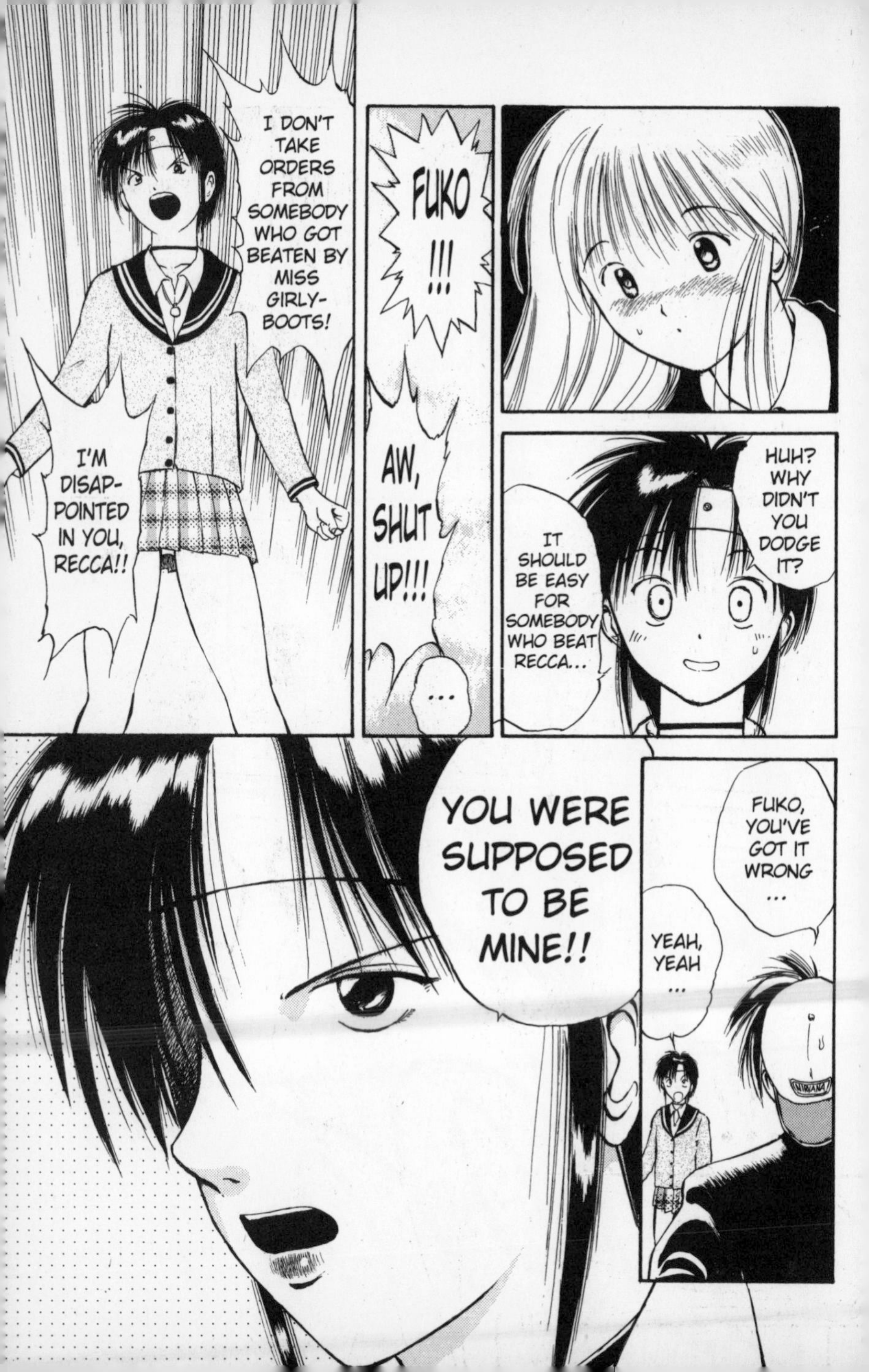
HUH? WHY DIDN'T YOU DODGE IT?
IT SHOULD BE EASY FOR SOMEBODY WHO BEAT RECCA...
FUKO!!!
AW, SHUT UP!!!
...
I DON'T TAKE ORDERS FROM SOMEBODY WHO GOT BEATEN BY MISS GIRLY-BOOTS!
I'M DISAP-POINTED IN YOU, RECCA!!
FUKO, YOU'VE GOT IT WRONG...
YEAH, YEAH...
YOU WERE SUPPOSED TO BE MINE!!

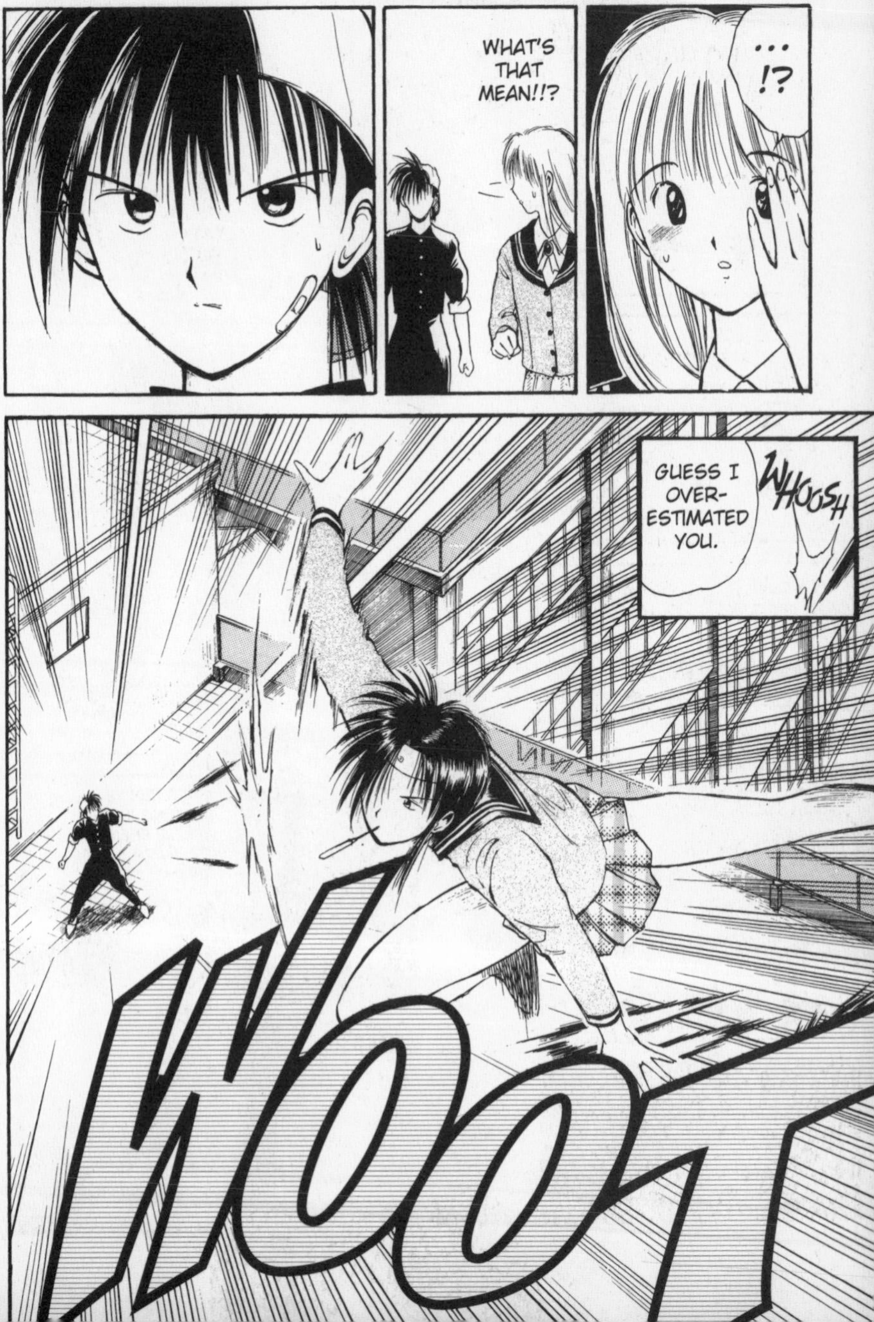
...!?
WHAT'S THAT MEAN!!?
GUESS I OVER-ESTIMATED YOU.
WHOOSH
WHOOT

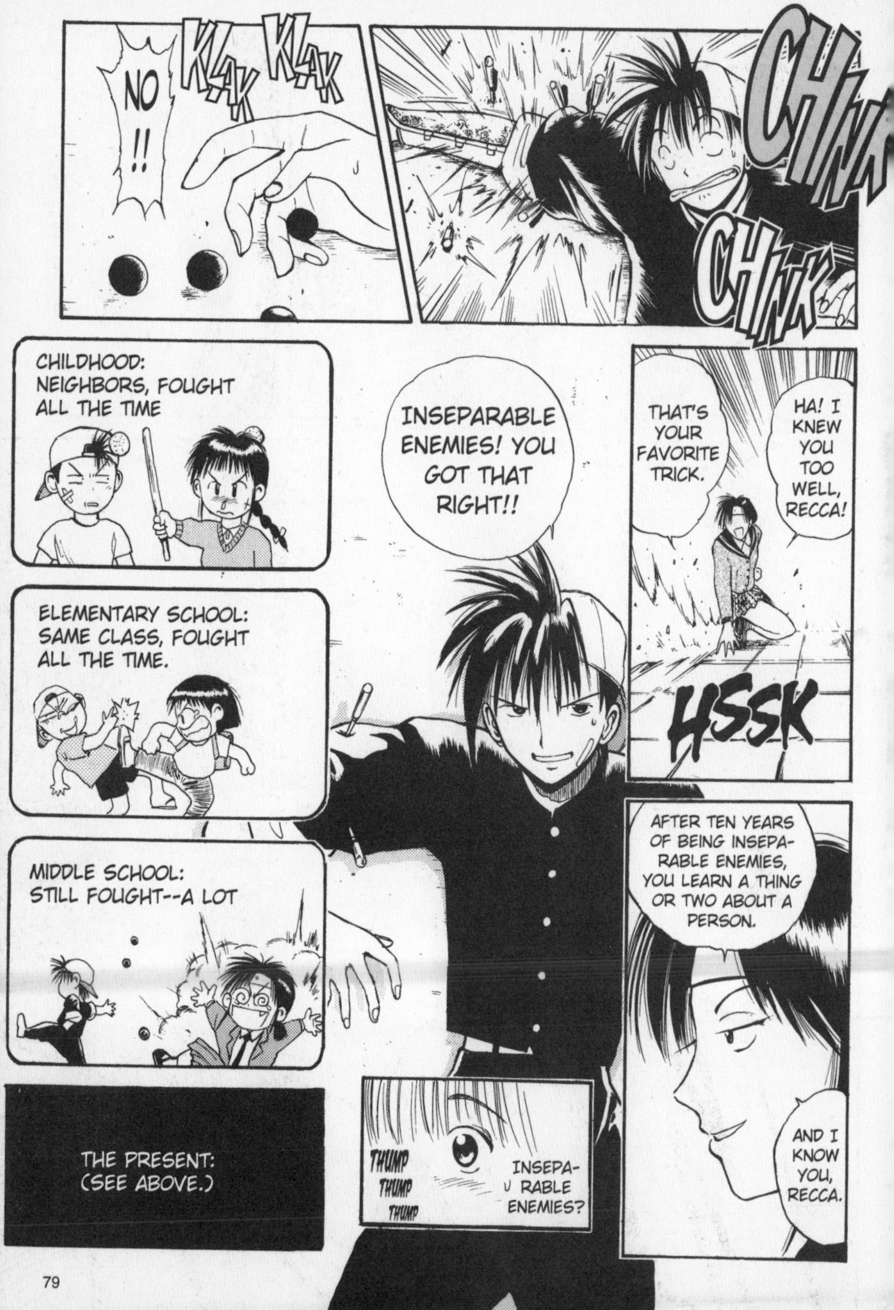
CHINK
CHINK
NO !!
KLAK KLAK
HA! I KNEW YOU TOO WELL, RECCA!
THAT'S YOUR FAVORITE TRICK.
HSSK
AFTER TEN YEARS OF BEING INSEPA-RABLE ENEMIES, YOU LEARN A THING OR TWO ABOUT A PERSON.
AND I KNOW YOU, RECCA.
INSEPARABLE ENEMIES! YOU GOT THAT RIGHT!!
THUMP THUMP THUMP
INSEPA-RABLE ENEMIES?
CHILDHOOD: NEIGHBORS, FOUGHT ALL THE TIME
ELEMENTARY SCHOOL: SAME CLASS, FOUGHT ALL THE TIME.
MIDDLE SCHOOL: STILL FOUGHT--A LOT
THE PRESENT: (SEE ABOVE.)

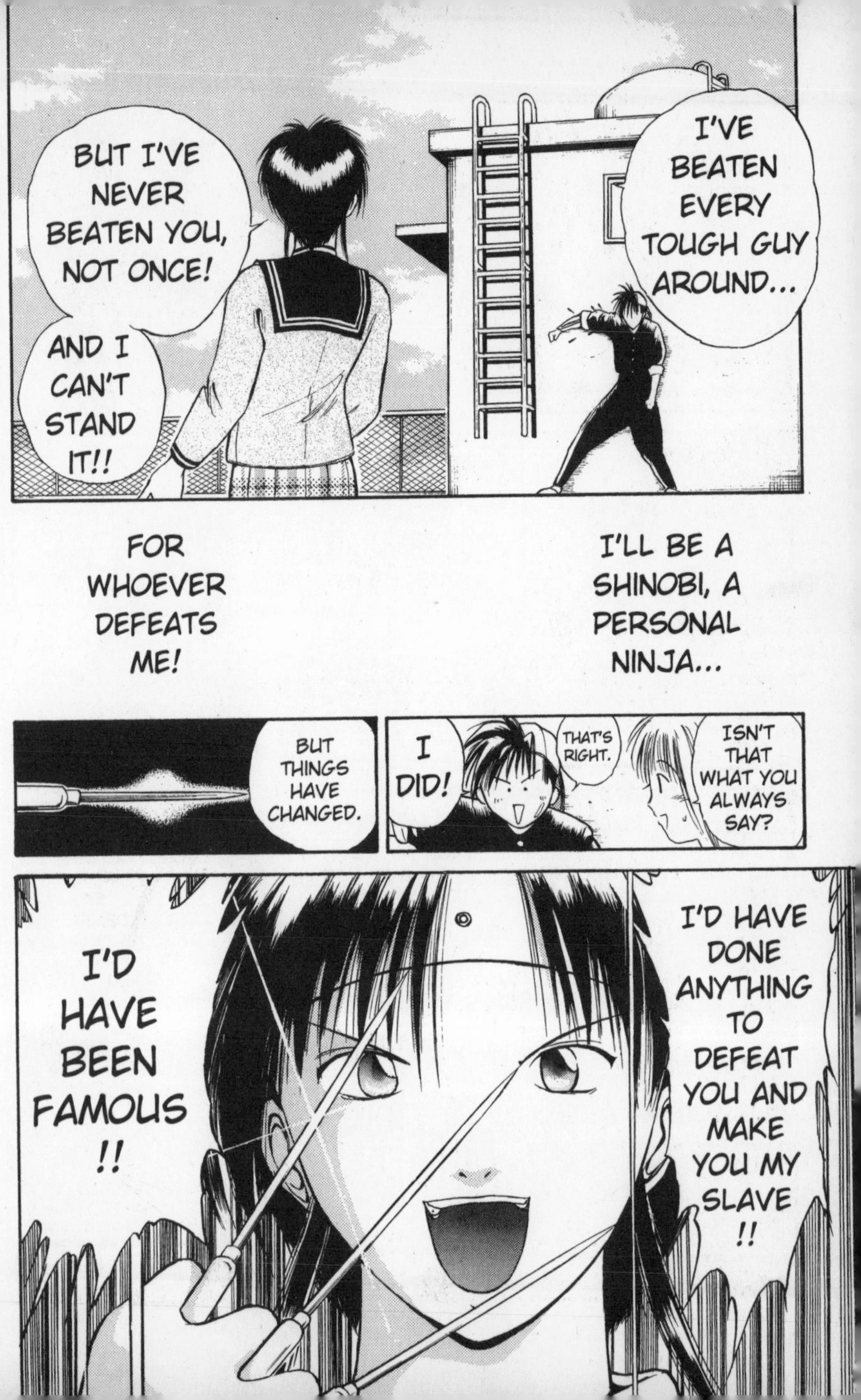
I'VE BEATEN EVERY TOUGH GUY AROUND...
BUT I'VE NEVER BEATEN YOU, NOT ONCE!
AND I CAN'T STAND IT!!
I'LL BE A SHINOBI, A PERSONAL NINJA...
FOR WHOEVER DEFEATS ME!
ISN'T THAT WHAT YOU ALWAYS SAY?
THAT'S RIGHT.
I DID!
BUT THINGS HAVE CHANGED.
I'D HAVE DONE ANYTHING TO DEFEAT YOU AND MAKE YOU MY SLAVE!!
I'D HAVE BEEN FAMOUS!!

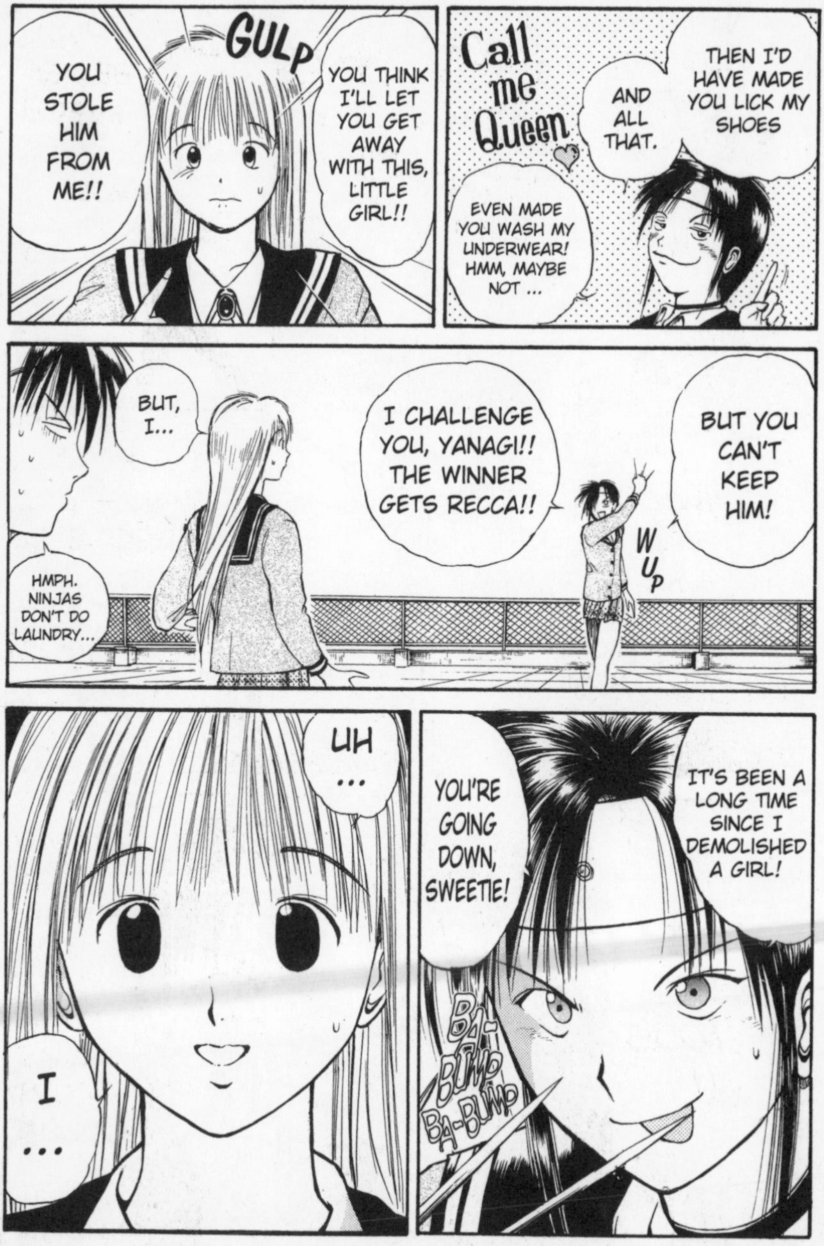
THEN I'D HAVE MADE YOU LICK MY SHOES
AND ALL THAT.
Call me Queen
EVEN MADE YOU WASH MY UNDERWEAR! HMM, MAYBE NOT ...
YOU THINK I'LL LET YOU GET AWAY WITH THIS, LITTLE GIRL!!
GULP
YOU STOLE HIM FROM ME!!
BUT YOU CAN'T KEEP HIM!
WUP
I CHALLENGE YOU, YANAGI!! THE WINNER GETS RECCA!!
BUT, I...
HMPH. NINJAS DON'T DO LAUNDRY...
IT'S BEEN A LONG TIME SINCE I DEMOLISHED A GIRL!
YOU'RE GOING DOWN, SWEETIE!
BA-BUMP BA-BUMP
UH ...
I ...

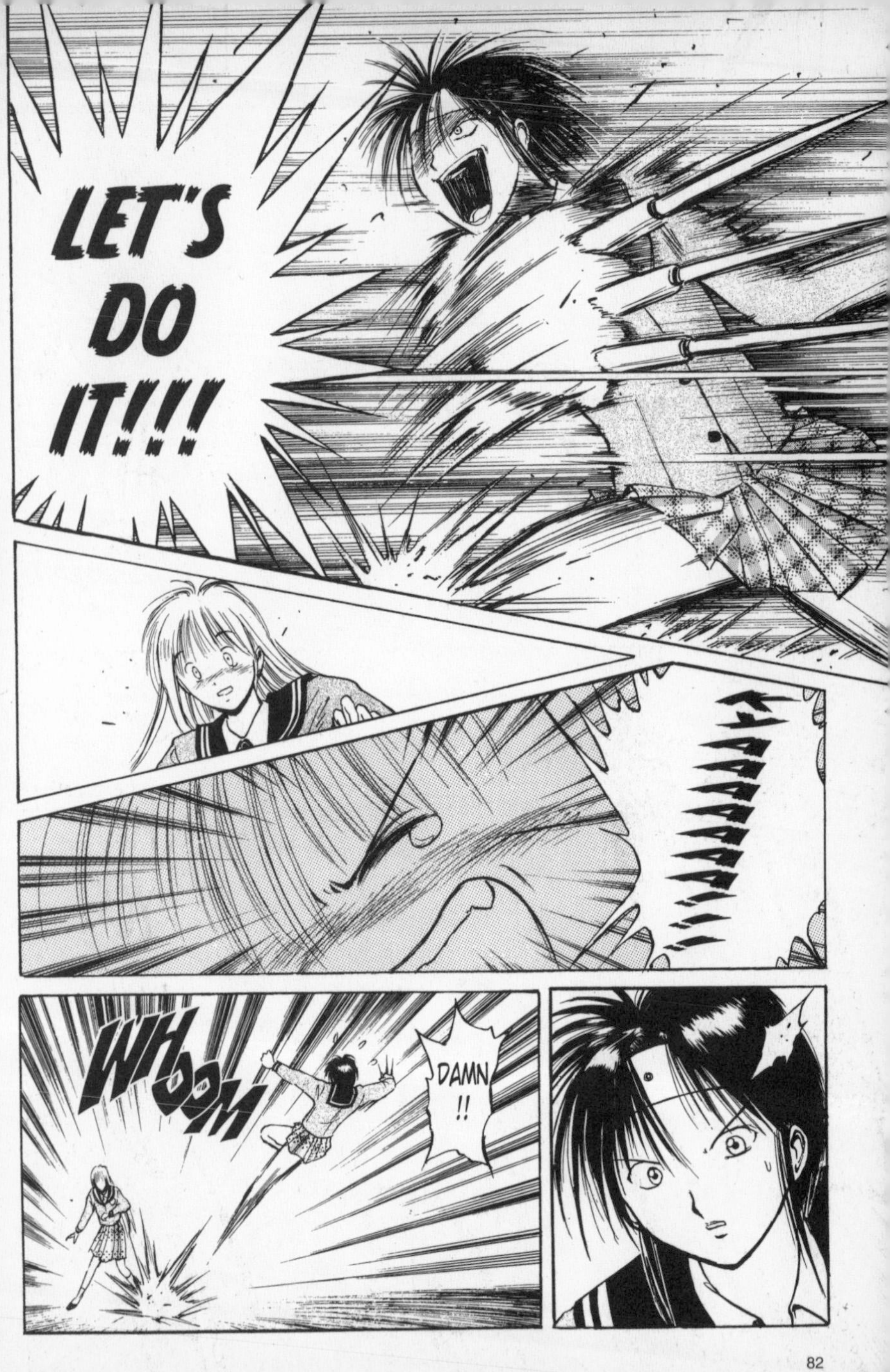
LET'S DO IT!!!
KYAAAAAAA!!!
WHOOM
DAMN !!

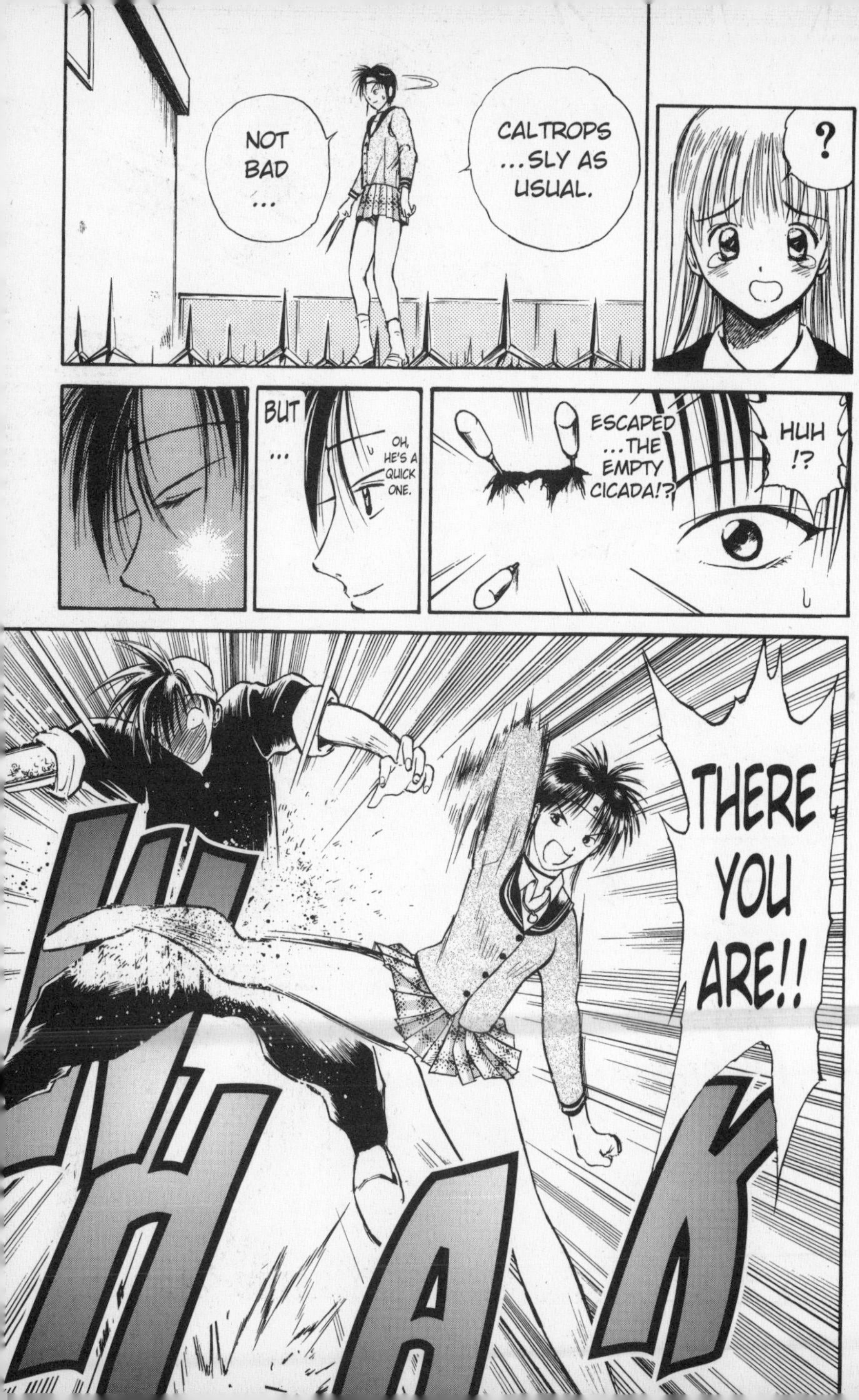
?
CALTROPS ...SLY AS USUAL.
NOT BAD ...
HUH !?
ESCAPED ...THE EMPTY CICADA!?
BUT ...
OH, HE'S A QUICK ONE.
THERE YOU ARE!!

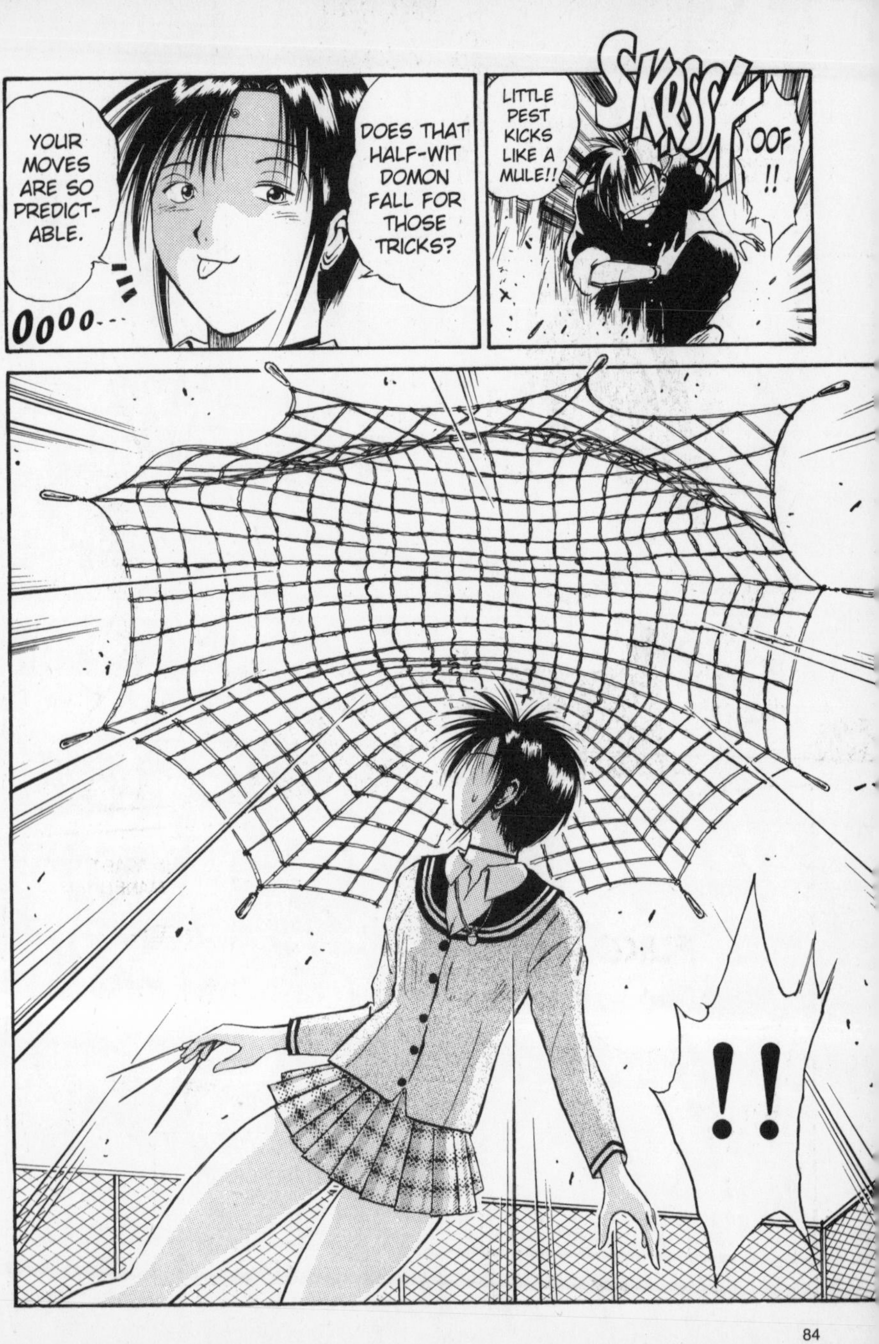
SKRSSK
OOF !!
LITTLE PEST KICKS LIKE A MULE!!
DOES THAT HALF-WIT DOMON FALL FOR THOSE TRICKS?
YOUR MOVES ARE SO PREDICT-ABLE.
OOOO...
!!

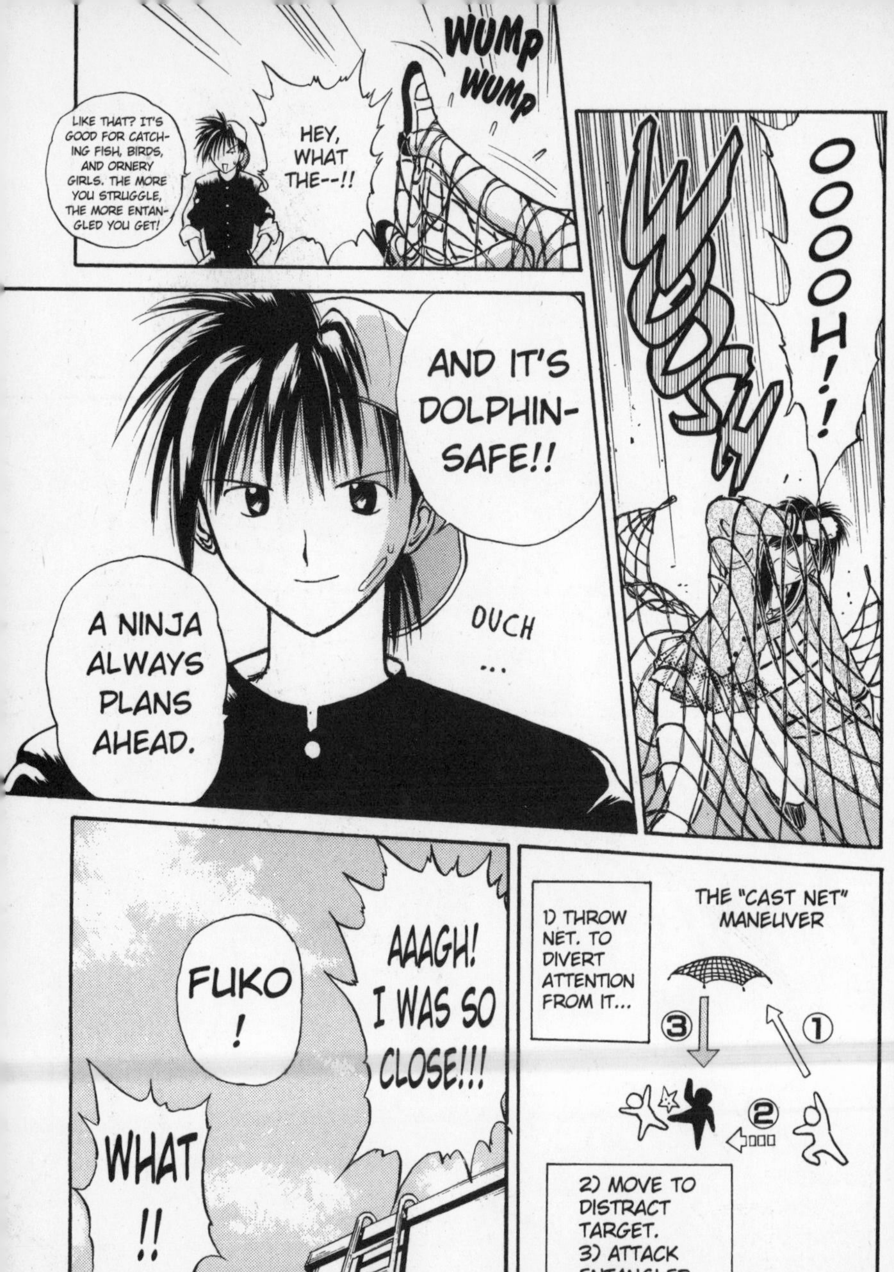
WHOOSH
OOOOH!!
WUMP WUMP
HEY, WHAT THE--!!
LIKE THAT? IT'S GOOD FOR CATCHING FISH, BIRDS, AND ORNERY GIRLS. THE MORE YOU STRUGGLE, THE MORE ENTANGLED YOU GET!
AND IT'S DOLPHIN-SAFE!!
OUCH ...
A NINJA ALWAYS PLANS AHEAD.
THE "CAST NET" MANEUVER
1) THROW NET. TO DIVERT ATTENTION FROM IT...
2) MOVE TO DISTRACT TARGET.
3) ATTACK ENTANGLED TARGET.
AAAGH! I WAS SO CLOSE!!!
FUKO!
WHAT!!

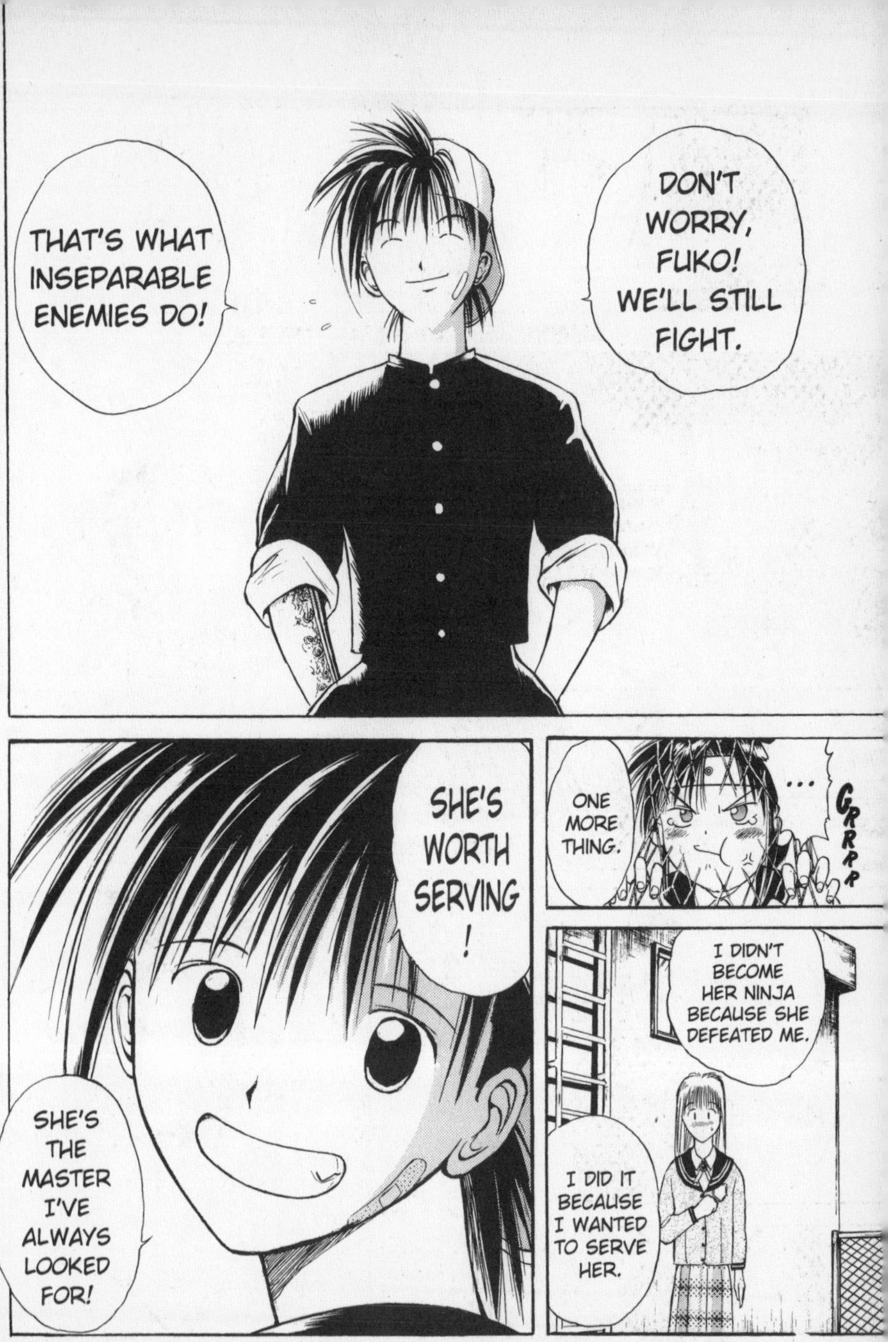
DON'T WORRY, FUKO! WE'LL STILL FIGHT.
THAT'S WHAT INSEPARABLE ENEMIES DO!
...
GRRRR
ONE MORE THING.
I DIDN'T BECOME HER NINJA BECAUSE SHE DEFEATED ME.
I DID IT BECAUSE I WANTED TO SERVE HER.
SHE'S WORTH SERVING!
SHE'S THE MASTER I'VE ALWAYS LOOKED FOR!

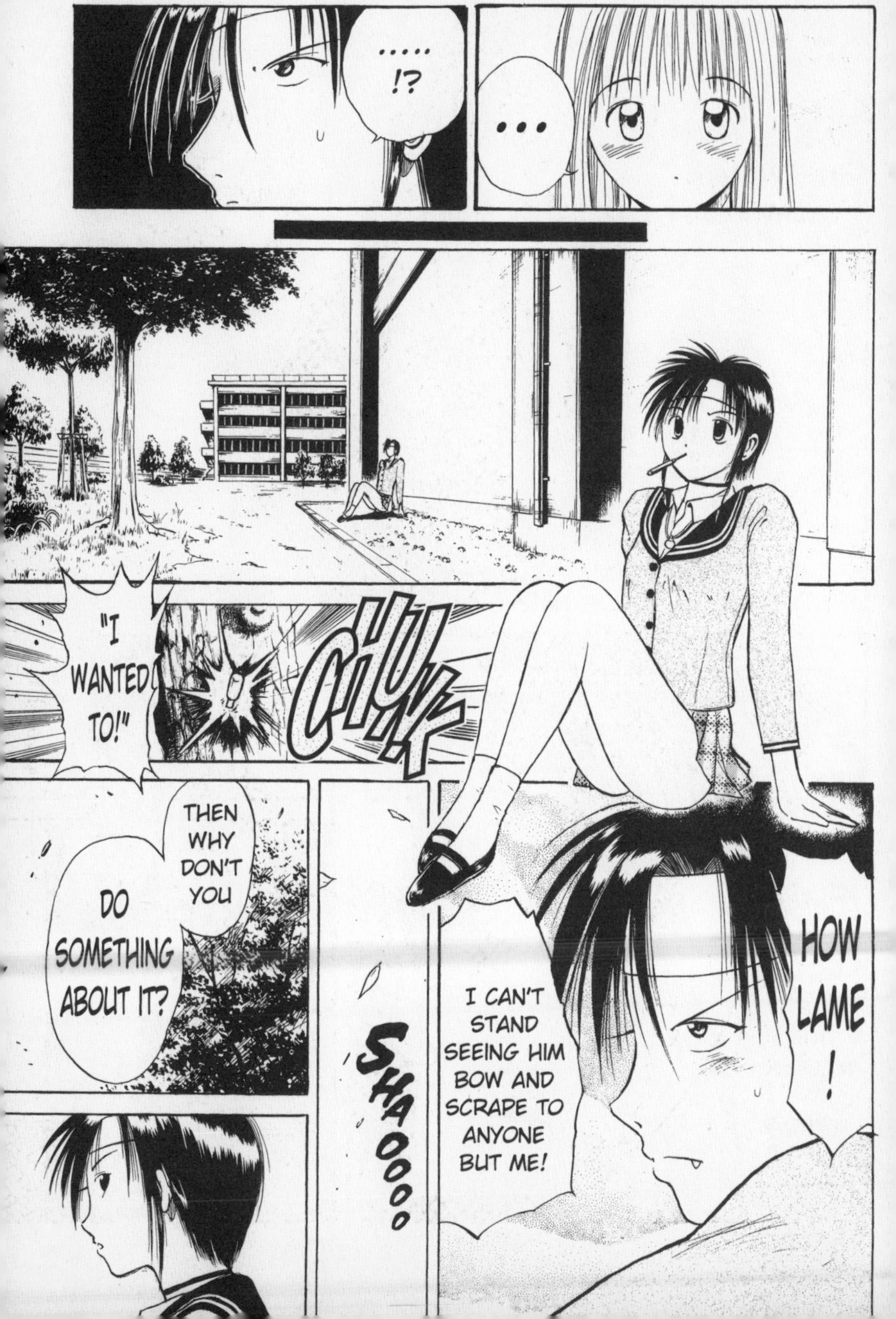
...
.....
!?
"I WANTED TO!"
CHINK
HOW LAME!
I CAN'T STAND SEEING HIM BOW AND SCRAPE TO ANYONE BUT ME!
SHAOOOO
THEN WHY DON'T YOU DO SOMETHING ABOUT IT?

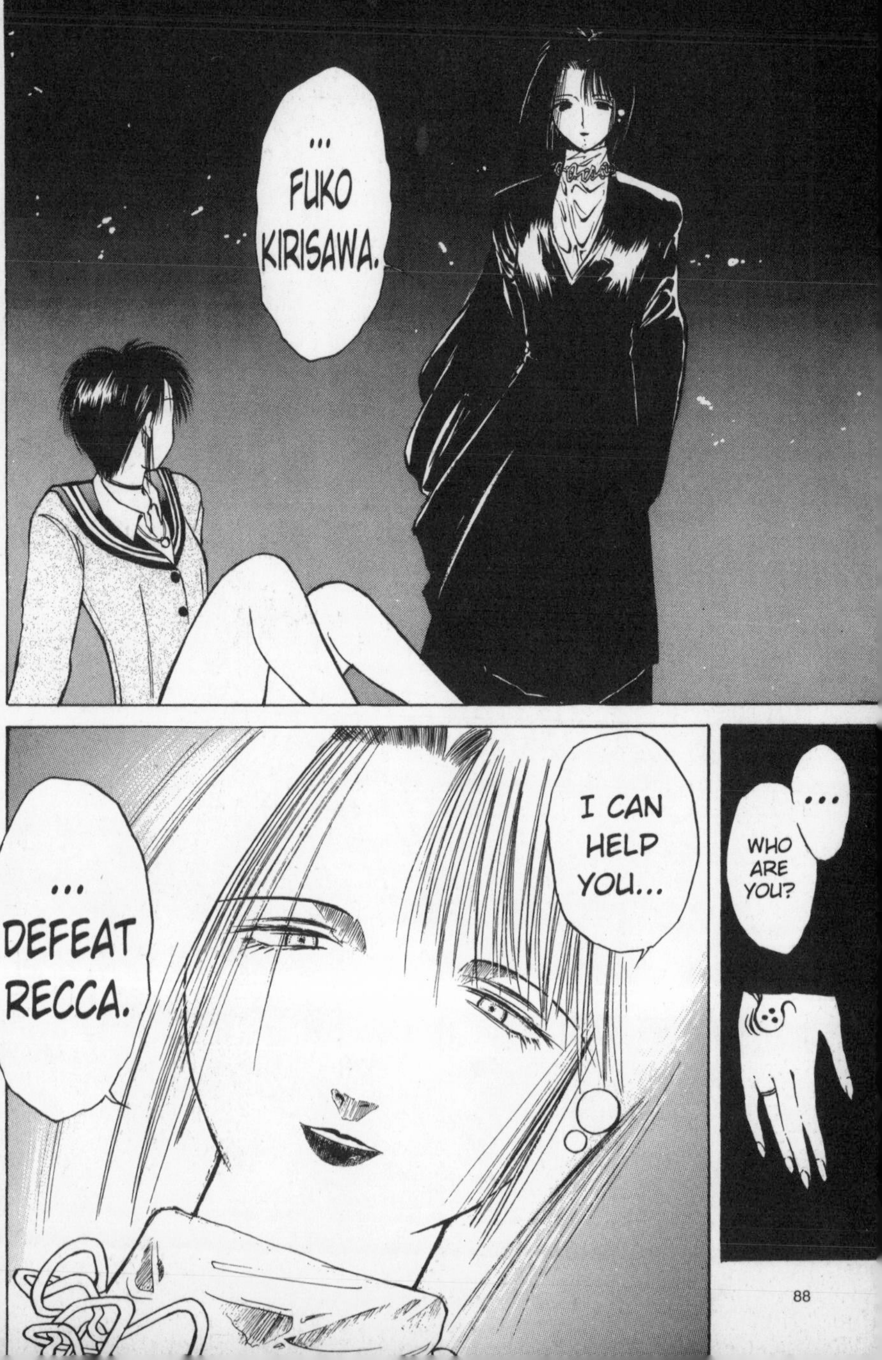
... FUKO KIRISAWA.
...
WHO ARE YOU?
I CAN HELP YOU...
... DEFEAT RECCA.

Part Five: God of Wind

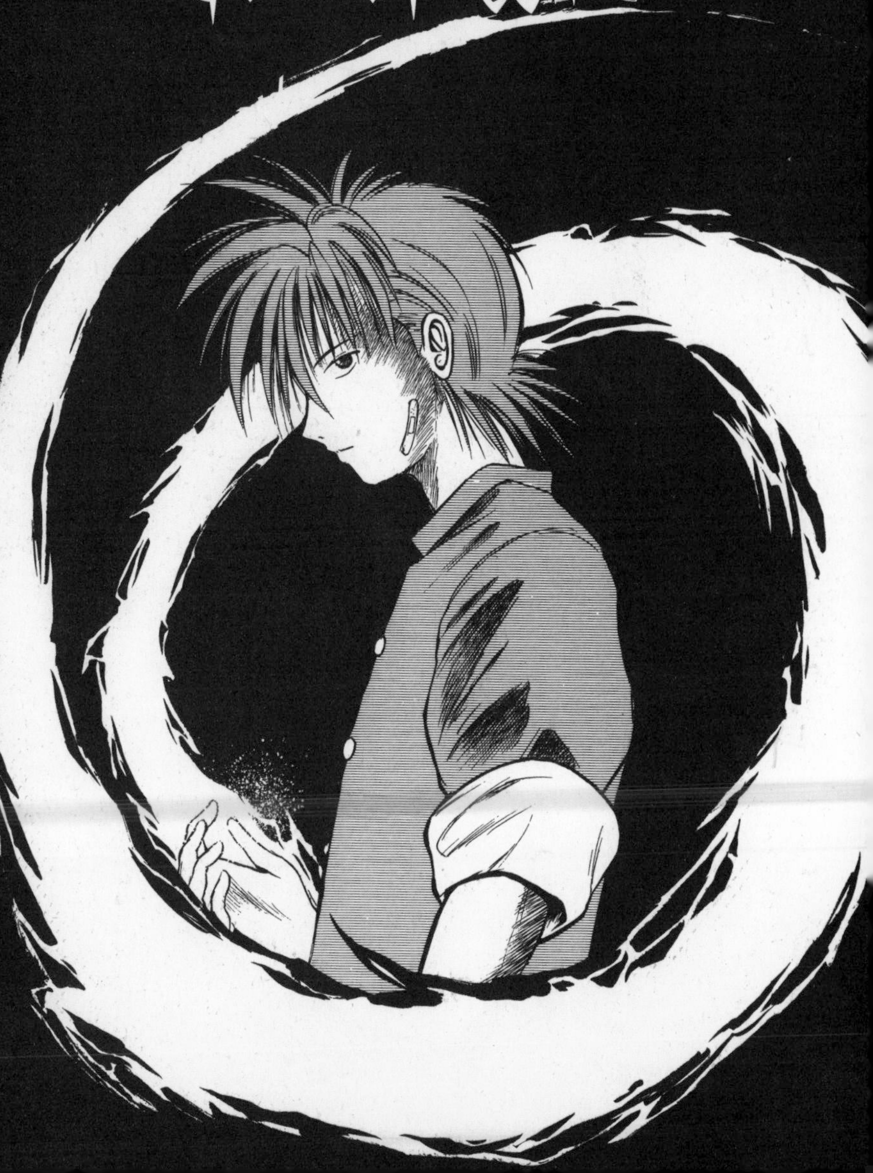

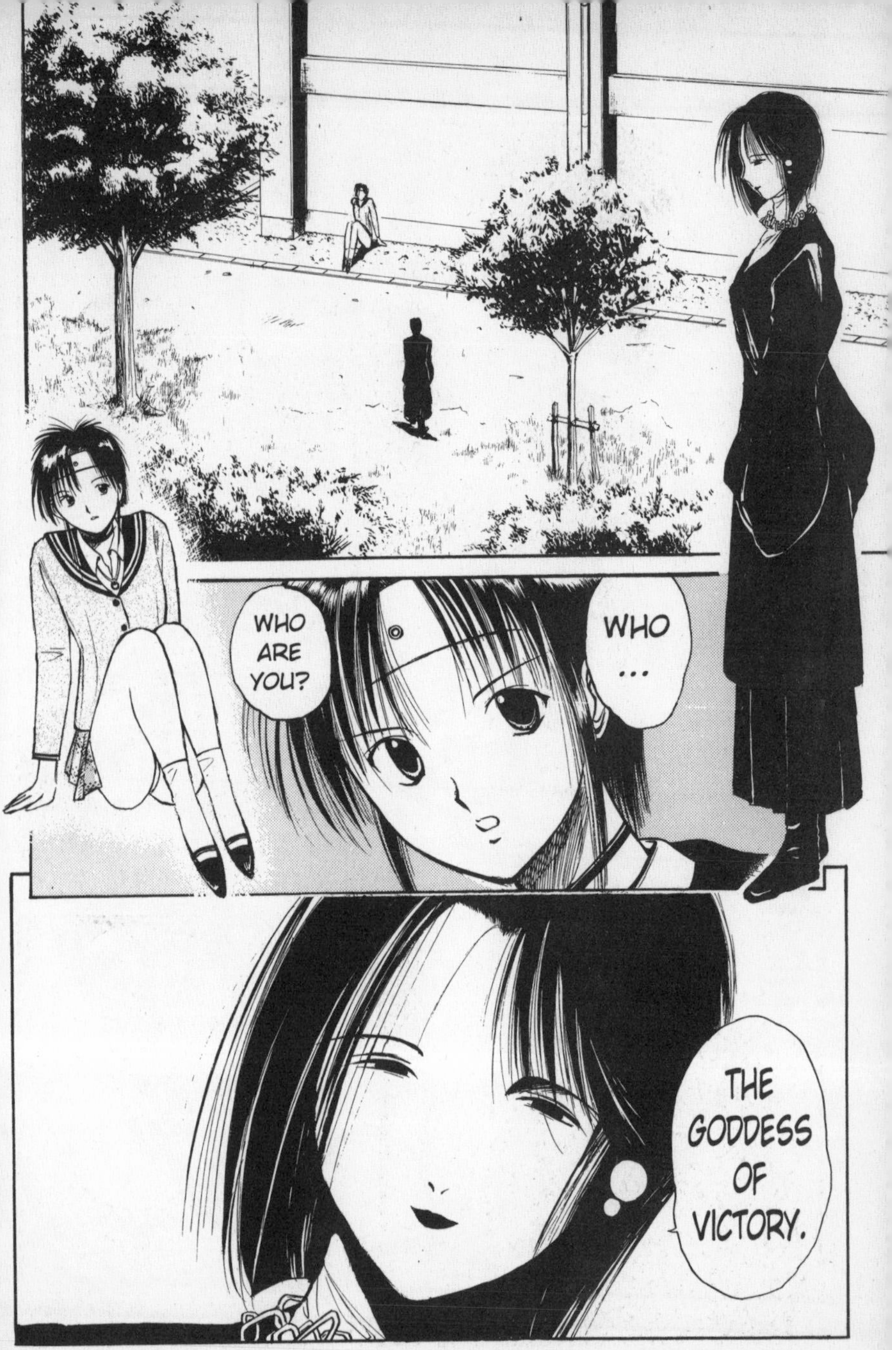
WHO ...
WHO ARE YOU?
THE GODDESS OF VICTORY.

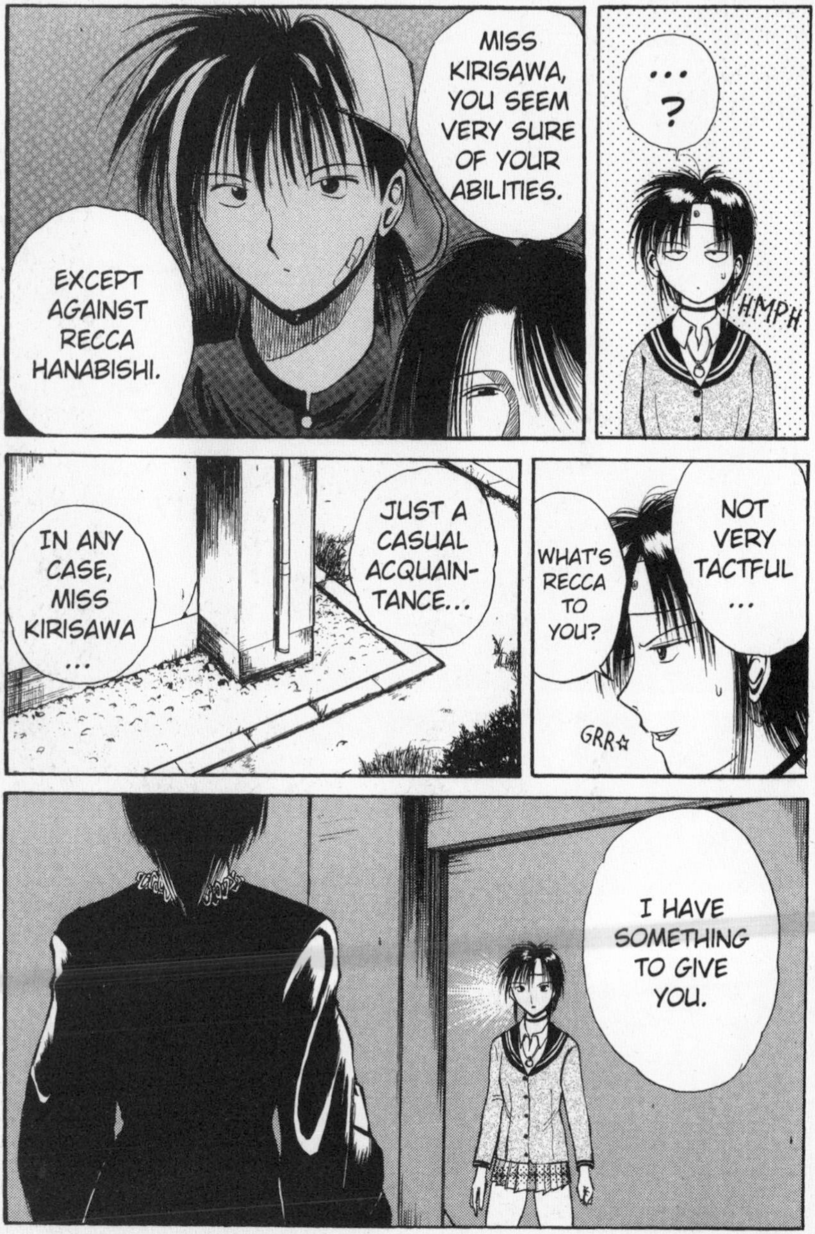
...?
HMPH
MISS KIRISAWA, YOU SEEM VERY SURE OF YOUR ABILITIES.
EXCEPT AGAINST RECCA HANABISHI.
NOT VERY TACTFUL...
WHAT'S RECCA TO YOU?
GRR☆
JUST A CASUAL ACQUAIN- TANCE...
IN ANY CASE, MISS KIRISAWA...
I HAVE SOMETHING TO GIVE YOU.

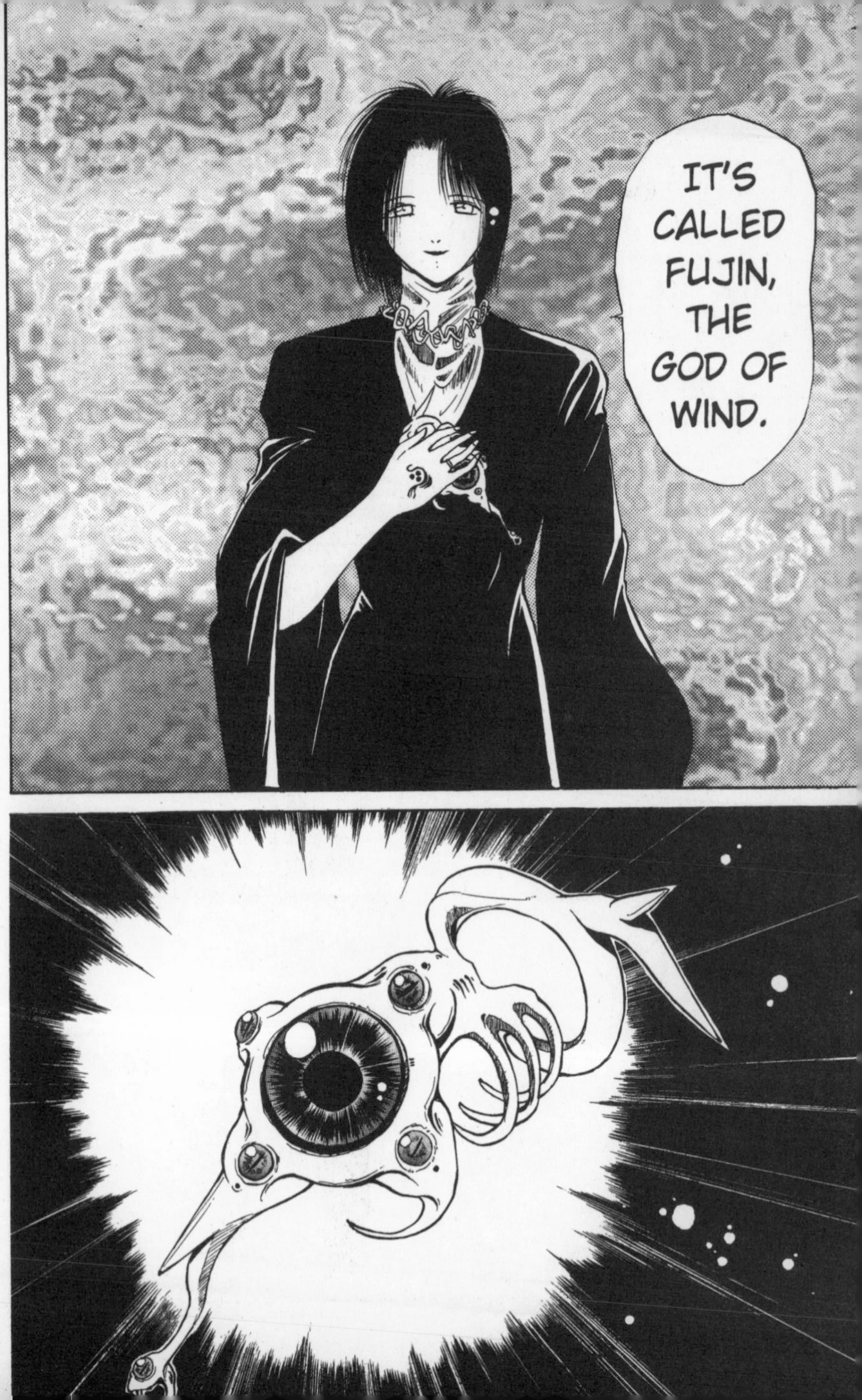
IT'S CALLED FUJIN, THE GOD OF WIND.

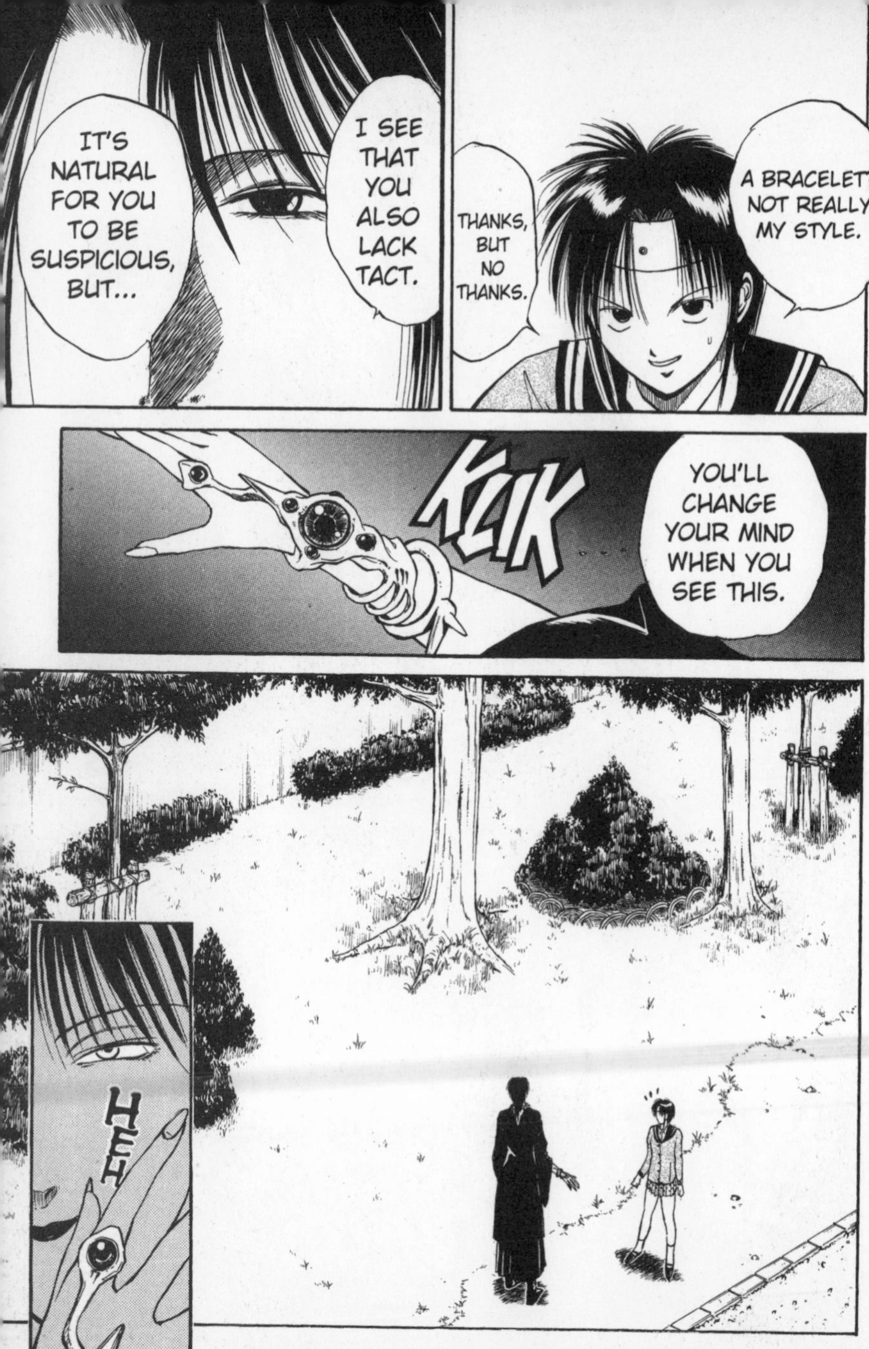
A BRACELET? NOT REALLY MY STYLE.
THANKS, BUT NO THANKS.
I SEE THAT YOU ALSO LACK TACT.
IT'S NATURAL FOR YOU TO BE SUSPICIOUS, BUT...
YOU'LL CHANGE YOUR MIND WHEN YOU SEE THIS.
KLIK
HEH

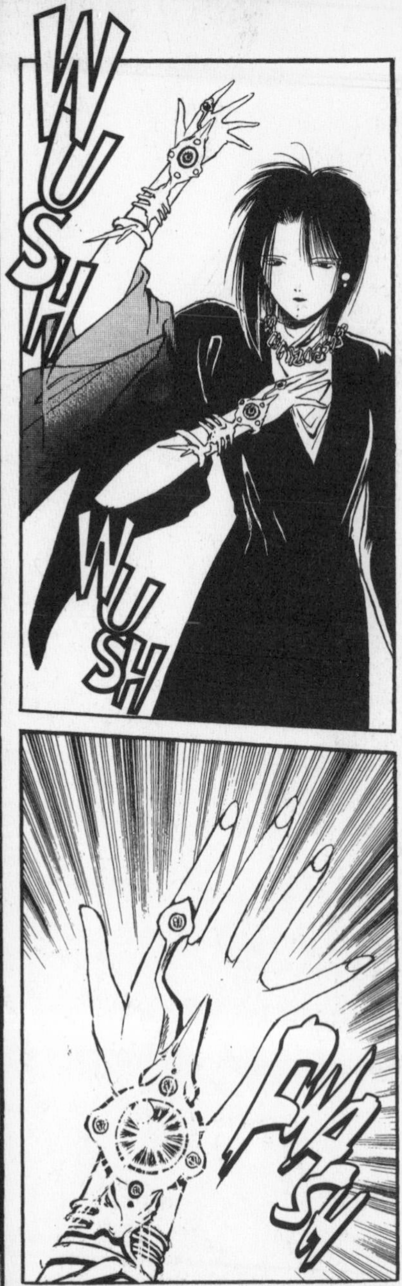
WUSH
WUSH
FWASH

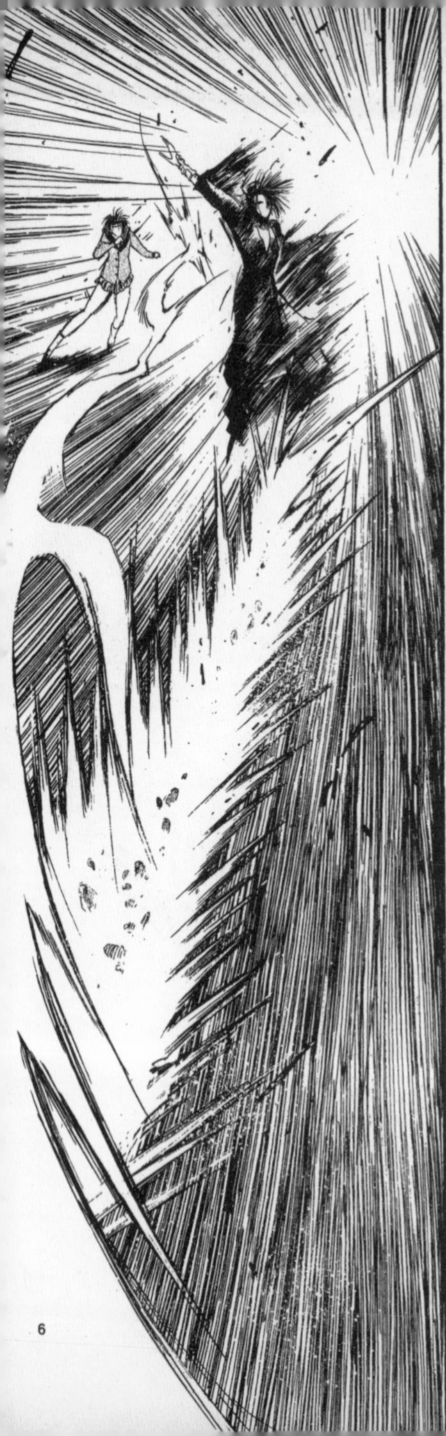

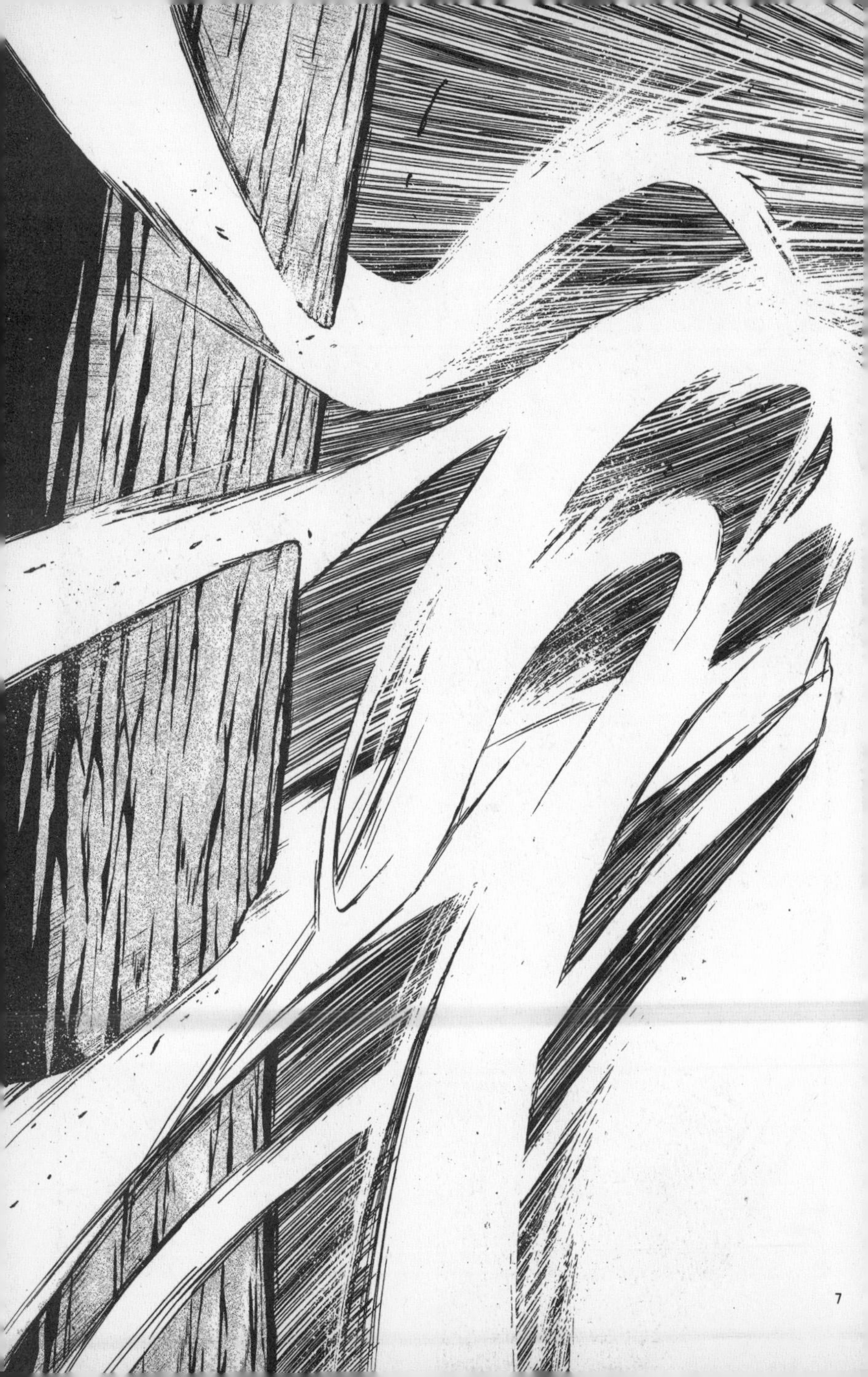

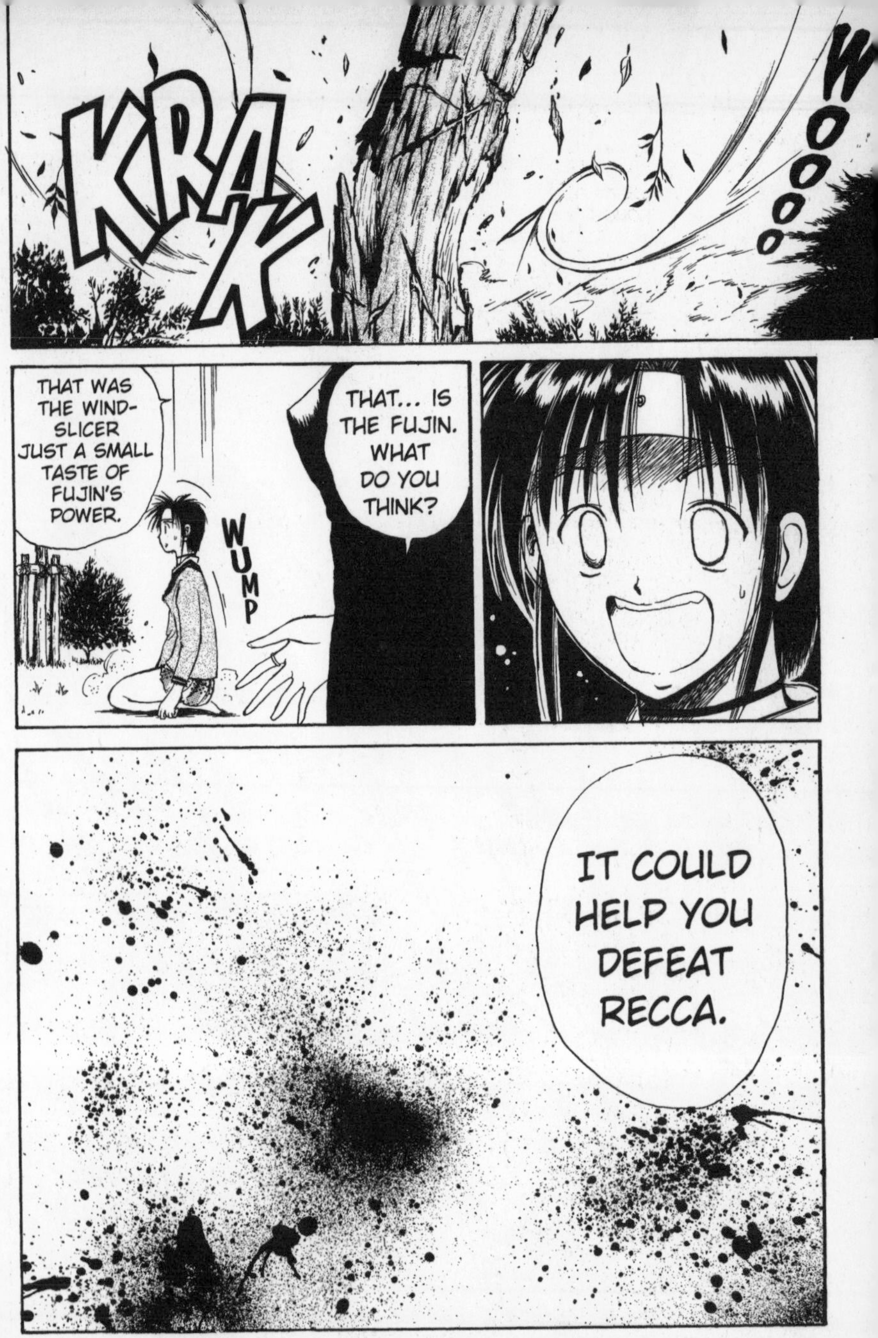
WOOOOOO
KRAK
THAT... IS THE FUJIN. WHAT DO YOU THINK?
THAT WAS THE WIND-SLICER JUST A SMALL TASTE OF FUJIN'S POWER.
WUMP
IT COULD HELP YOU DEFEAT RECCA.

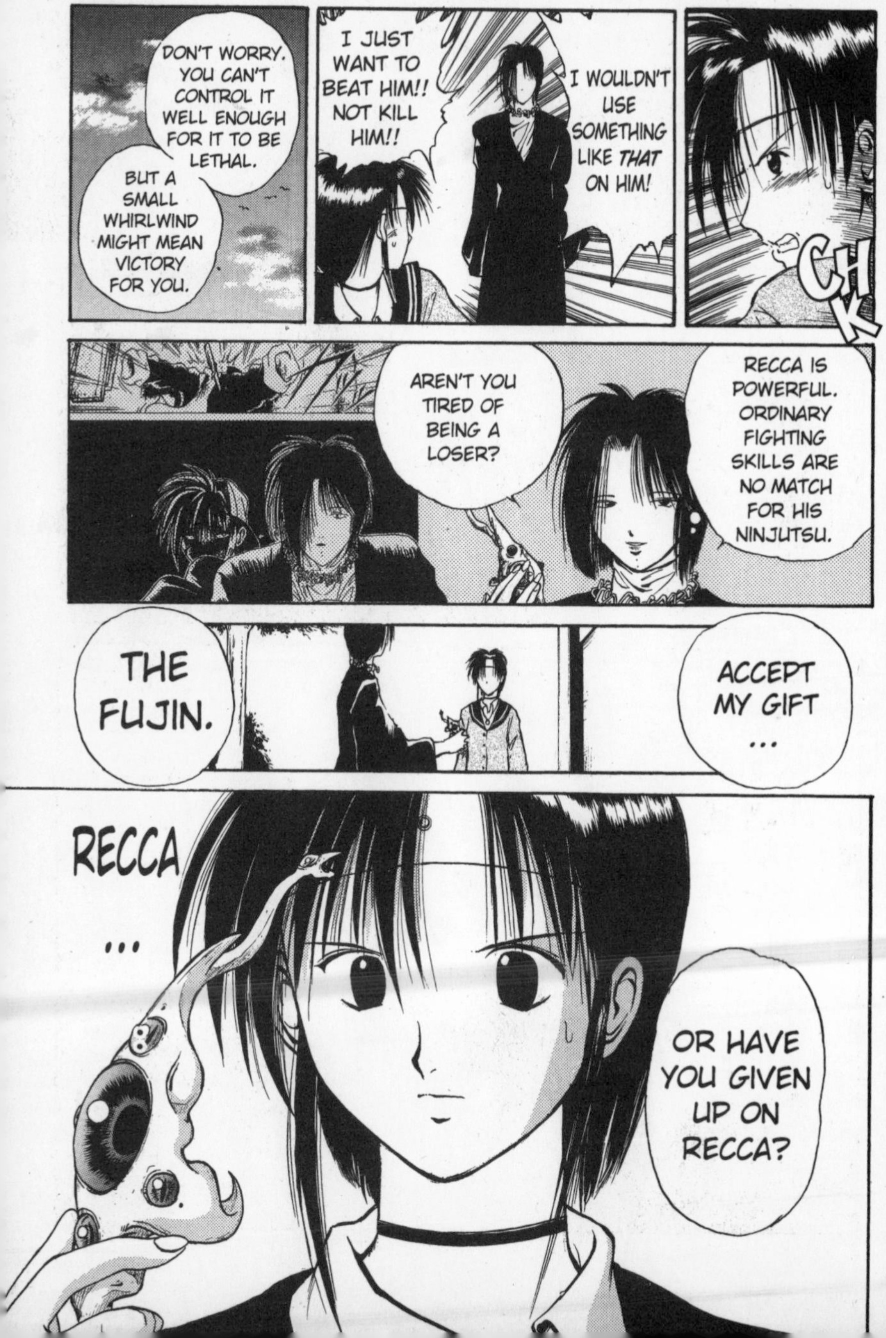
CHK
I WOULDN'T USE SOMETHING LIKE THAT ON HIM!
I JUST WANT TO BEAT HIM!! NOT KILL HIM!!
DON'T WORRY. YOU CAN'T CONTROL IT WELL ENOUGH FOR IT TO BE LETHAL.
BUT A SMALL WHIRLWIND MIGHT MEAN VICTORY FOR YOU.
RECCA IS POWERFUL. ORDINARY FIGHTING SKILLS ARE NO MATCH FOR HIS NINJUTSU.
AREN'T YOU TIRED OF BEING A LOSER?
ACCEPT MY GIFT ...
THE FUJIN.
OR HAVE YOU GIVEN UP ON RECCA?
RECCA ...

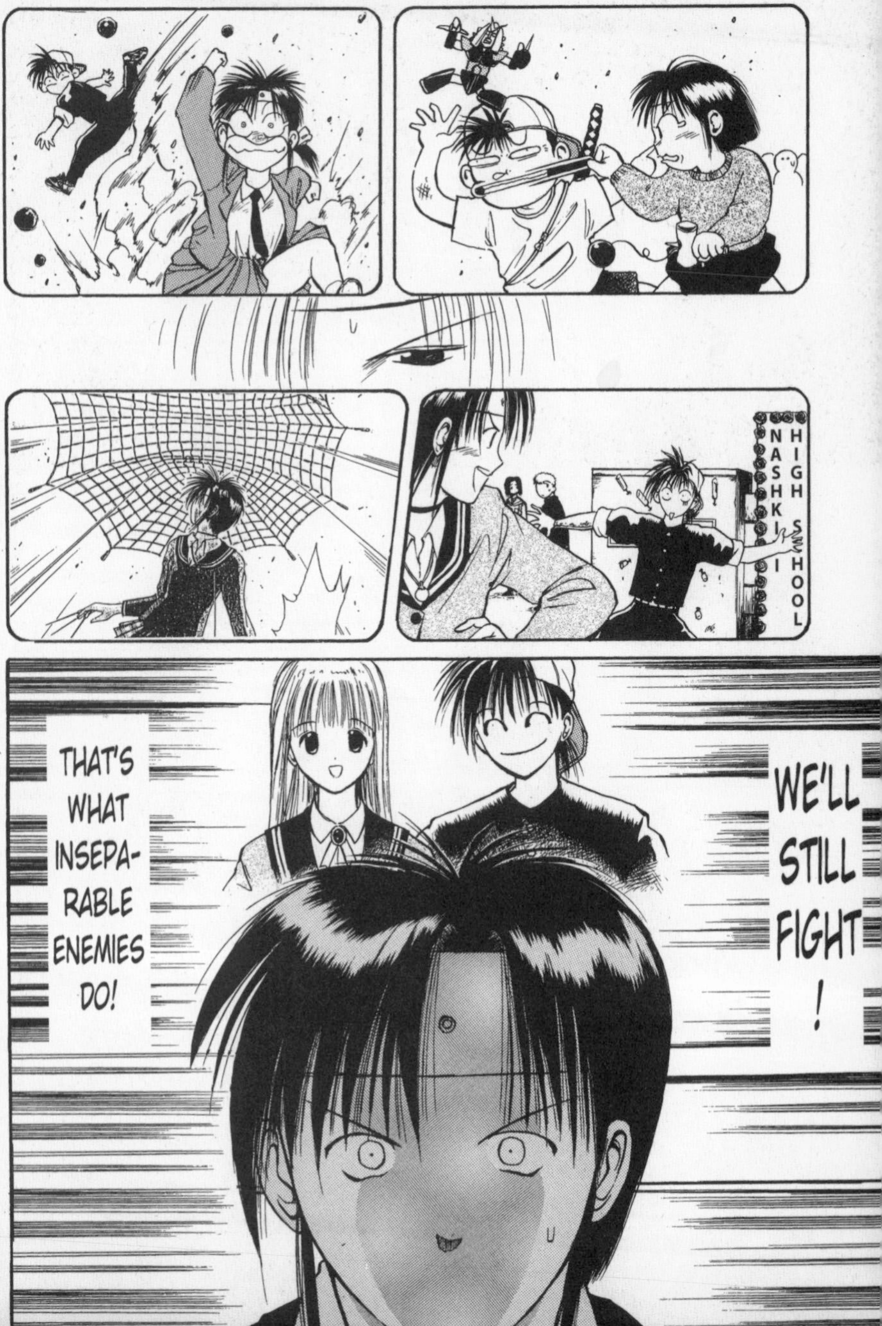
NASHIKI HIGH SCHOOL
WE'LL STILL FIGHT!
THAT'S WHAT INSEPARABLE ENEMIES DO!

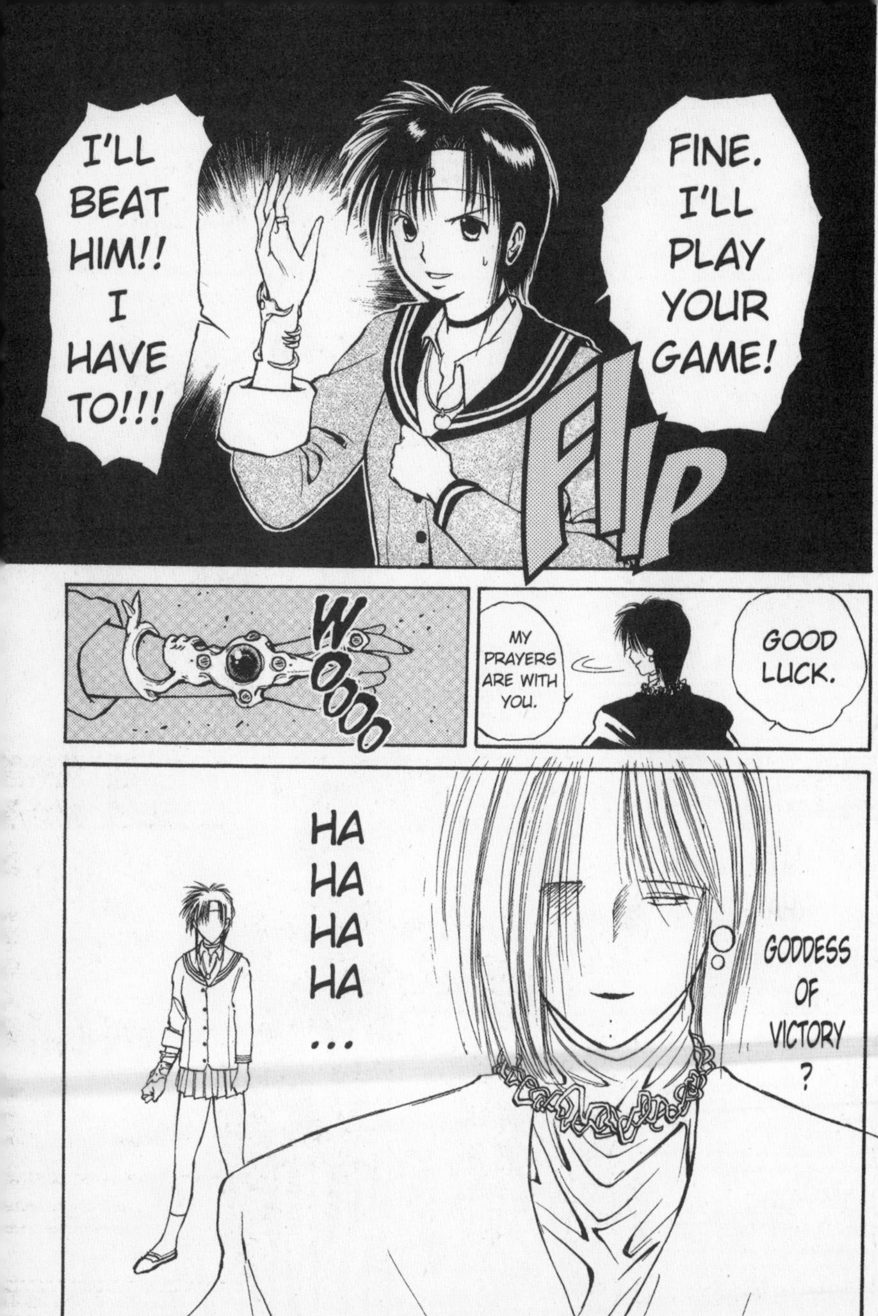
FINE. I'LL PLAY YOUR GAME!
FLIP
I'LL BEAT HIM!! I HAVE TO!!!
GOOD LUCK.
MY PRAYERS ARE WITH YOU.
WOOOO
GODDESS OF VICTORY ?
HA HA HA HA ...

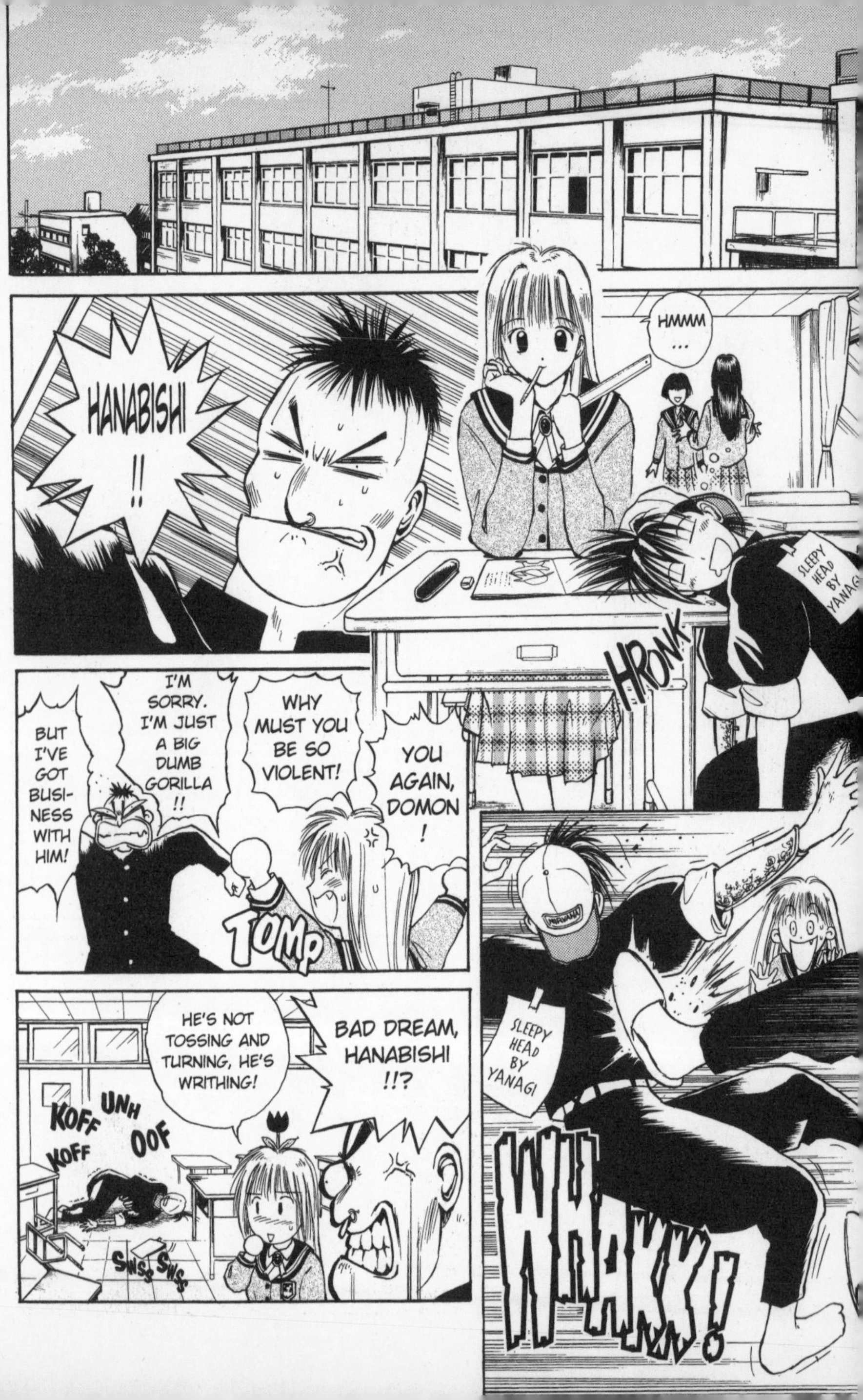
HMMM
...
SLEEPY HEAD BY YANAGI
HRONK
HANABISHI
!!
SLEEPY HEAD BY YANAGI
WHAKK!
YOU AGAIN, DOMON!
WHY MUST YOU BE SO VIOLENT!
I'M SORRY. I'M JUST A BIG DUMB GORILLA !!
BUT I'VE GOT BUSI-NESS WITH HIM!
TOMP
BAD DREAM, HANABISHI !!?
HE'S NOT TOSSING AND TURNING, HE'S WRITHING!
UNH
KOFF
OOF
KOFF
SWSS SWSS

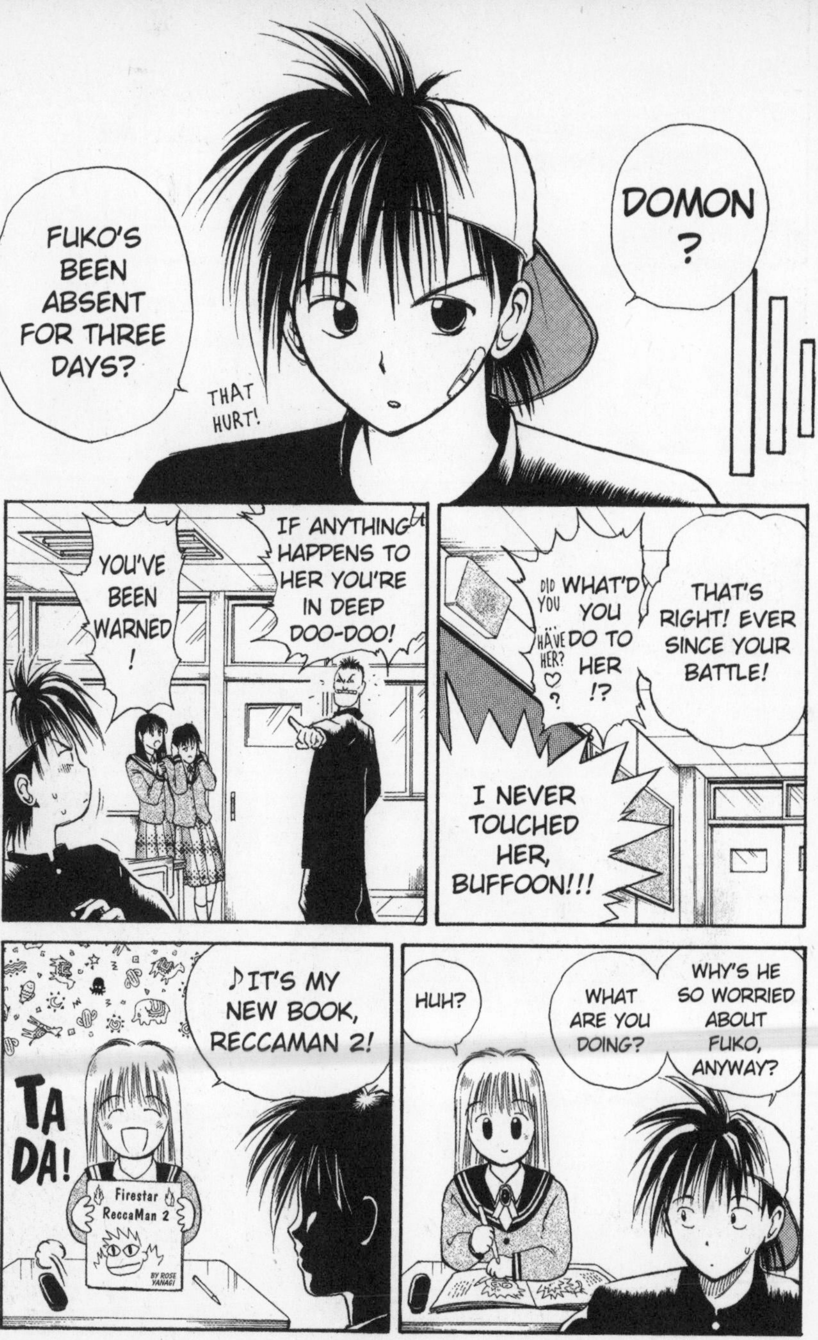
DOMON ?
FUKO'S BEEN ABSENT FOR THREE DAYS?
THAT HURT!
THAT'S RIGHT! EVER SINCE YOUR BATTLE!
WHAT'D YOU DO TO HER !?
DID YOU HÄVE HER? ♡ ?
I NEVER TOUCHED HER, BUFFOON!!!
IF ANYTHING HAPPENS TO HER YOU'RE IN DEEP DOO-DOO!
YOU'VE BEEN WARNED !
WHY'S HE SO WORRIED ABOUT FUKO, ANYWAY?
WHAT ARE YOU DOING?
HUH?
♪IT'S MY NEW BOOK, RECCAMAN 2!
TA DA!
Firestar ReccaMan 2
BY ROSE YANAGI

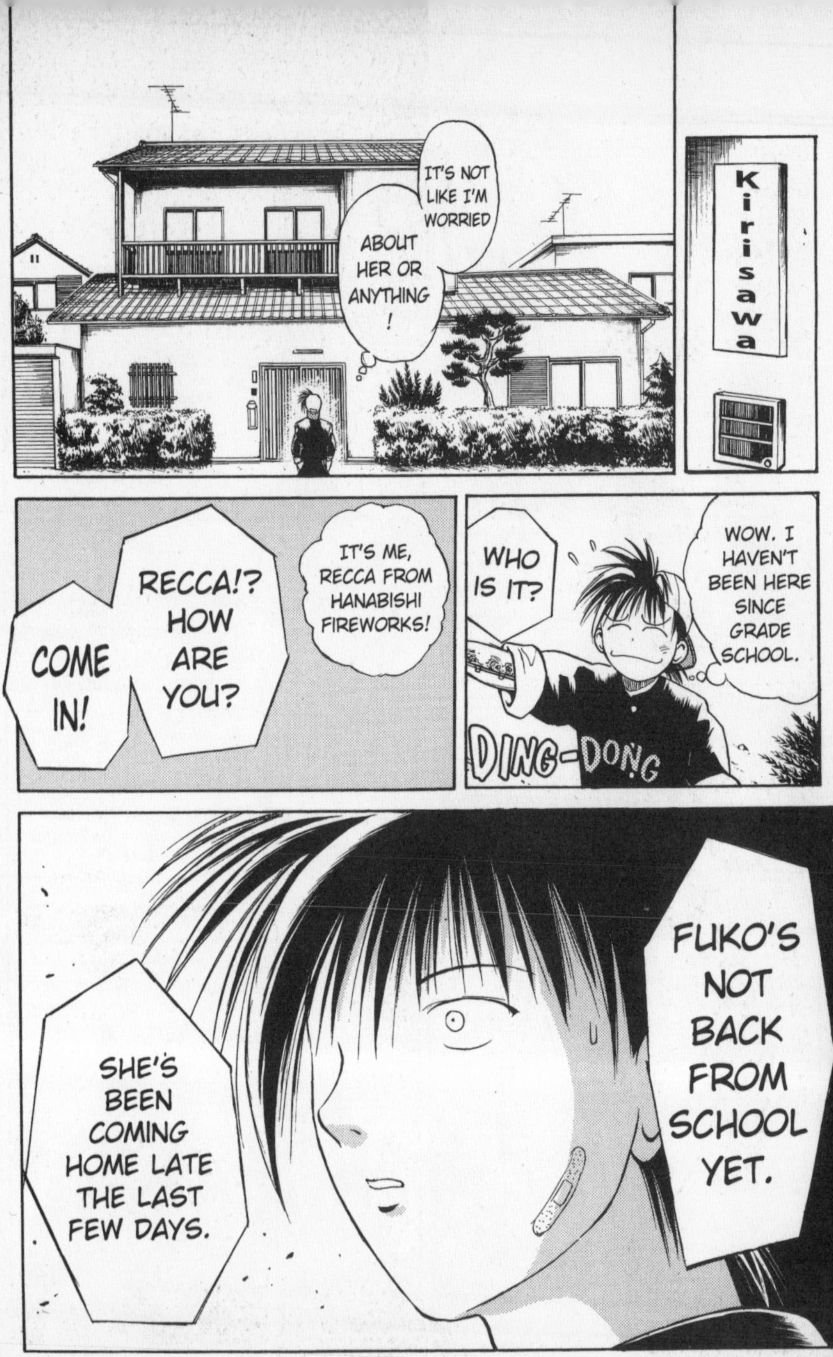
Kirisawa
IT'S NOT LIKE I'M WORRIED
ABOUT HER OR ANYTHING!
WOW. I HAVEN'T BEEN HERE SINCE GRADE SCHOOL.
WHO IS IT?
DING-DONG
IT'S ME, RECCA FROM HANABISHI FIREWORKS!
RECCA!? HOW ARE YOU?
COME IN!
FUKO'S NOT BACK FROM SCHOOL YET.
SHE'S BEEN COMING HOME LATE THE LAST FEW DAYS.

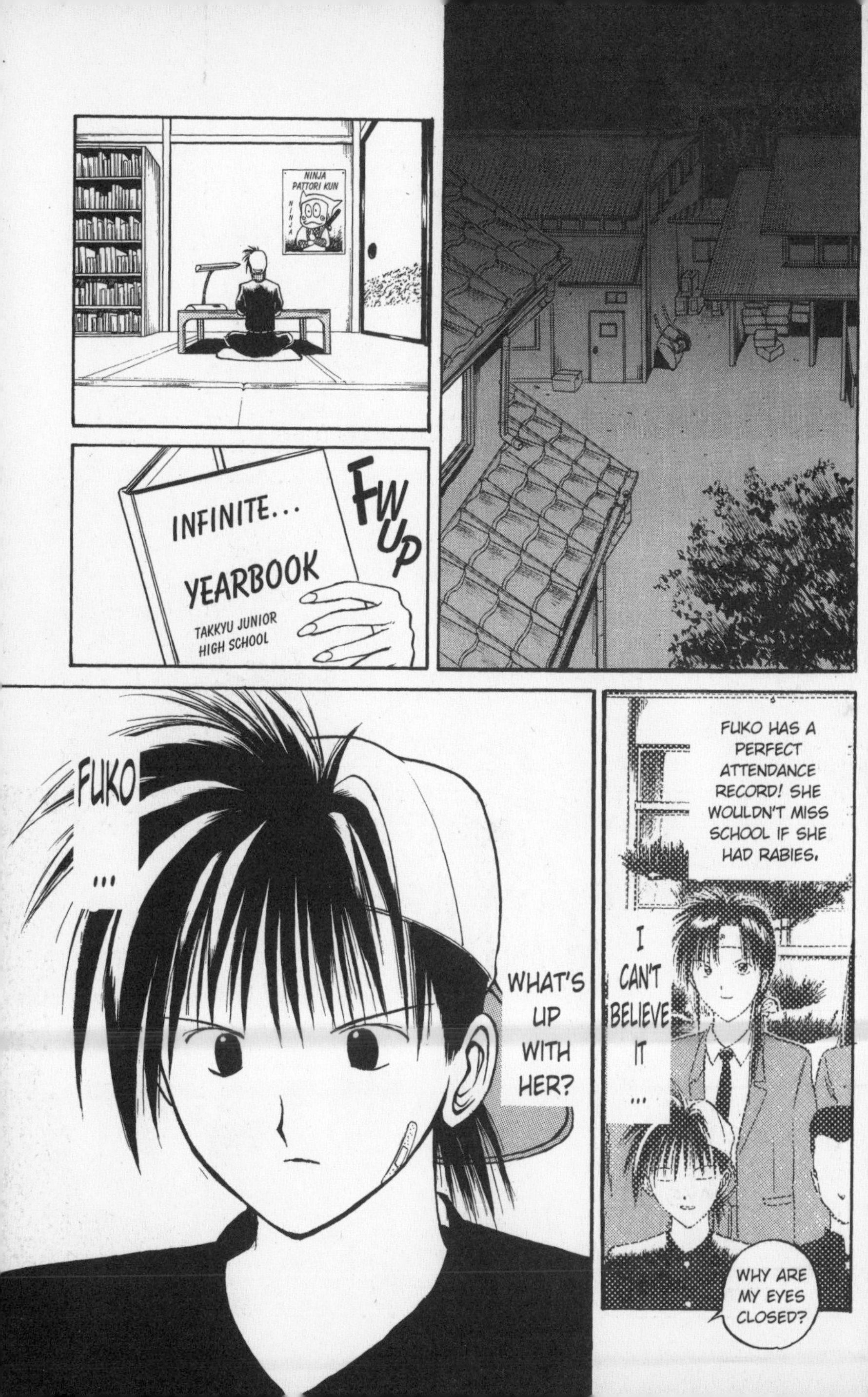
NINJA PATTORI KUN
INFINITE...
YEARBOOK
TAKKYU JUNIOR HIGH SCHOOL
FWUP
FUKO HAS A PERFECT ATTENDANCE RECORD! SHE WOULDN'T MISS SCHOOL IF SHE HAD RABIES.
I CAN'T BELIEVE IT ...
WHY ARE MY EYES CLOSED?
WHAT'S UP WITH HER?
FUKO ...

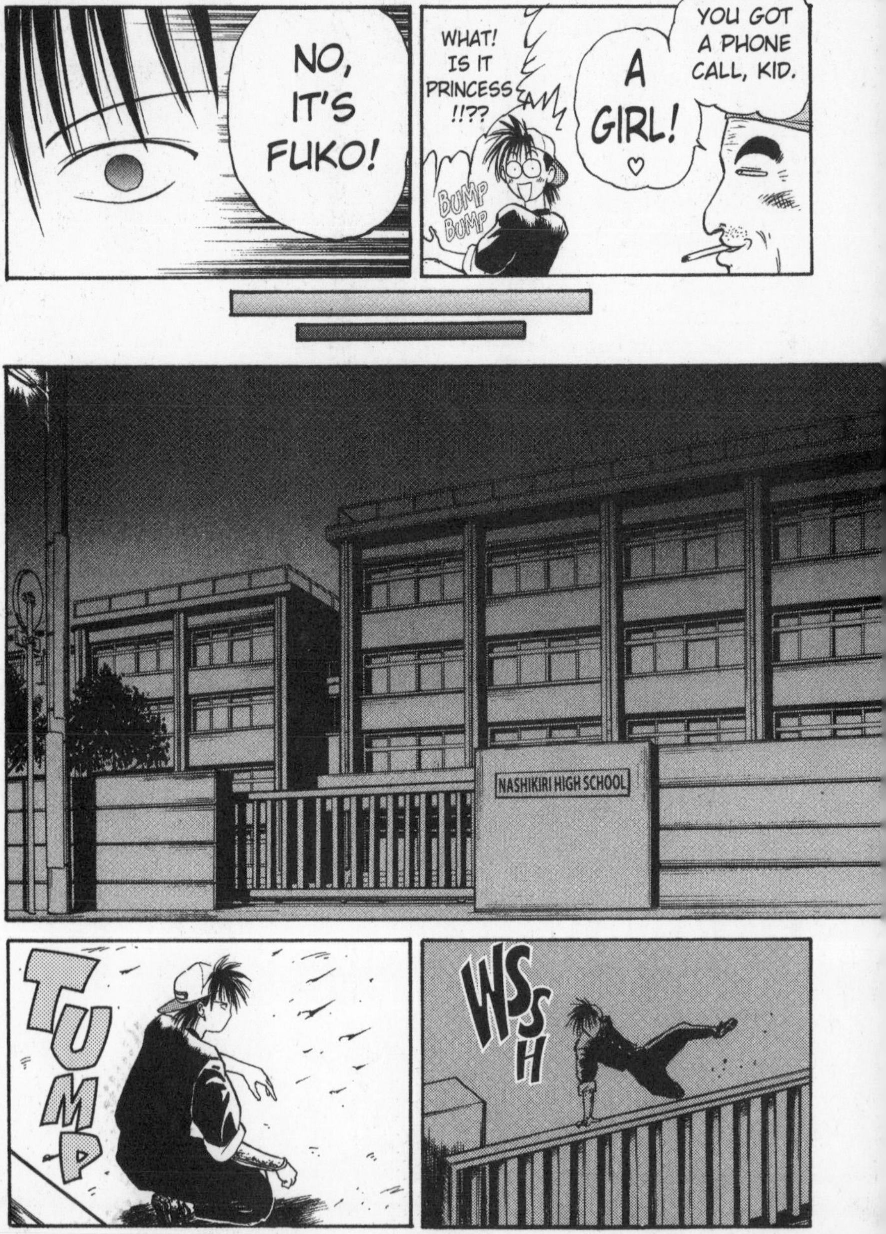
YOU GOT A PHONE CALL, KID.
A GIRL! ♡
WHAT! IS IT PRINCESS !!??
BUMP BUMP
NO, IT'S FUKO!
NASHIKIRI HIGH SCHOOL
WSSH
TUMP

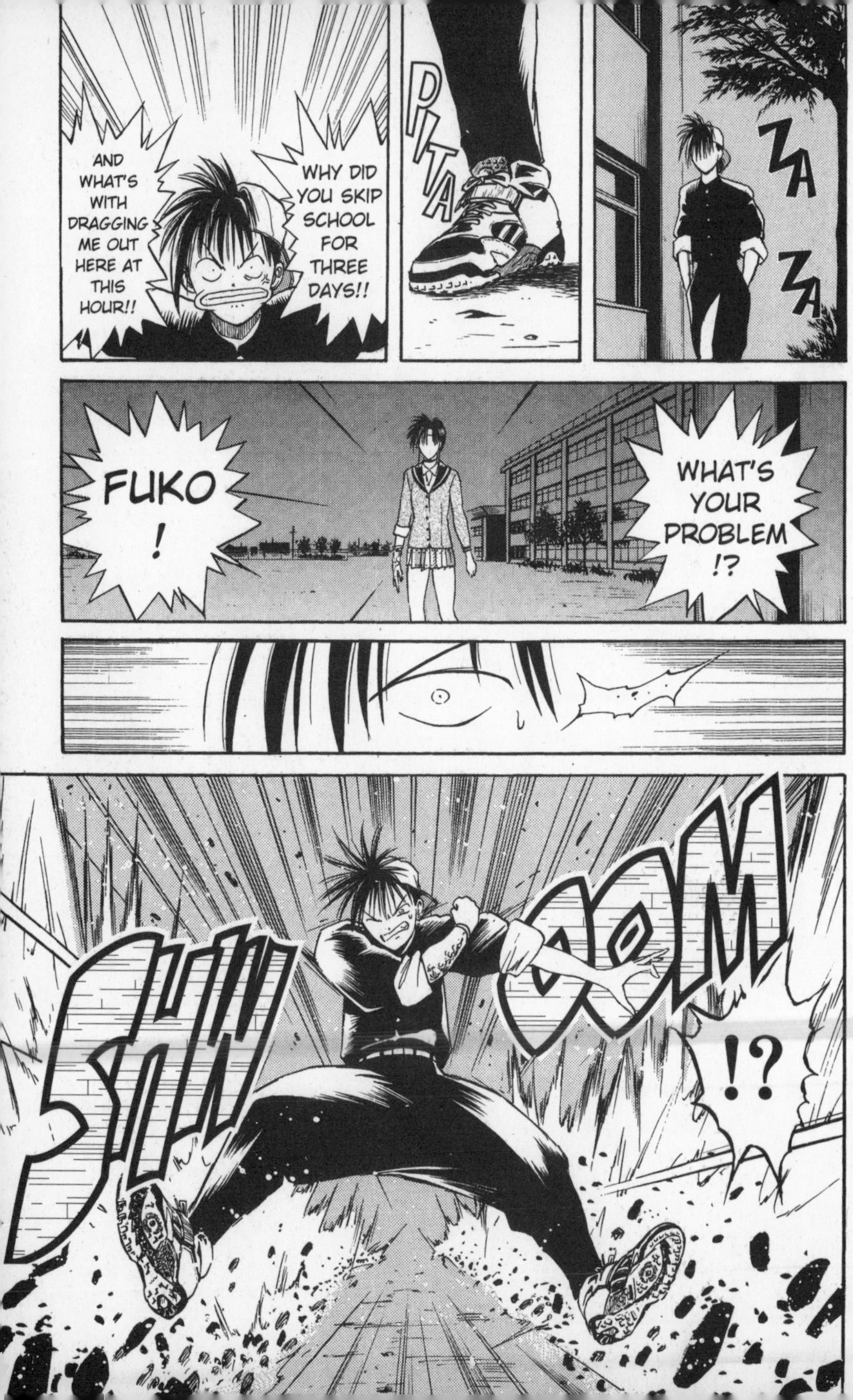
ZA ZA
PITA
WHY DID YOU SKIP SCHOOL FOR THREE DAYS!!
AND WHAT'S WITH DRAGGING ME OUT HERE AT THIS HOUR!!
WHAT'S YOUR PROBLEM !?
FUKO !
SHHOOM
!?

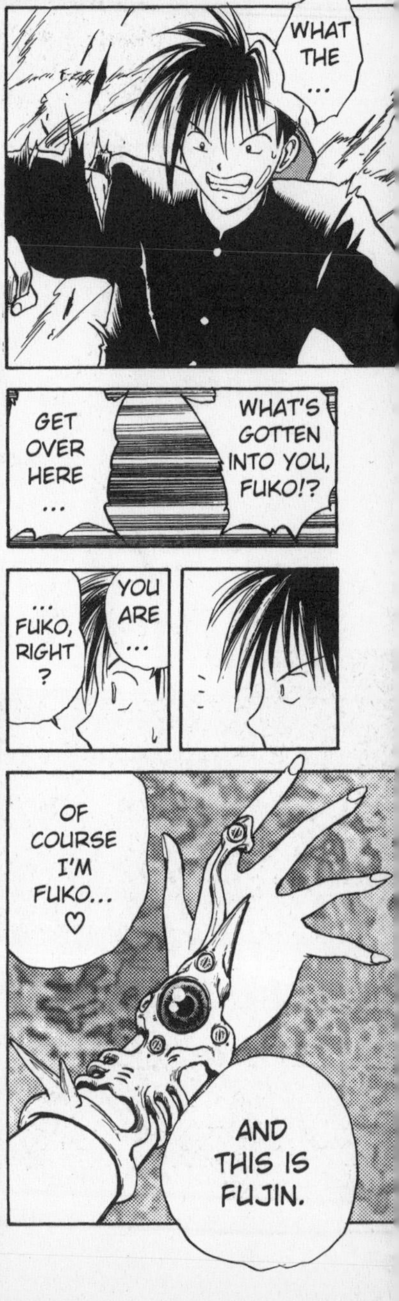
WHAT THE ...
WHAT'S GOTTEN INTO YOU, FUKO!?
GET OVER HERE ...
YOU ARE ...
... FUKO, RIGHT ?
OF COURSE I'M FUKO... ♡
AND THIS IS FUJIN.
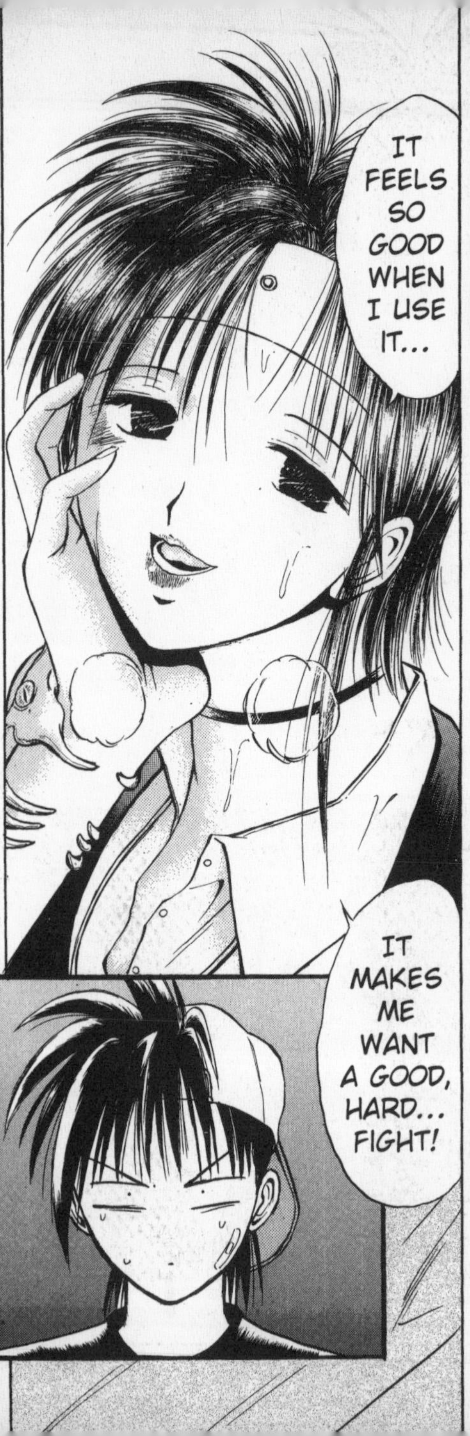
IT FEELS SO GOOD WHEN I USE IT...
IT MAKES ME WANT A GOOD, HARD... FIGHT!

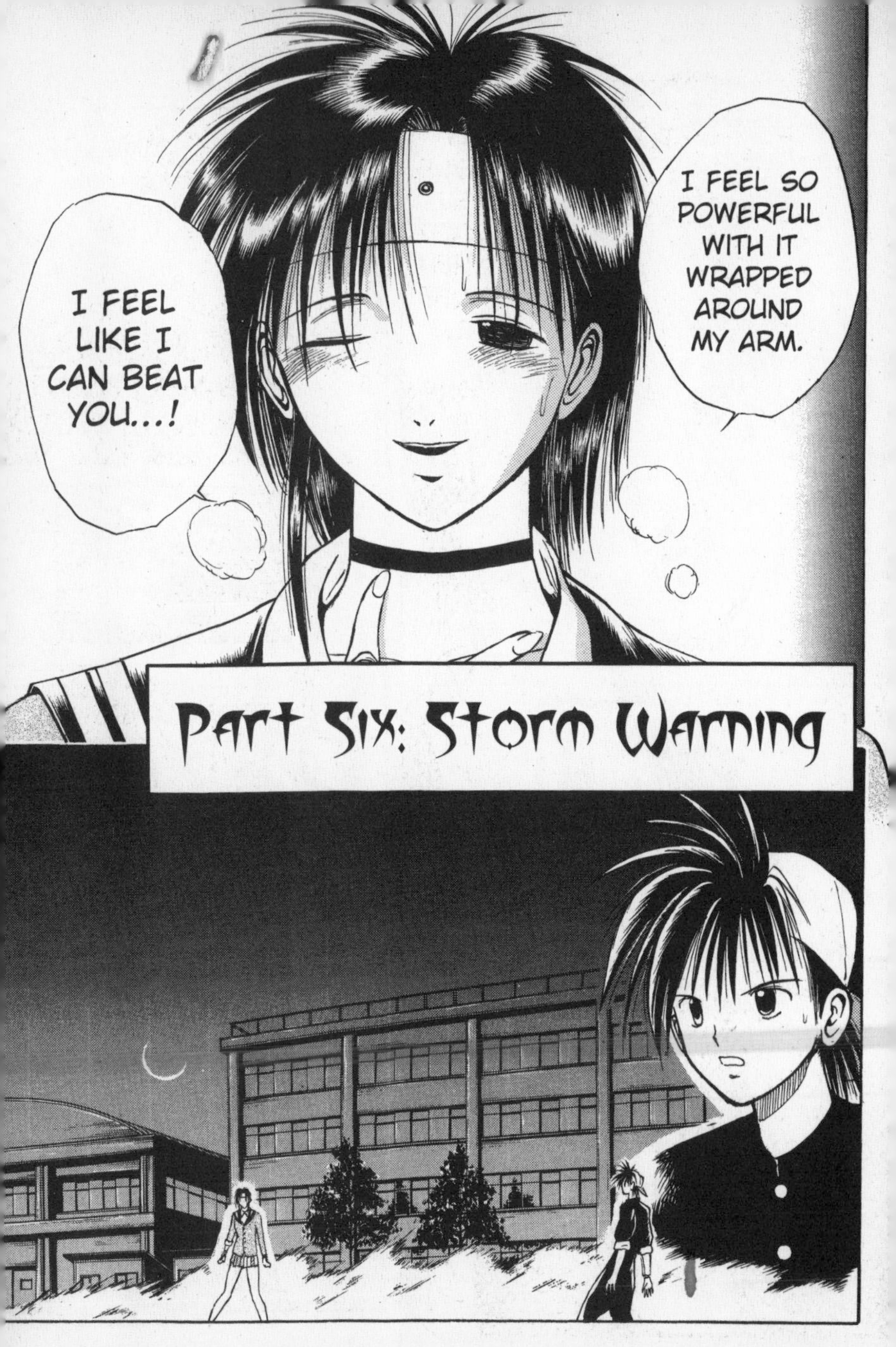
I FEEL SO POWERFUL WITH IT WRAPPED AROUND MY ARM.
I FEEL LIKE I CAN BEAT YOU...!
Part Six: Storm Warning

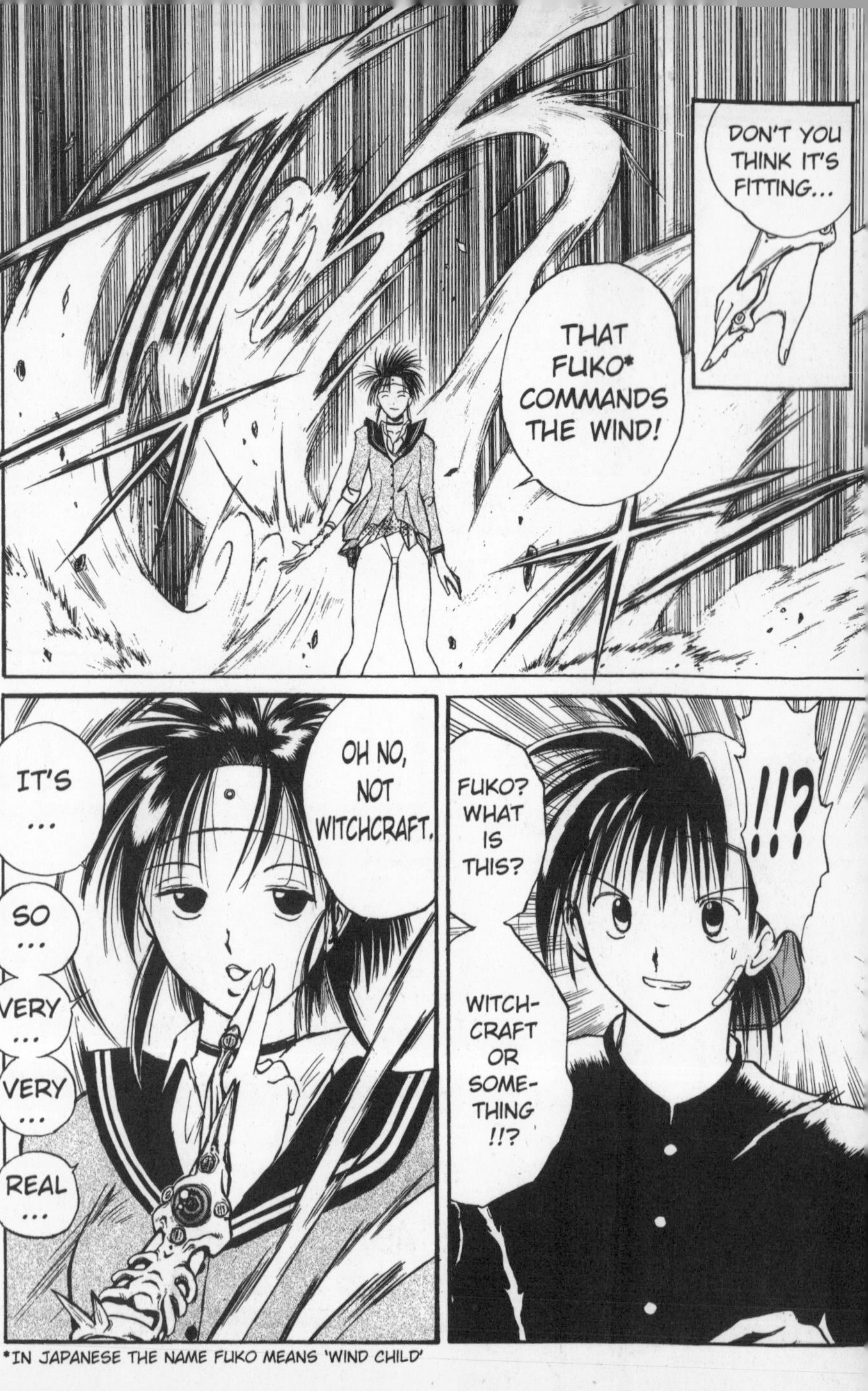
DON'T YOU THINK IT'S FITTING...
THAT FUKO* COMMANDS THE WIND!
!!?
FUKO? WHAT IS THIS?
WITCH-CRAFT OR SOME-THING !!?
OH NO, NOT WITCHCRAFT.
IT'S ...
SO ...
VERY ...
VERY ...
REAL ...

*IN JAPANESE THE NAME FUKO MEANS 'WIND CHILD'

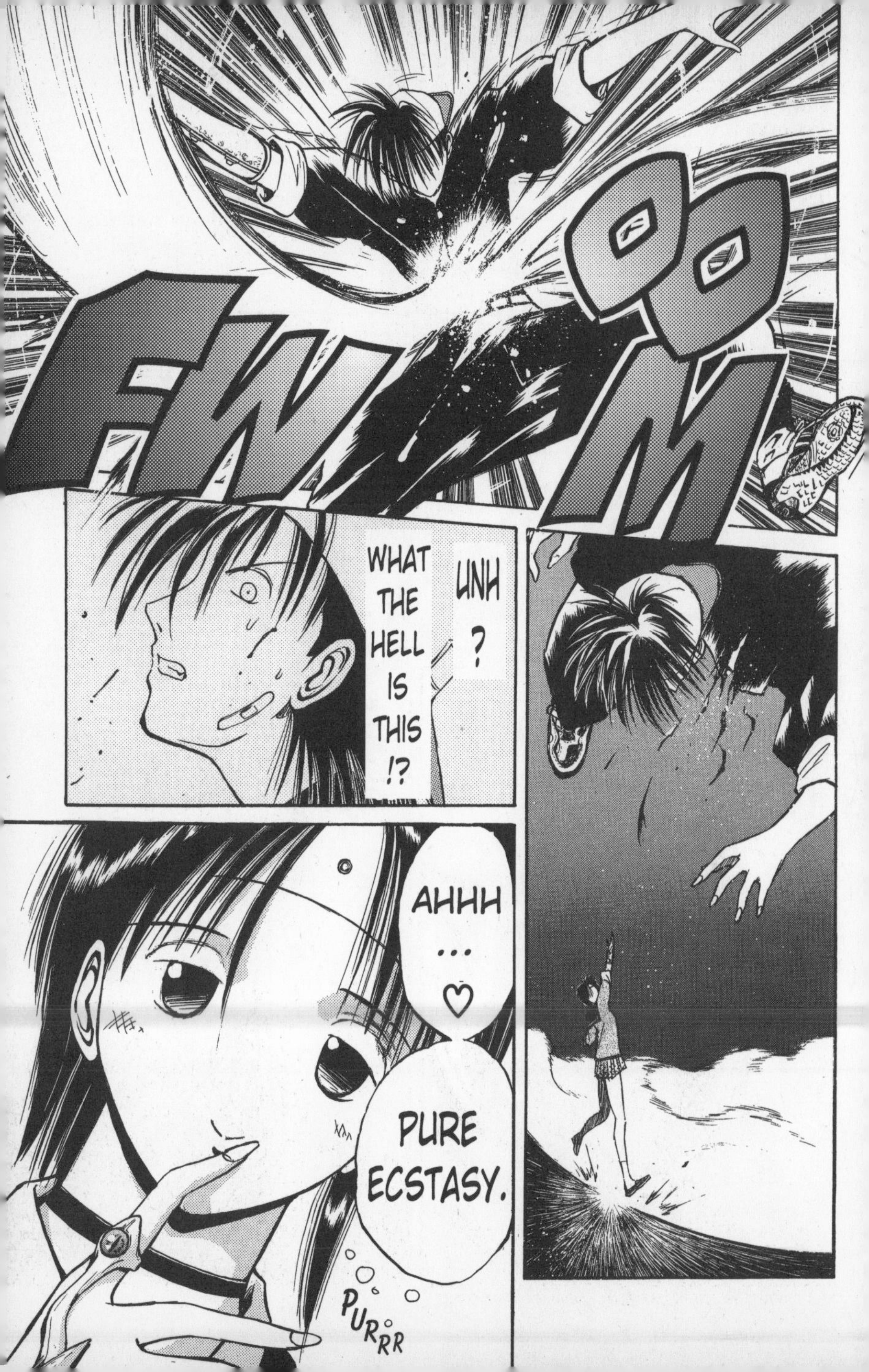

FWOOM
UNH ?
WHAT THE HELL IS THIS !?
AHHH ... ♡
PURE ECSTASY.
PURRR

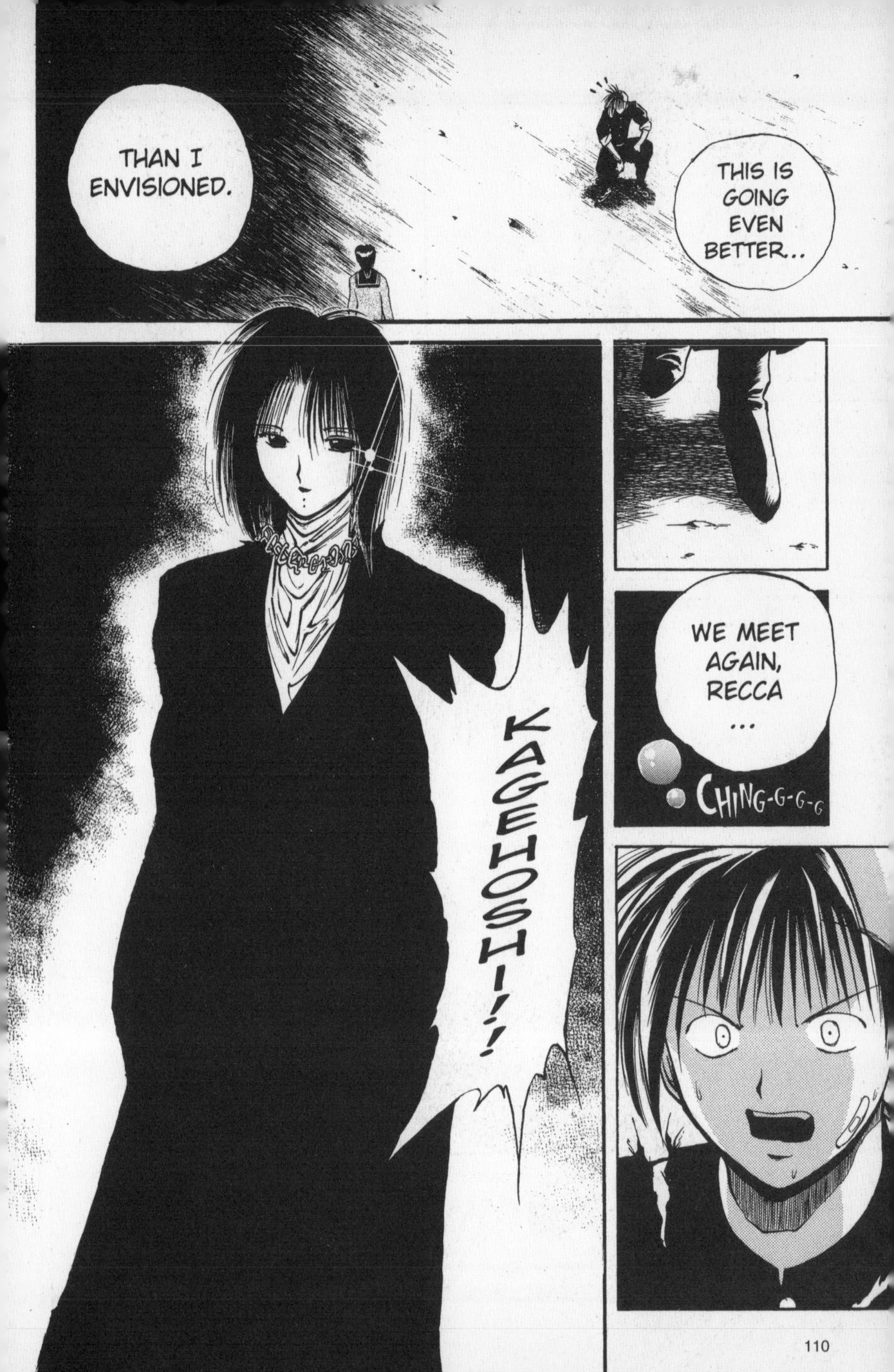
THIS IS GOING EVEN BETTER...
THAN I ENVISIONED.
WE MEET AGAIN, RECCA ...
CHING-G-G-G
KAGEHOSHI!!!

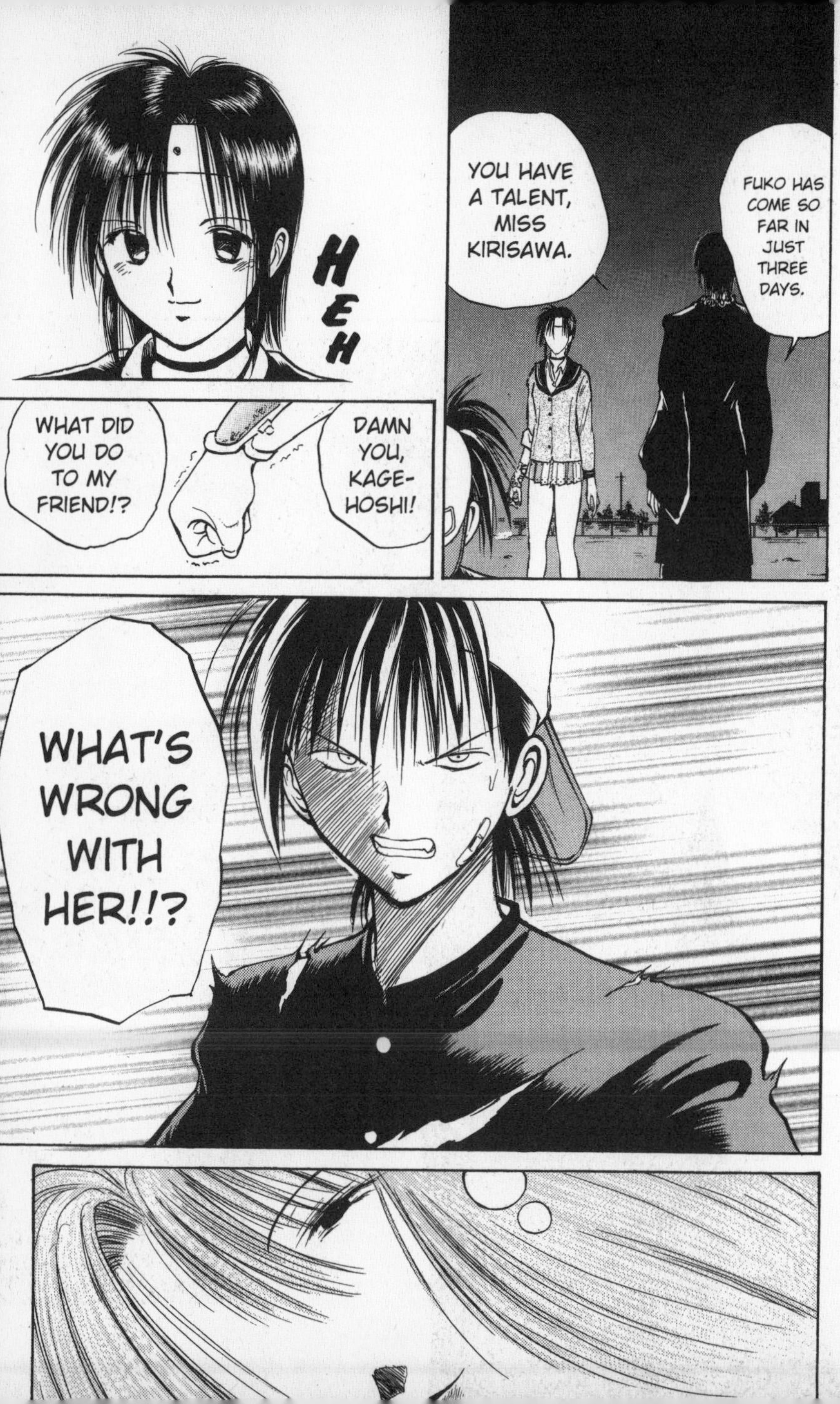
FUKO HAS COME SO FAR IN JUST THREE DAYS.
YOU HAVE A TALENT, MISS KIRISAWA.
HEH
DAMN YOU, KAGE-HOSHI!
WHAT DID YOU DO TO MY FRIEND!?
WHAT'S WRONG WITH HER!!?

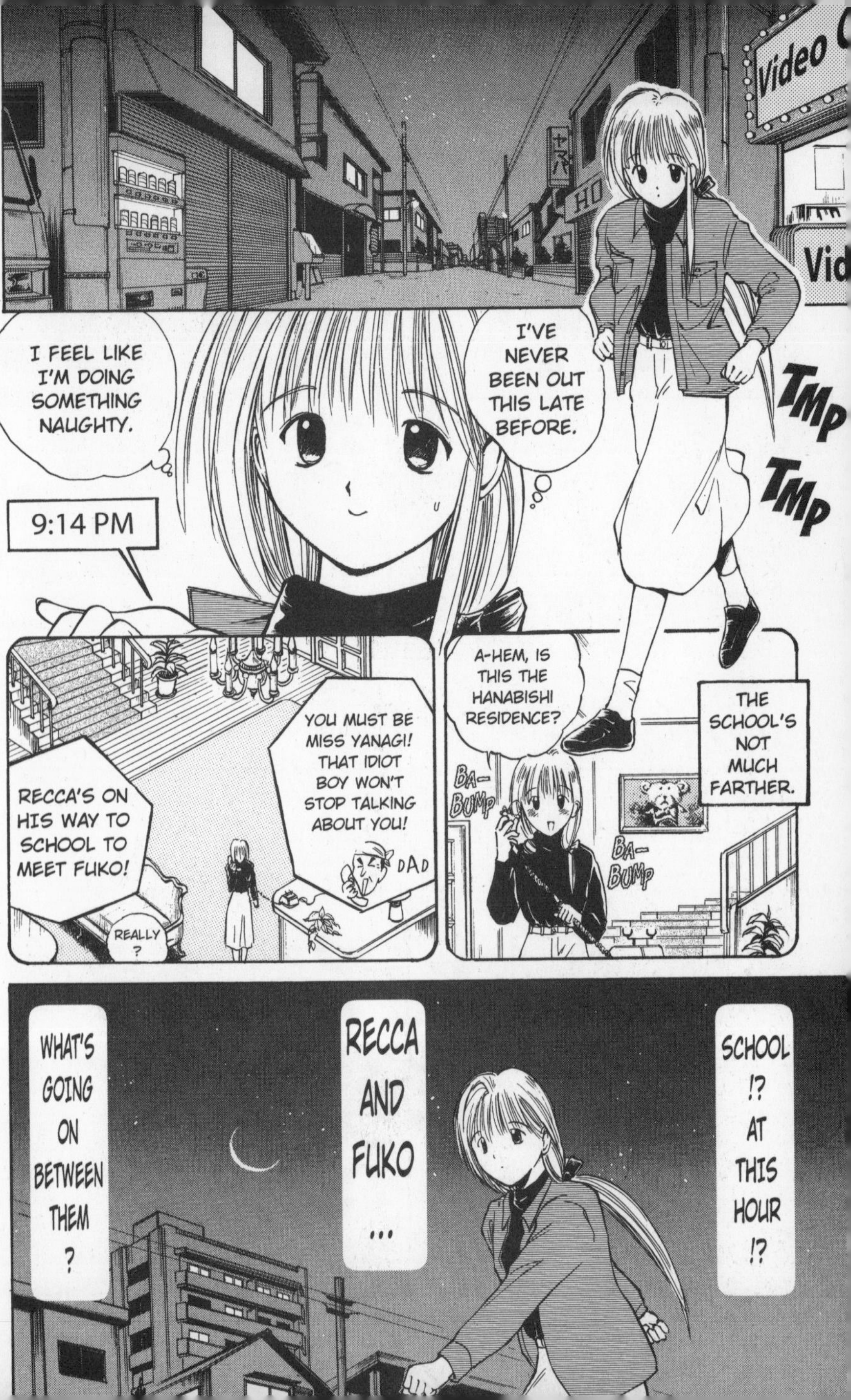
TMP TMP
I'VE NEVER BEEN OUT THIS LATE BEFORE.
I FEEL LIKE I'M DOING SOMETHING NAUGHTY.
9:14 PM
THE SCHOOL'S NOT MUCH FARTHER.
A-HEM, IS THIS THE HANABISHI RESIDENCE?
BA-BUMP
BA-BUMP
YOU MUST BE MISS YANAGI! THAT IDIOT BOY WON'T STOP TALKING ABOUT YOU!
DAD
RECCA'S ON HIS WAY TO SCHOOL TO MEET FUKO!
REALLY?
SCHOOL!? AT THIS HOUR!?
RECCA AND FUKO...
WHAT'S GOING ON BETWEEN THEM?

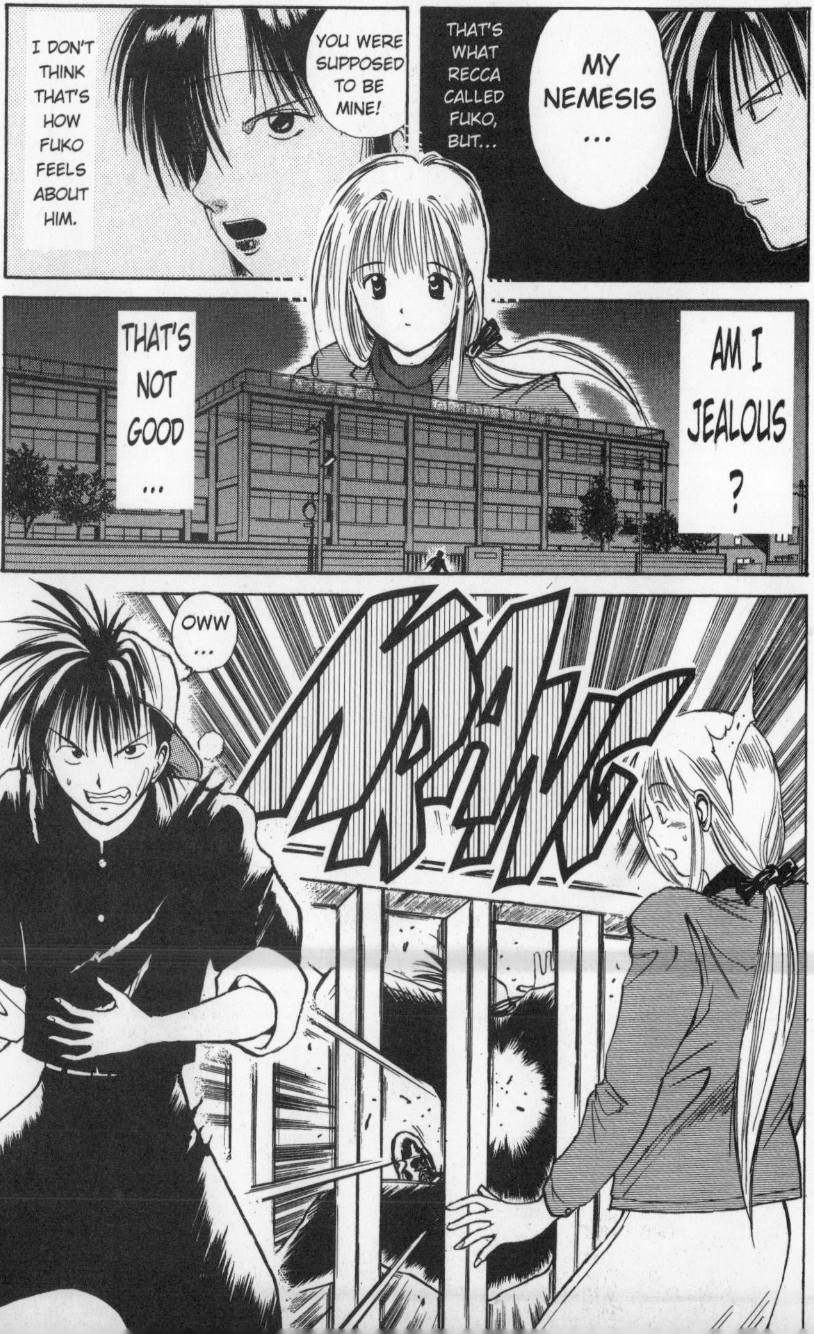
MY NEMESIS ...
THAT'S WHAT RECCA CALLED FUKO, BUT...
YOU WERE SUPPOSED TO BE MINE!
I DON'T THINK THAT'S HOW FUKO FEELS ABOUT HIM.
AM I JEALOUS ?
THAT'S NOT GOOD ...
OWW ...

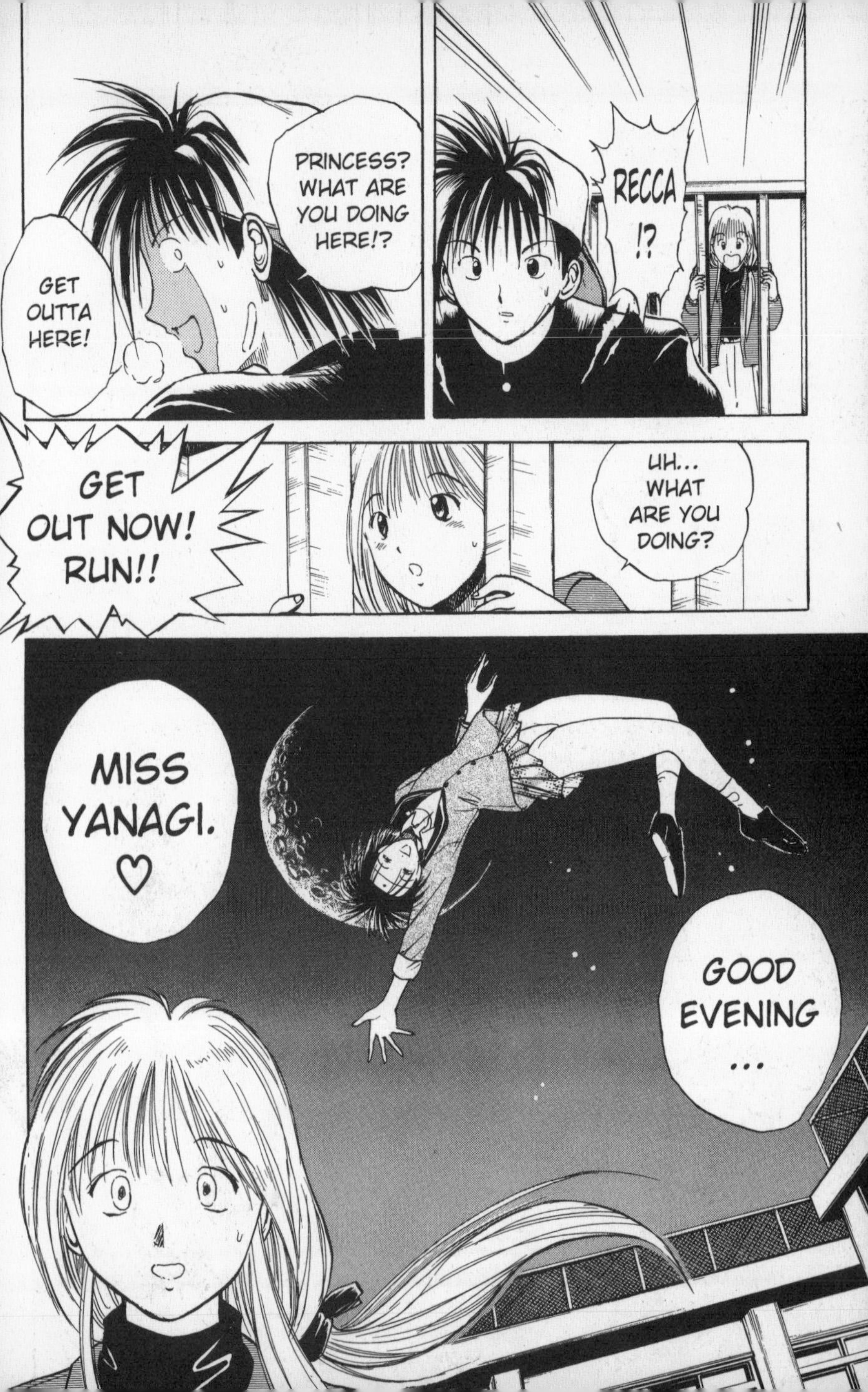
RECCA !?
PRINCESS? WHAT ARE YOU DOING HERE!?
GET OUTTA HERE!
UH... WHAT ARE YOU DOING?
GET OUT NOW! RUN!!
GOOD EVENING ...
MISS YANAGI. ♡

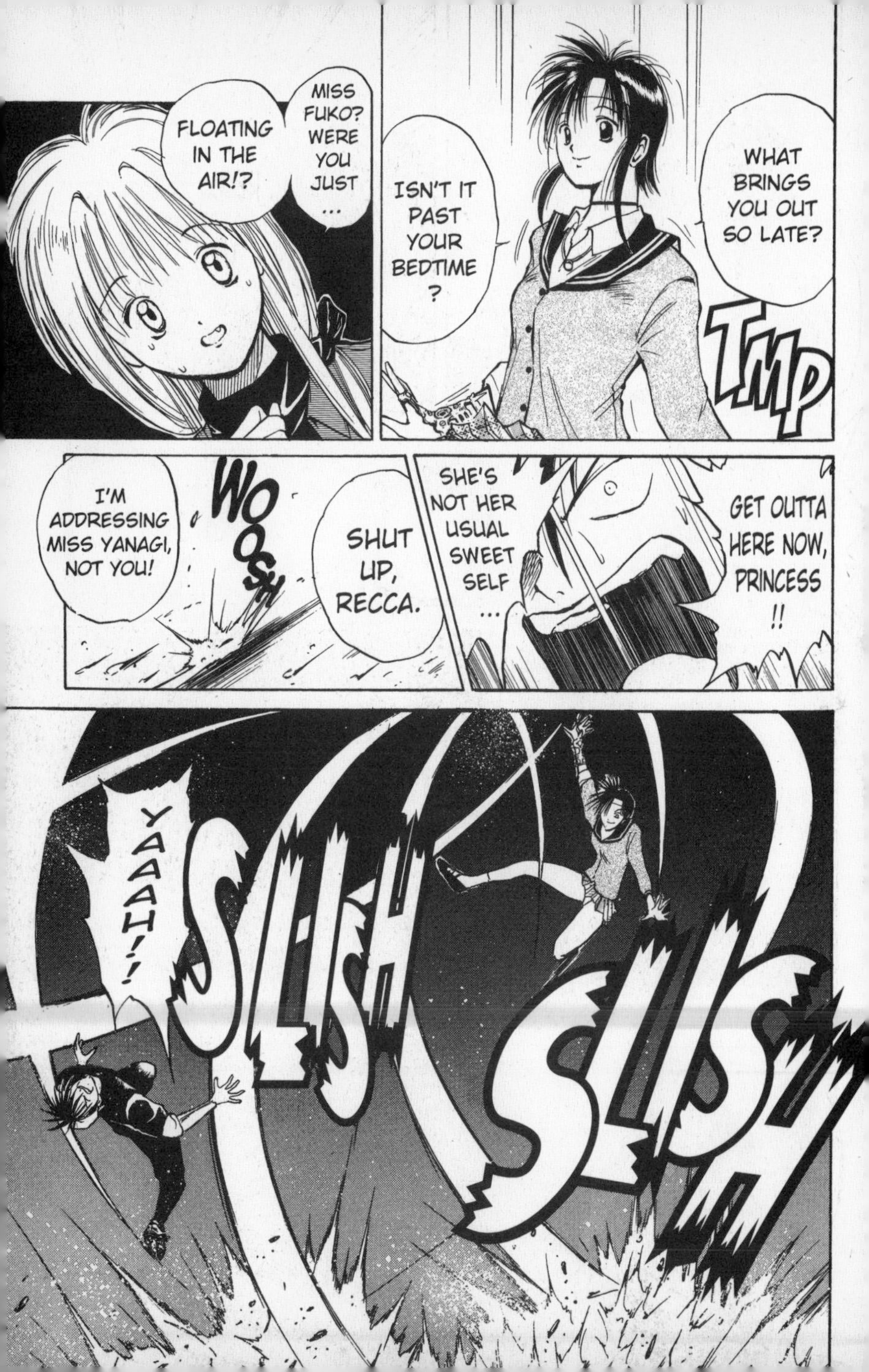
WHAT BRINGS YOU OUT SO LATE?
TMP
ISN'T IT PAST YOUR BEDTIME?
MISS FUKO? WERE YOU JUST ...
FLOATING IN THE AIR!?
GET OUTTA HERE NOW, PRINCESS!!
SHE'S NOT HER USUAL SWEET SELF ...
SHUT UP, RECCA.
WOOSH
I'M ADDRESSING MISS YANAGI, NOT YOU!
SLISH
SLISH
YAAAH!!

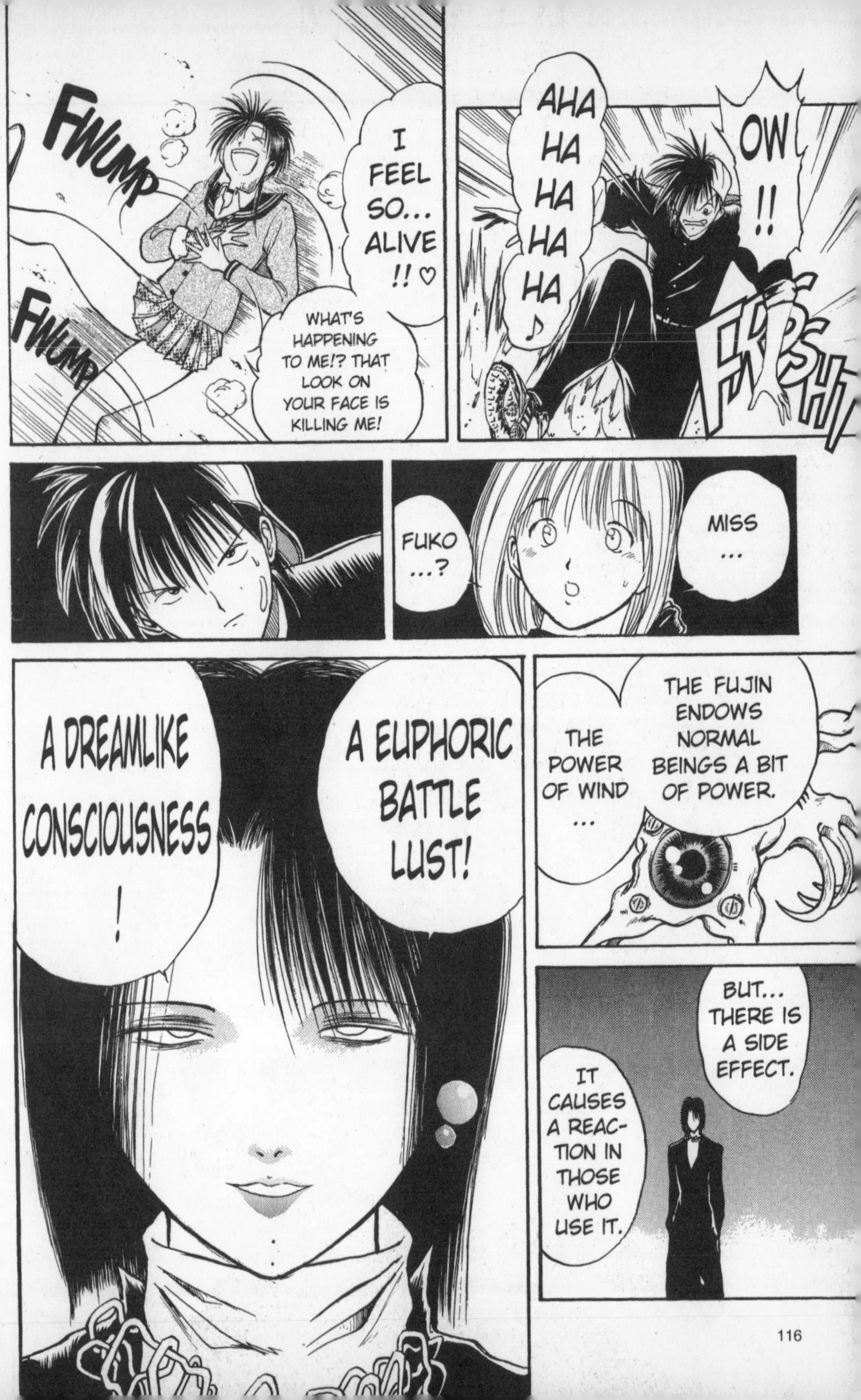
OW !!
AHA HA HA HA HA ♪
I FEEL SO... ALIVE !! ♡
WHAT'S HAPPENING TO ME!? THAT LOOK ON YOUR FACE IS KILLING ME!
FWUMP
FWUMP
MISS ...
FUKO ...?
THE FUJIN ENDOWS NORMAL BEINGS A BIT OF POWER.
THE POWER OF WIND ...
BUT... THERE IS A SIDE EFFECT.
IT CAUSES A REACTION IN THOSE WHO USE IT.
A EUPHORIC BATTLE LUST!
A DREAMLIKE CONSCIOUSNESS !

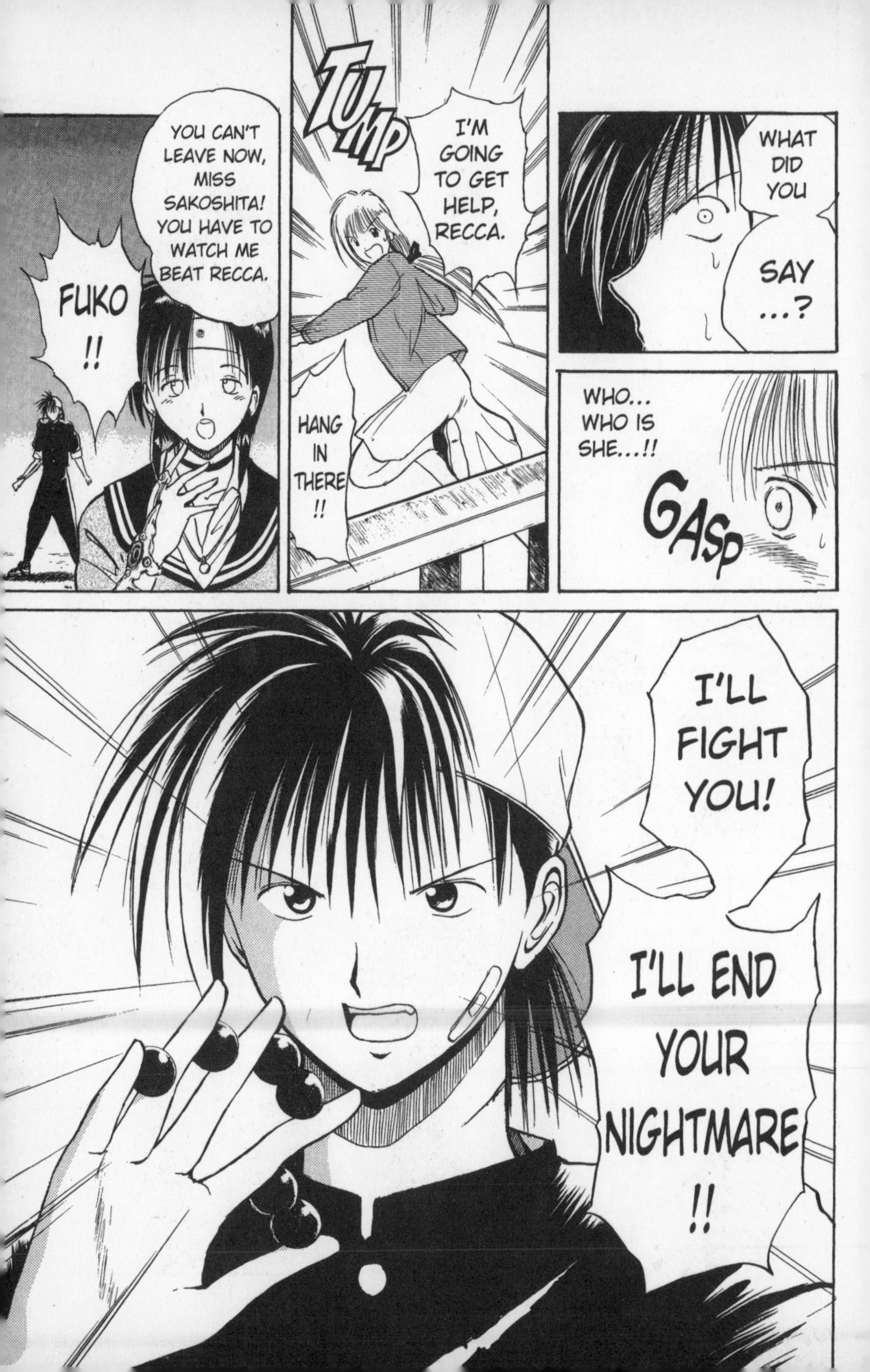
WHAT DID YOU SAY ...?
WHO... WHO IS SHE...!!
GASP
TUMP
I'M GOING TO GET HELP, RECCA.
HANG IN THERE !!
YOU CAN'T LEAVE NOW, MISS SAKOSHITA! YOU HAVE TO WATCH ME BEAT RECCA.
FUKO !!
I'LL FIGHT YOU!
I'LL END YOUR NIGHTMARE !!

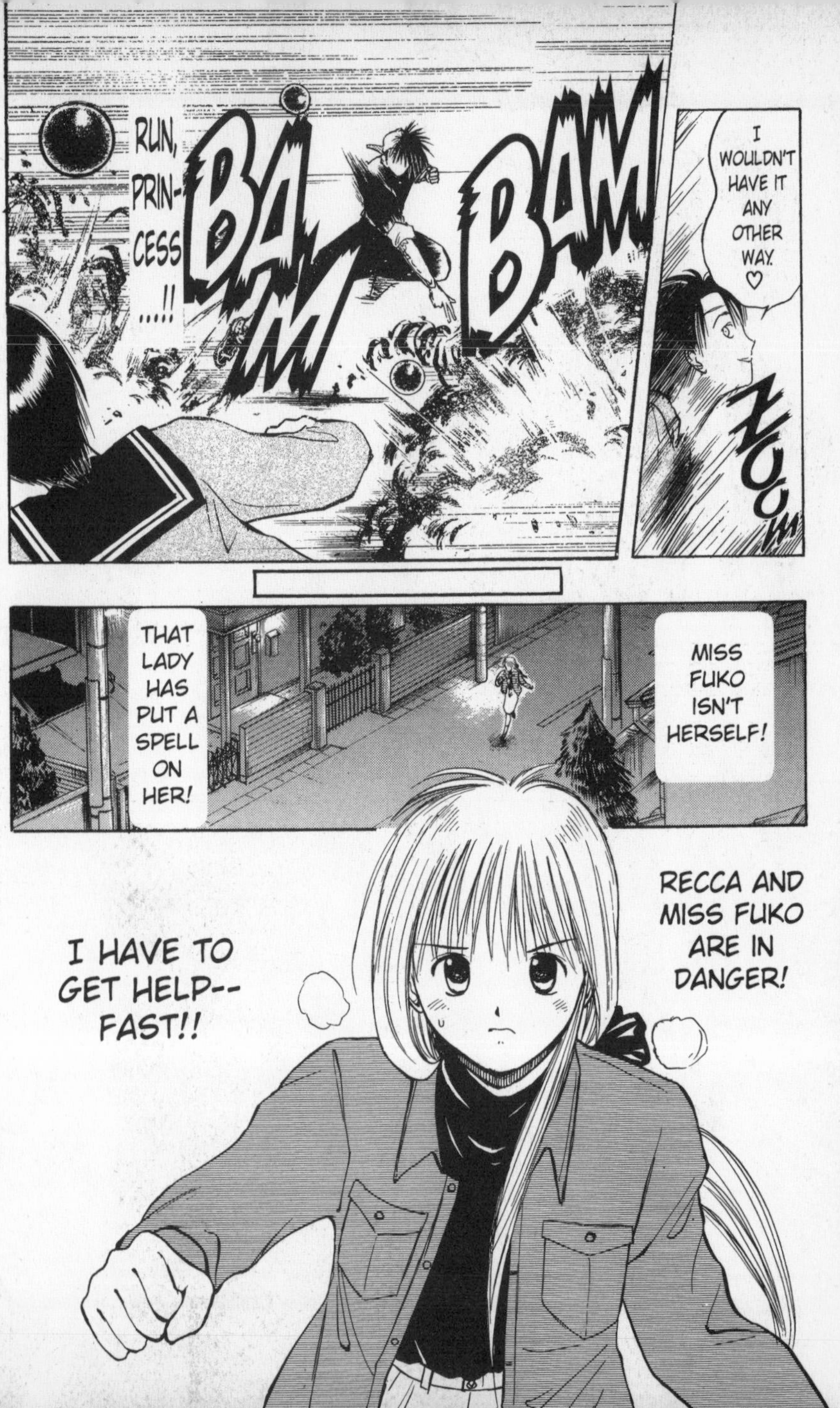
I WOULDN'T HAVE IT ANY OTHER WAY. ♡
ZOOOM
BAM BAM
RUN, PRIN-CESS ...!!
MISS FUKO ISN'T HERSELF!
THAT LADY HAS PUT A SPELL ON HER!
RECCA AND MISS FUKO ARE IN DANGER!
I HAVE TO GET HELP-- FAST!!

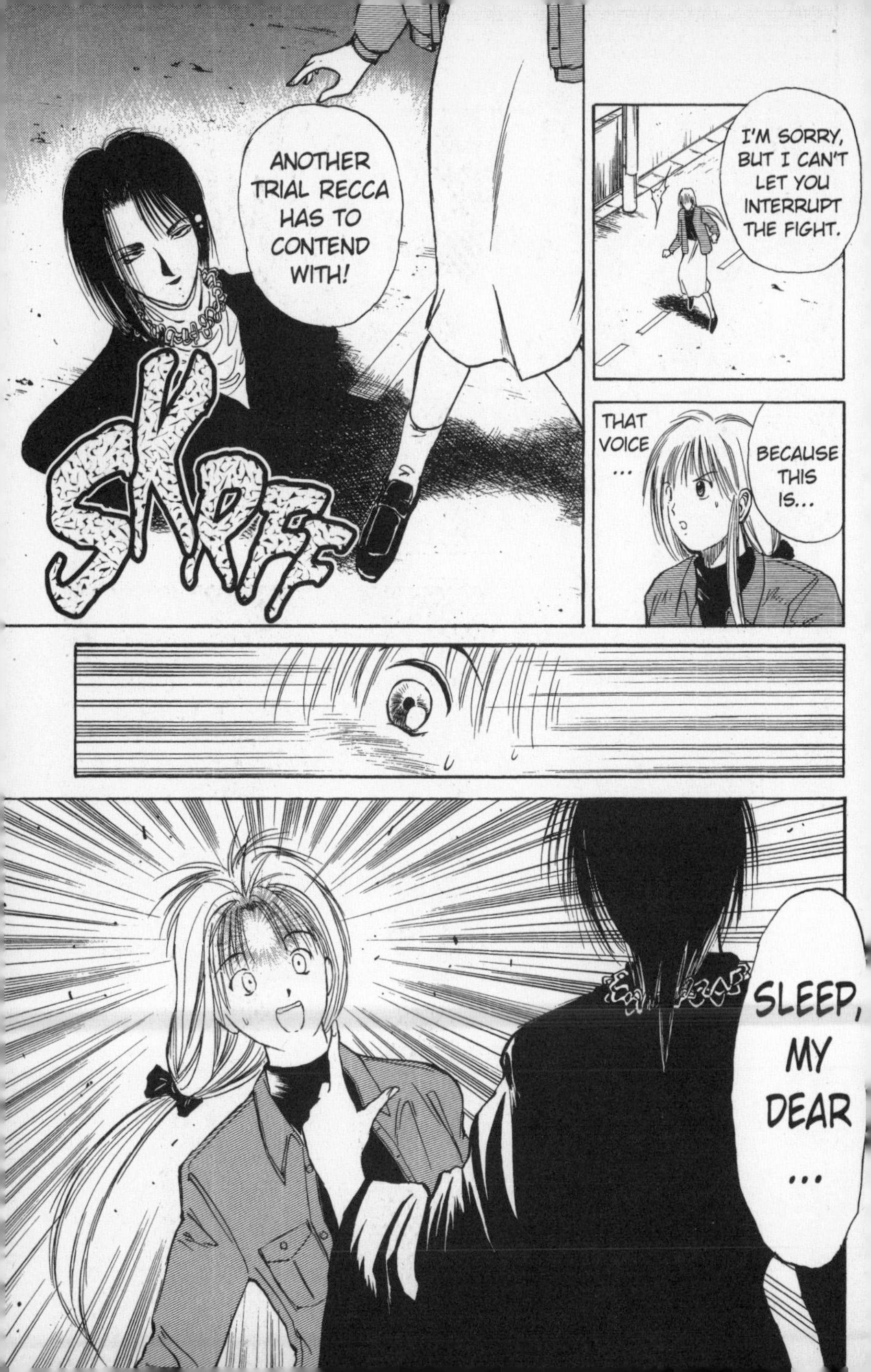
I'M SORRY, BUT I CAN'T LET YOU INTERRUPT THE FIGHT.
BECAUSE THIS IS...
THAT VOICE ...
ANOTHER TRIAL RECCA HAS TO CONTEND WITH!
SKRFF
SLEEP, MY DEAR ...

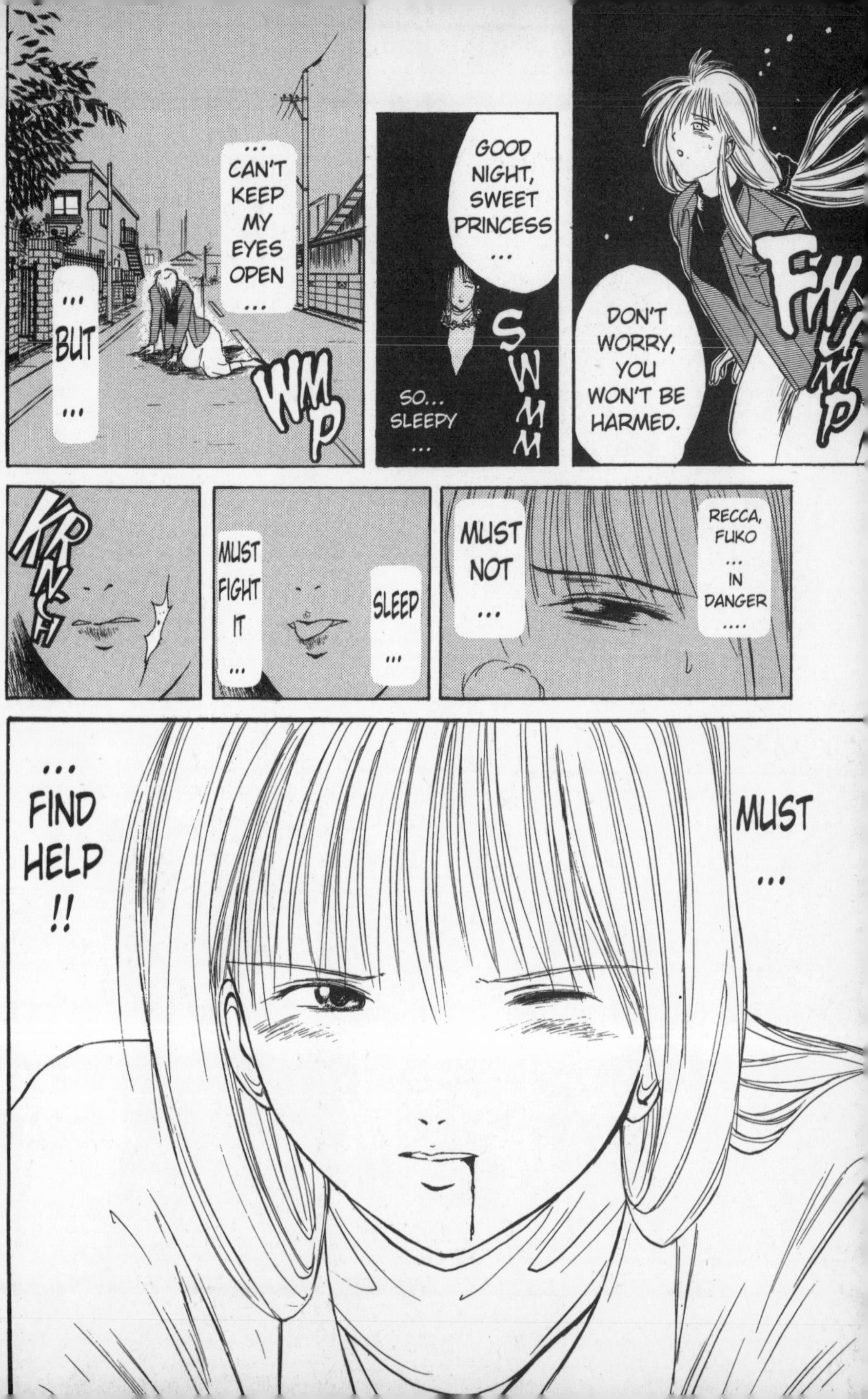

DON'T WORRY, YOU WON'T BE HARMED.
FWUMP
GOOD NIGHT, SWEET PRINCESS ...
SWMM
SO... SLEEPY ...
... CAN'T KEEP MY EYES OPEN ...
... BUT ...
WMP
RECCA, FUKO ... IN DANGER ....
MUST NOT ...
SLEEP ...
MUST FIGHT IT ...
KRANCH
MUST ...
... FIND HELP !!

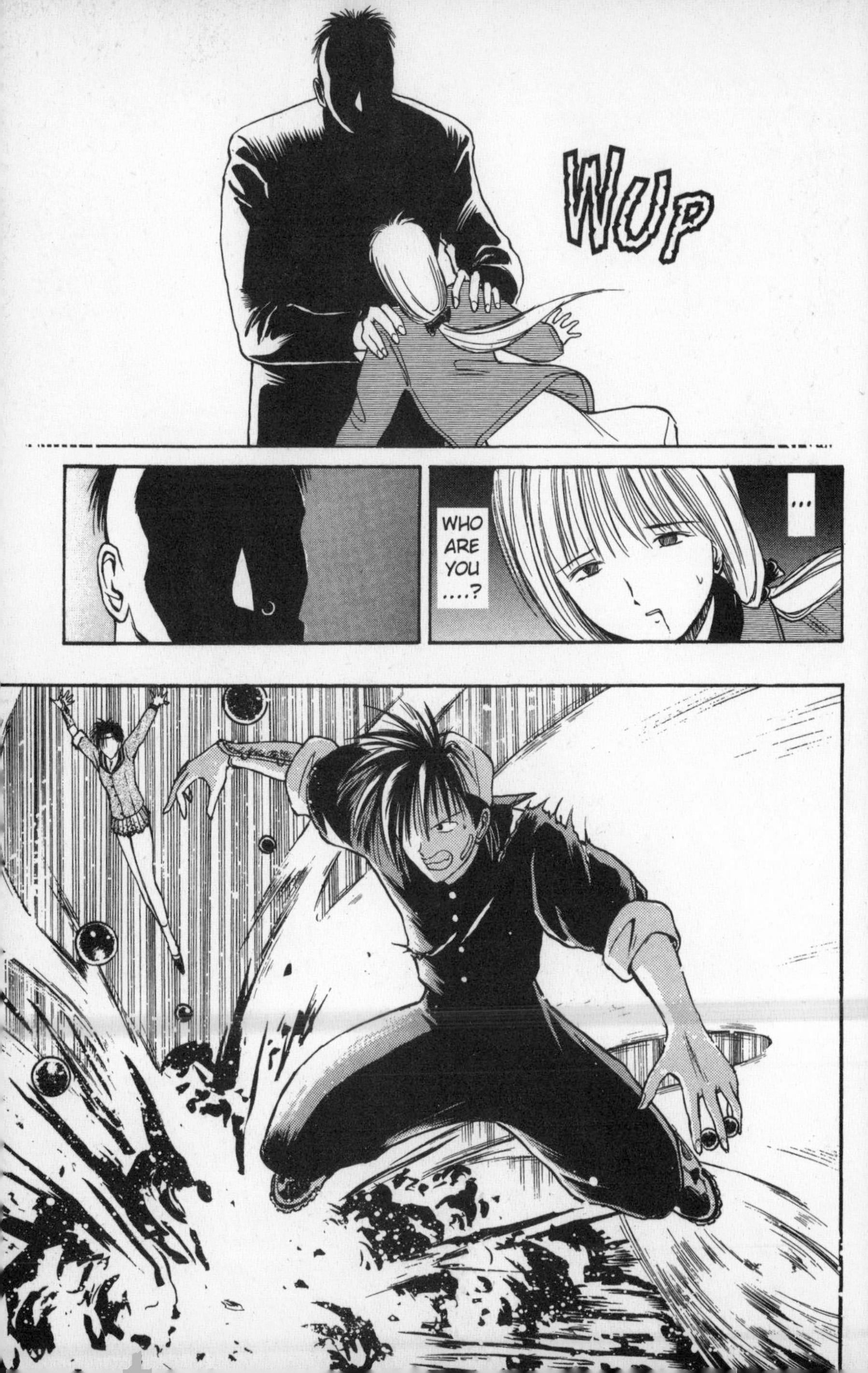
WUP
...
WHO ARE YOU ....?

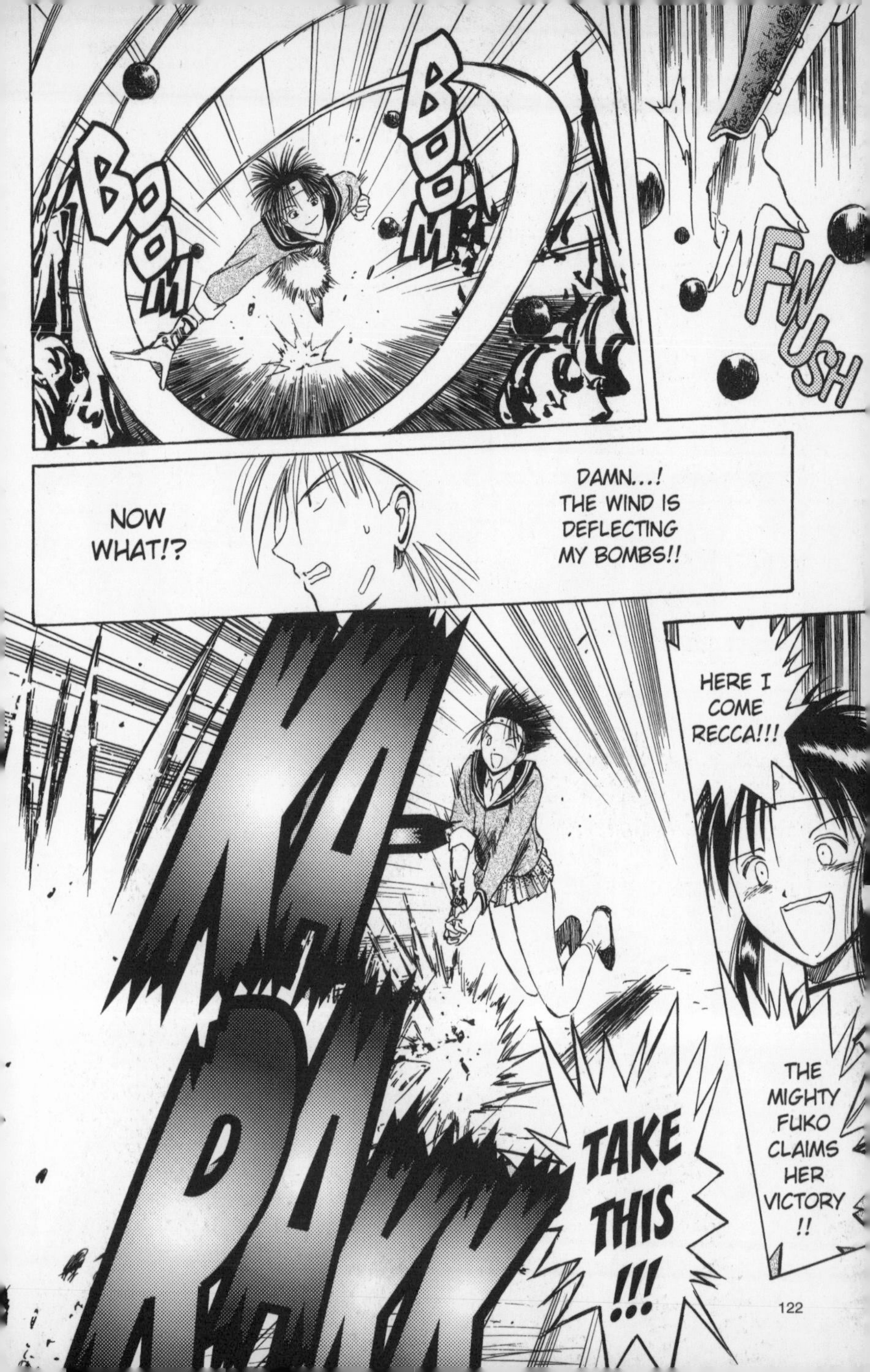
FWUSH
BOOM
BOOM
DAMN...! THE WIND IS DEFLECTING MY BOMBS!!
NOW WHAT!?
HERE I COME RECCA!!!
THE MIGHTY FUKO CLAIMS HER VICTORY !!
TAKE THIS !!!

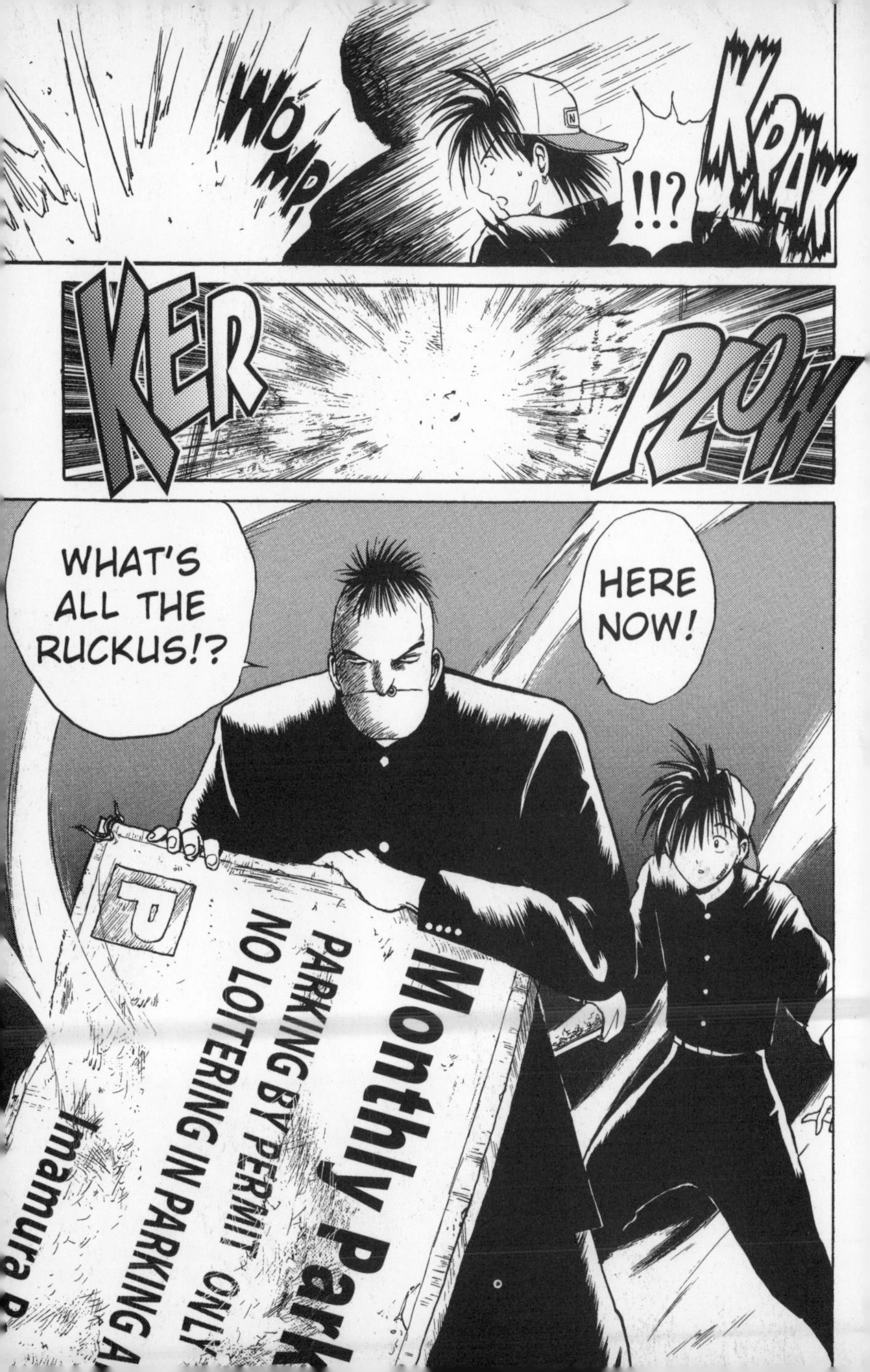
KDAK
!!?
WOMP
KER
PLOW
HERE NOW!
WHAT'S ALL THE RUCKUS!?
Monthly Park
PARKING BY PERMIT ONLY
NO LOITERING IN PARKING A
Imamura

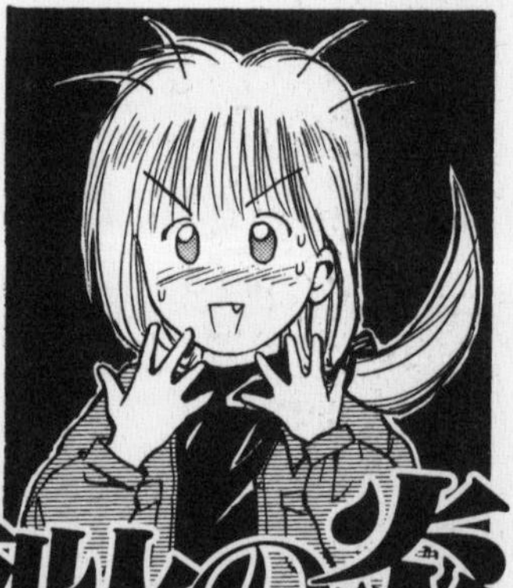

烈火の炎

~FLAME OF RECCA~

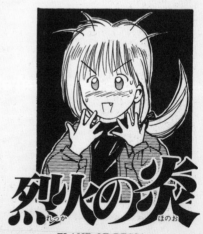

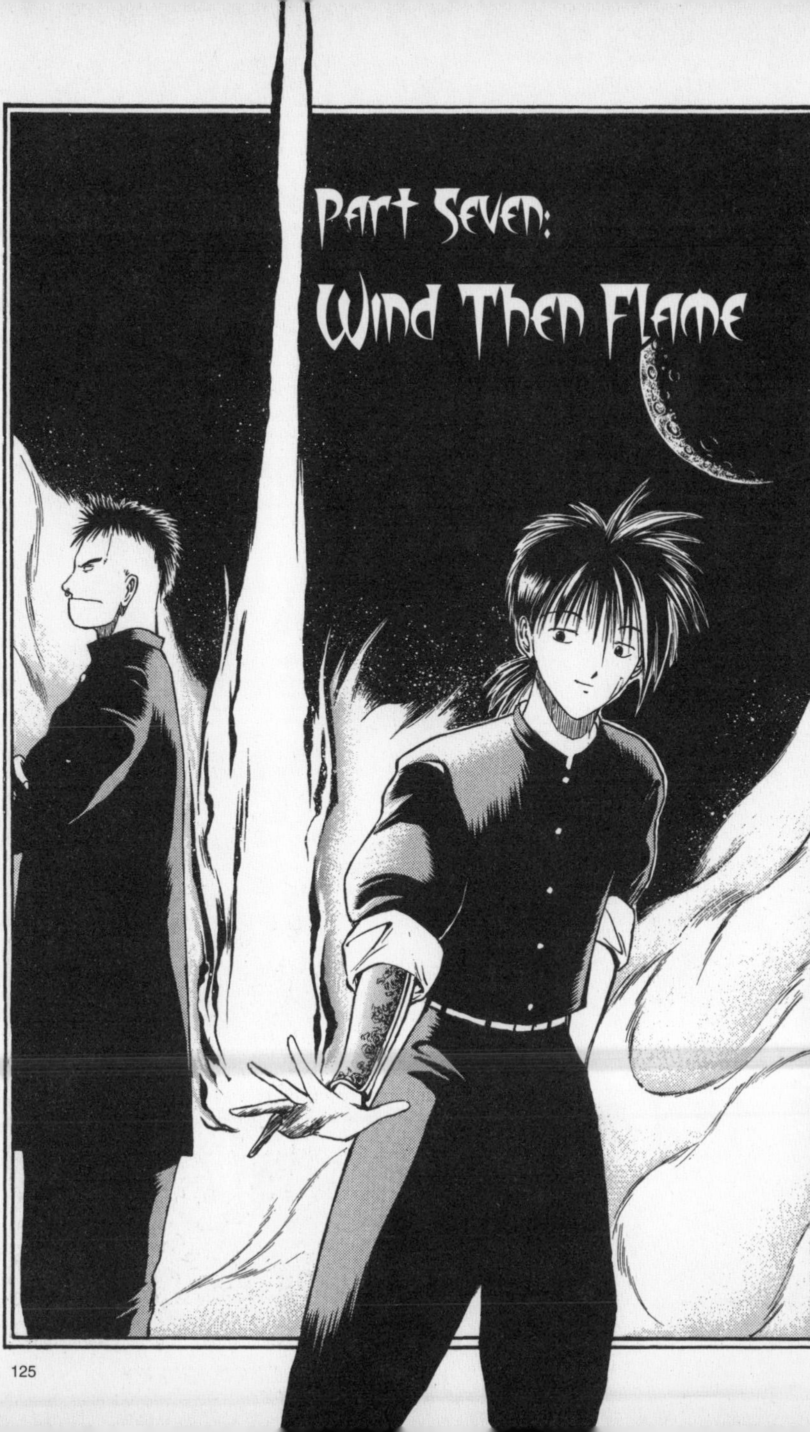
Part Seven:
Wind Then Flame

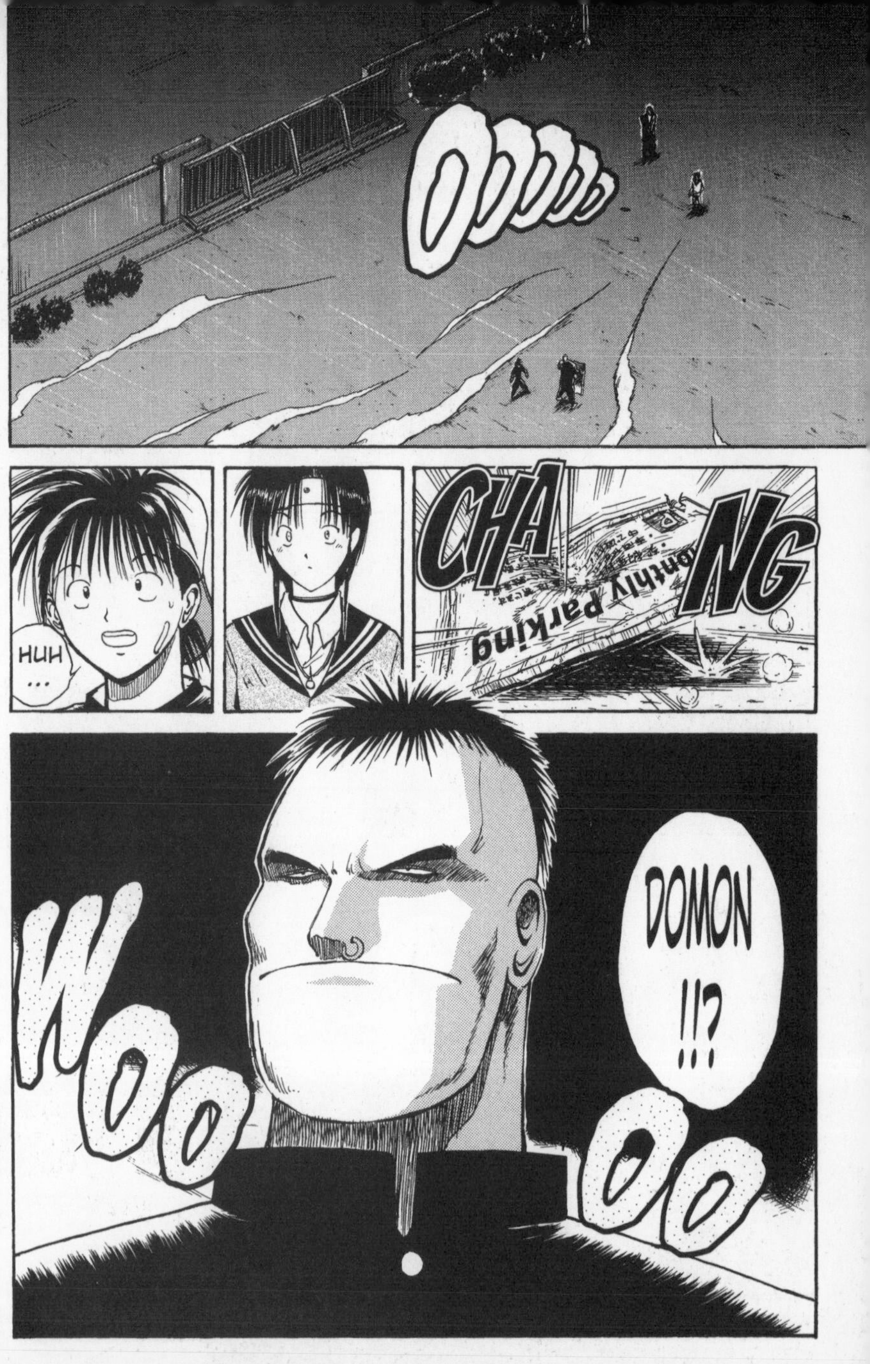
OOOOOO
CHANG
onthly parking
HUH ...
DOMON !!?
WOOOOO

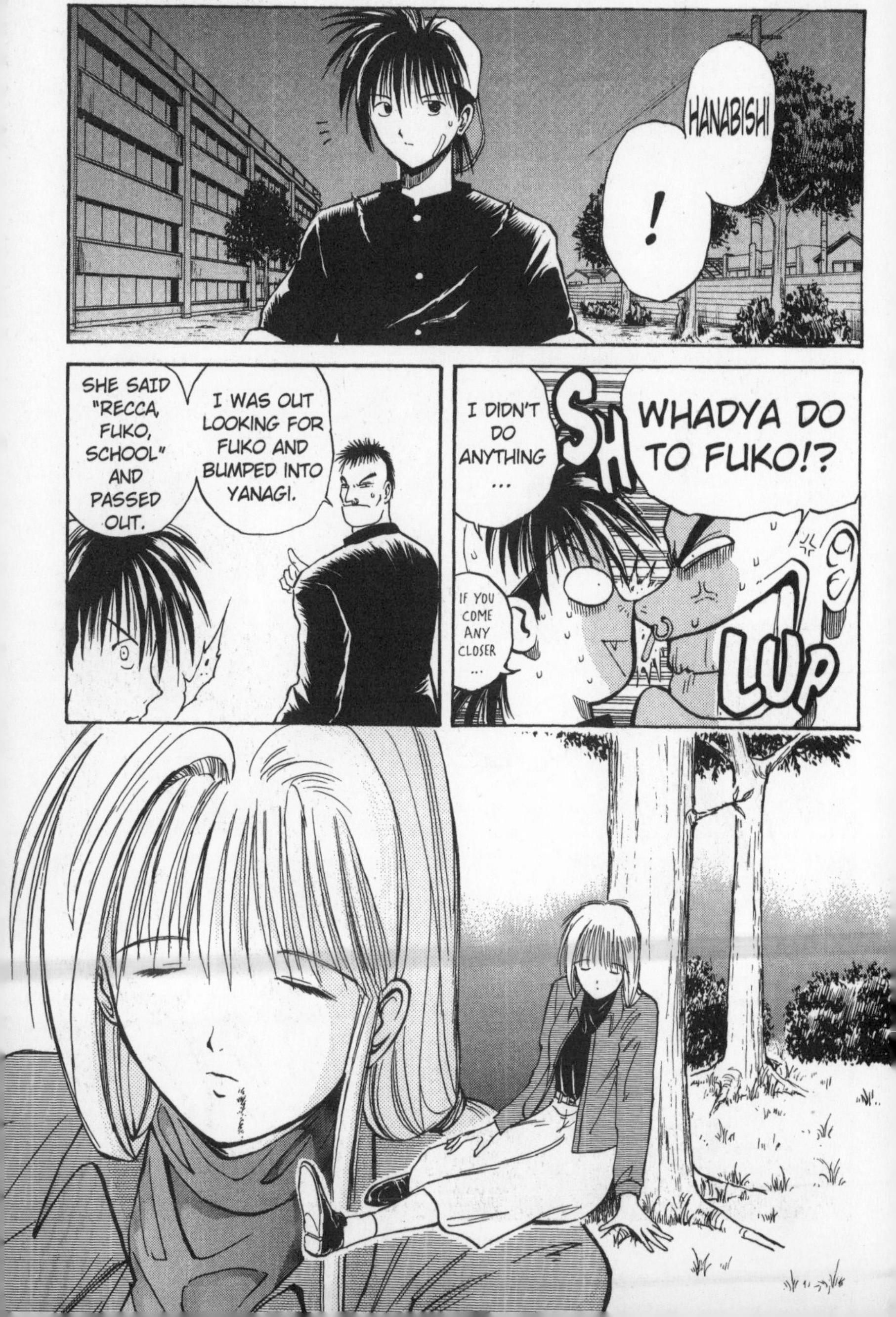
HANABISHI
!
WHADYA DO TO FUKO!?
SH
I DIDN'T DO ANYTHING ...
IF YOU COME ANY CLOSER ...
LUP
I WAS OUT LOOKING FOR FUKO AND BUMPED INTO YANAGI.
SHE SAID "RECCA, FUKO, SCHOOL" AND PASSED OUT.

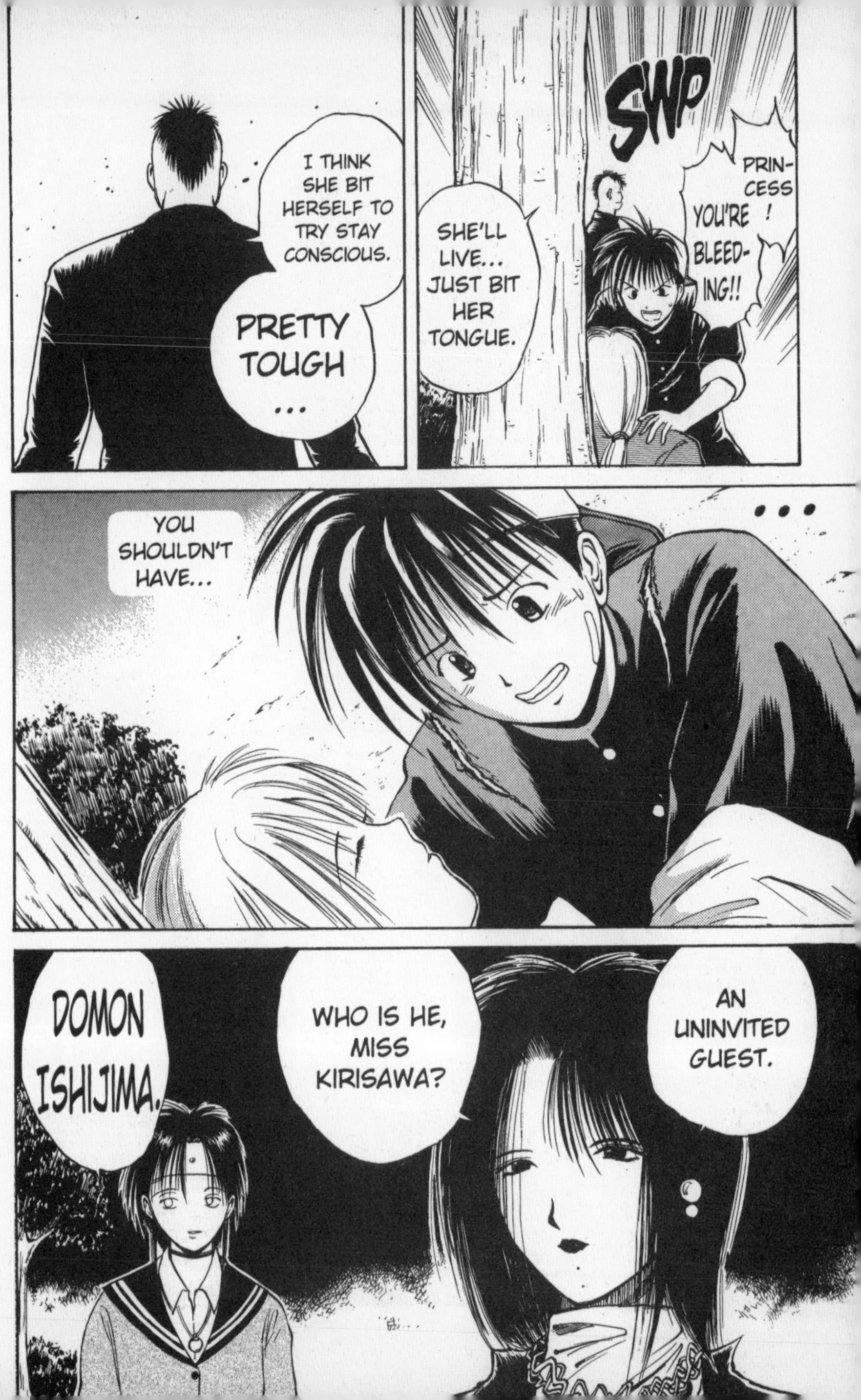
SWP
PRINCESS! YOU'RE BLEEDING!!
SHE'LL LIVE... JUST BIT HER TONGUE.
I THINK SHE BIT HERSELF TO TRY STAY CONSCIOUS.
PRETTY TOUGH ...
...
YOU SHOULDN'T HAVE...
AN UNINVITED GUEST.
WHO IS HE, MISS KIRISAWA?
DOMON ISHIJIMA.

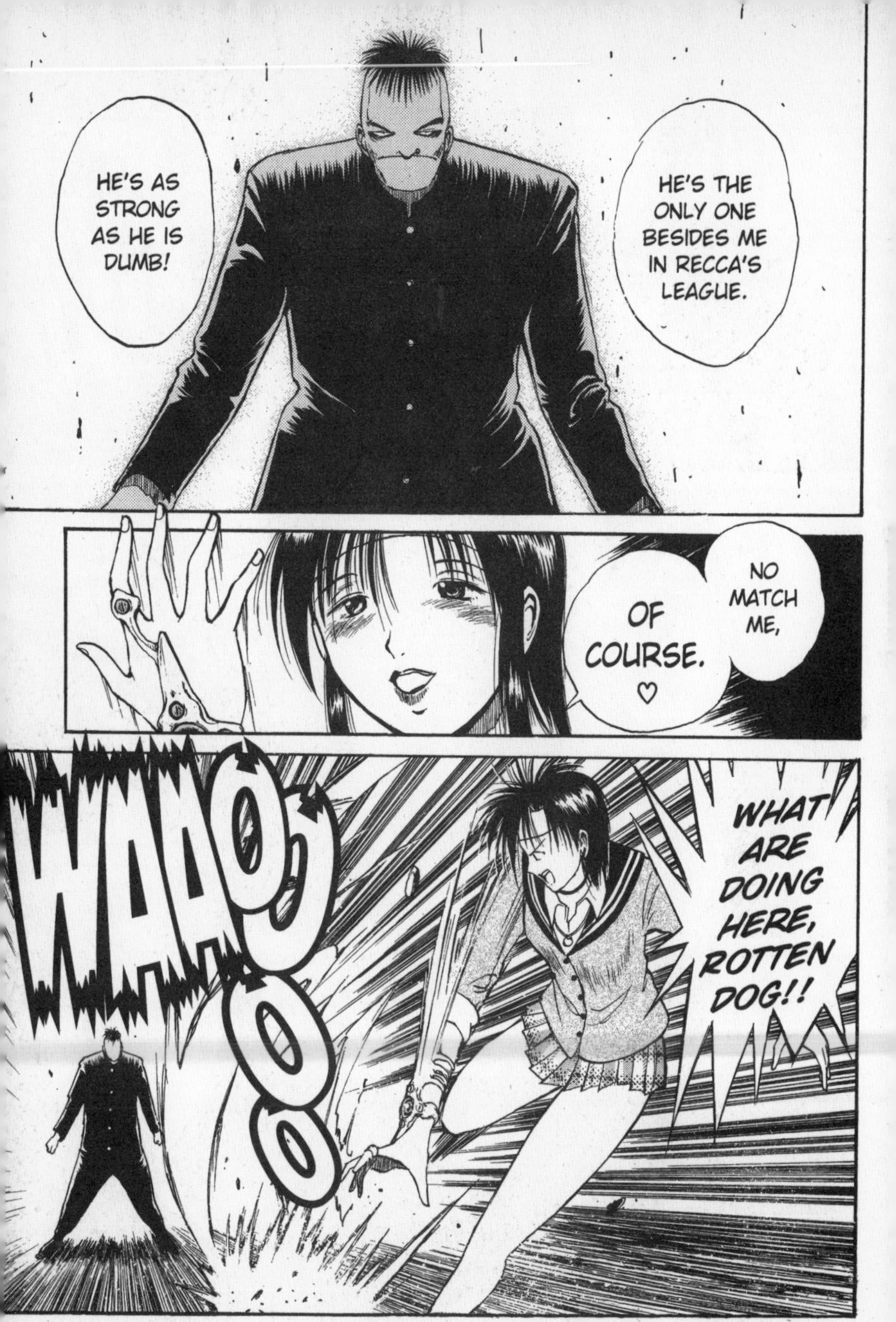
HE'S THE ONLY ONE BESIDES ME IN RECCA'S LEAGUE.
HE'S AS STRONG AS HE IS DUMB!
NO MATCH ME,
OF COURSE. ♡
WHAT ARE DOING HERE, ROTTEN DOG!!
WAAOOOO

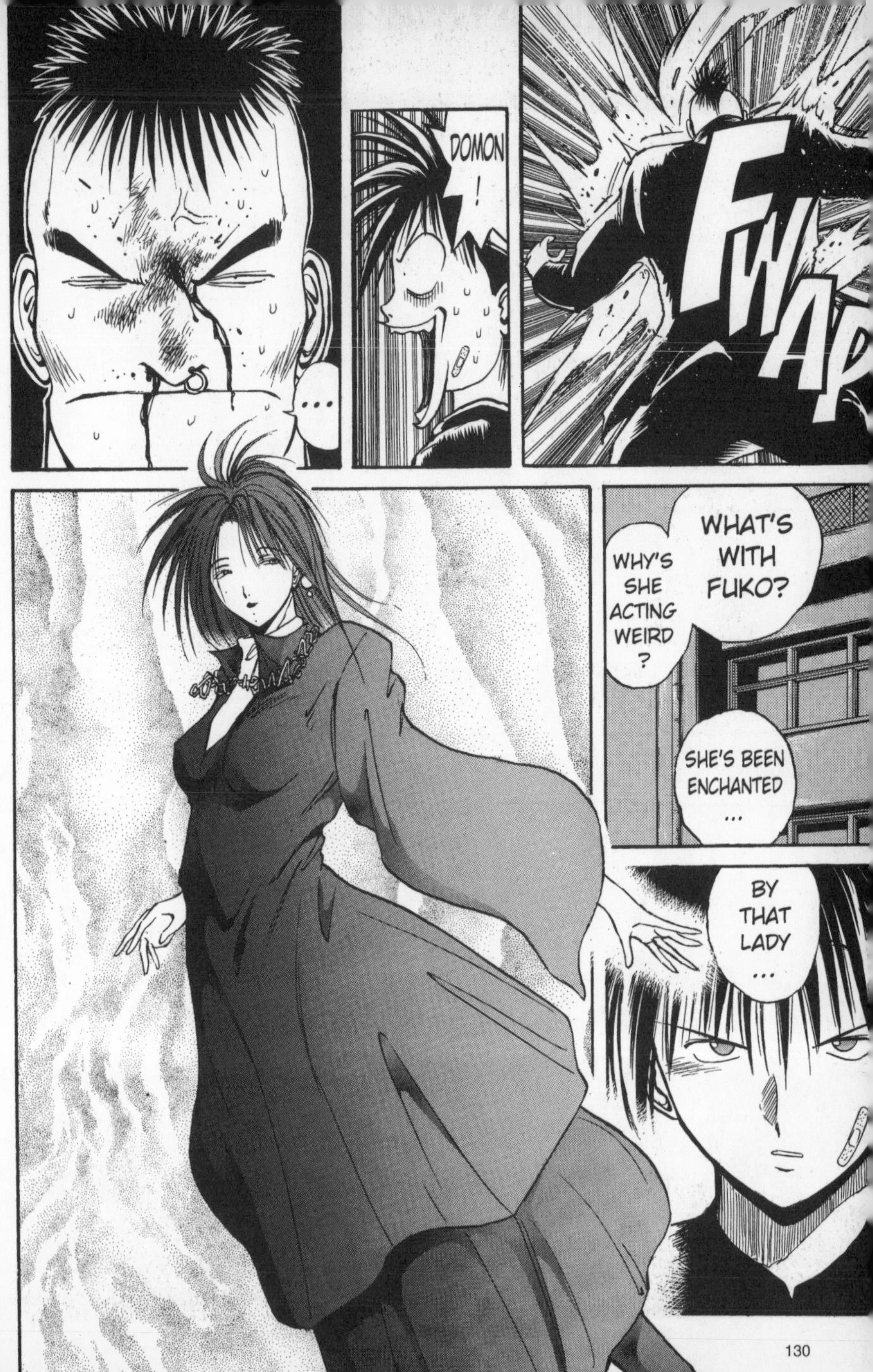
FWAP
DOMON!
...
WHAT'S WITH FUKO?
WHY'S SHE ACTING WEIRD?
SHE'S BEEN ENCHANTED ...
BY THAT LADY ...

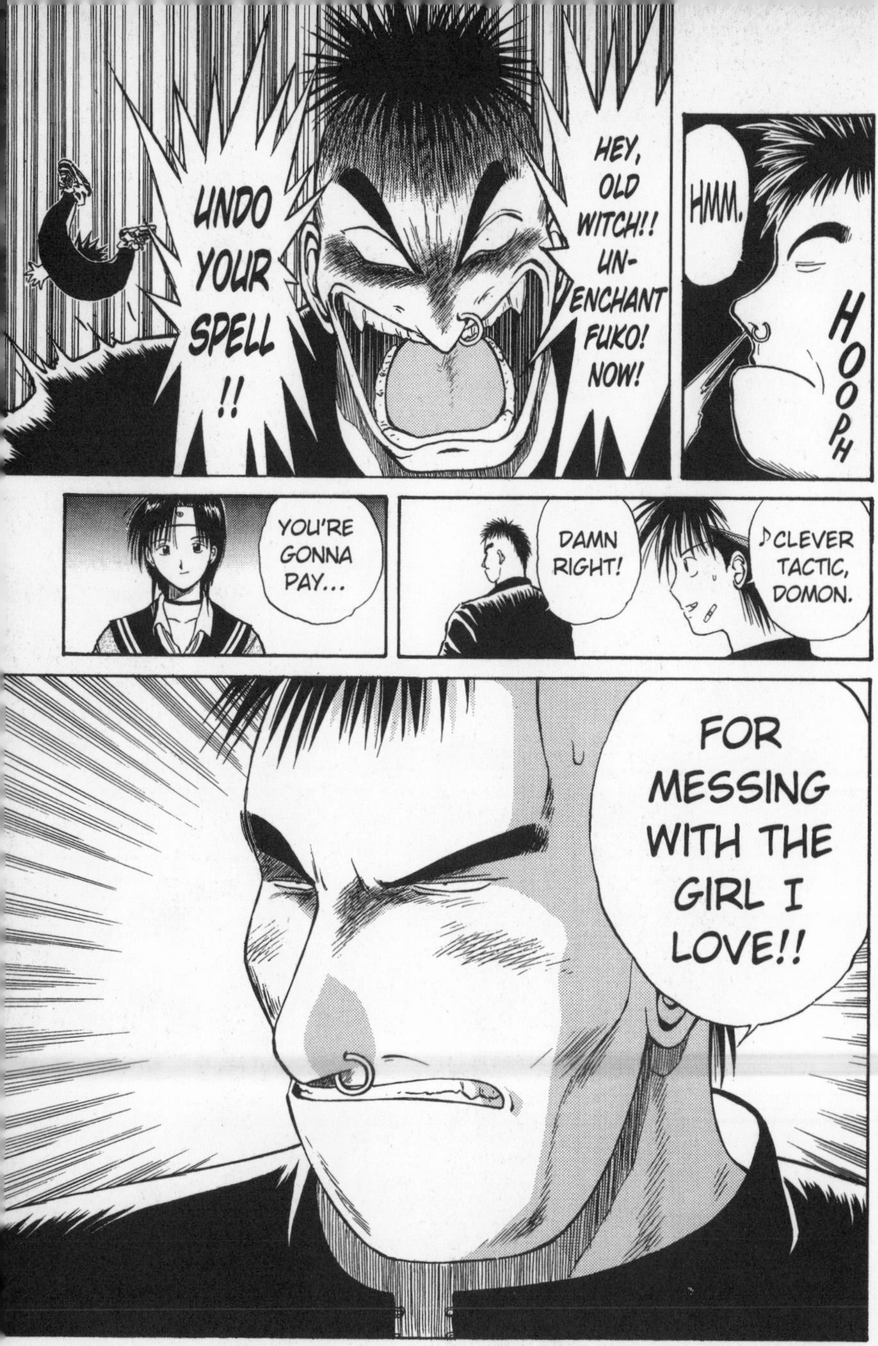
HMM.
HOOOPH
HEY, OLD WITCH!! UN-ENCHANT FUKO! NOW!
UNDO YOUR SPELL!!
♪CLEVER TACTIC, DOMON.
DAMN RIGHT!
YOU'RE GONNA PAY...
FOR MESSING WITH THE GIRL I LOVE!!

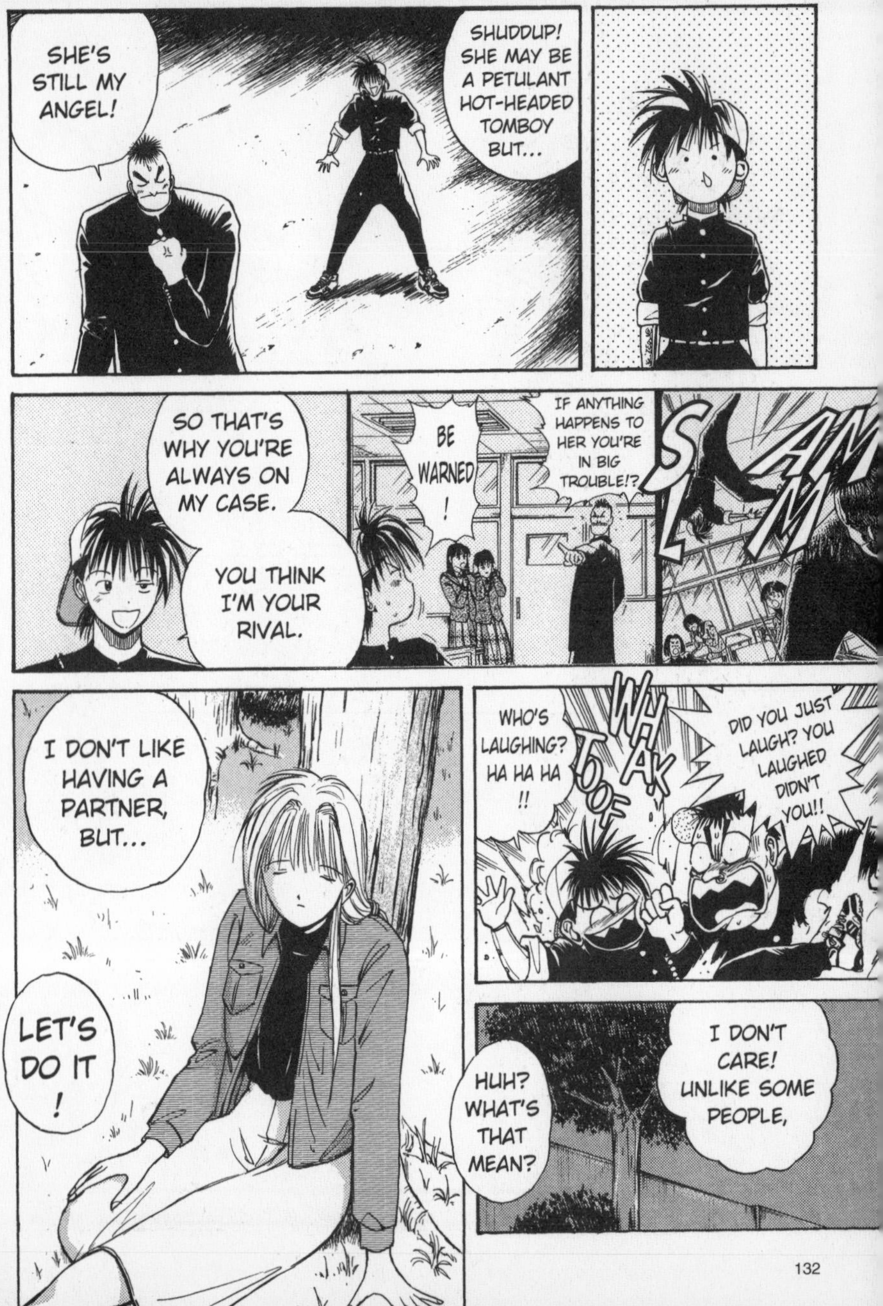
SHUDDUP! SHE MAY BE A PETULANT HOT-HEADED TOMBOY BUT...
SHE'S STILL MY ANGEL!
SLAM
IF ANYTHING HAPPENS TO HER YOU'RE IN BIG TROUBLE!?
BE WARNED!
SO THAT'S WHY YOU'RE ALWAYS ON MY CASE.
YOU THINK I'M YOUR RIVAL.
DID YOU JUST LAUGH? YOU LAUGHED DIDN'T YOU!!
WHAK
WHO'S LAUGHING? HA HA HA!!
TOOF
I DON'T CARE! UNLIKE SOME PEOPLE,
HUH? WHAT'S THAT MEAN?
I DON'T LIKE HAVING A PARTNER, BUT...
LET'S DO IT!

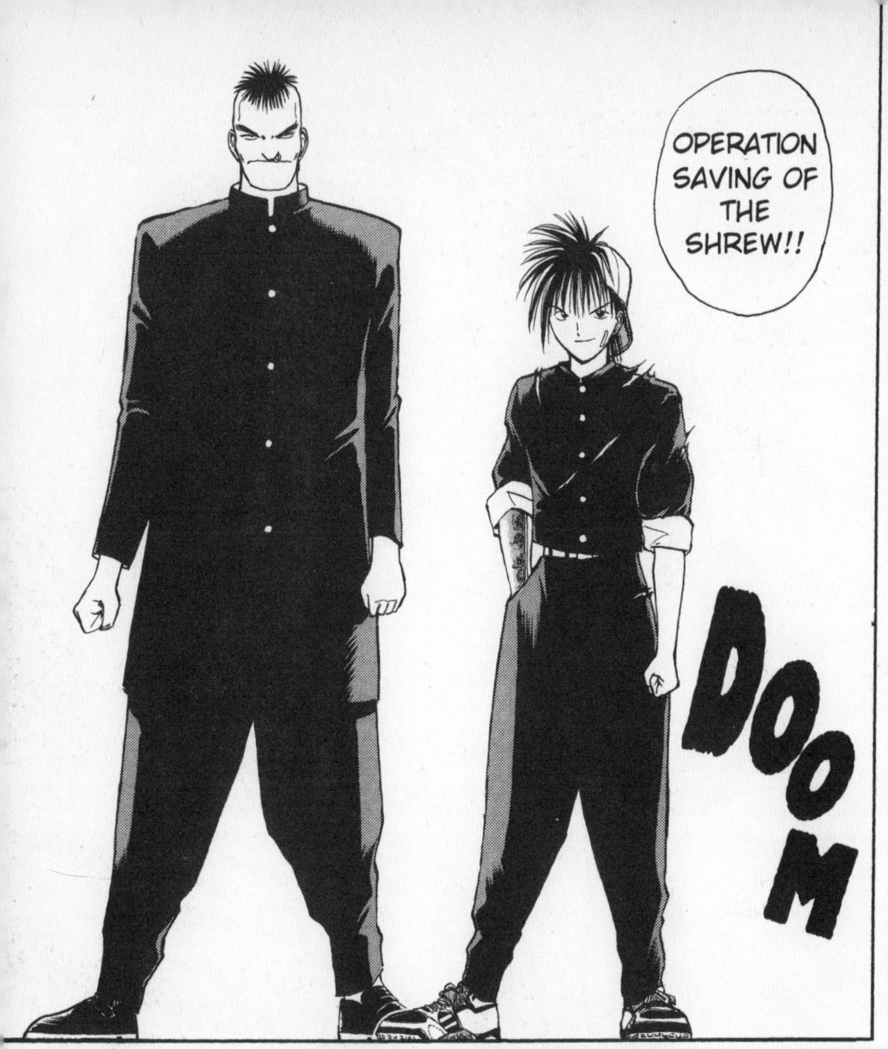
OPERATION SAVING OF THE SHREW!!
DOOOM

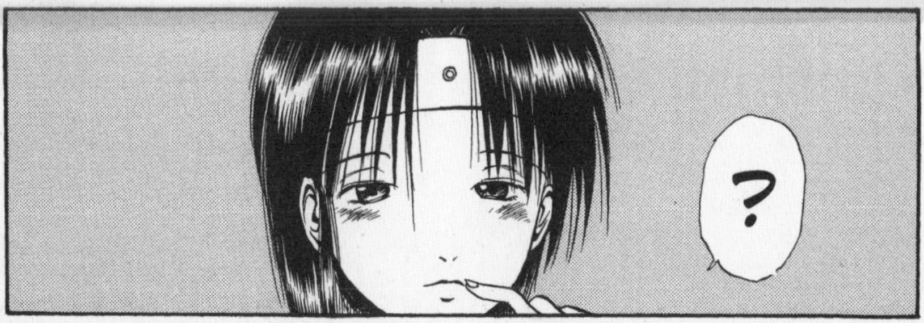
?

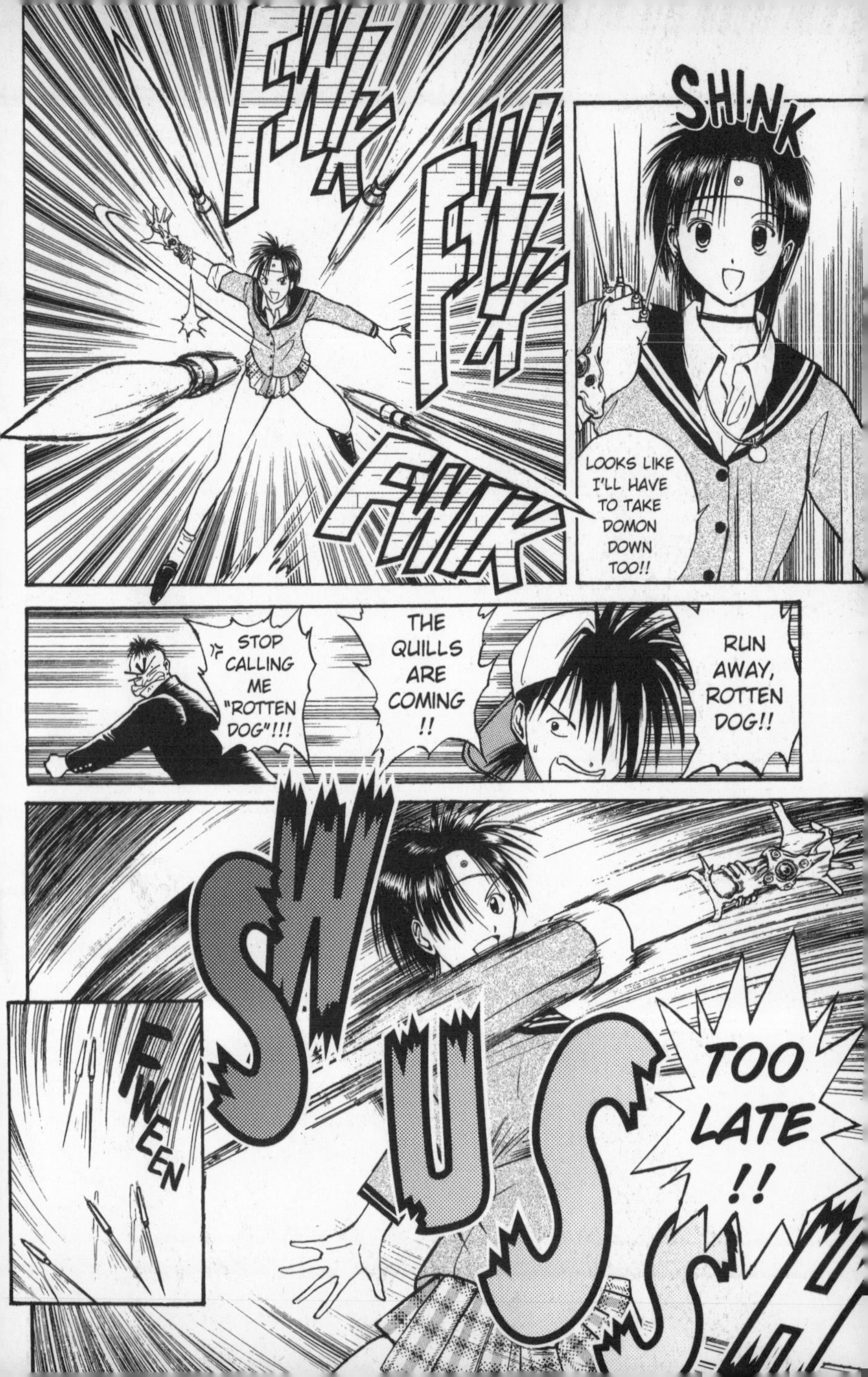
SHINK
LOOKS LIKE I'LL HAVE TO TAKE DOMON DOWN TOO!!
RUN AWAY, ROTTEN DOG!!
THE QUILLS ARE COMING!!
STOP CALLING ME "ROTTEN DOG"!!!
TOO LATE!!
FWEEN

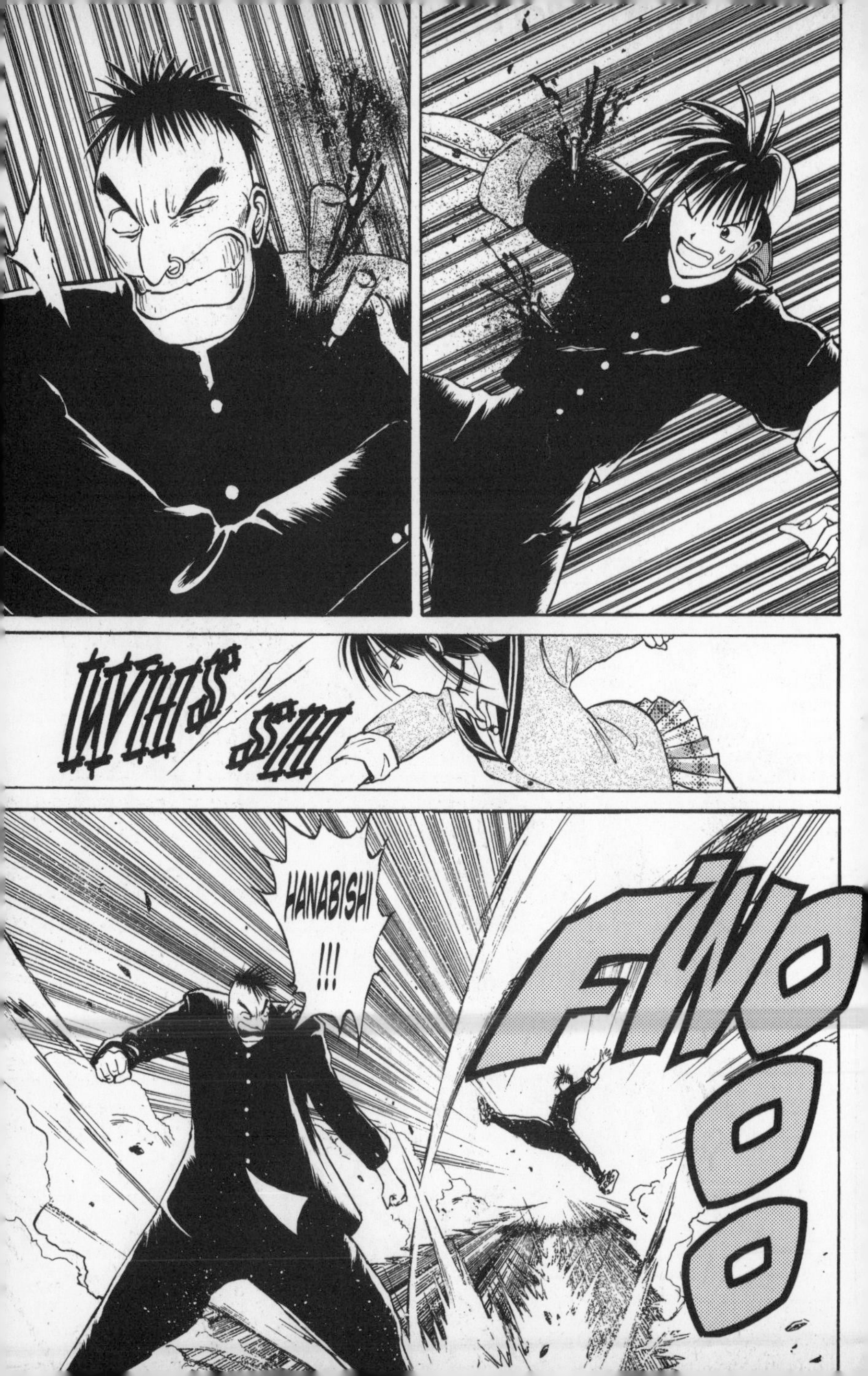
HANABISHI !!!
FWOOOO

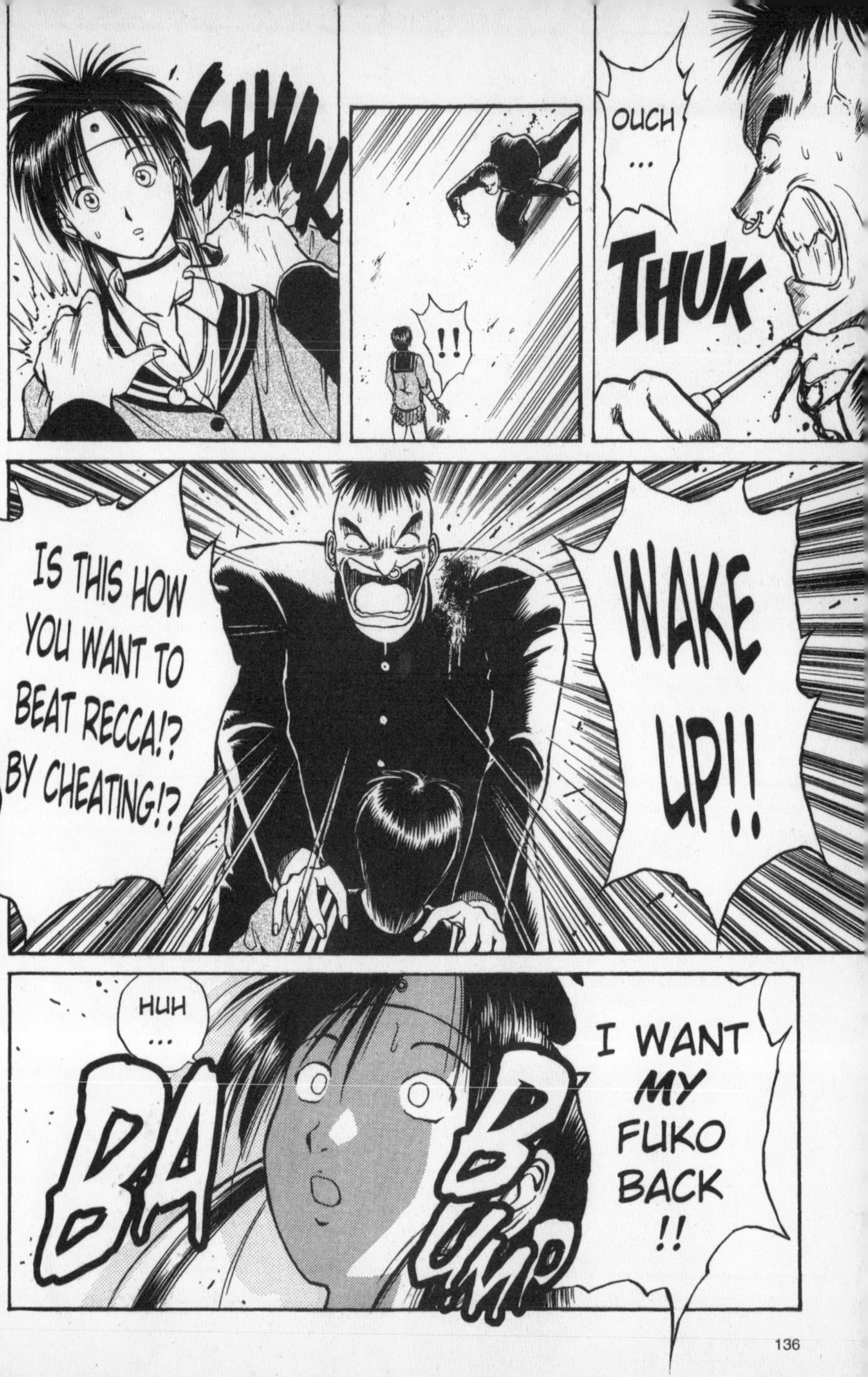
OUCH ...
THUK
!!
SHUK
WAKE UP!!
IS THIS HOW YOU WANT TO BEAT RECCA!? BY CHEATING!?
I WANT MY FUKO BACK !!
HUH ...
BA BUMP

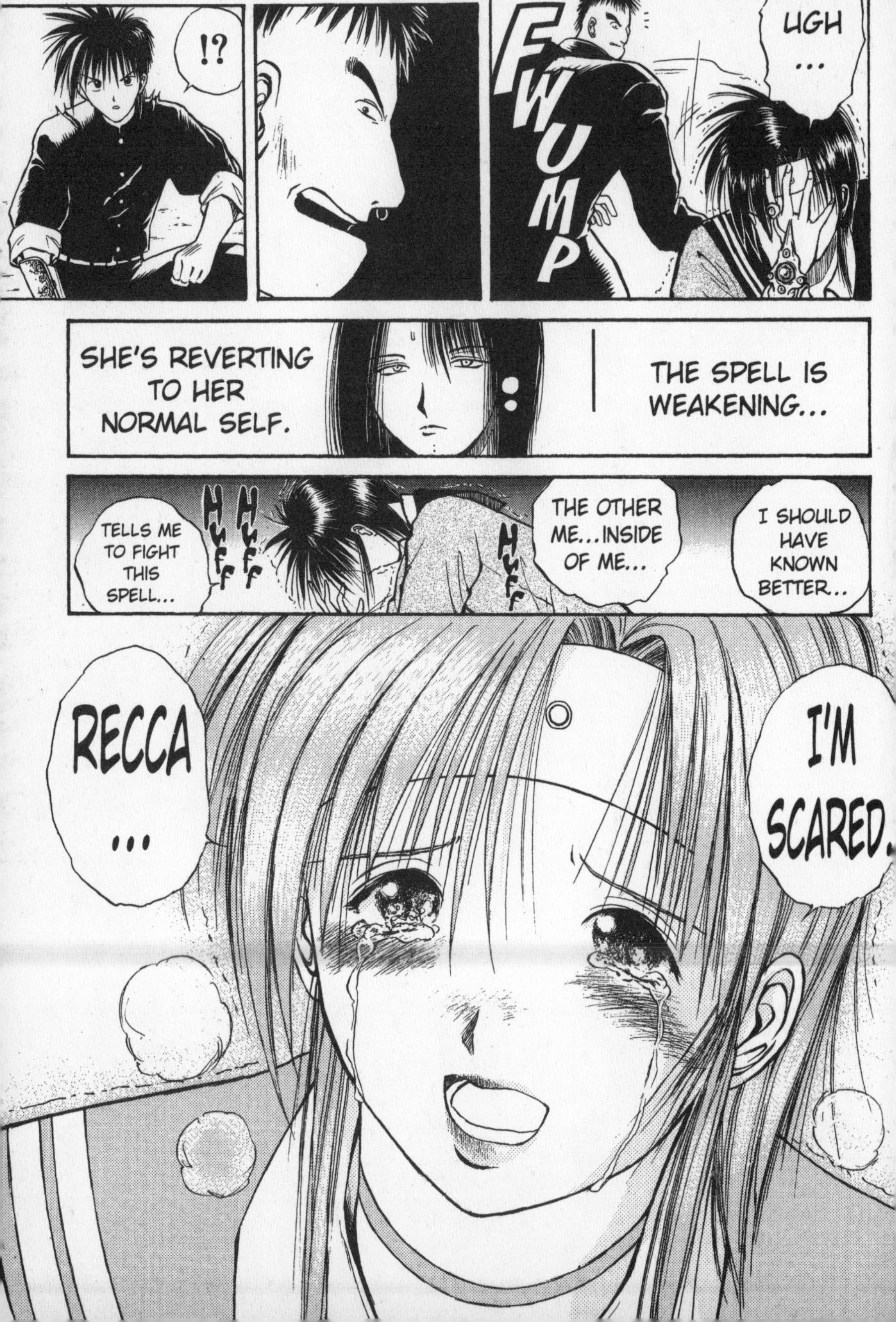
UGH ...
FWUMP
!?
THE SPELL IS WEAKENING...
SHE'S REVERTING TO HER NORMAL SELF.
I SHOULD HAVE KNOWN BETTER...
THE OTHER ME...INSIDE OF ME...
HUFF
HUFF HUFF
TELLS ME TO FIGHT THIS SPELL...
I'M SCARED.
RECCA ...

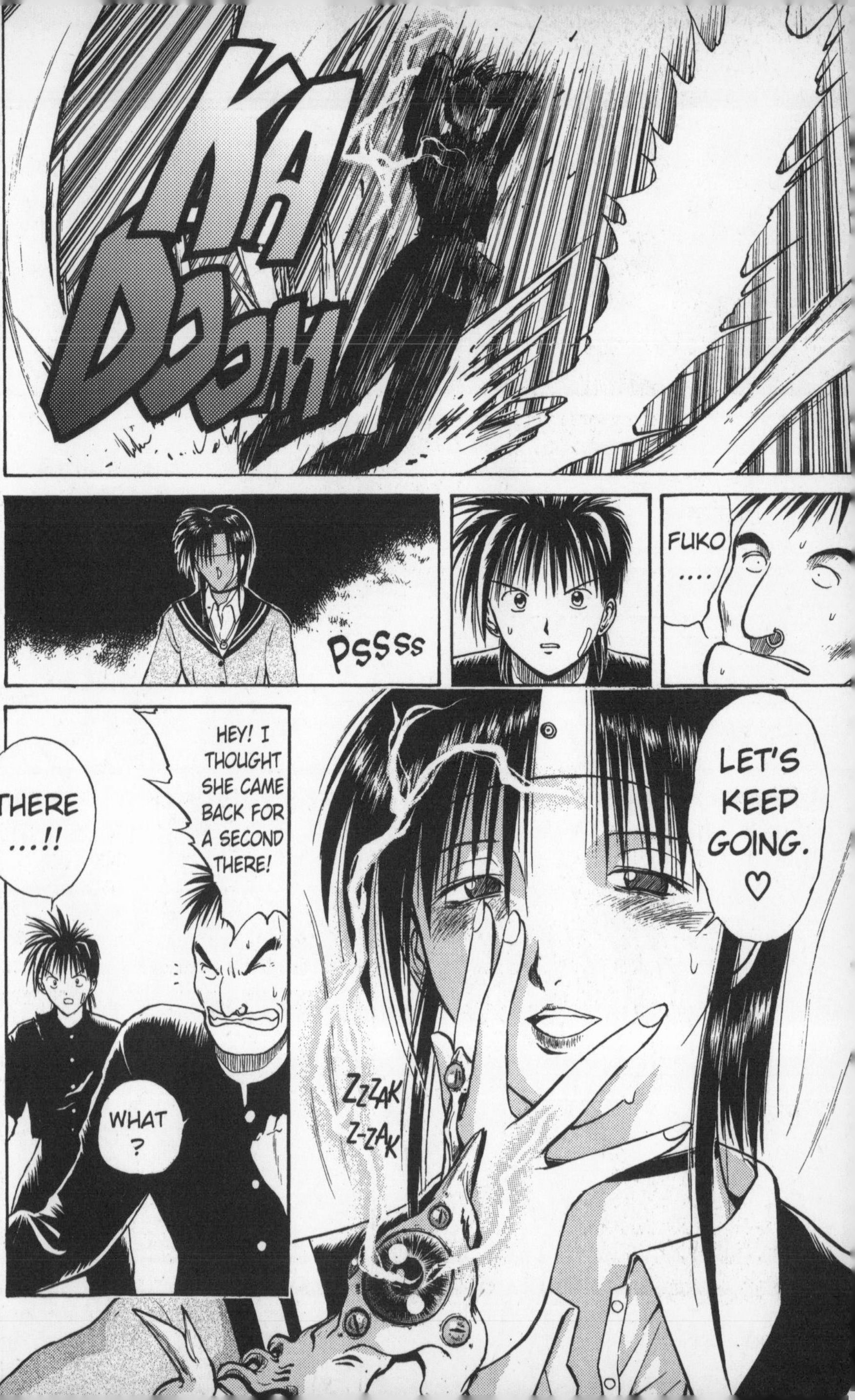
KA DOOM
FUKO ....
PSSSS
LET'S KEEP GOING. ♥
ZZZAK
Z-ZAK
HEY! I THOUGHT SHE CAME BACK FOR A SECOND THERE!
THERE ...!!
WHAT ?

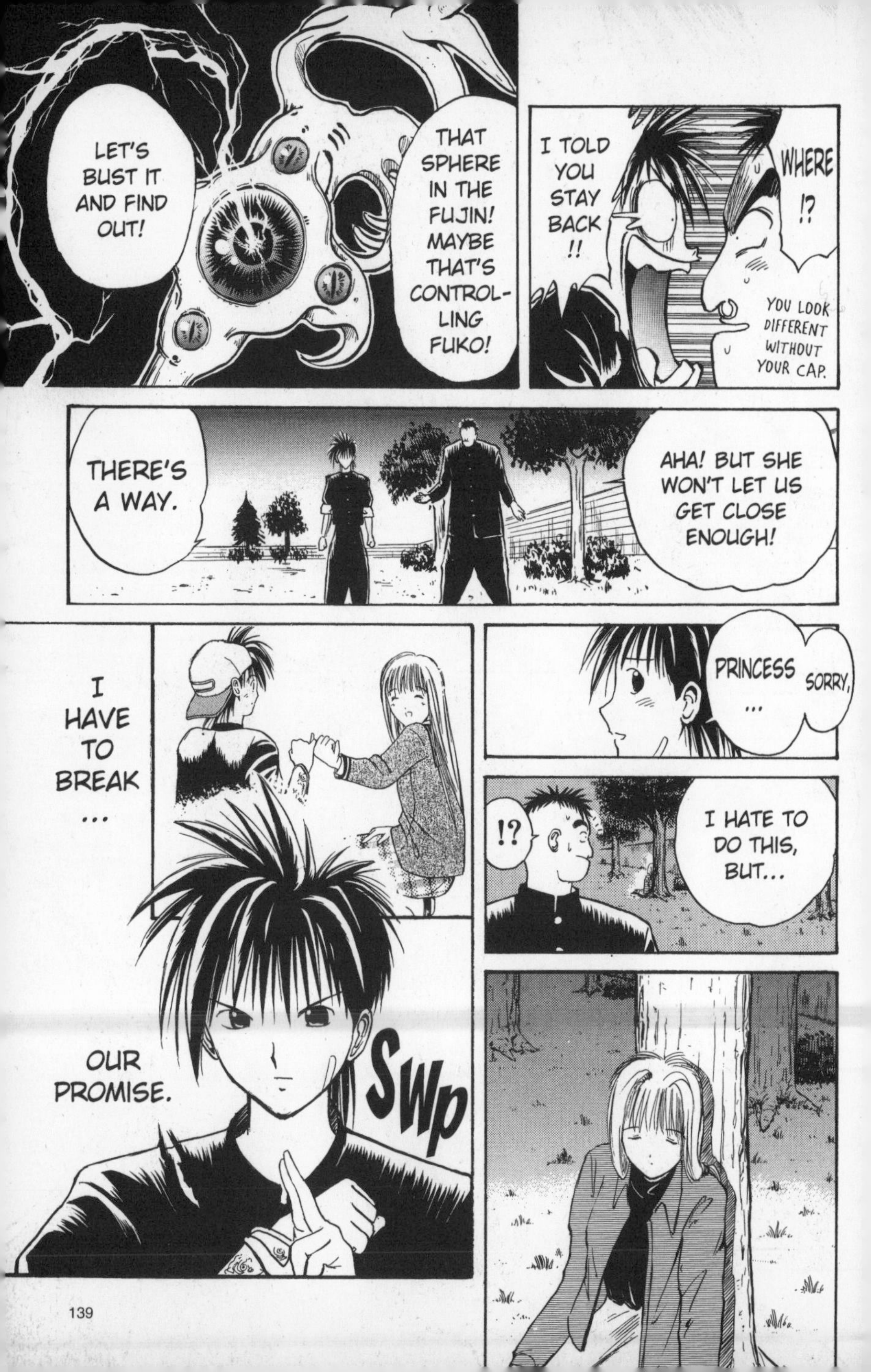
WHERE !?
I TOLD YOU STAY BACK !!
YOU LOOK DIFFERENT WITHOUT YOUR CAP.
THAT SPHERE IN THE FUJIN! MAYBE THAT'S CONTROL-LING FUKO!
LET'S BUST IT AND FIND OUT!
AHA! BUT SHE WON'T LET US GET CLOSE ENOUGH!
THERE'S A WAY.
SORRY,
PRINCESS ...
I HATE TO DO THIS, BUT...
!?
I HAVE TO BREAK ...
OUR PROMISE.
SWP

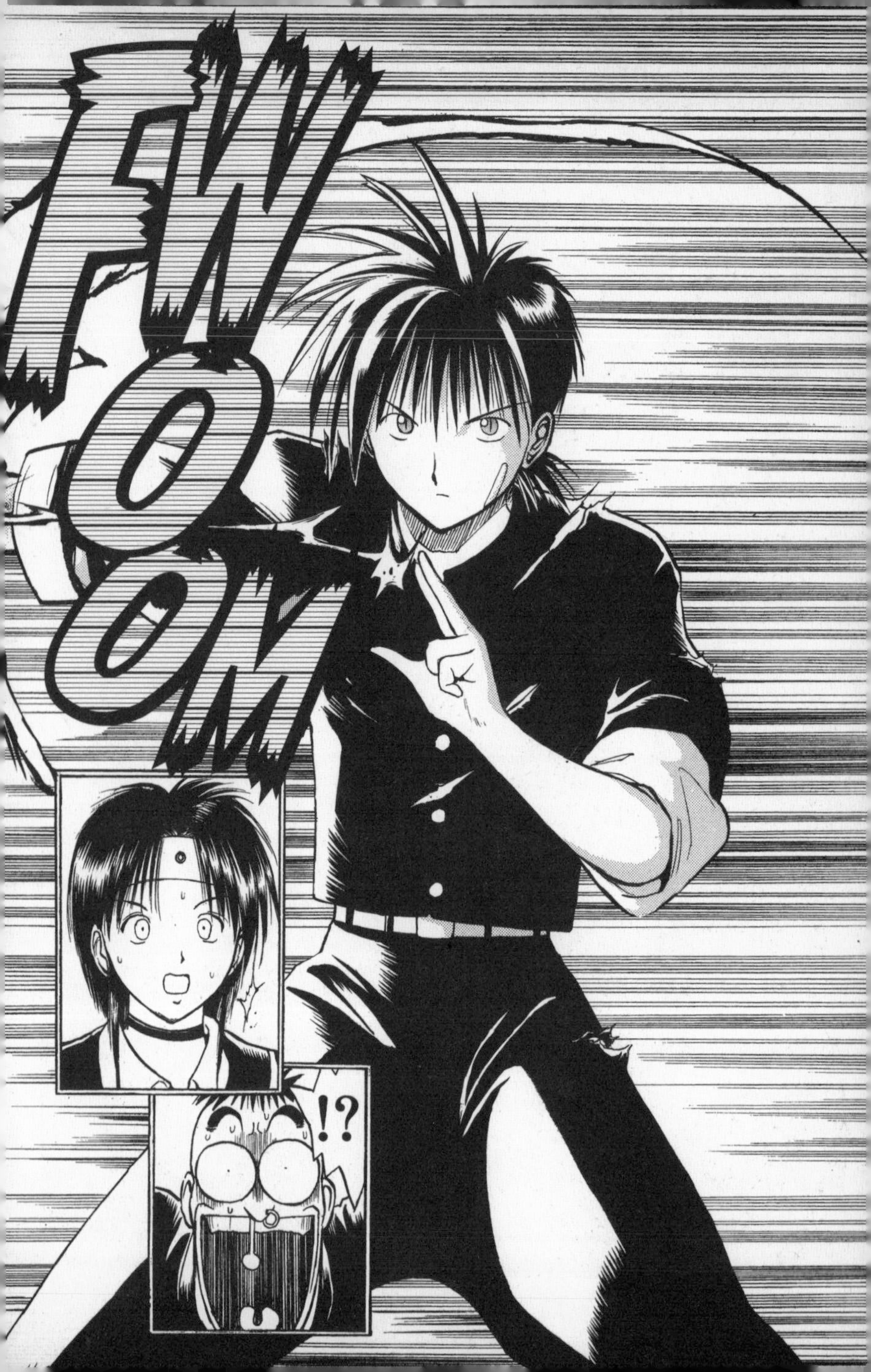
FWOOM
!?

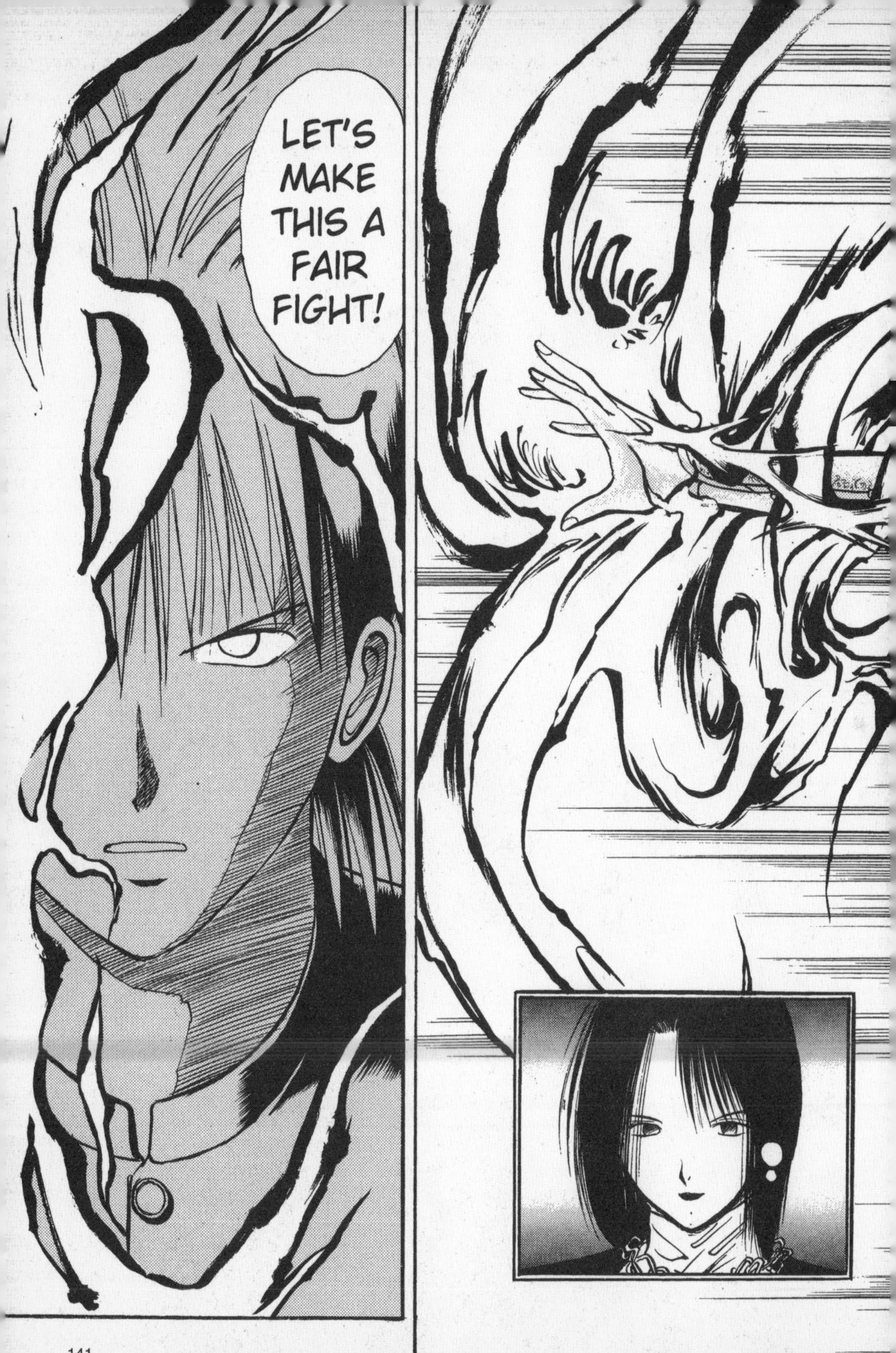
LET'S MAKE THIS A FAIR FIGHT!

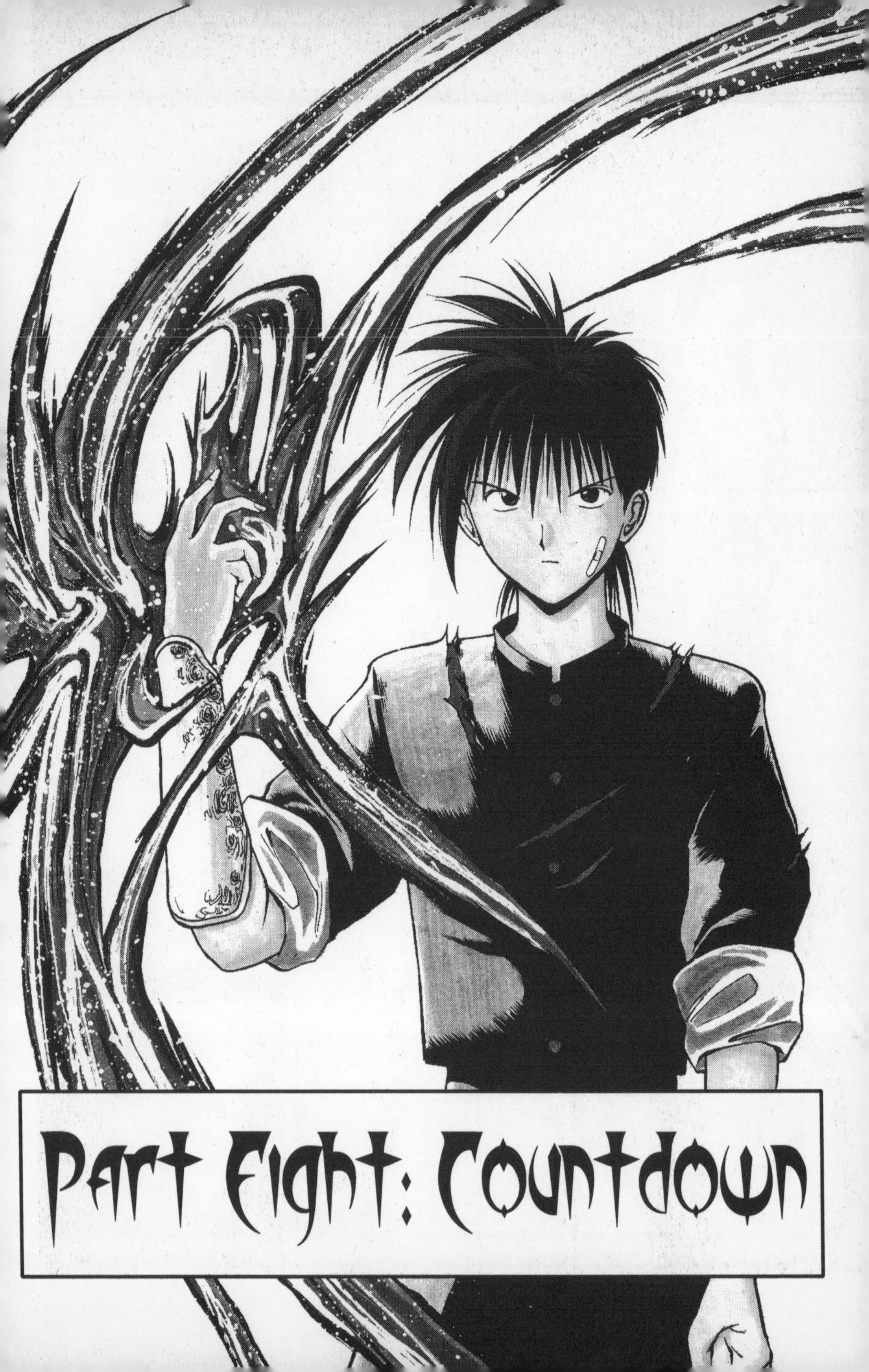
Part Eight: Countdown

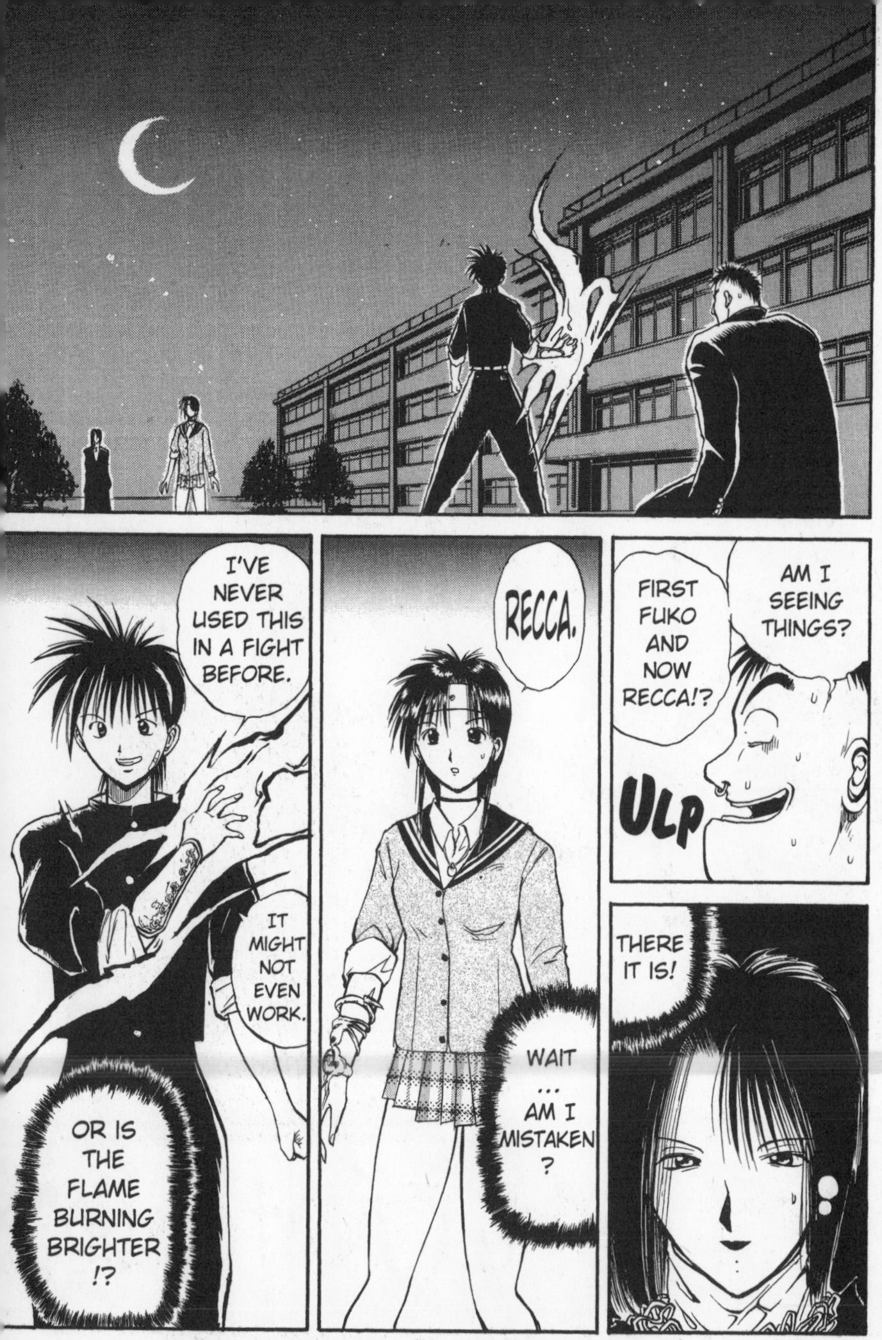
AM I SEEING THINGS?
FIRST FUKO AND NOW RECCA!?
ULP
THERE IT IS!
RECCA.
WAIT ... AM I MISTAKEN?
I'VE NEVER USED THIS IN A FIGHT BEFORE.
IT MIGHT NOT EVEN WORK.
OR IS THE FLAME BURNING BRIGHTER!?

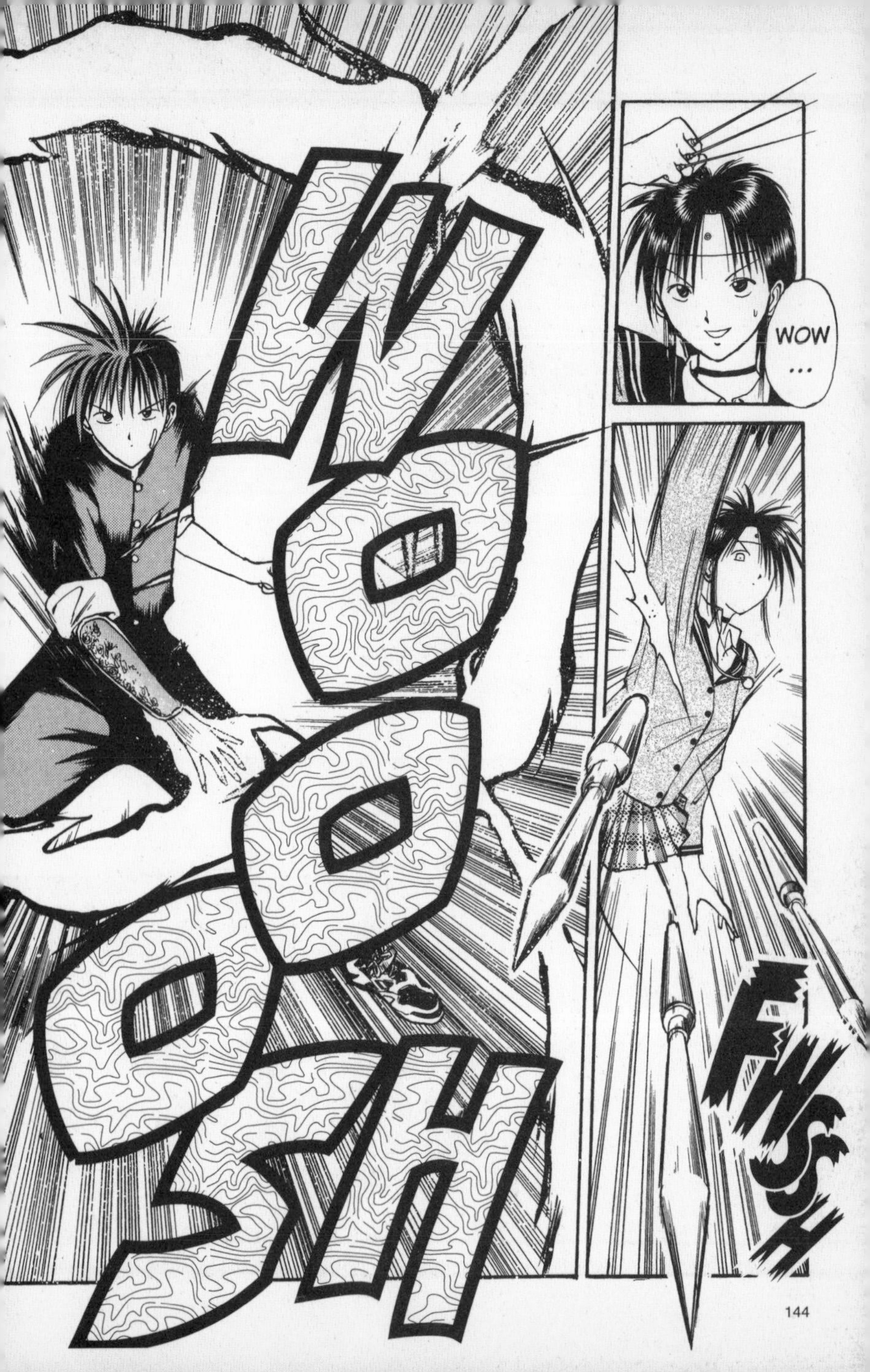
WOW ...
FWSH
WOOOSH

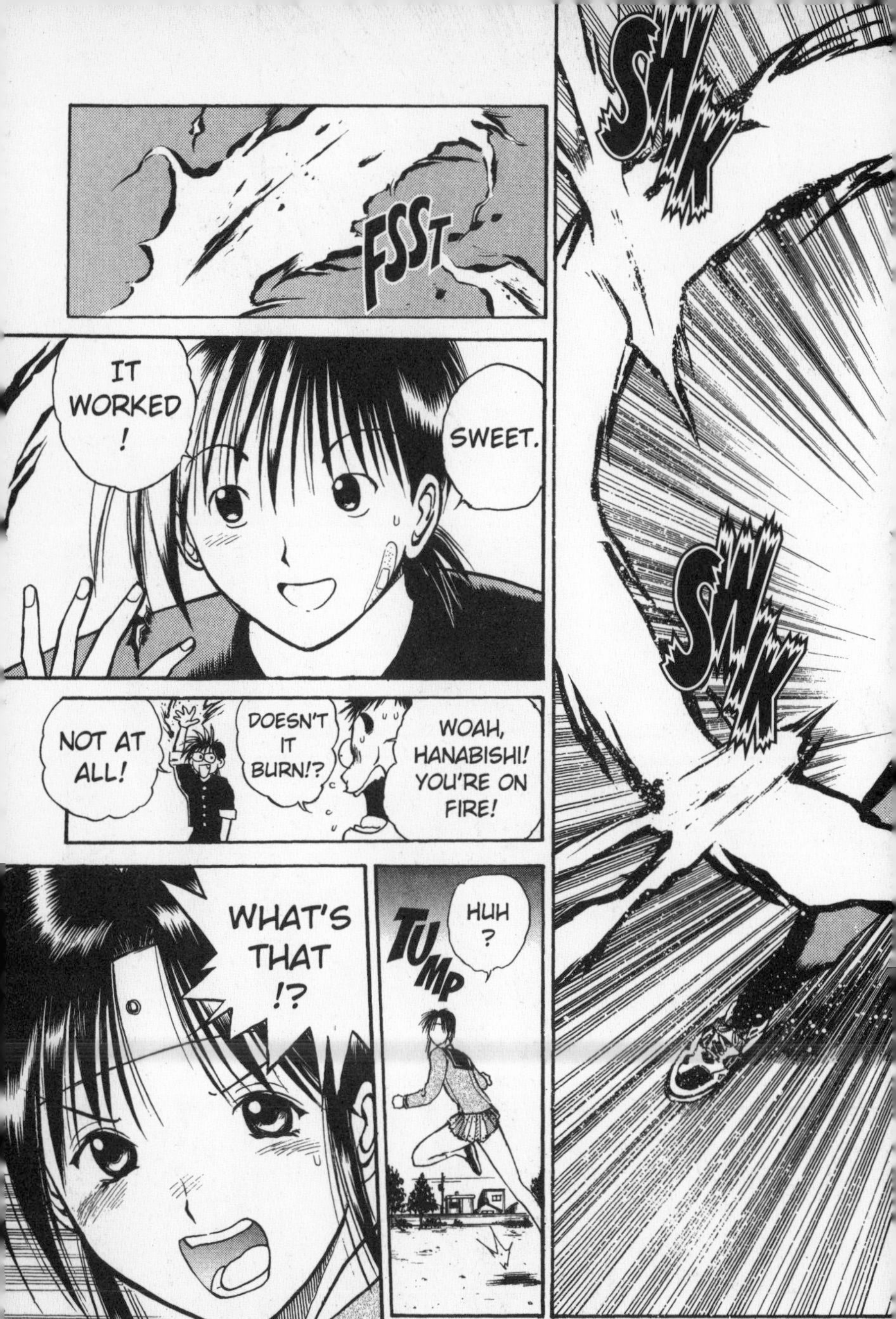
SHK
SHK
FSST
SWEET.
IT WORKED!
WOAH, HANABISHI! YOU'RE ON FIRE!
DOESN'T IT BURN!?
NOT AT ALL!
HUH?
TUMP
WHAT'S THAT!?

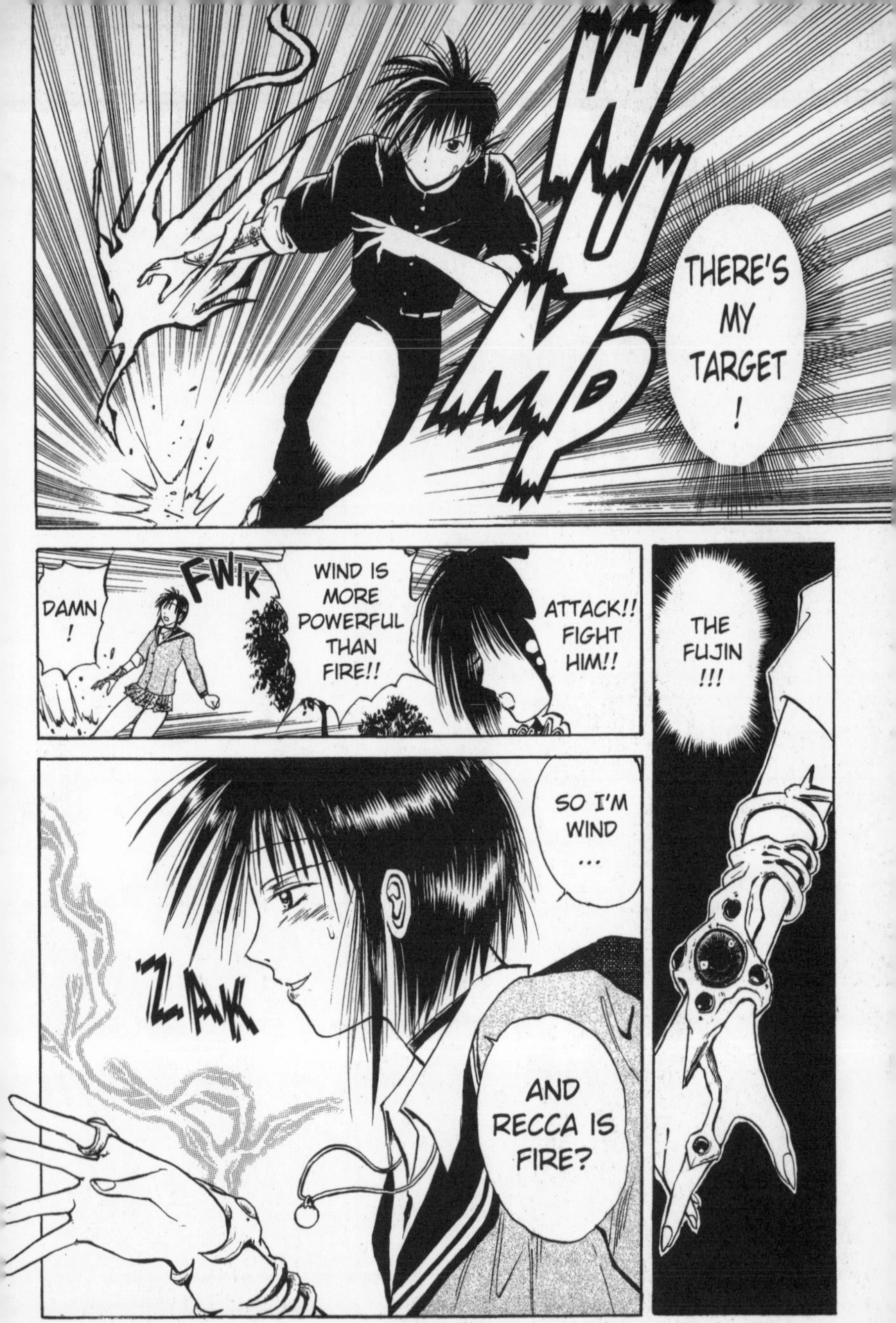
WHUMP
THERE'S MY TARGET!
THE FUJIN!!!
ATTACK!! FIGHT HIM!!
WIND IS MORE POWERFUL THAN FIRE!!
FWIK
DAMN!
SO I'M WIND...
AND RECCA IS FIRE?
ZAK

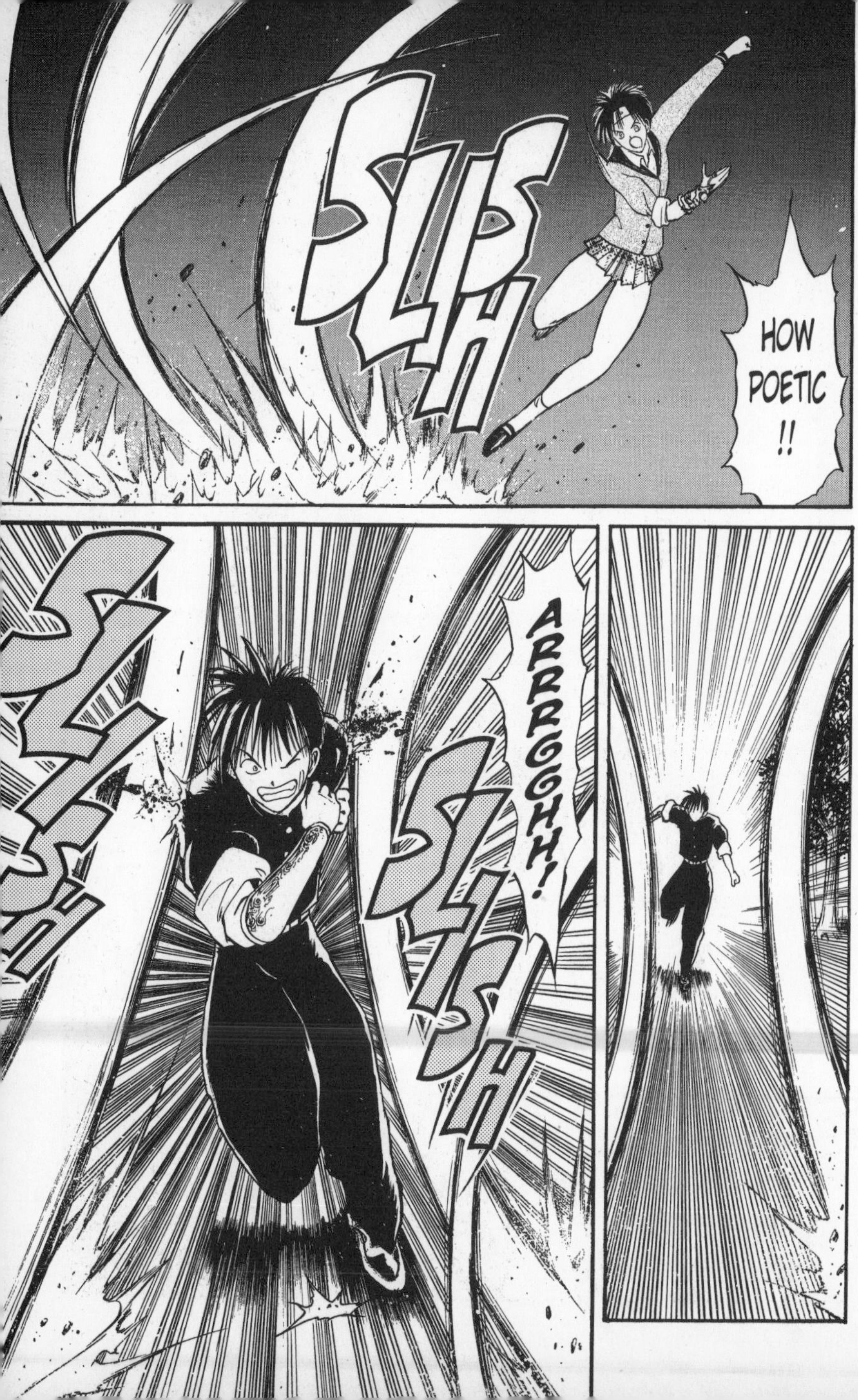
HOW POETIC !!
SLISH
ARRRGGHH!
SLISH
SLISH

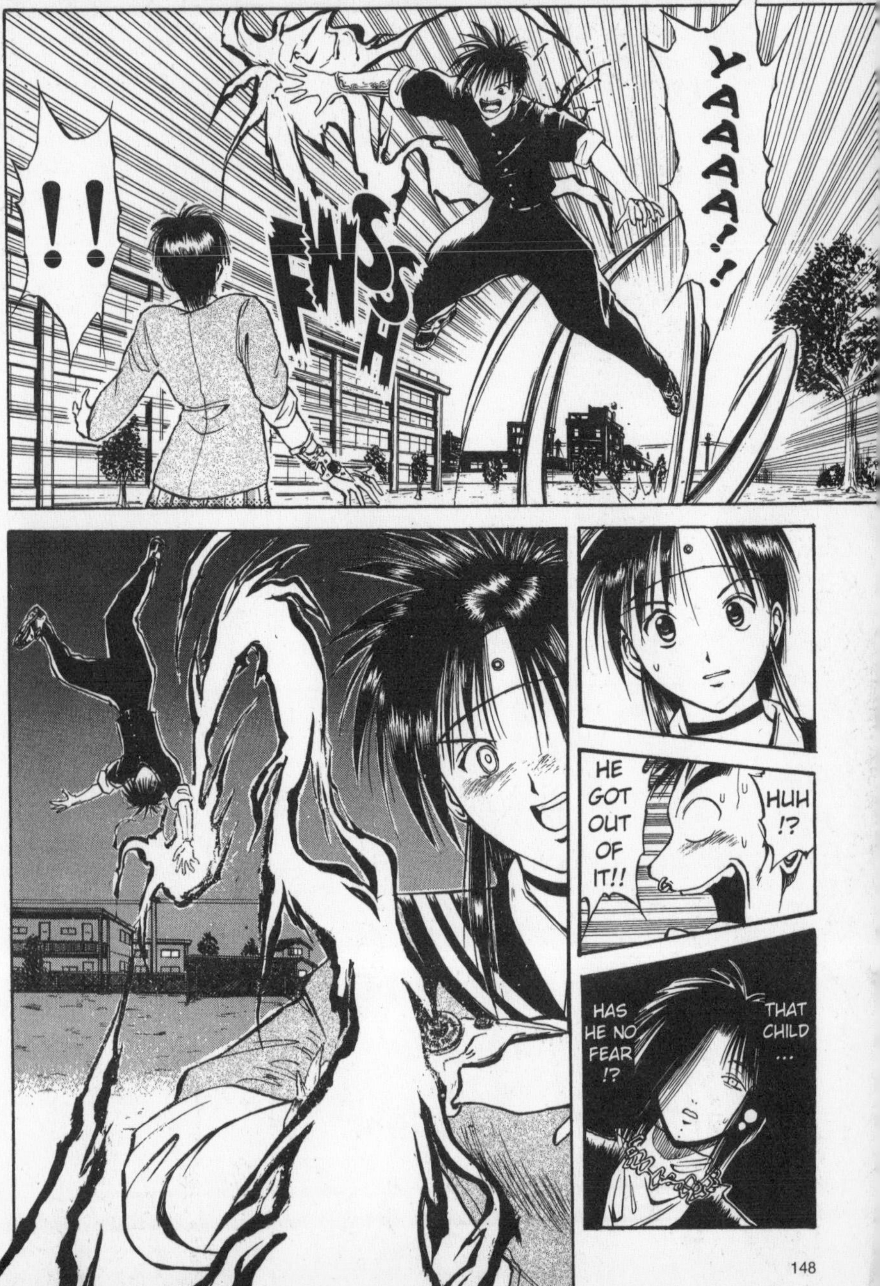
YAAAAA!!
FWSSH
!!
HUH!?
HE GOT OUT OF IT!!
THAT CHILD ...
HAS HE NO FEAR!?

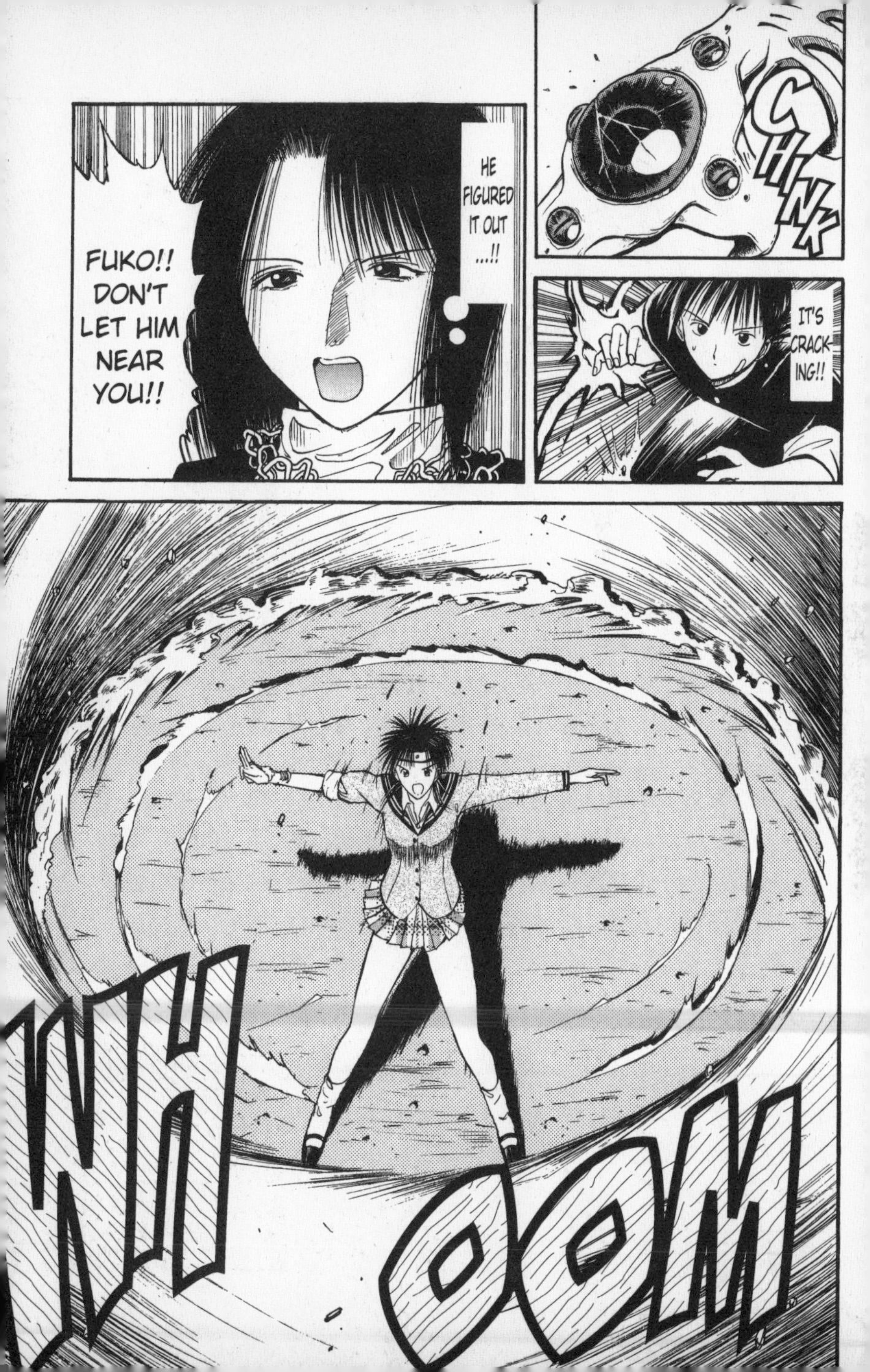
CHINK
IT'S CRACKING!!
HE FIGURED IT OUT ...!!
FUKO!! DON'T LET HIM NEAR YOU!!
WHOOM

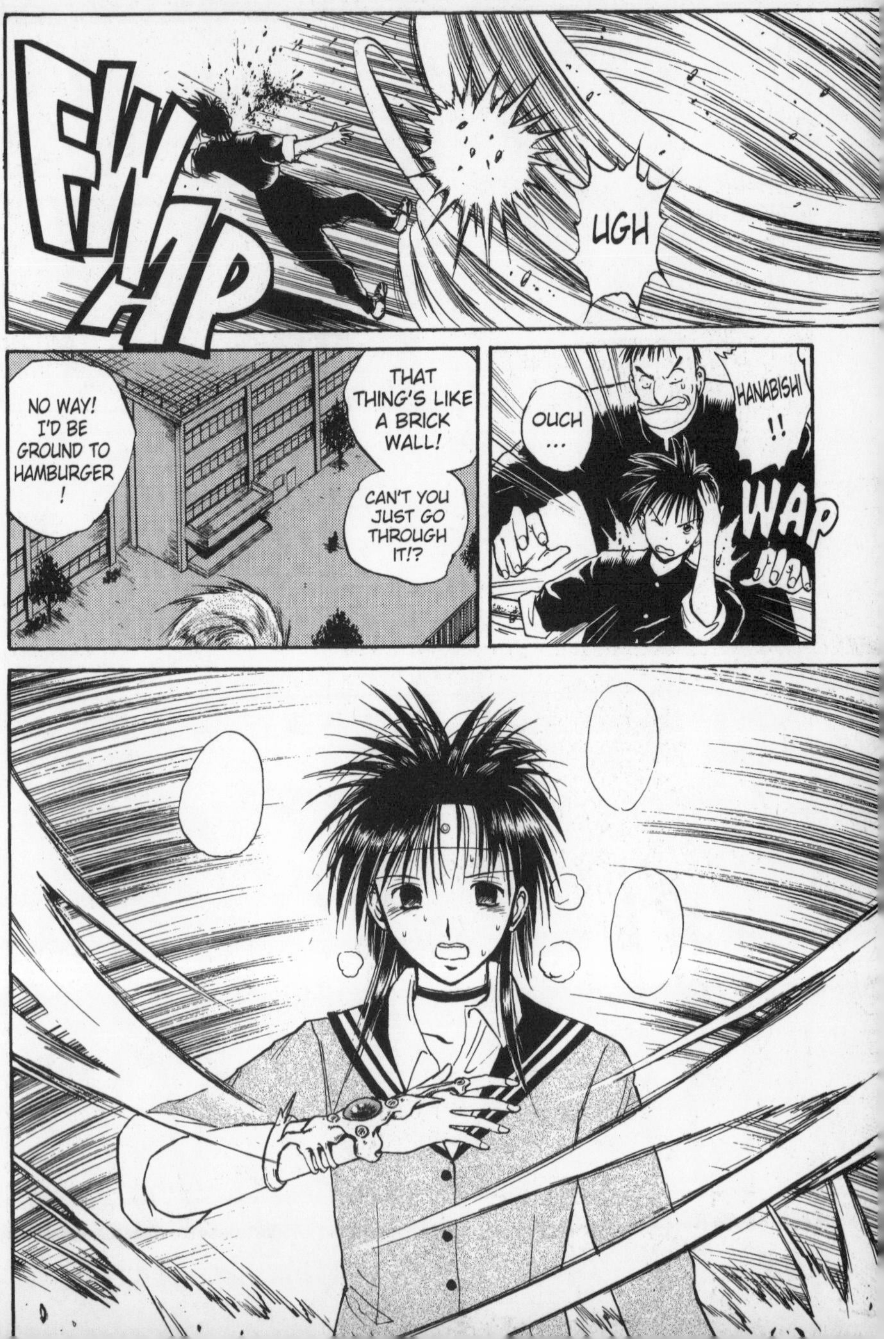
FWAP
UGH
HANABISHI !!
OUCH ...
WAP
THAT THING'S LIKE A BRICK WALL!
CAN'T YOU JUST GO THROUGH IT!?
NO WAY! I'D BE GROUND TO HAMBURGER !

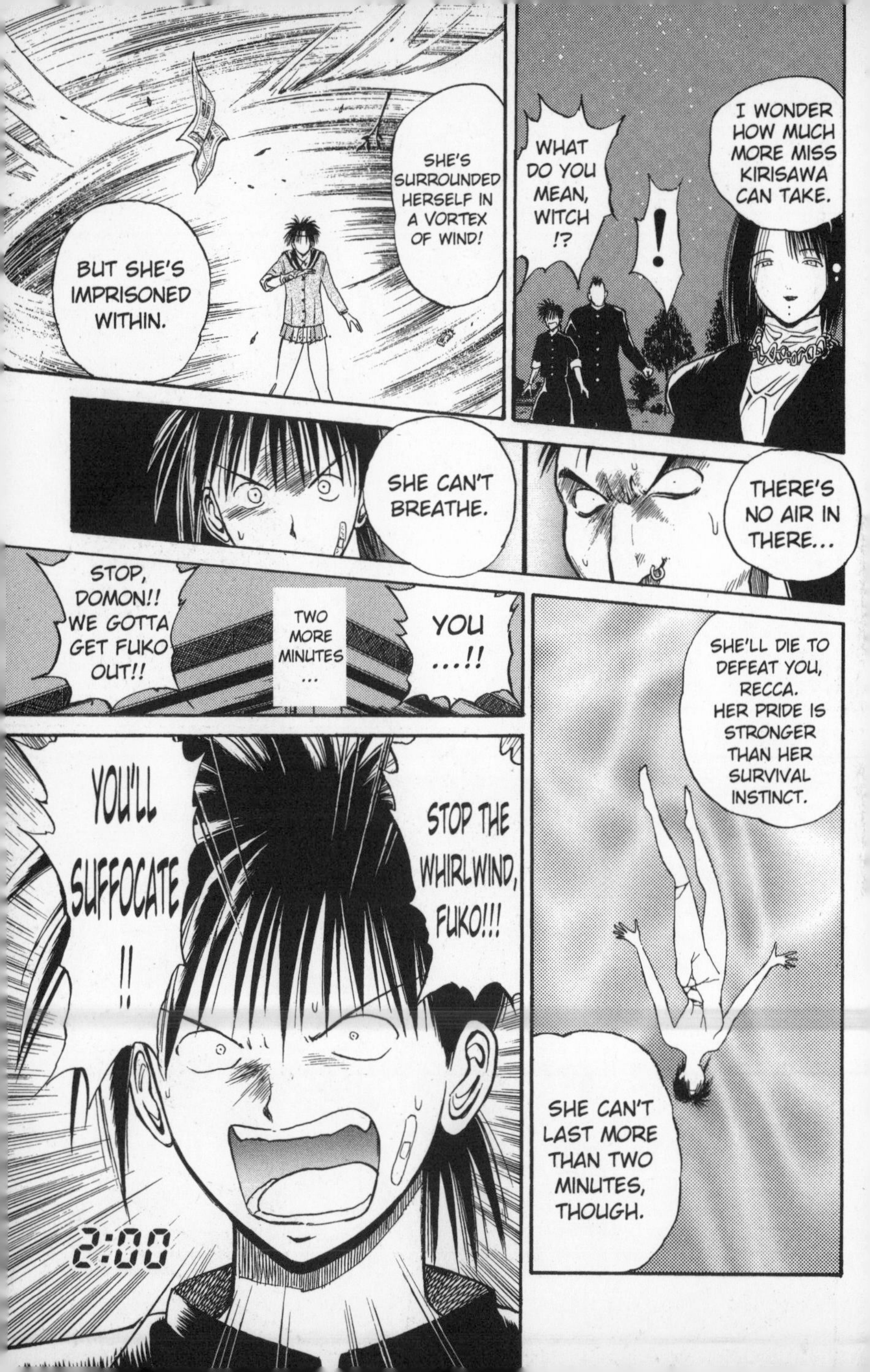
I WONDER HOW MUCH MORE MISS KIRISAWA CAN TAKE.
!
WHAT DO YOU MEAN, WITCH !?
SHE'S SURROUNDED HERSELF IN A VORTEX OF WIND!
BUT SHE'S IMPRISONED WITHIN.
THERE'S NO AIR IN THERE...
SHE CAN'T BREATHE.
SHE'LL DIE TO DEFEAT YOU, RECCA. HER PRIDE IS STRONGER THAN HER SURVIVAL INSTINCT.
SHE CAN'T LAST MORE THAN TWO MINUTES, THOUGH.
YOU ...!!
TWO MORE MINUTES ...
STOP, DOMON!! WE GOTTA GET FUKO OUT!!
STOP THE WHIRLWIND, FUKO!!!
YOU'LL SUFFOCATE !!
2:00

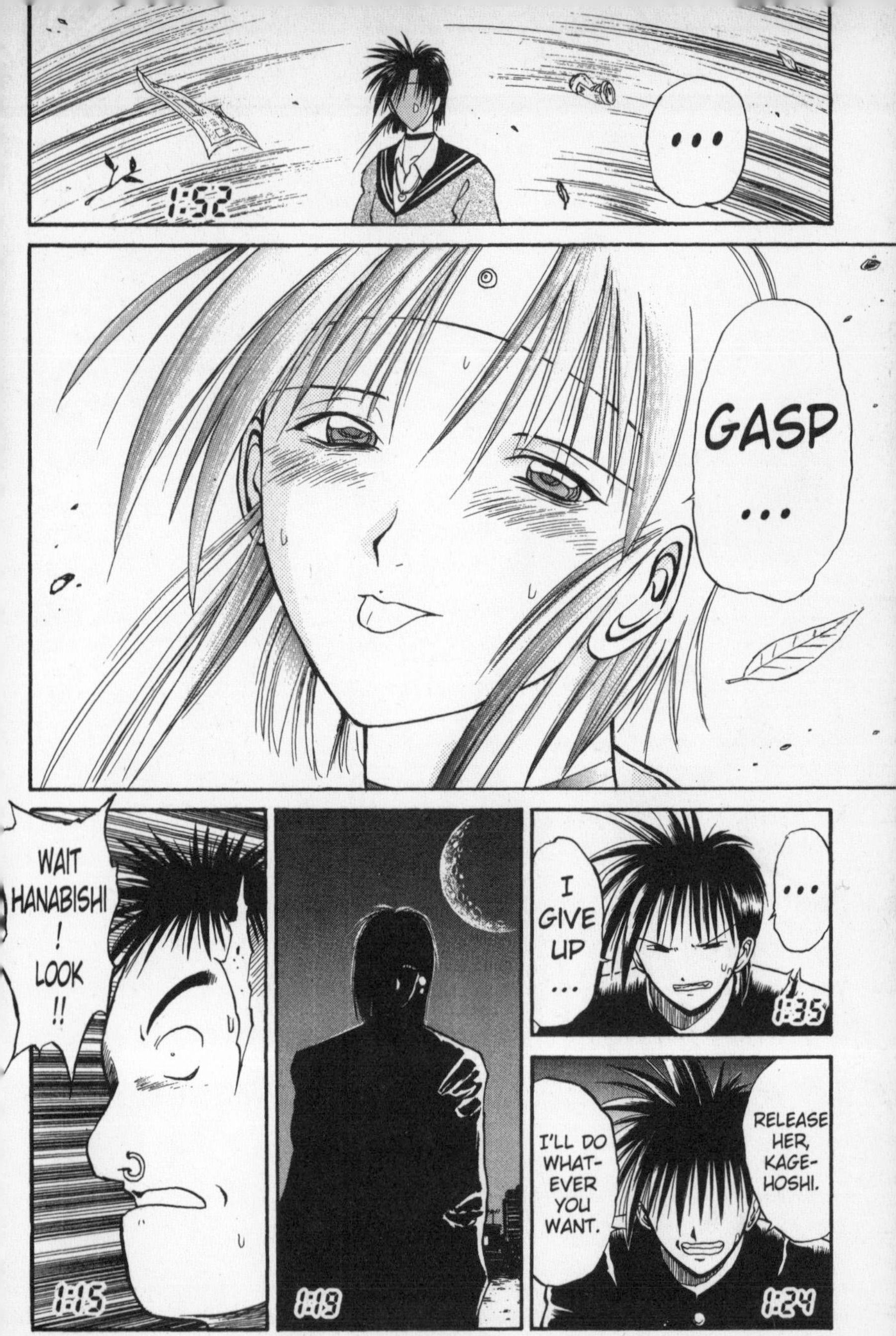
...
1:52
GASP ...
...
I GIVE UP ...
1:35
RELEASE HER, KAGE-HOSHI.
I'LL DO WHATEVER YOU WANT.
1:24
1:19
WAIT HANABISHI! LOOK!!
1:15

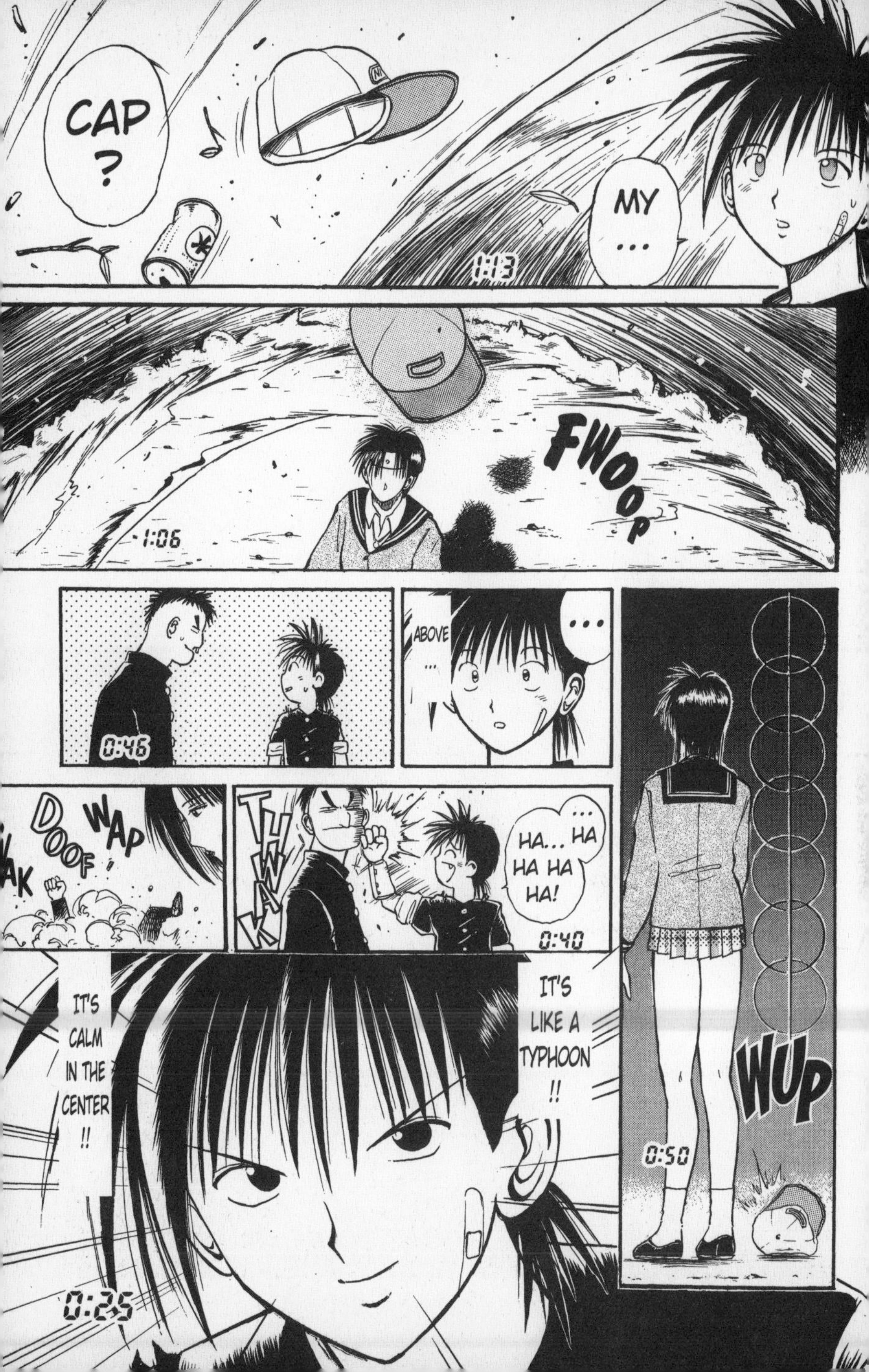
MY ...
CAP ?
1:13
FWOOP
1:06
WUP
0:50
...
ABOVE ...
0:46
... HA... HA HA HA HA!
THWAK
0:40
WAP
DOOF
WAK
IT'S LIKE A TYPHOON !!
IT'S CALM IN THE CENTER !!
0:25

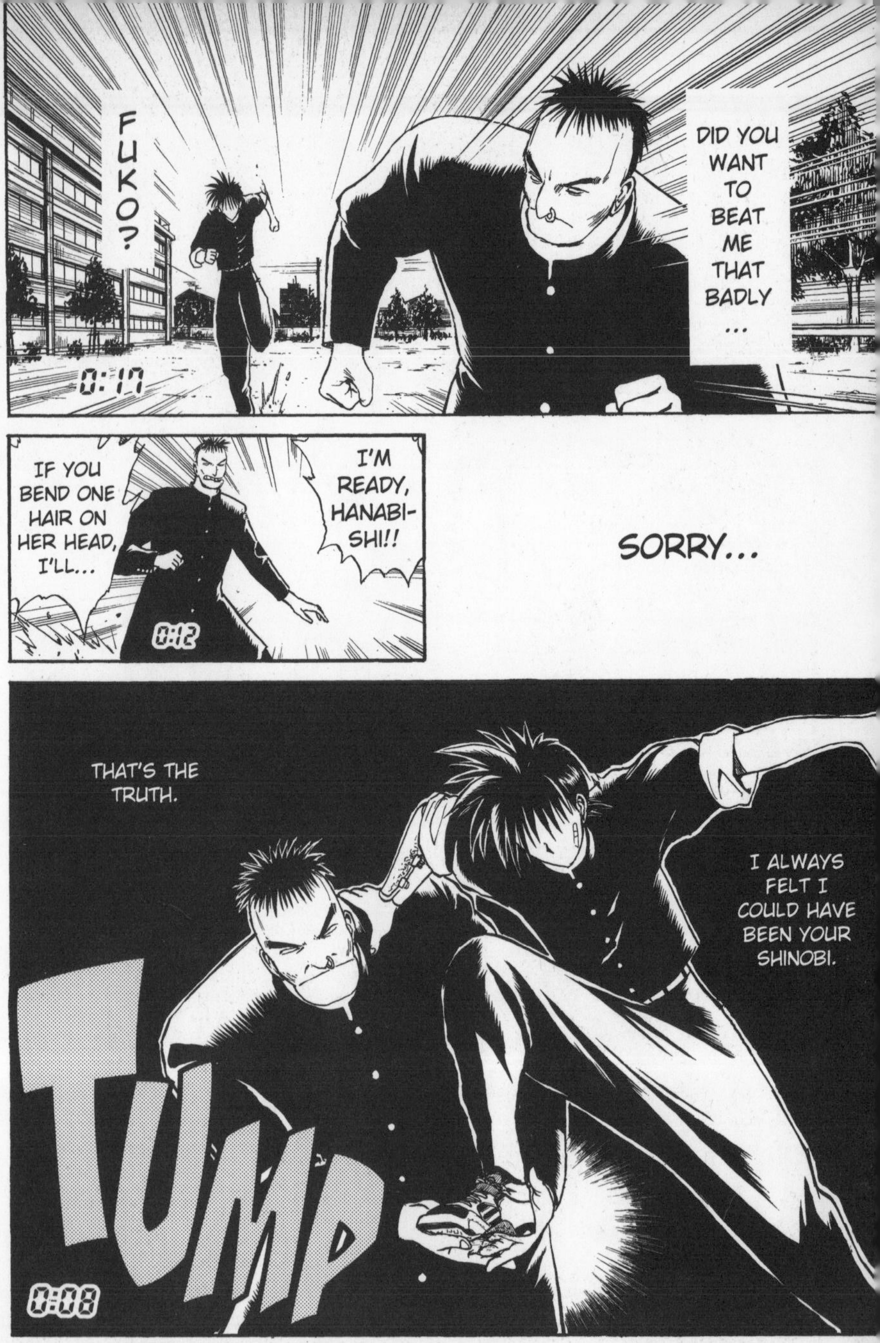
DID YOU WANT TO BEAT ME THAT BADLY ...
FUKO?
0:17
SORRY...
I'M READY, HANABISHI!!
IF YOU BEND ONE HAIR ON HER HEAD, I'LL...
0:12
I ALWAYS FELT I COULD HAVE BEEN YOUR SHINOBI.
THAT'S THE TRUTH.
TUMP
0:08

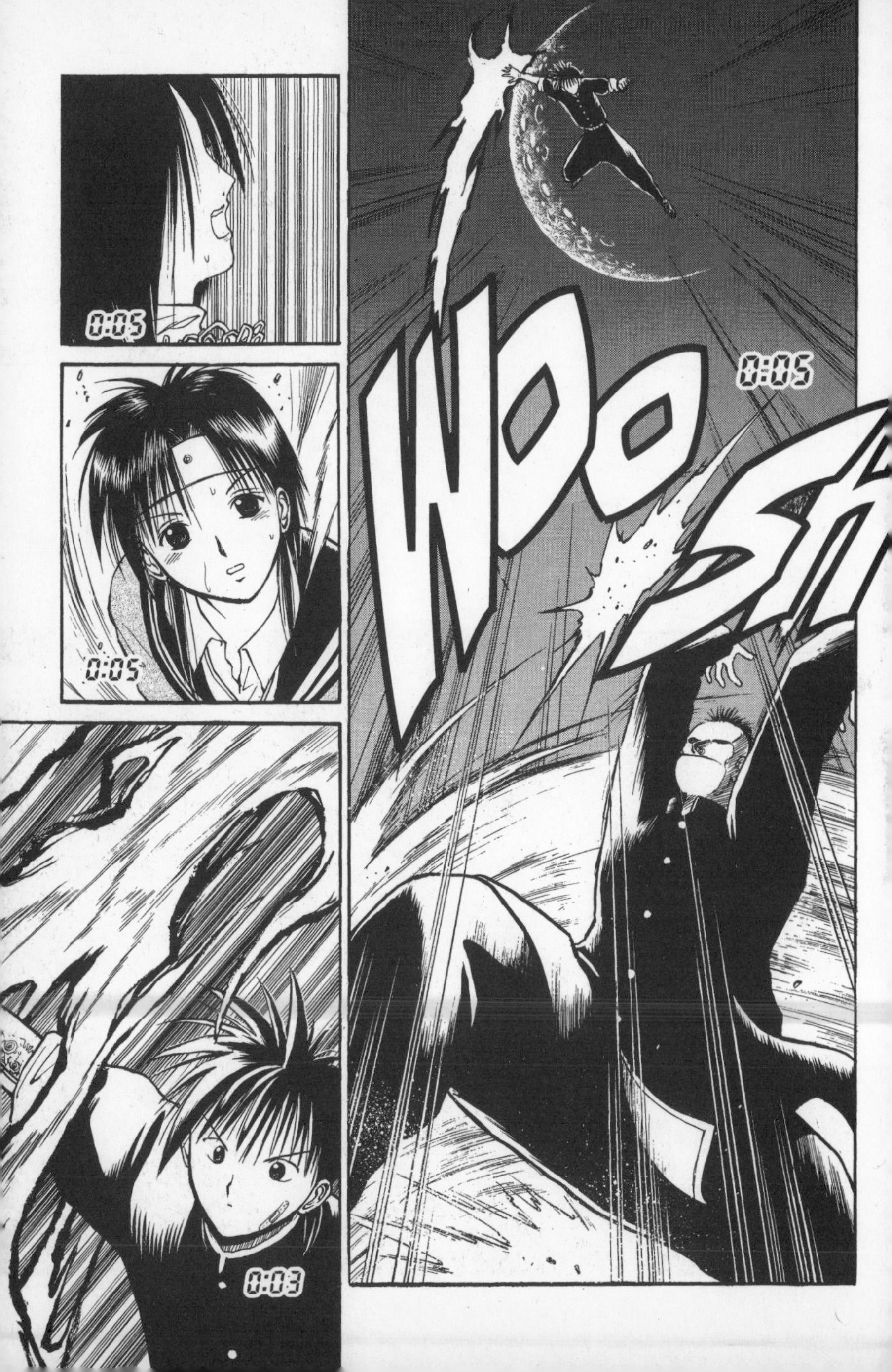
WHOOSH
0:05
0:05
0:05
0:03

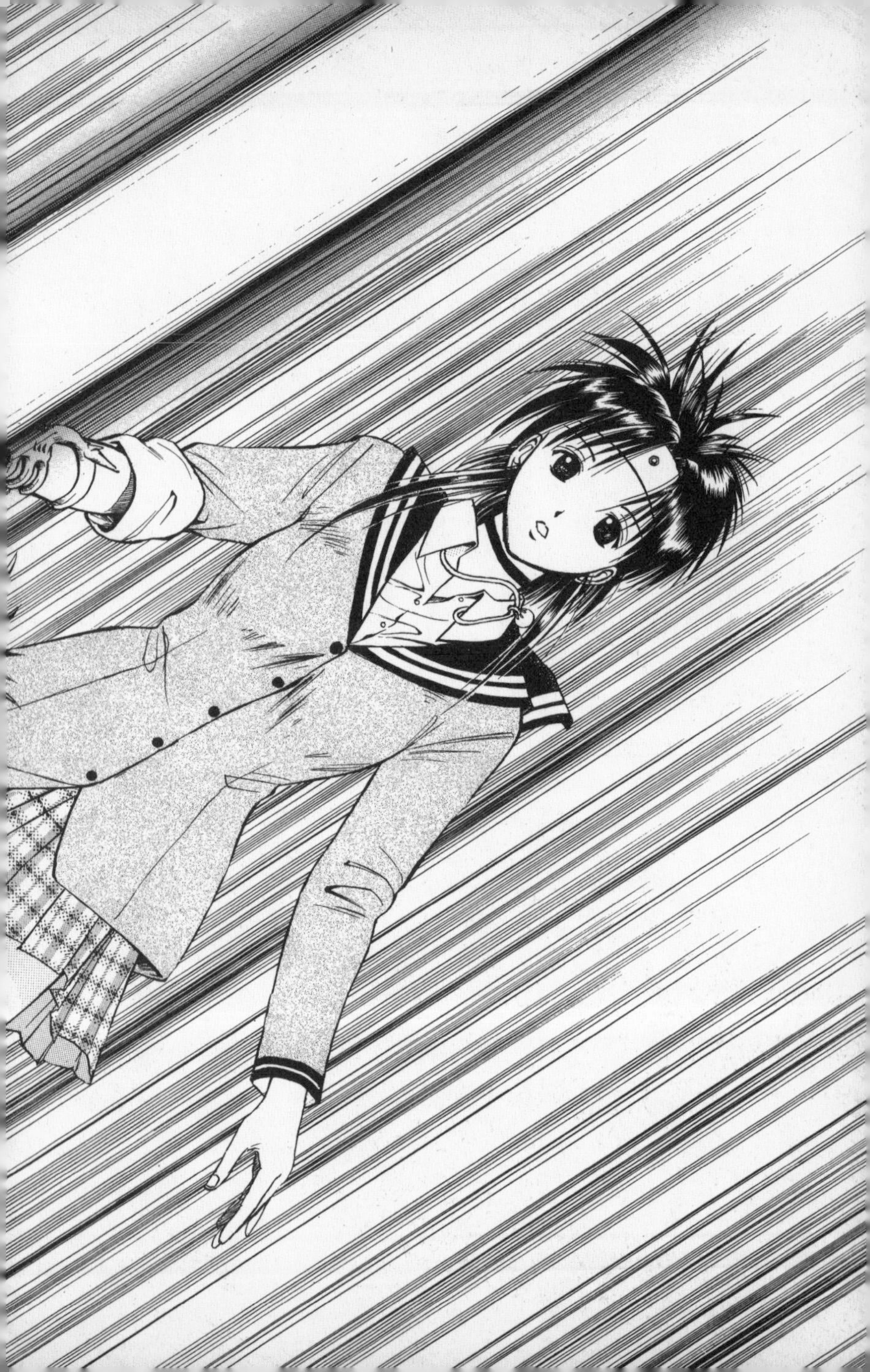

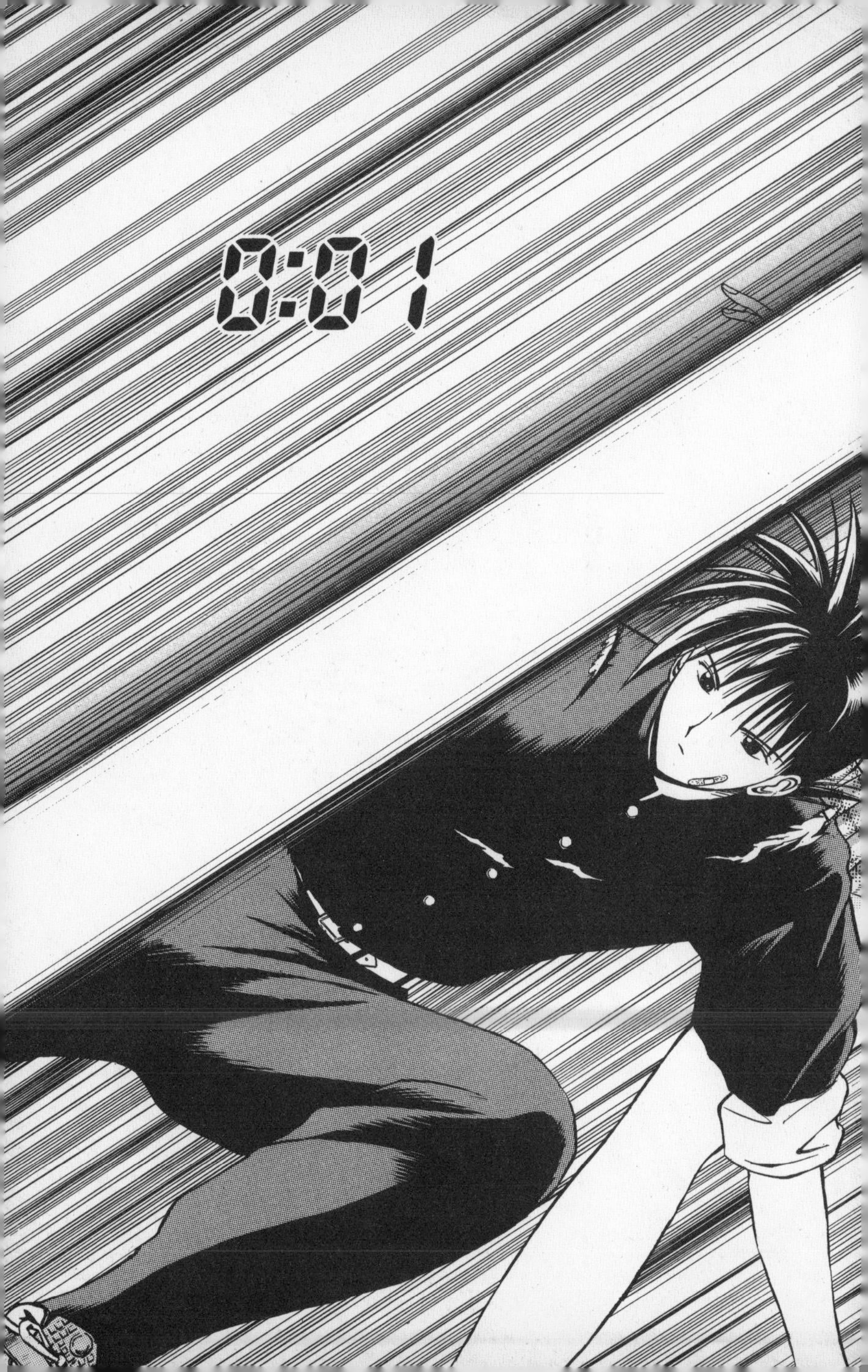
0:01

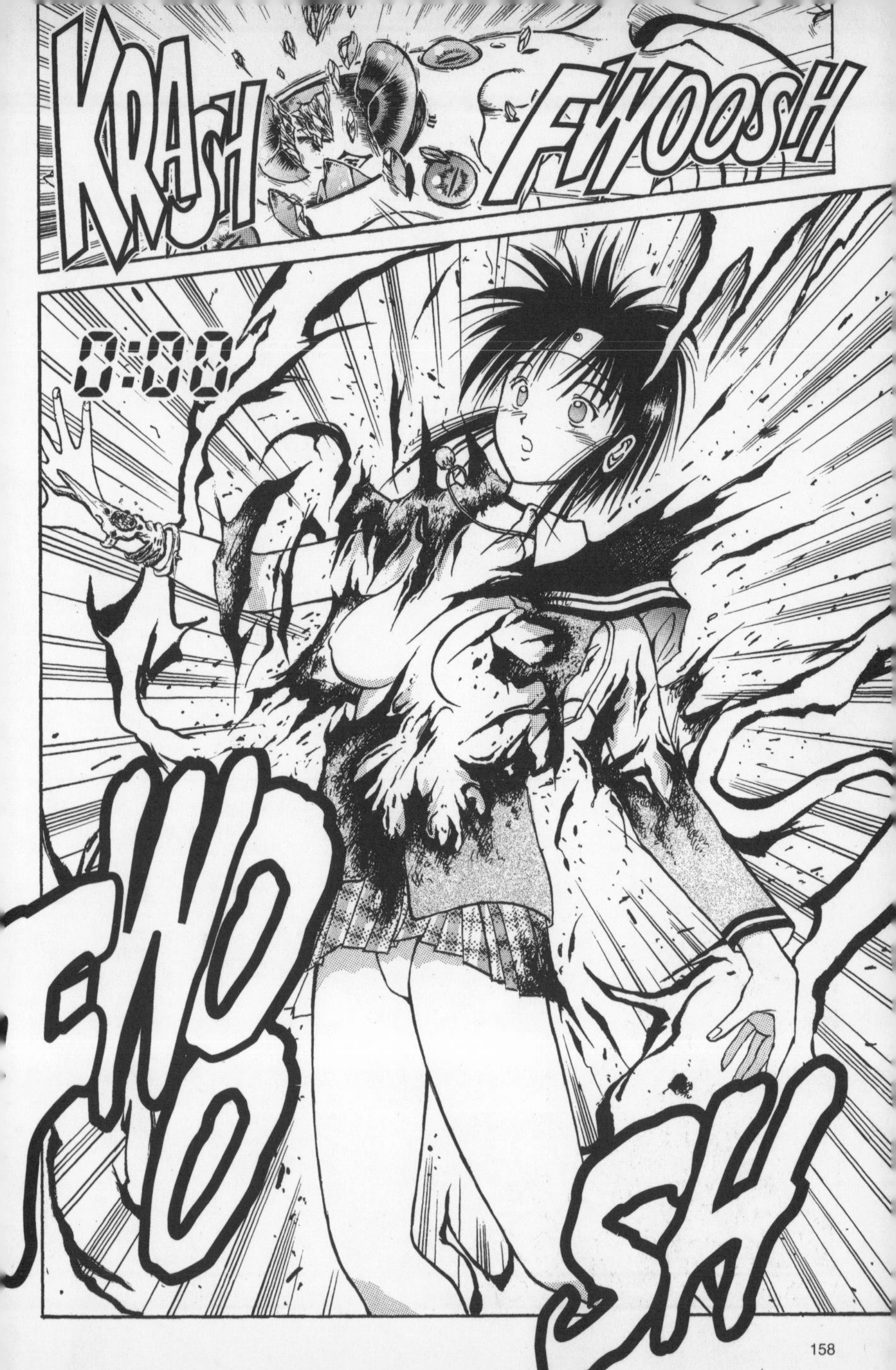
FWOOSH
KRASH
0:00
FWOOSH

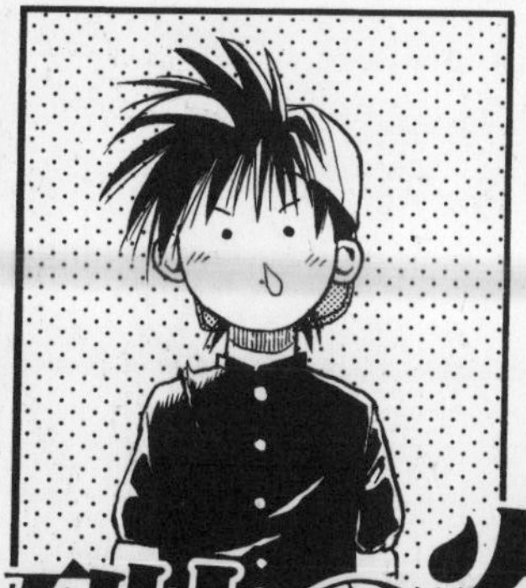

烈火（れっか）の炎（ほのお）

~FLAME OF RECCA~

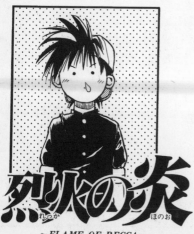

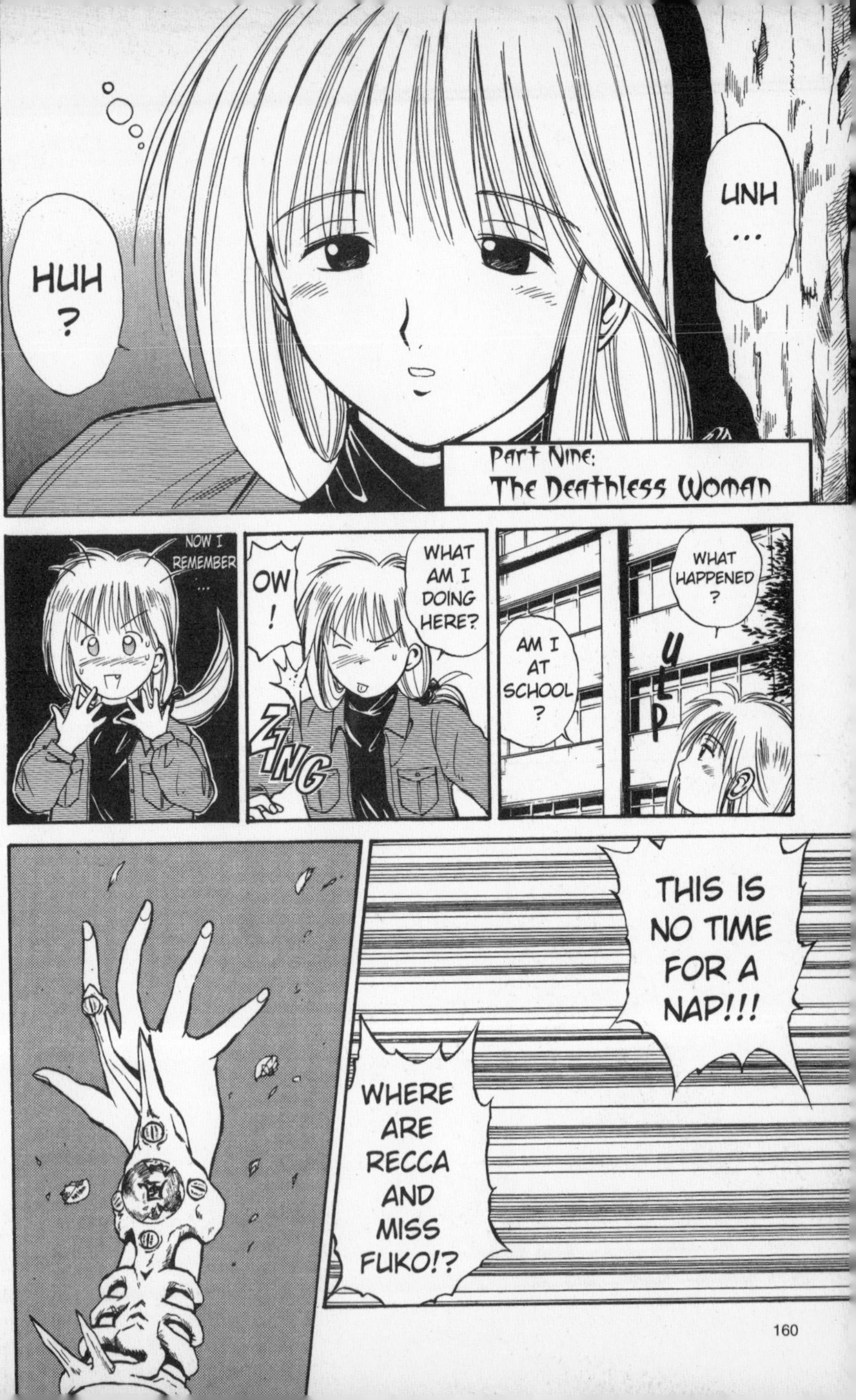
UNH ...
HUH ?
Part Nine:
The Deathless Woman
WHAT HAPPENED ?
AM I AT SCHOOL ?
ULP
WHAT AM I DOING HERE?
OW !
ZING
NOW I REMEMBER ...
THIS IS NO TIME FOR A NAP!!!
WHERE ARE RECCA AND MISS FUKO!?

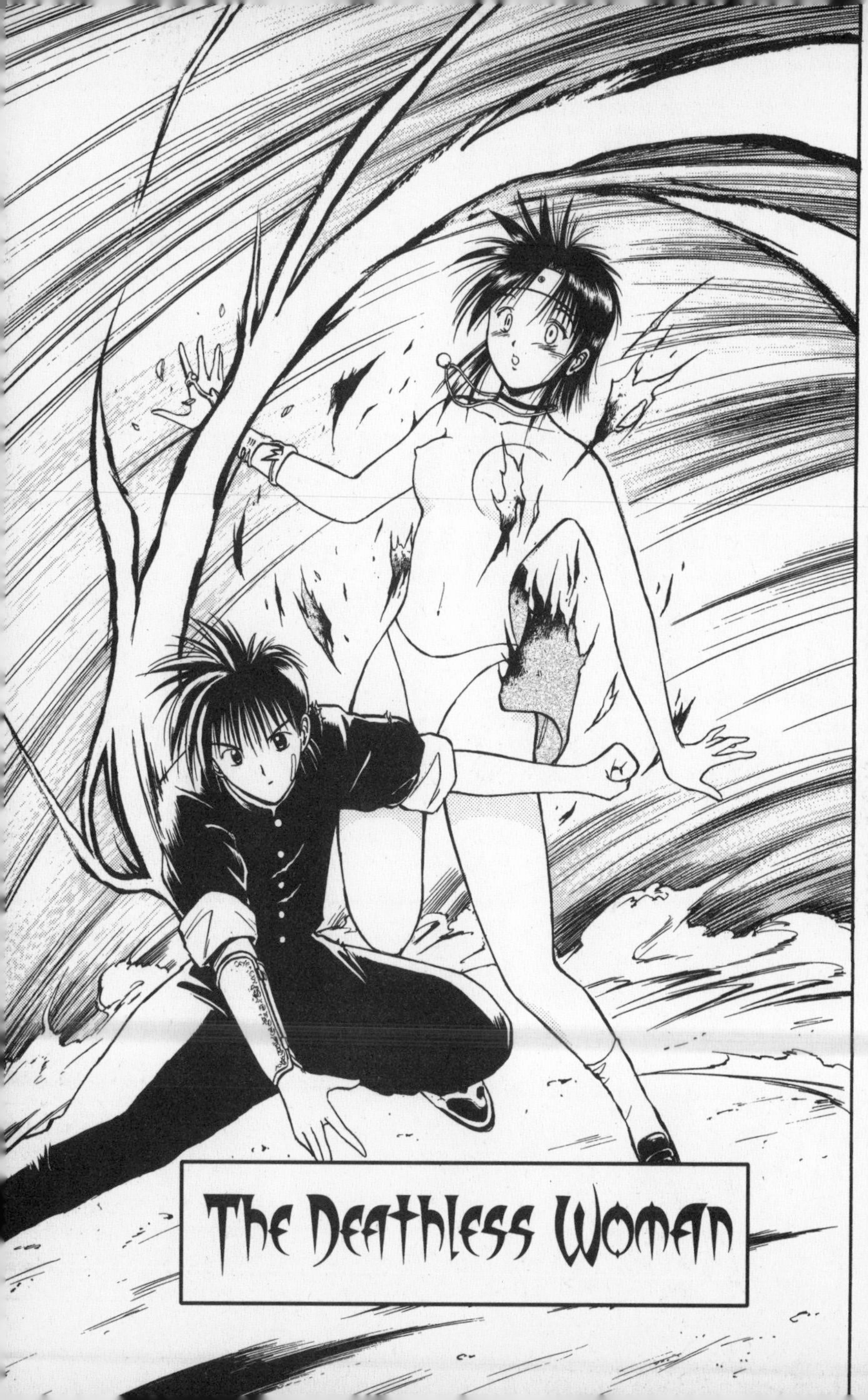
The Deathless Woman

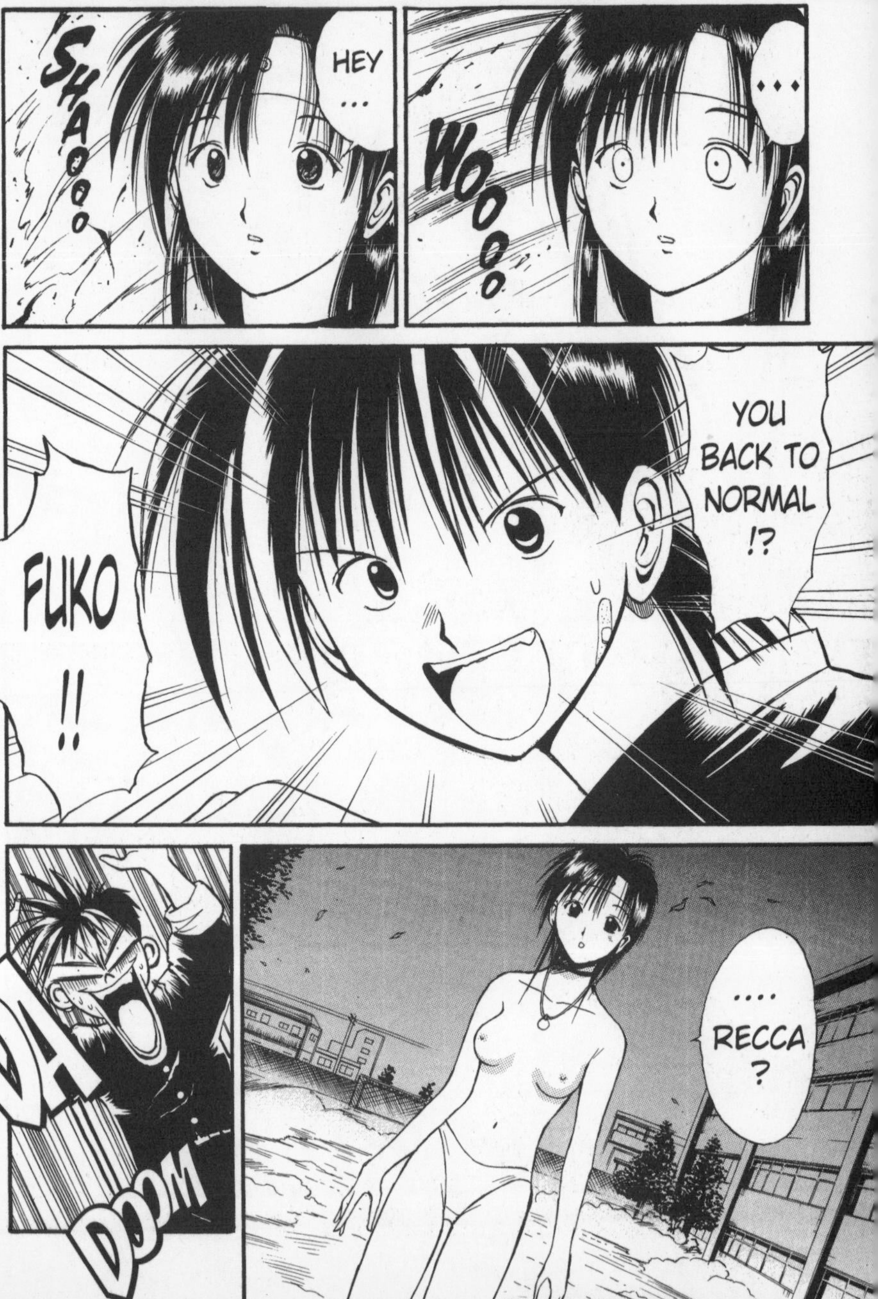
...
WOOOOOO
HEY ...
SHAOOOO
YOU BACK TO NORMAL !?
FUKO !!
.... RECCA ?
DA
DOOM

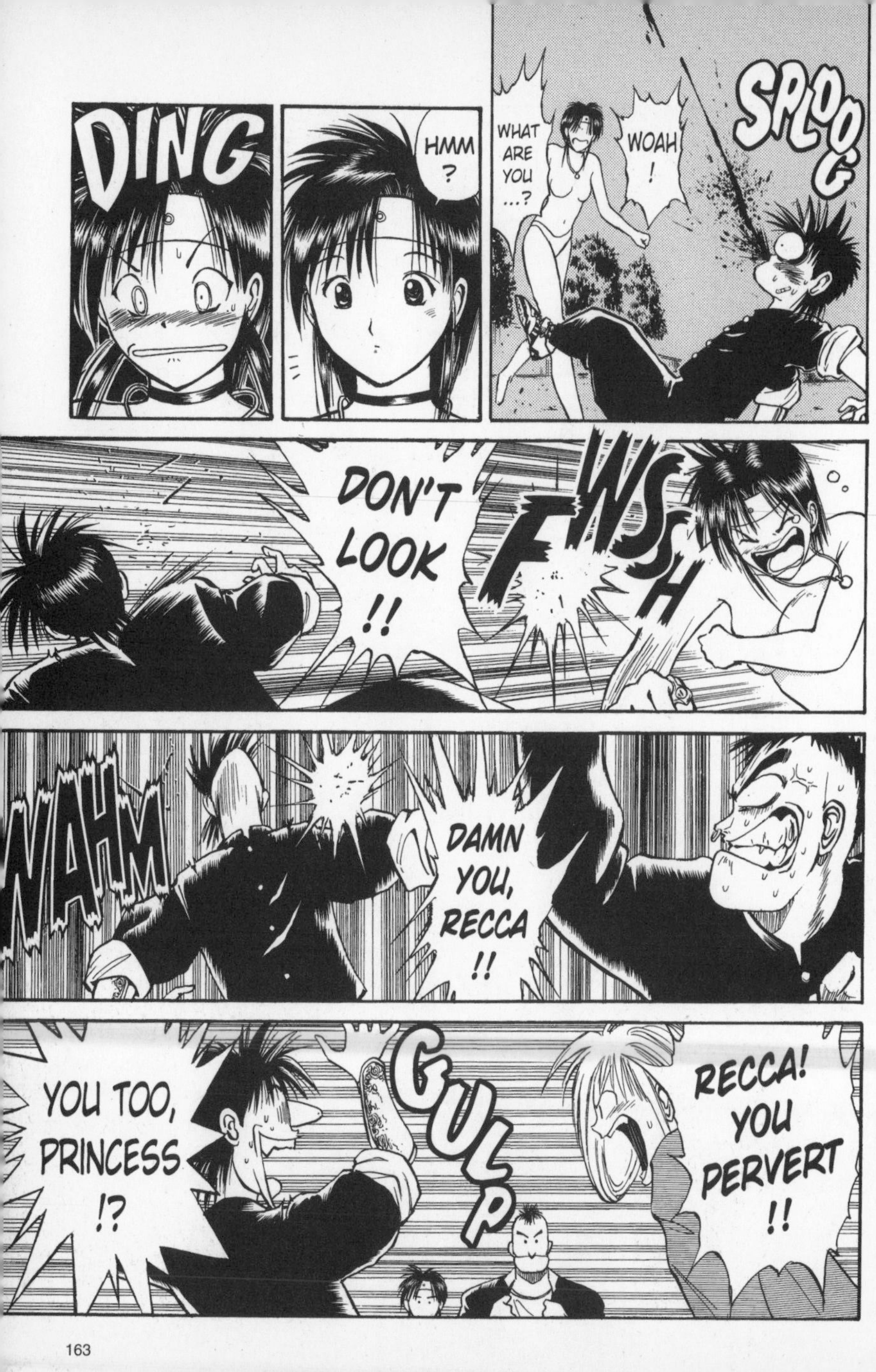
SPLOOG
WOAH!
WHAT ARE YOU ...?
HMM ?
DING
FWSH
DON'T LOOK !!
DAMN YOU, RECCA !!
WAHM
RECCA! YOU PERVERT !!
GULP
YOU TOO, PRINCESS !?

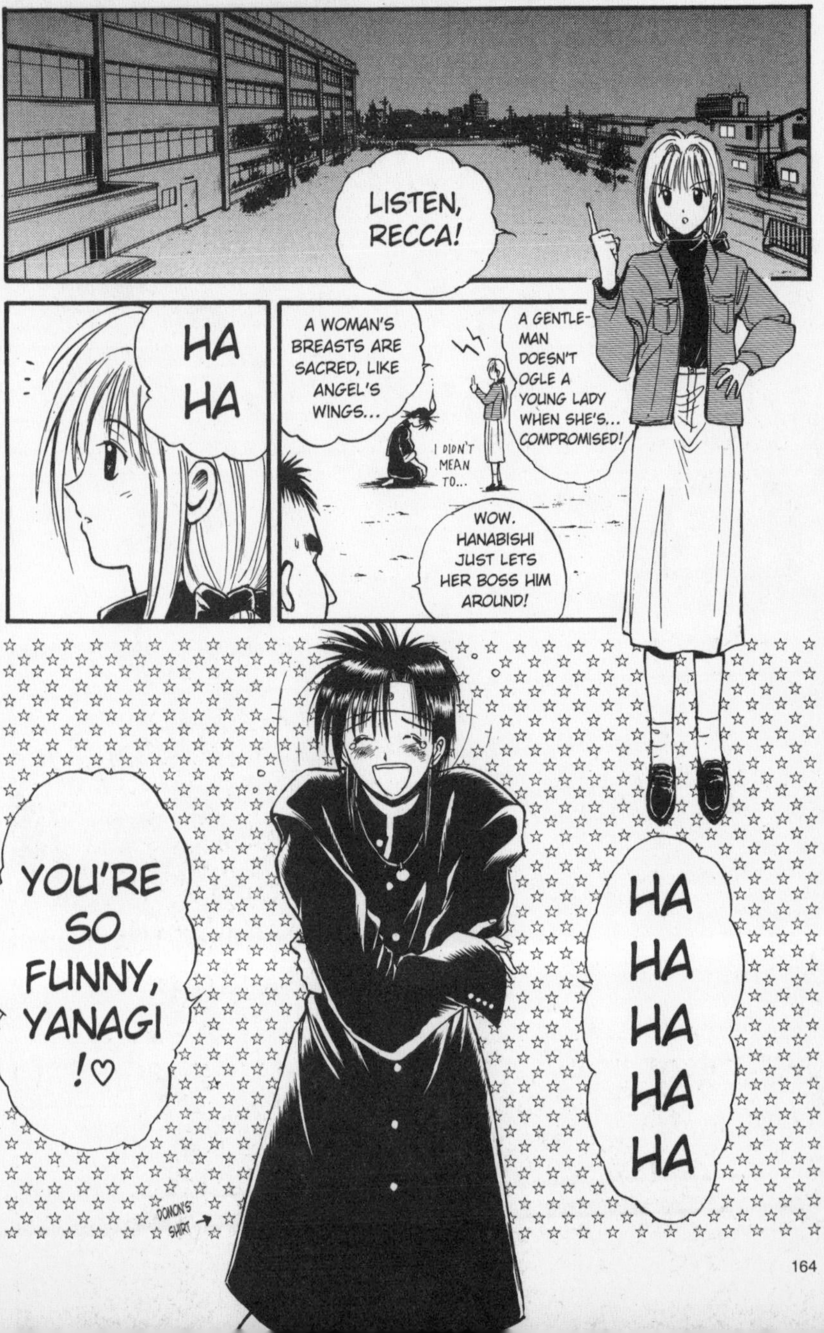
LISTEN, RECCA!
A GENTLEMAN DOESN'T OGLE A YOUNG LADY WHEN SHE'S... COMPROMISED!
A WOMAN'S BREASTS ARE SACRED, LIKE ANGEL'S WINGS...
I DIDN'T MEAN TO...
WOW. HANABISHI JUST LETS HER BOSS HIM AROUND!
HA HA
HA HA HA HA HA
YOU'RE SO FUNNY, YANAGI!♡
DOMON'S SHIRT

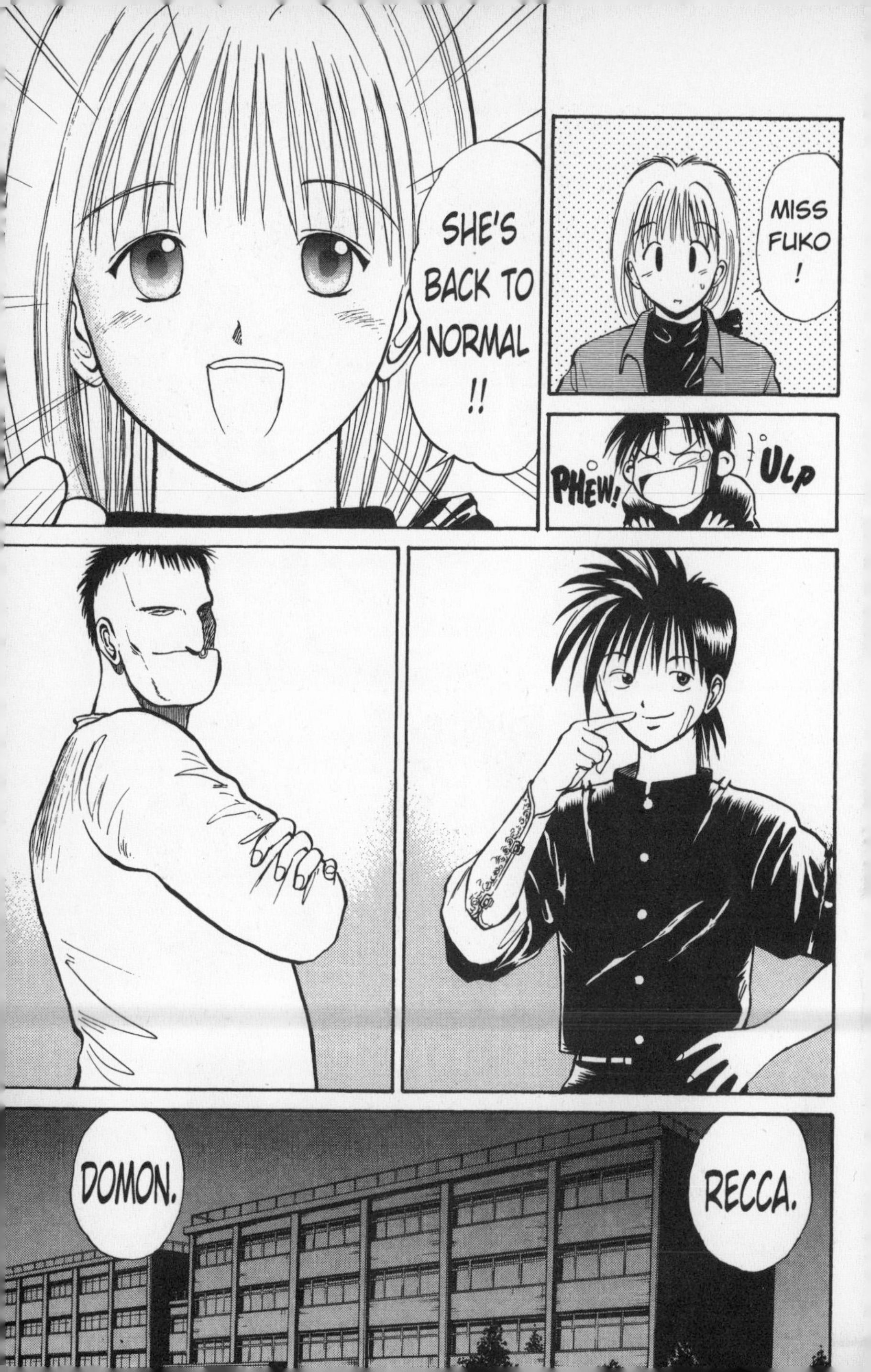
MISS FUKO!
PHEW!
ULP
SHE'S BACK TO NORMAL!!
RECCA.
DOMON.

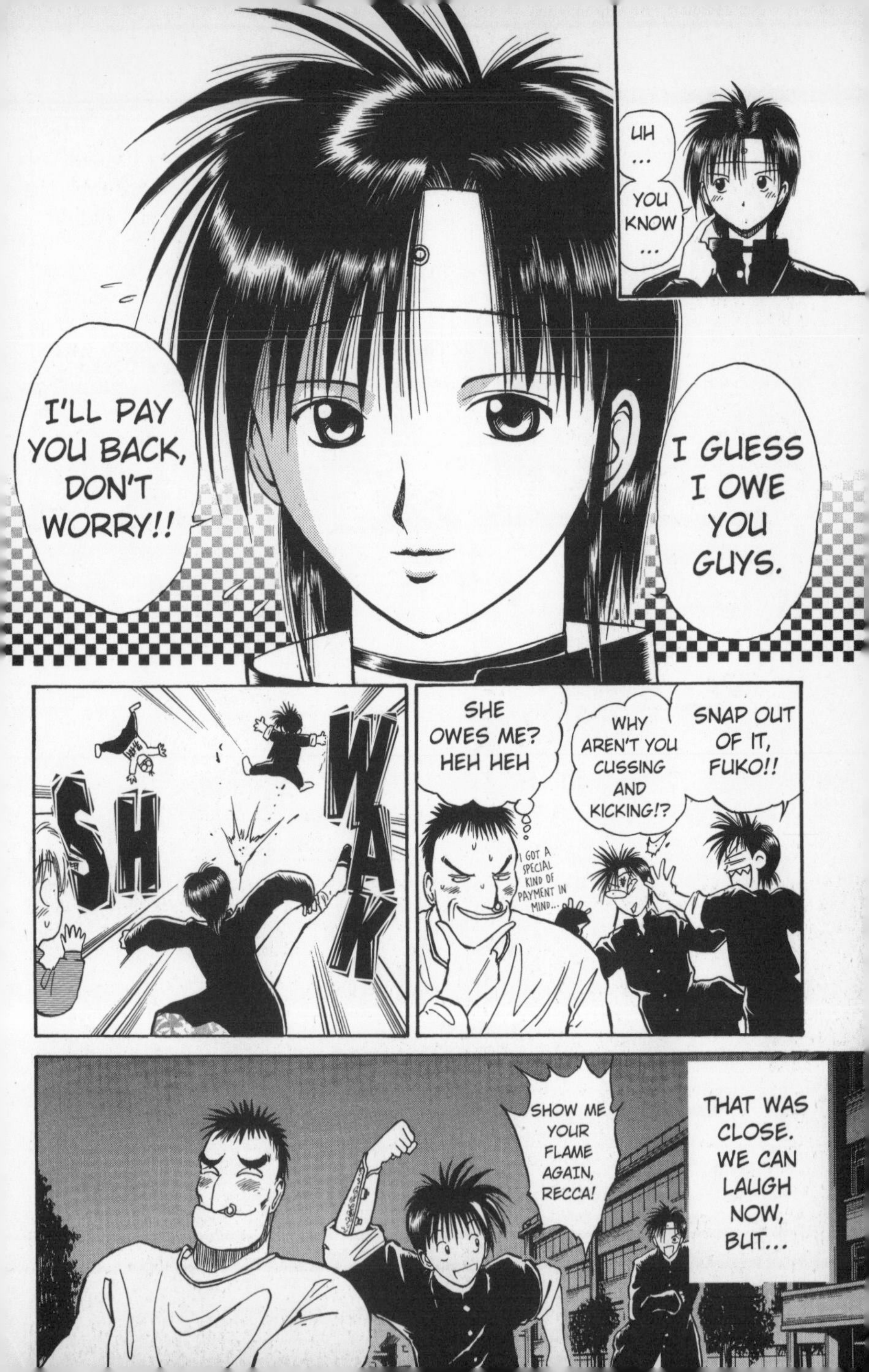
UH ... YOU KNOW ...
I GUESS I OWE YOU GUYS.
I'LL PAY YOU BACK, DON'T WORRY!!
SNAP OUT OF IT, FUKO!!
WHY AREN'T YOU CUSSING AND KICKING!?
SHE OWES ME? HEH HEH
I GOT A SPECIAL KIND OF PAYMENT IN MIND...
SH
THAT WAS CLOSE. WE CAN LAUGH NOW, BUT...
SHOW ME YOUR FLAME AGAIN, RECCA!

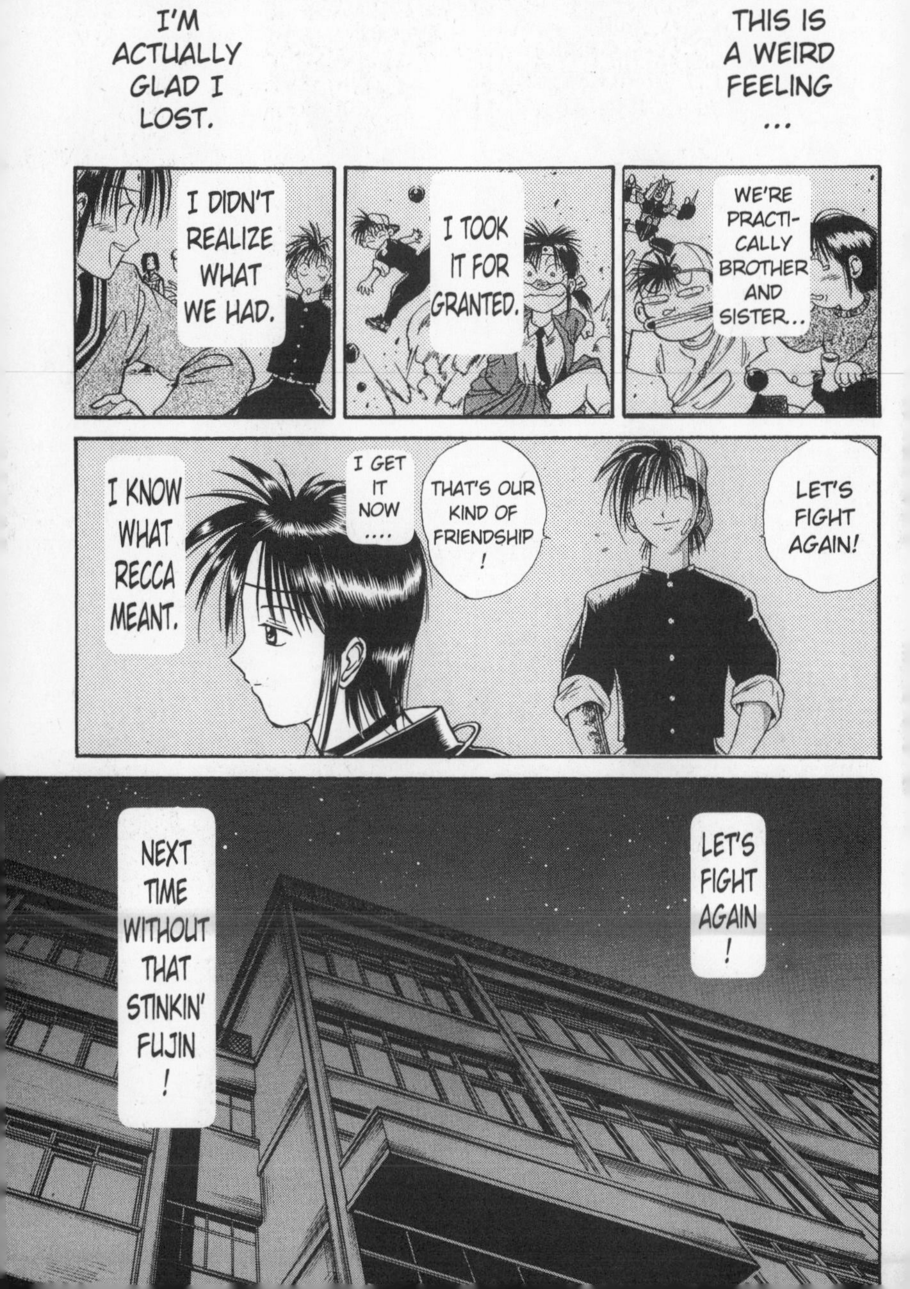
THIS IS A WEIRD FEELING ...
I'M ACTUALLY GLAD I LOST.
WE'RE PRACTI-CALLY BROTHER AND SISTER...
I TOOK IT FOR GRANTED.
I DIDN'T REALIZE WHAT WE HAD.
LET'S FIGHT AGAIN!
THAT'S OUR KIND OF FRIENDSHIP!
I GET IT NOW ....
I KNOW WHAT RECCA MEANT.
LET'S FIGHT AGAIN!
NEXT TIME WITHOUT THAT STINKIN' FUJIN!

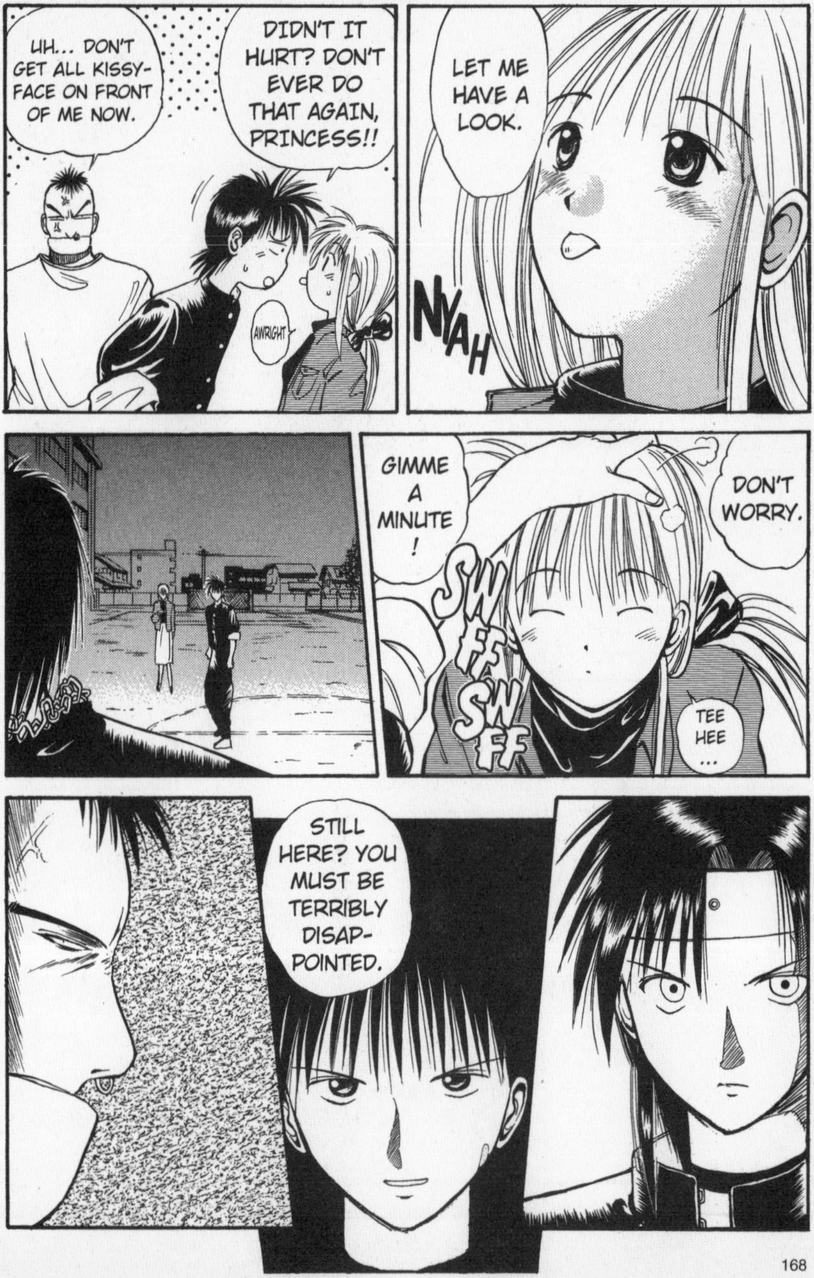
LET ME HAVE A LOOK.
NYAH
DIDN'T IT HURT? DON'T EVER DO THAT AGAIN, PRINCESS!!
UH... DON'T GET ALL KISSY-FACE ON FRONT OF ME NOW.
AWRIGHT
DON'T WORRY.
GIMME A MINUTE!
SWFF SWFF
TEE HEE...
STILL HERE? YOU MUST BE TERRIBLY DISAP-POINTED.

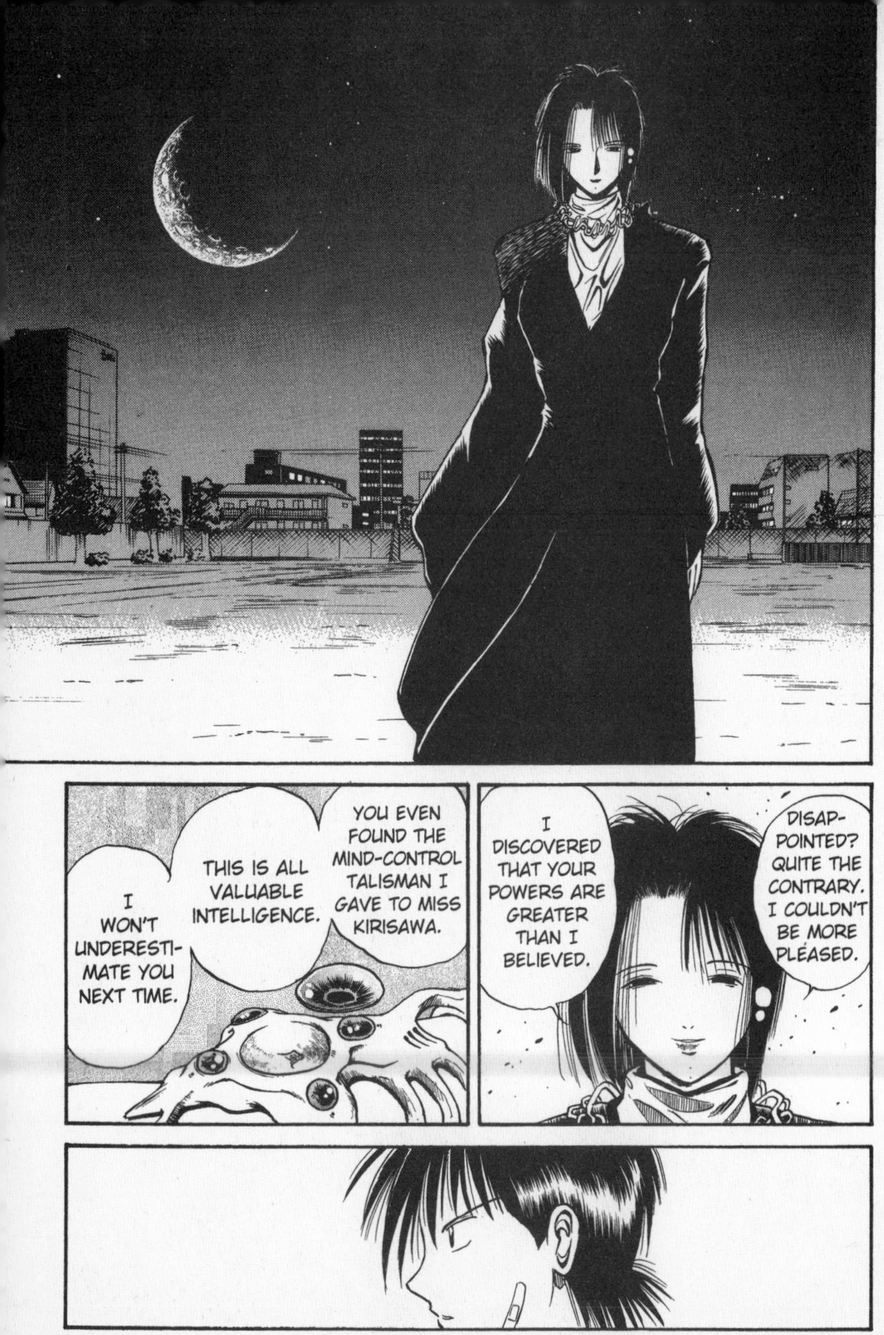
DISAPPOINTED? QUITE THE CONTRARY. I COULDN'T BE MORE PLEASED.
I DISCOVERED THAT YOUR POWERS ARE GREATER THAN I BELIEVED.
YOU EVEN FOUND THE MIND-CONTROL TALISMAN I GAVE TO MISS KIRISAWA.
THIS IS ALL VALUABLE INTELLIGENCE.
I WON'T UNDERESTIMATE YOU NEXT TIME.

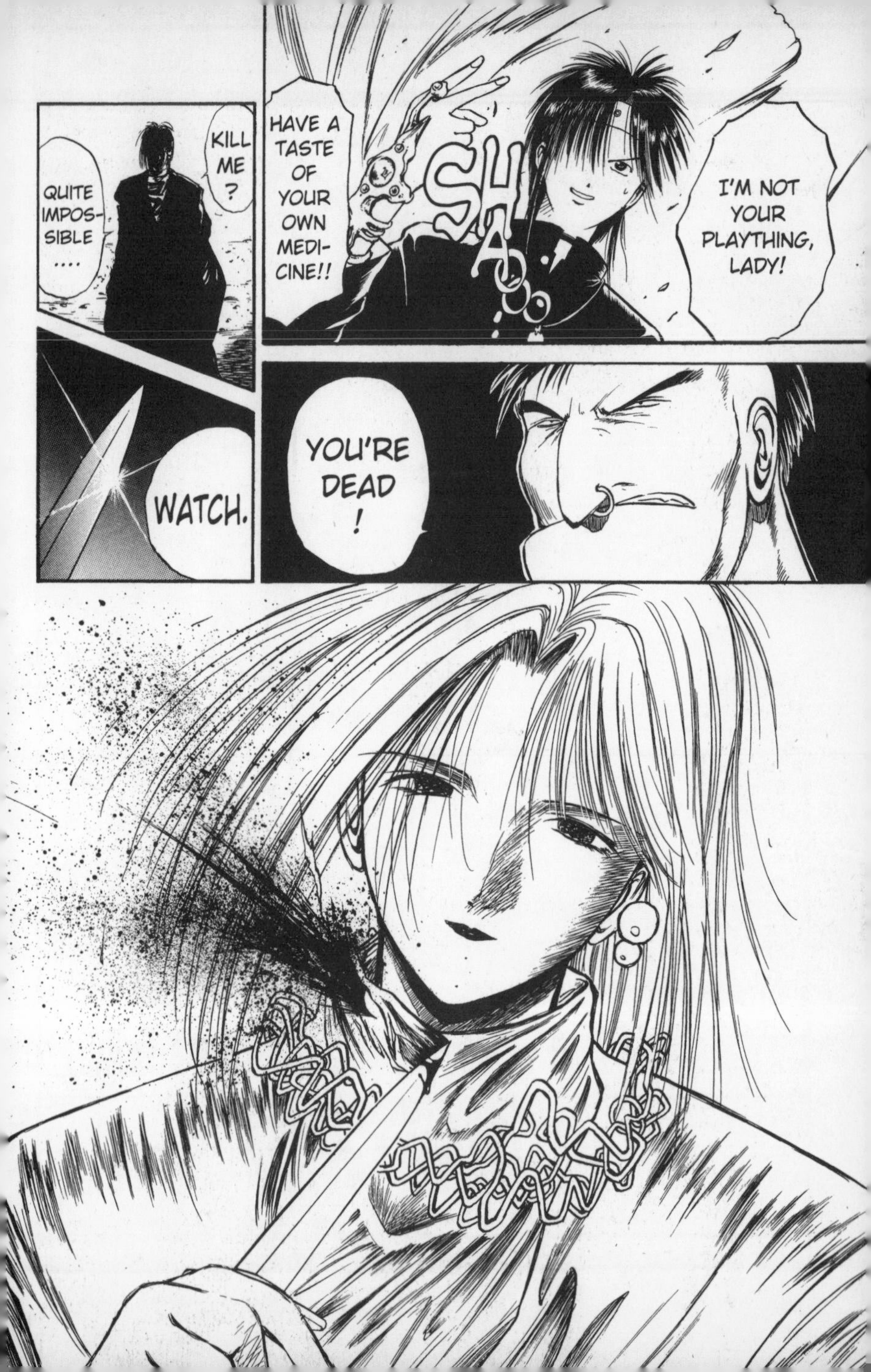
I'M NOT YOUR PLAYTHING, LADY!
SHA
HAVE A TASTE OF YOUR OWN MEDI-CINE!!
KILL ME?
QUITE IMPOS-SIBLE ....
YOU'RE DEAD!
WATCH.

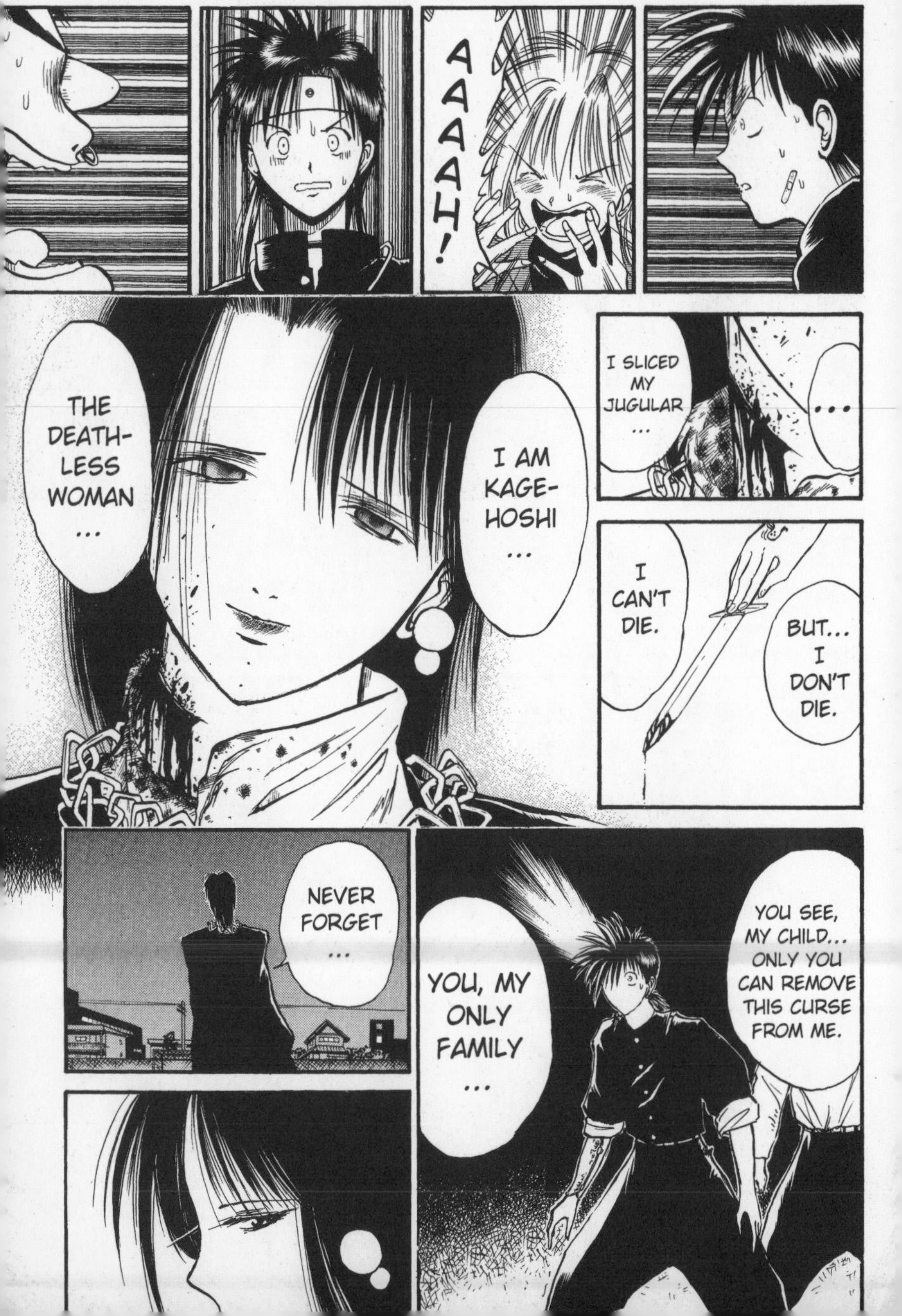
AAAAAH!
...
I SLICED MY JUGULAR ...
I CAN'T DIE.
BUT... I DON'T DIE.
I AM KAGE-HOSHI ...
THE DEATH-LESS WOMAN ...
YOU SEE, MY CHILD... ONLY YOU CAN REMOVE THIS CURSE FROM ME.
YOU, MY ONLY FAMILY ...
NEVER FORGET ...

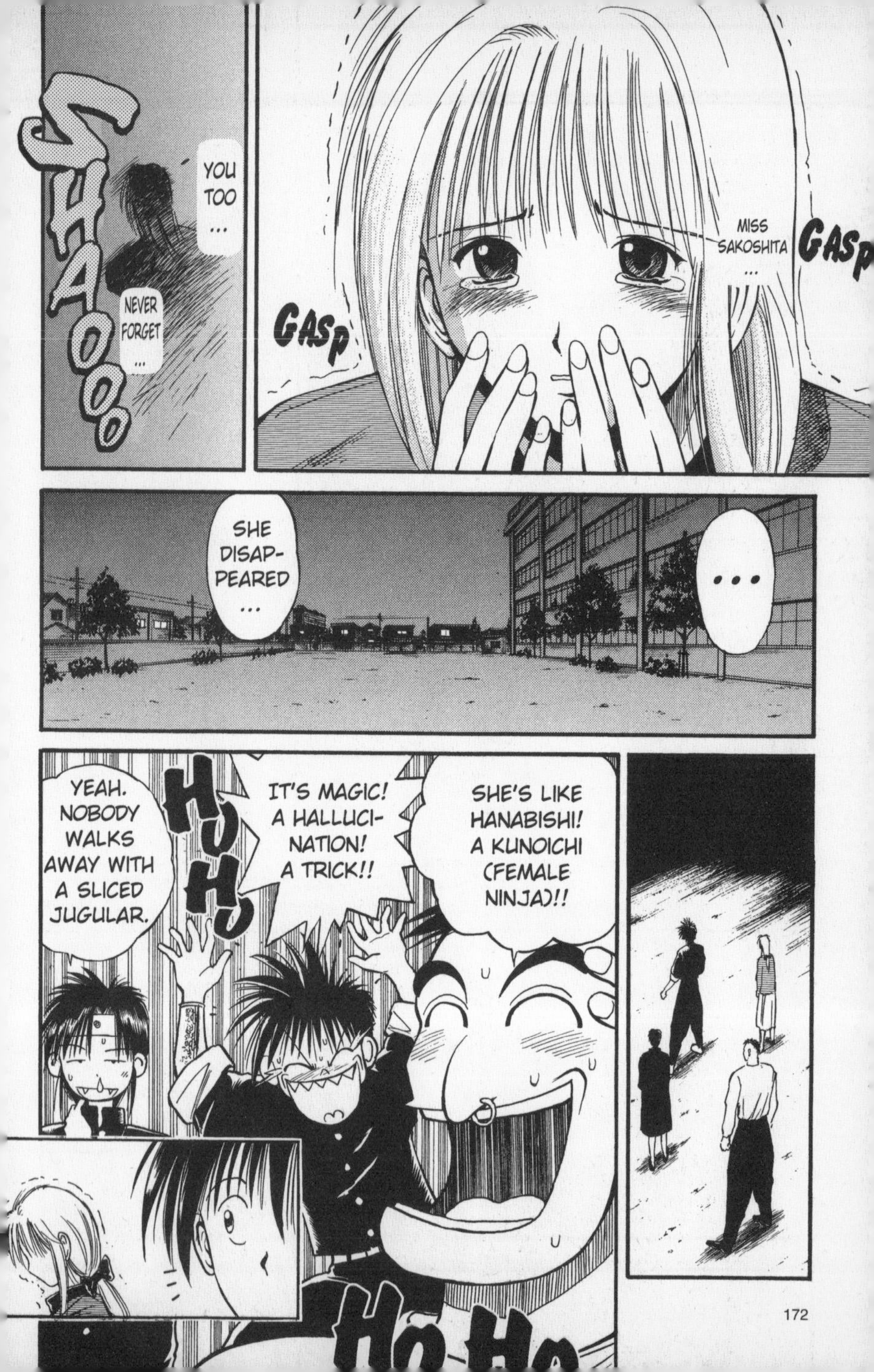
MISS SAKOSHITA ...
GASP
GASP
SHAOOO
YOU TOO ...
NEVER FORGET ...
...
SHE DISAP-PEARED ...
SHE'S LIKE HANABISHI! A KUNOICHI (FEMALE NINJA)!!
IT'S MAGIC! A HALLUCI-NATION! A TRICK!!
HOHO
YEAH. NOBODY WALKS AWAY WITH A SLICED JUGULAR.
HO-HO

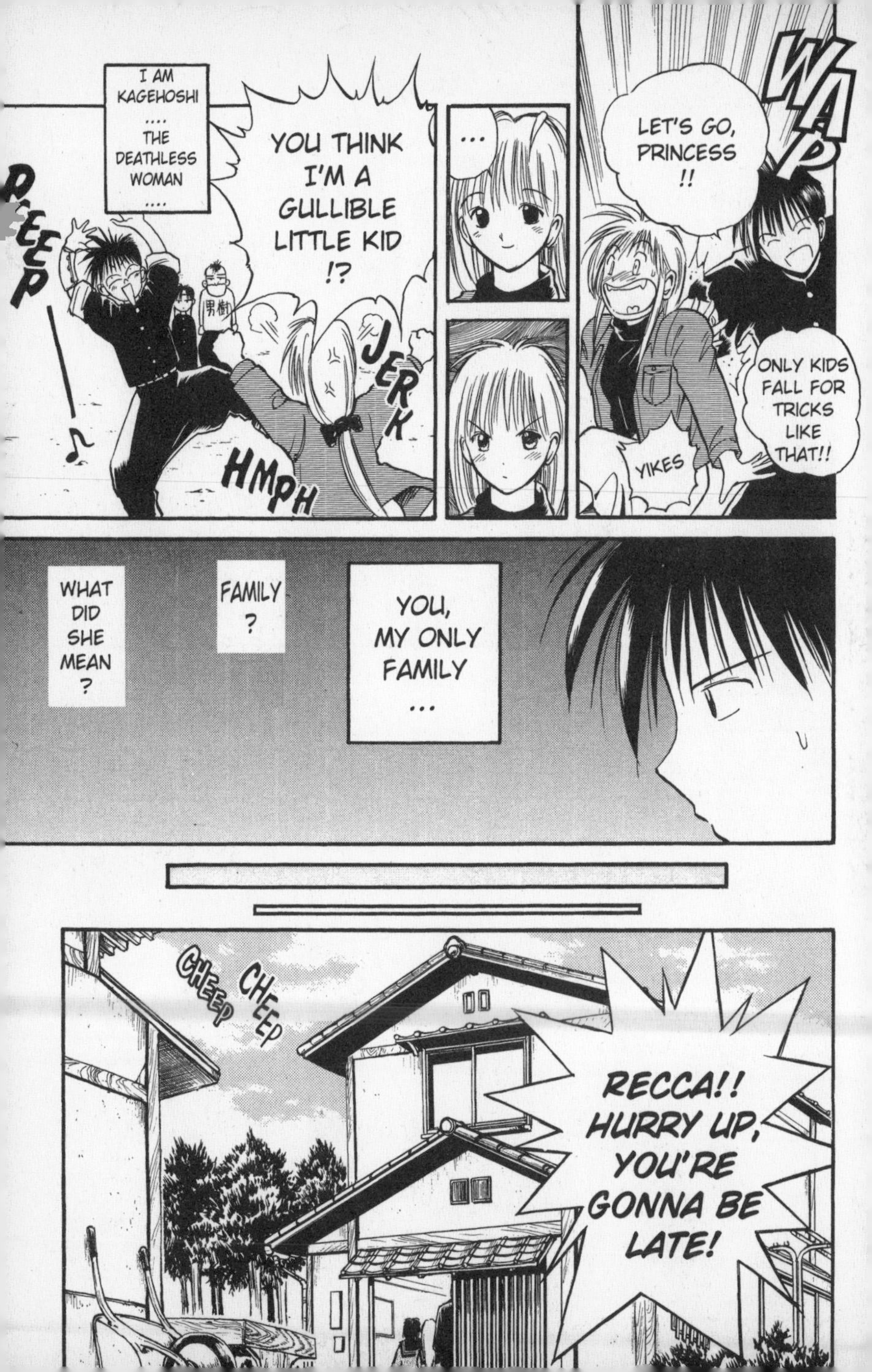
WAP
LET'S GO, PRINCESS !!
ONLY KIDS FALL FOR TRICKS LIKE THAT!!
YIKES
...
YOU THINK I'M A GULLIBLE LITTLE KID !?
JERK
HMPH
I AM KAGEHOSHI .... THE DEATHLESS WOMAN ....
YOU, MY ONLY FAMILY ...
FAMILY ?
WHAT DID SHE MEAN ?
RECCA!! HURRY UP, YOU'RE GONNA BE LATE!
CHEEP
CHEEP

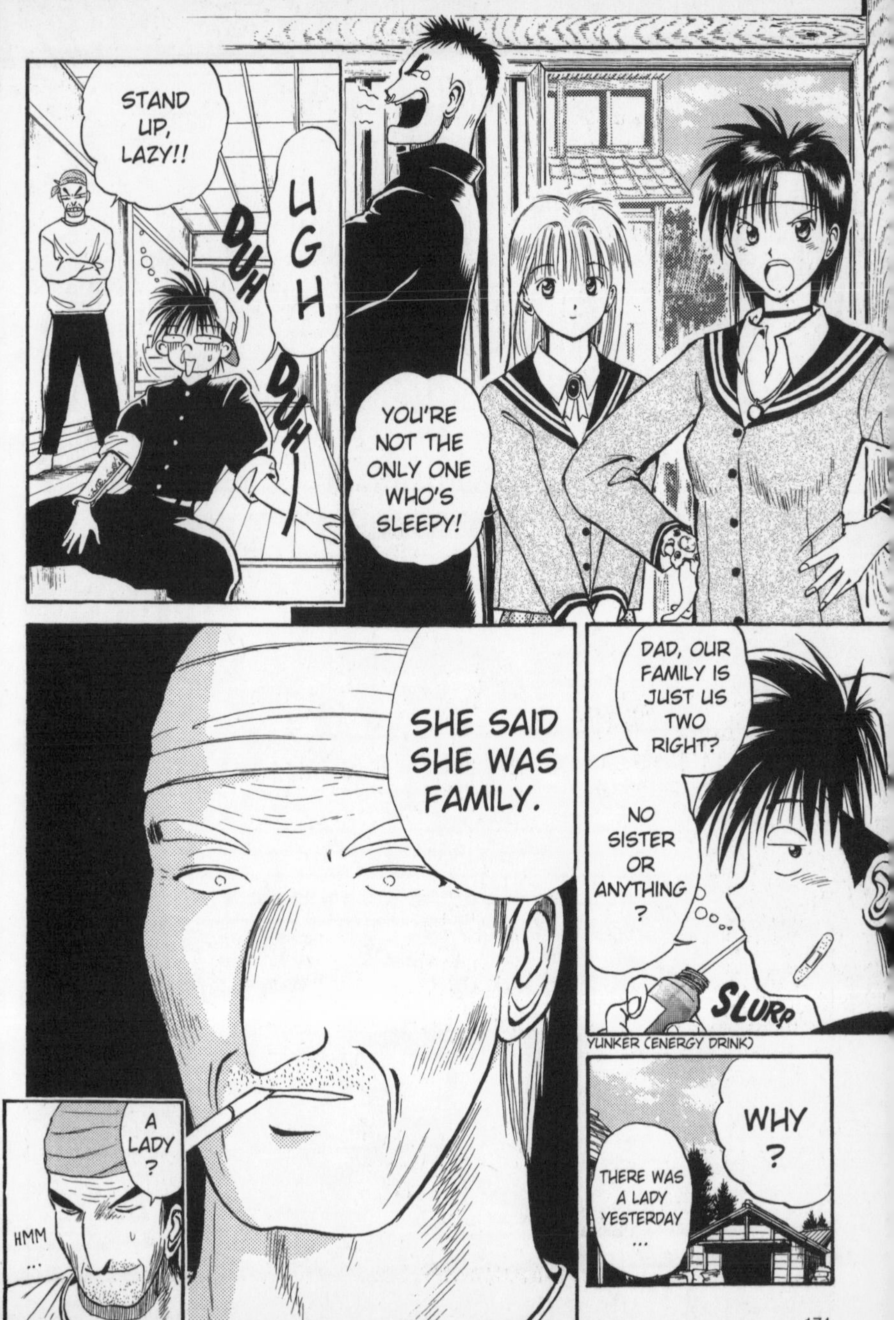
YOU'RE NOT THE ONLY ONE WHO'S SLEEPY!
STAND UP, LAZY!!
UGH
DUH DUH
DAD, OUR FAMILY IS JUST US TWO RIGHT?
NO SISTER OR ANYTHING?
SLURP
YUNKER (ENERGY DRINK)
WHY?
THERE WAS A LADY YESTERDAY ...
A LADY?
HMM ...
SHE SAID SHE WAS FAMILY.

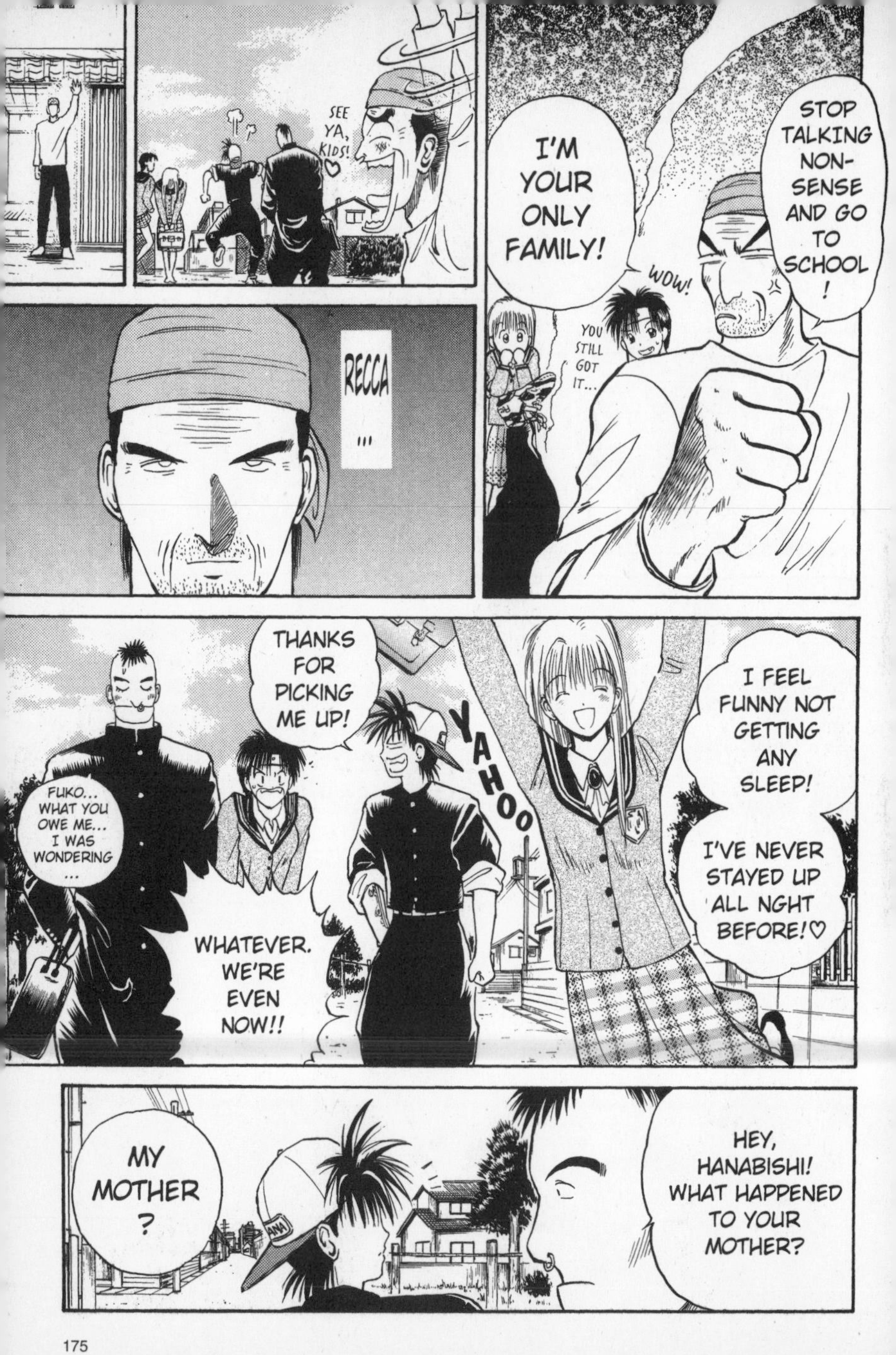
STOP TALKING NON-SENSE AND GO TO SCHOOL!
I'M YOUR ONLY FAMILY!
WOW!
YOU STILL GOT IT...
SEE YA, KIDS! ♡
RECCA ...
I FEEL FUNNY NOT GETTING ANY SLEEP!
I'VE NEVER STAYED UP ALL NGHT BEFORE! ♡
YAHOO
THANKS FOR PICKING ME UP!
FUKO... WHAT YOU OWE ME... I WAS WONDERING ...
WHATEVER. WE'RE EVEN NOW!!
HEY, HANABISHI! WHAT HAPPENED TO YOUR MOTHER?
MY MOTHER ?

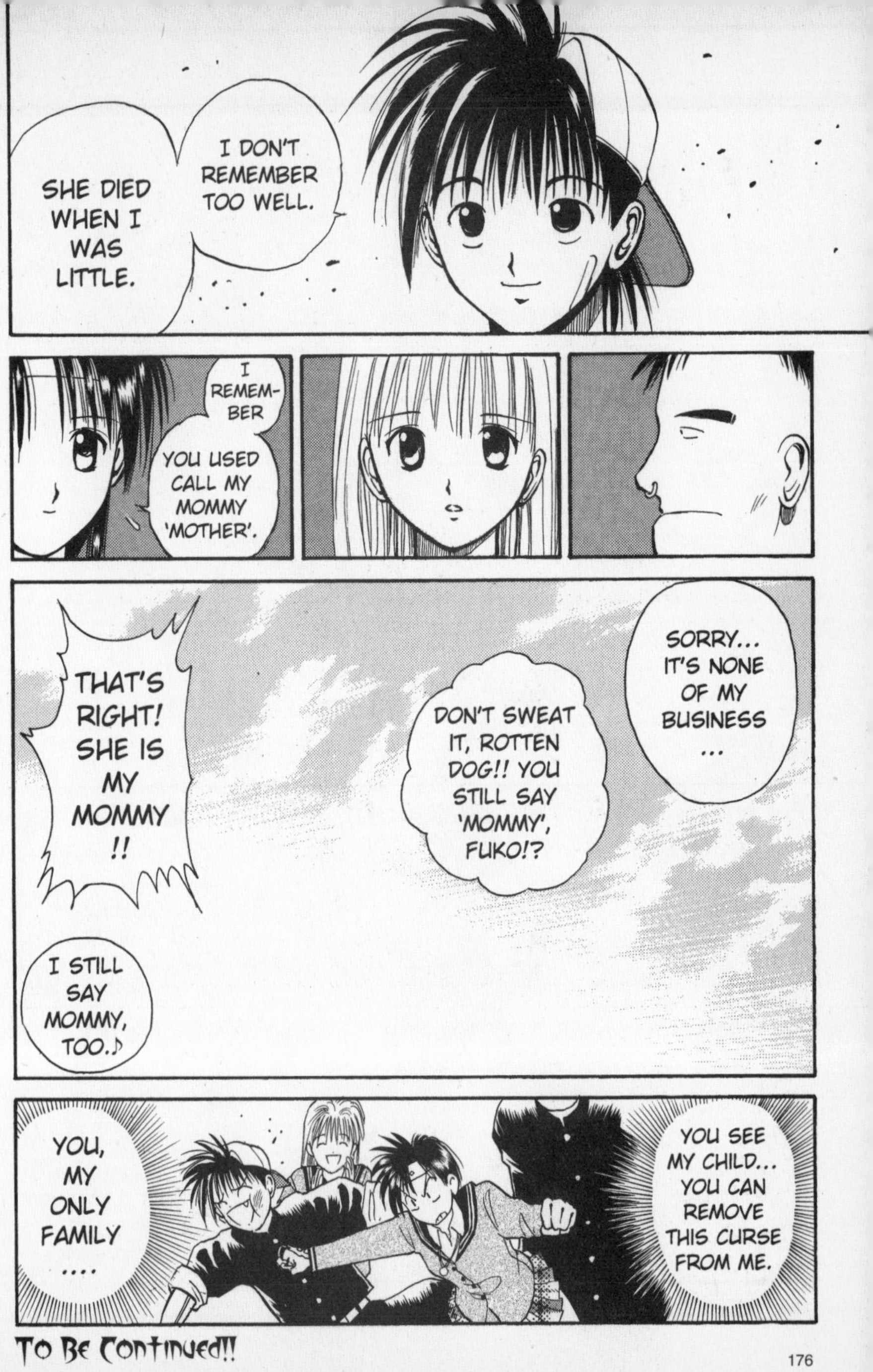
I DON'T REMEMBER TOO WELL.
SHE DIED WHEN I WAS LITTLE.
I REMEMBER
YOU USED CALL MY MOMMY 'MOTHER'.
SORRY... IT'S NONE OF MY BUSINESS ...
DON'T SWEAT IT, ROTTEN DOG!! YOU STILL SAY 'MOMMY', FUKO!?
THAT'S RIGHT! SHE IS MY MOMMY !!
I STILL SAY MOMMY, TOO.♪
YOU SEE MY CHILD... YOU CAN REMOVE THIS CURSE FROM ME.
YOU, MY ONLY FAMILY ....

To Be Continued!!

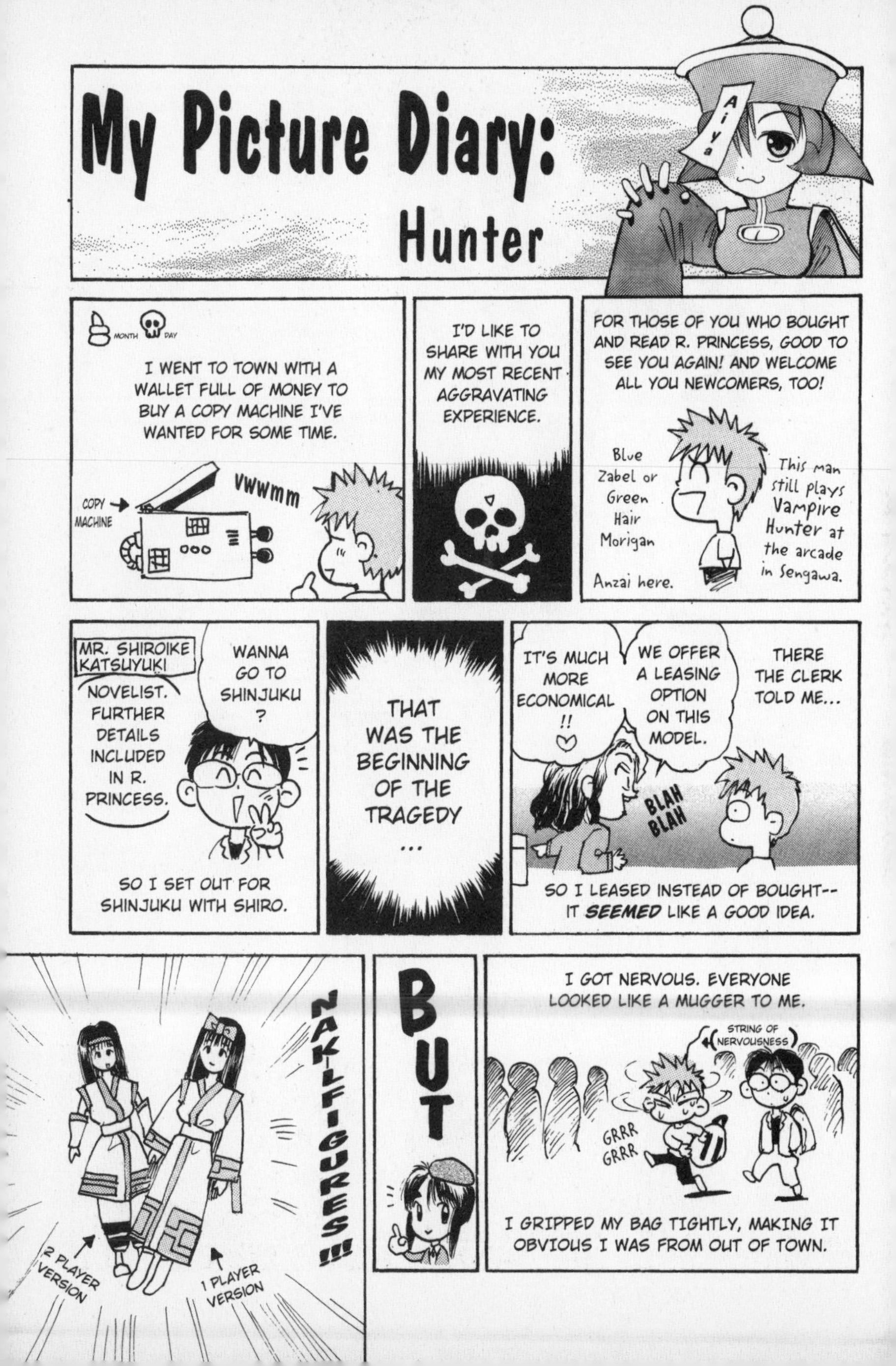
My Picture Diary:
Hunter
Aiya
MONTH DAY
I WENT TO TOWN WITH A WALLET FULL OF MONEY TO BUY A COPY MACHINE I'VE WANTED FOR SOME TIME.
COPY MACHINE
VWWMM
I'D LIKE TO SHARE WITH YOU MY MOST RECENT AGGRAVATING EXPERIENCE.
FOR THOSE OF YOU WHO BOUGHT AND READ R. PRINCESS, GOOD TO SEE YOU AGAIN! AND WELCOME ALL YOU NEWCOMERS, TOO!
Blue Zabel or Green Hair Morigan
Anzai here.
This man still plays Vampire Hunter at the arcade in Sengawa.
MR. SHIROIKE KATSUYUKI
NOVELIST. FURTHER DETAILS INCLUDED IN R. PRINCESS.
WANNA GO TO SHINJUKU ?
SO I SET OUT FOR SHINJUKU WITH SHIRO.
THAT WAS THE BEGINNING OF THE TRAGEDY ...
THERE THE CLERK TOLD ME...
WE OFFER A LEASING OPTION ON THIS MODEL.
IT'S MUCH MORE ECONOMICAL !!
BLAH BLAH
SO I LEASED INSTEAD OF BOUGHT-- IT *SEEMED* LIKE A GOOD IDEA.
NAKIL FIGURES!!!
2 PLAYER VERSION
1 PLAYER VERSION
BUT
I GOT NERVOUS. EVERYONE LOOKED LIKE A MUGGER TO ME.
STRING OF NERVOUSNESS
GRRR GRRR
I GRIPPED MY BAG TIGHTLY, MAKING IT OBVIOUS I WAS FROM OUT OF TOWN.

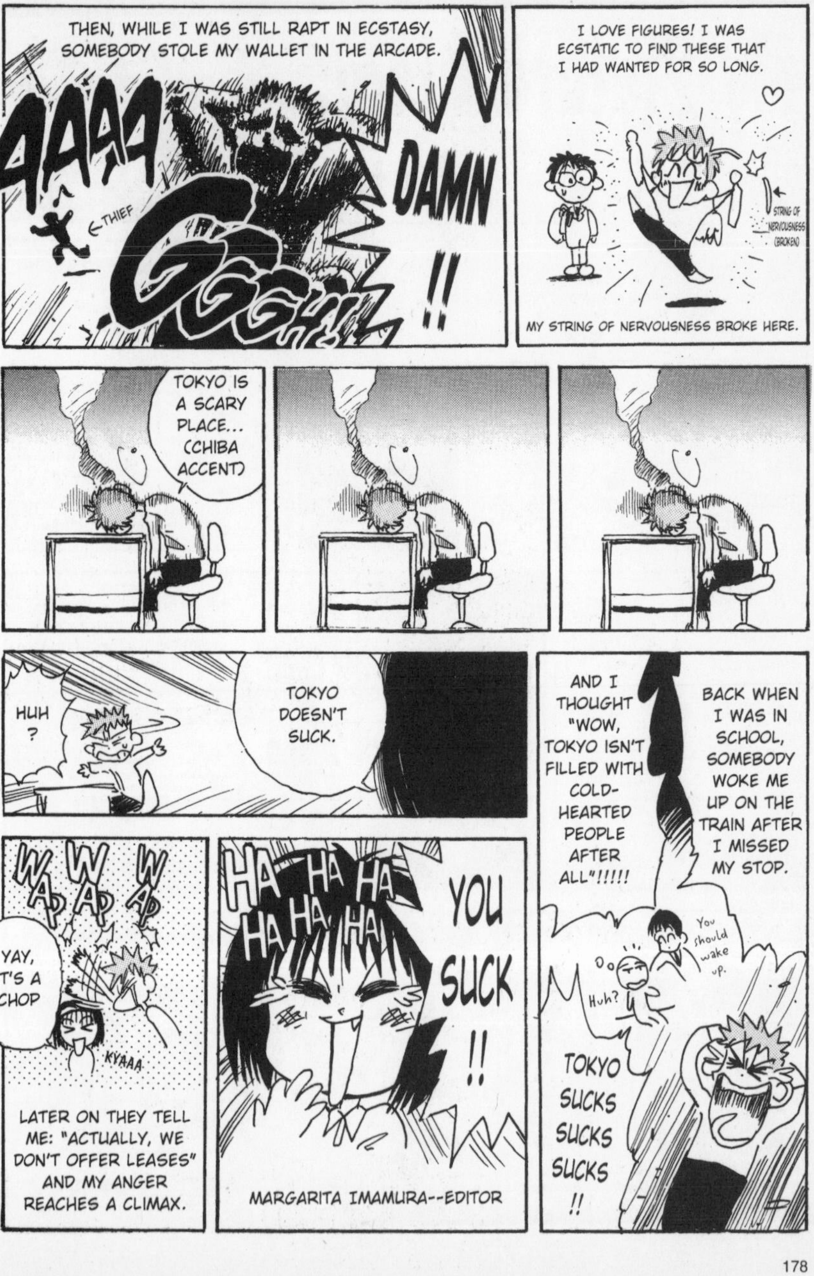
I LOVE FIGURES! I WAS ECSTATIC TO FIND THESE THAT I HAD WANTED FOR SO LONG.
STRING OF NERVOUSNESS (BROKEN)
MY STRING OF NERVOUSNESS BROKE HERE.
THEN, WHILE I WAS STILL RAPT IN ECSTASY, SOMEBODY STOLE MY WALLET IN THE ARCADE.
DAMN !!
AAAA
GGGH!!
THIEF
TOKYO IS A SCARY PLACE... (CHIBA ACCENT)
BACK WHEN I WAS IN SCHOOL, SOMEBODY WOKE ME UP ON THE TRAIN AFTER I MISSED MY STOP.
AND I THOUGHT "WOW, TOKYO ISN'T FILLED WITH COLD-HEARTED PEOPLE AFTER ALL"!!!!!
You should wake up.
Huh?
TOKYO SUCKS SUCKS SUCKS !!
TOKYO DOESN'T SUCK.
HUH ?
YOU SUCK !!
HA HA HA HA HA HA
MARGARITA IMAMURA--EDITOR
WAP WAP WAP
YAY, IT'S A CHOP
KYAAA
LATER ON THEY TELL ME: "ACTUALLY, WE DON'T OFFER LEASES" AND MY ANGER REACHES A CLIMAX.

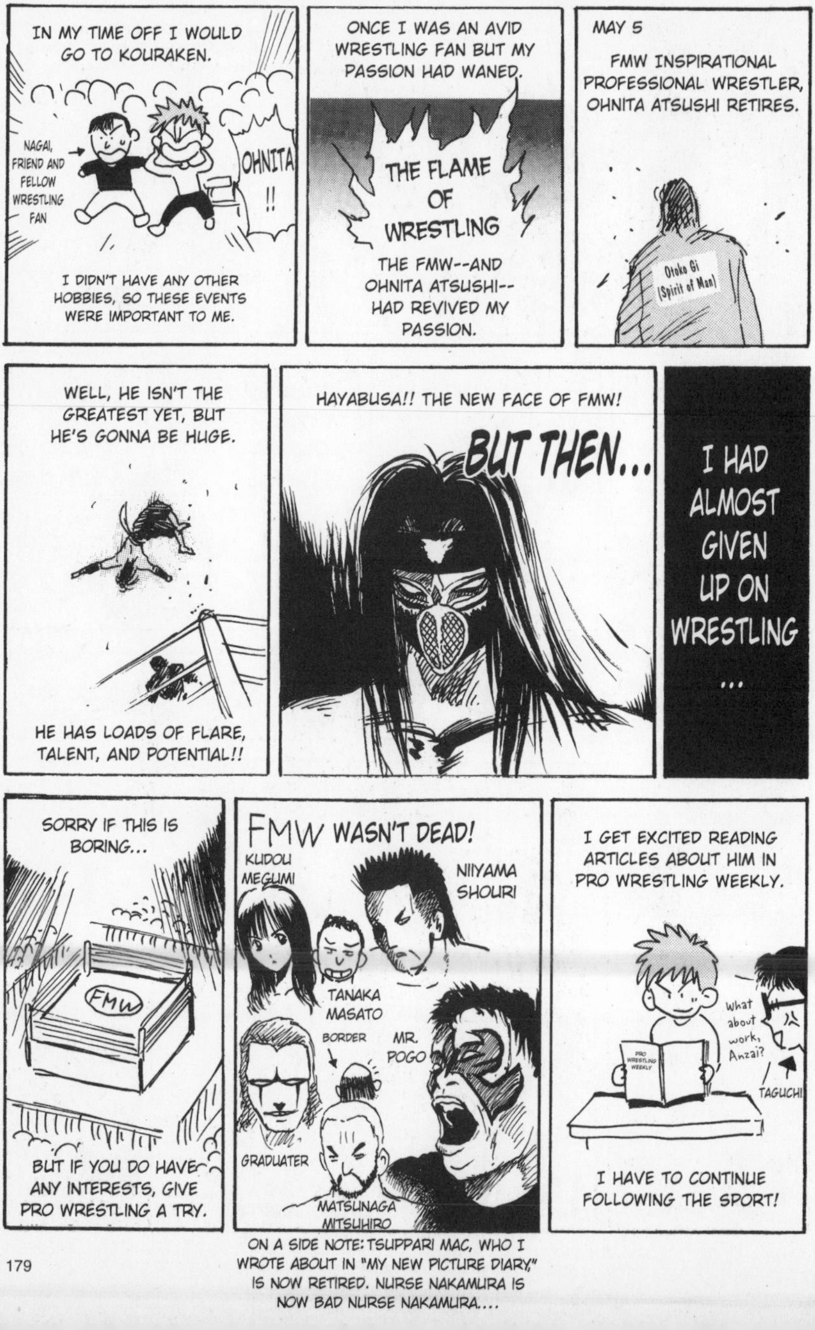
MAY 5
FMW INSPIRATIONAL PROFESSIONAL WRESTLER, OHNITA ATSUSHI RETIRES.
Otoko Gi (Spirit of Man)
ONCE I WAS AN AVID WRESTLING FAN BUT MY PASSION HAD WANED.
THE FLAME OF WRESTLING
THE FMW--AND OHNITA ATSUSHI--HAD REVIVED MY PASSION.
IN MY TIME OFF I WOULD GO TO KOURAKEN.
OHNITA !!
NAGAI, FRIEND AND FELLOW WRESTLING FAN
I DIDN'T HAVE ANY OTHER HOBBIES, SO THESE EVENTS WERE IMPORTANT TO ME.
I HAD ALMOST GIVEN UP ON WRESTLING ...
HAYABUSA!! THE NEW FACE OF FMW!
BUT THEN...
WELL, HE ISN'T THE GREATEST YET, BUT HE'S GONNA BE HUGE.
HE HAS LOADS OF FLARE, TALENT, AND POTENTIAL!!
I GET EXCITED READING ARTICLES ABOUT HIM IN PRO WRESTLING WEEKLY.
What about work, Anzai?
TAGUCHI
PRO WRESTLING WEEKLY
I HAVE TO CONTINUE FOLLOWING THE SPORT!
FMW WASN'T DEAD!
NIIYAMA SHOURI
KUDOU MEGUMI
TANAKA MASATO
MR. POGO
BORDER
GRADUATER
MATSUNAGA MITSUHIRO
SORRY IF THIS IS BORING...
FMW
BUT IF YOU DO HAVE ANY INTERESTS, GIVE PRO WRESTLING A TRY.

ON A SIDE NOTE: TSUPPARI MAC, WHO I WROTE ABOUT IN "MY NEW PICTURE DIARY," IS NOW RETIRED. NURSE NAKAMURA IS NOW BAD NURSE NAKAMURA....

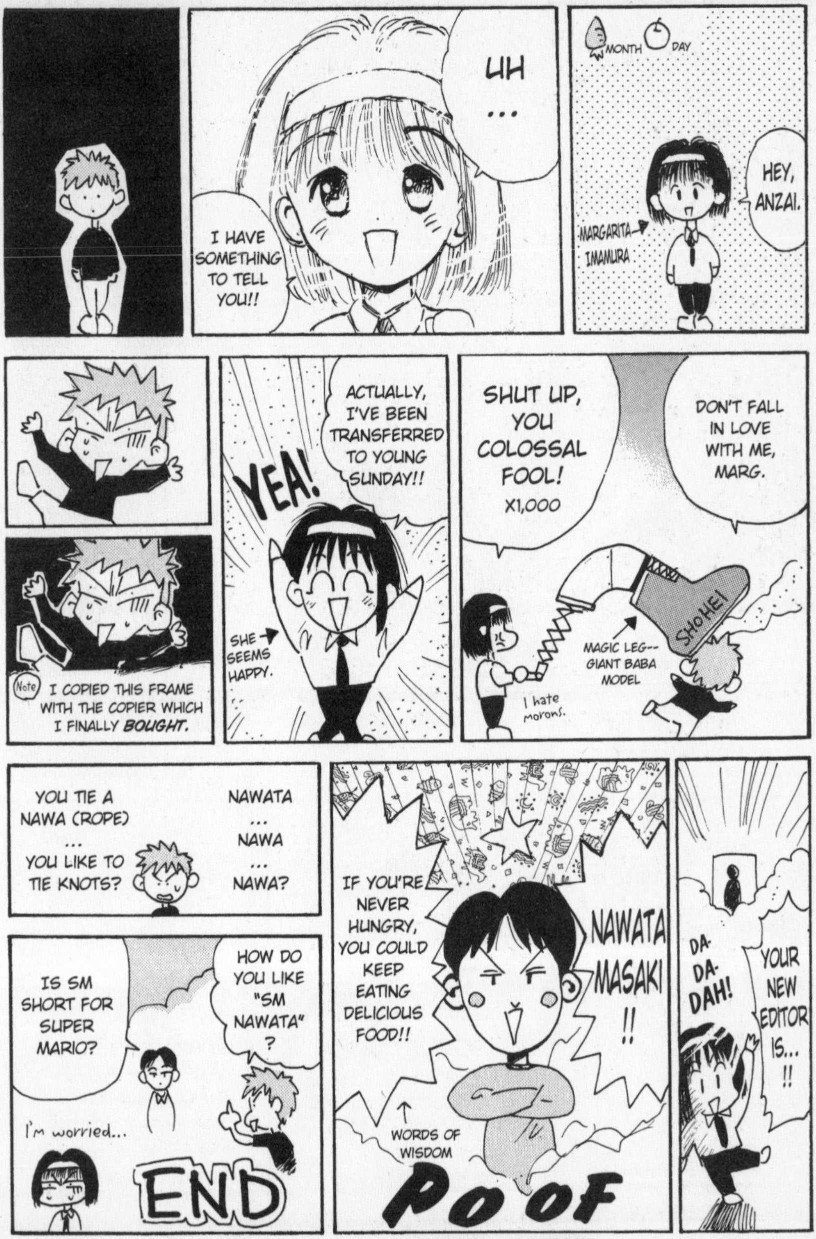
MONTH DAY
HEY, ANZAI.
MARGARITA IMAMURA
UH ...
I HAVE SOMETHING TO TELL YOU!!
DON'T FALL IN LOVE WITH ME, MARG.
SHUT UP, YOU COLOSSAL FOOL! X1,000
SHOHEI
MAGIC LEG-- GIANT BABA MODEL
I hate morons.
ACTUALLY, I'VE BEEN TRANSFERRED TO YOUNG SUNDAY!!
YEA!
SHE SEEMS HAPPY.
Note I COPIED THIS FRAME WITH THE COPIER WHICH I FINALLY BOUGHT.
YOUR NEW EDITOR IS... !!
DA-DA-DAH!
NAWATA MASAKI !!
IF YOU'RE NEVER HUNGRY, YOU COULD KEEP EATING DELICIOUS FOOD!!
WORDS OF WISDOM
POOF
NAWATA ... NAWA ... NAWA?
YOU TIE A NAWA (ROPE) ... YOU LIKE TO TIE KNOTS?
HOW DO YOU LIKE "SM NAWATA" ?
IS SM SHORT FOR SUPER MARIO?
I'm worried...
END

ACTUALLY, HE DOESN'T LOOK ANYTHING LIKE THIS.

Flame on!

Jaded manga readers in the U.S. might unjustly dismiss **FLAME OF RECCA** as just another exercise in karate chops and panty shots. That's too bad.

Oh sure, this volume contains lots of super-kinetic sparring and plenty of female undergarments. But there's more to **FLAME OF RECCA** than just that.

Between the years of 1995 and 2001, readers in Japan enjoyed the weekly adventures of Recca Hanabishi in **SHONEN SUNDAY**. If the series simply pandered to a narrow vision of young male fantasy, it never would have lasted so long. Nobuyuki Anzai's creation became so popular, in fact, it was eventually compiled into 33 graphic novels. You have to admit, that's pretty impressive.

More than anything, **FLAME OF RECCA** is a story about commitment. In an era that values quick kicks and disposable culture, the story of a teenage boy and his unflagging devotion to traditional values struck a chord with millions of Japanese readers.

Guaranteed, there will be plenty of karate chops and panty shots in future issues. But there will also be plenty of universal truths about friendship and love sprinkled in the mix. In Japan, the series has ended. The flame in Recca, however, continues to burn bright here at Viz.

Eric Searleman
Editor, **FLAME OF RECCA**

DID YOU ENJOY FLAME OF RECCA? IF SO, HERE'S SOME ADDITIONAL BOOKS THE EDITOR RECOMMENDS:

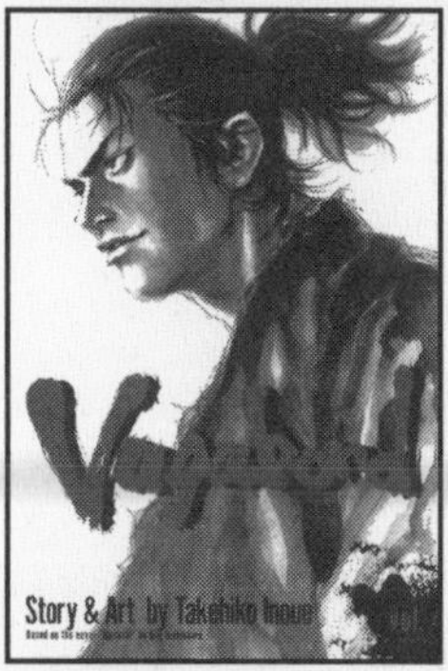
Story & Art by Takehiko Inoue

Vagabond: The continuing saga of a young samurai on a spiritual quest to become the greatest swordsman of Japan. Easily, one of the most beautifully illustrated comics in the world.

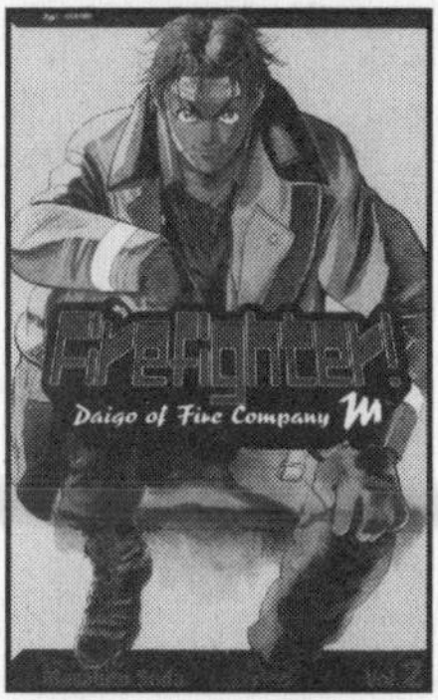
Daigo of Fire Company M

Firefighter! Daigo of Fire Company M: Rookie firefighter Daigo struggles to earn the respect of his fellow firefighters while battling blazes, rivals and tigers. Yes, that's right: tigers!

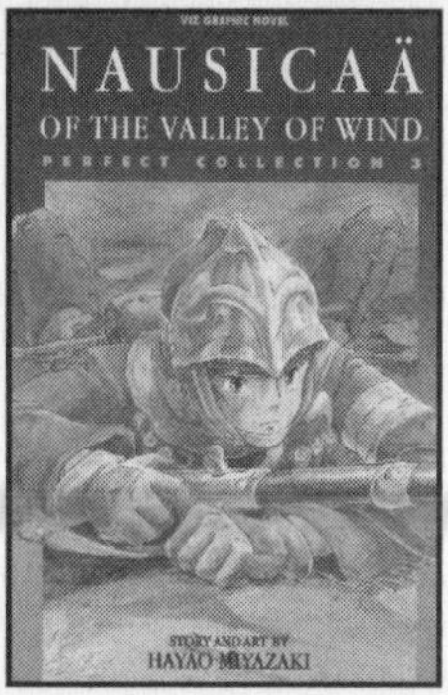
NAUSICAÄ
OF THE VALLEY OF WIND
PERFECT COLLECTION 3
STORY AND ART BY
HAYAO MIYAZAKI

Nausicaä of the Valley of Wind: From the pen of Academy Award-winning director Hayao Miyazaki, comes this epic fable of a world crippled by ecological disaster. Get the complete four-volume set from Viz. You won't regret it.

COMPLETE OUR SURVEY AND LET US KNOW WHAT YOU THINK!

☐ Please check here if you DO NOT wish to receive information or future offers from VIZ

Name: _____

Address: _____

City: _____ State: _____ Zip: _____

E-mail: _____

☐ Male ☐ Female   Date of Birth (mm/dd/yyyy): ___/___/_____   (Under 13? Parental consent required)

What race/ethnicity do you consider yourself? (please check one)

☐ Asian/Pacific Islander   ☐ Black/African American   ☐ Hispanic/Latino

☐ Native American/Alaskan Native ☐ White/Caucasian   ☐ Other: _____

What VIZ product did you purchase? (check all that apply and indicate title purchased)

☐ DVD/VHS _____

☐ Graphic Novel _____

☐ Magazines _____

☐ Merchandise _____

Reason for purchase: (check all that apply)

☐ Special offer   ☐ Favorite title   ☐ Gift

☐ Recommendation   ☐ Other _____

Where did you make your purchase? (please check one)

☐ Comic store   ☐ Bookstore   ☐ Mass/Grocery Store

☐ Newsstand   ☐ Video/Video Game Store ☐ Other: _____

☐ Online (site: _____)

What other VIZ properties have you purchased/own? _____

_____

How many anime and/or manga titles have you purchased in the last year? How many were VIZ titles? (please check one from each column)

ANIME	MANGA	VIZ
☐ None	☐ None	☐ None
☐ 1-4	☐ 1-4	☐ 1-4
☐ 5-10	☐ 5-10	☐ 5-10
☐ 11+	☐ 11+	☐ 11+

I find the pricing of VIZ products to be: (please check one)

☐ Cheap ☐ Reasonable ☐ Expensive

What genre of manga and anime would you like to see from VIZ? (please check two)

☐ Adventure ☐ Comic Strip ☐ Detective ☐ Fighting

☐ Horror ☐ Romance ☐ Sci-Fi/Fantasy ☐ Sports

What do you think of VIZ's new look?

☐ Love It ☐ It's OK ☐ Hate It ☐ Didn't Notice ☐ No Opinion

THANK YOU! Please send the completed form to:

NJW Research
42 Catharine St.
Poughkeepsie, NY 12601

All information provided will be used for internal purposes only. We promise not to sell or otherwise divulge your information.